"The theology of revelation has long been the subject of ecumenical disagreement. Dmytro Bintsarovskyi's comparison of Herman Bavinck and John Meyendorff offers a meticulous and thorough analysis of the key issues involved. Fair-minded but decisive in his evaluation of both the Reformed and Palamite approaches, Bintsarovskyi charts his own path in assessing the knowability of God, rightly centering on God's revelation in Jesus Christ. This is ecumenical dialogue at its best."

—**Hans Boersma,** Saint Benedict Servants of Christ Chair in Ascetical Theology, Nashotah House Theological Seminary

"In this book Dr. Dmytro Bintsarovskyi engages in a valuable ecumenical task by comparing the understanding of the hiddenness of God in the thought of two figures, who might well be thought to be poles apart: the Dutch Reformed theologian, Herman Bavinck, and the Orthodox theologian of Russian descent, John Meyendorff, whose academic career was mostly in America. He shows how their different understandings of God's hiddenness contain at their heart a fundamental affirmation of transcendence in immanence."

—**Andrew Louth,** professor emeritus, Durham University

"This masterfully researched and well conceived dialogue between Reformed and Orthodox theology enters into core issues: the essence-energies distinction, apophatic theology and human language, analogy and univocity, and divine incomprehensibility and divine revelation. The choice of Bavinck and Meyendorff as the central voices in the dialogue turns out to be inspired, with Bavinck representing a broadly 'Augustinian' position and Meyendorff representing a broadly 'neo-Palamite' position. Bintsarovskyi takes Bavinck's side on some of the central issues, but he demonstrates himself willing to criticize both sides, and he does so with verve and clarity. Everyone interested in these issues, whatever their allegiances, will benefit from this lucid and stimulating book."

—**Matthew Levering,** James N. and Mary D. Perry Jr. Chair of Theology, Mundelein Seminary

"The true test of a theologian's catholicity is a capacity to engage both Western and Eastern Christianity. Dmytro Bintsarovskyi's careful comparison between Reformed theologian Herman Bavinck and Eastern Orthodox theologian John Meyendorff is a model of sound ecumenical theology. The focus on the doctrine of God as hidden and revealed is an inspired choice by which to measure Bavinck's catholicity; it is true to Bavinck's own method of always engaging different traditions on their own terms and in the very place where they are strongest and distinctive. Bintsarovskyi honors both men and the traditions they represent with his convincing demonstration that the theologies of both men had this capacity for engagement with the other tradition and thus were true, albeit imperfectly, to their own catholic intentions."

—**John Bolt,** Jean and Kenneth Baker Professor of Systematic Theology, Calvin Theological Seminary

"One of history's great theological questions is that of how to describe God's transcendence and immanence, the fact that he is beyond our comprehension and yet has revealed himself to us, that he is at once both hidden from us and known. In this fascinating study, Bintsarovskyi sheds fresh light on this perennial question through a comparison of a great Reformed theologian, Herman Bavinck, with a great Eastern Orthodox thinker, John Meyendorff. Bintsarovskyi's investigation touches on many aspects of the doctrine of God and provides not only an insightful critique of two traditions that have more in common than meets the eye, but also valuable suggestions for our further thinking about God's revelation of himself. I am delighted to recommend this book."

—**Donald Fairbairn,** Robert E. Cooley Professor of Early Christianity, Gordon-Conwell Theological Seminary

HIDDEN *and* REVEALED

The Doctrine of God in the Reformed and Eastern Orthodox Traditions

STUDIES IN HISTORICAL & SYSTEMATIC THEOLOGY

H S S T

HIDDEN *and* REVEALED

The Doctrine of God in the Reformed and Eastern Orthodox Traditions

DMYTRO BINTSAROVSKYI

STUDIES IN HISTORICAL AND SYSTEMATIC THEOLOGY

LEXHAM ACADEMIC

Hidden and Revealed: The Doctrine of God in the Reformed and Eastern Orthodox Traditions
Studies in Historical and Systematic Theology

Lexham Academic, an imprint of Lexham Press
1313 Commercial St., Bellingham, WA 98225
LexhamPress.com

Print ISBN 9781683594895
Digital ISBN 9781683594901
Library of Congress Control Number 2021933216

Lexham Editorial Team: Todd Hains, Kelsey Matthews, Jessi Strong
Cover Design: Brittany Schrock
Typesetting: Danielle Thevenaz

This book was made possible by
the Neo-Calvinism Research Institute.

The Neo-Calvinism Research Institute
at Theological Kampen University
examines the relationship among
religion, life, and thought,
how it takes shape, and
how it develops over
time in the global
tradition of
Neo-Calvinism.

The Neo-Calvinism Research Institute

CONTENTS

ACKNOWLEDGMENTS

The present book is the product of doctoral research at Kampen Theological University. It would not have been possible without the help and support of many individuals, some of whom I would like to mention by name.

First, I am grateful to my dissertation advisers, each of whom contributed to this work in unique and invaluable ways. Prof. Barend Kamphuis kindly accepted me as a PhD student, patiently oversaw the research, and provided important feedback throughout my writing. His wise and unobtrusive guidance gave me the intellectual freedom to find my own path into the subject. I owe my gratitude also to Dr. Hans Burger, who made insightful comments and drew my attention to new aspects of the issues I wrestle with. Our conversations were always enjoyable and led to further refinements of the text. I have also greatly benefited from Prof. Hans Boersma's solid encouragement and his meticulous reading of my work. His academic excellence has motivated me to strive for rigorous thought and constantly reminded me of how much I still have to learn.

Several people have commented on parts of this work. My particular thanks are extended to Prof. Joost van Rossum, Vladimir Kharlamov, and Wolter Huttinga, who closely read significant portions of my work and suggested ways to improve it. Further, I am deeply indebted to Jos Colijn, not only for his particular observations and suggestions, but also for his constant encouragement throughout all the stages of this project. A special word of gratitude is due to Henk van ter Meij for his helpful suggestions, and to Alister Torrens for his thorough job of correcting my English.

Finally and above all, my thanks are due to my wife for her love, understanding, and numerous sacrifices. My wife and my daughter are my most precious treasure and the source of my joy and inspiration.

ABBREVIATIONS

ANF	*Ante-Nicene Fathers*
BavRev	*The Bavinck Review*
CD I	Barth, Karl, *Church Dogmatics*. Vol. 1, *The Doctrine of the Word of God*, Part 1. Translated by Geoffrey W. Bromiley. Edinburgh: T&T Clark, 2004.
CD II	Barth, Karl. *Church Dogmatics*. Vol. 2, *The Doctrine of God*, Part 1. Translated by T. H. L. Parker et al. Edinburgh: T&T Clark, 2004.
CTJ	*Calvin Theological Journal*
ECR	*Eastern Churches Review*
GD[1]	Bavinck, Herman. *Gereformeerde Dogmatiek*. 4 vols. Kampen: Bos, 1895–1901
GD[4]	Bavinck, Herman. *Gereformeerde Dogmatiek*. 4th ed. 4 vols. Kampen: Kok, 1928–1930
IJST	*International Journal of Systematic Theology*
NPNF[2]	*Nicene and Post-Nicene Fathers*, Series 2
PG	Patrologia Graeca [= Patrologiae Cursus Completus: Series Graeca]. Edited by Jacques-Paul Migne. 162 vols. Paris: 1857–1886
PL	Patrologia Latina [= Patrologiae Cursus Completus: Series Latina]. Edited by Jacques-Paul Migne. 217 vols. Paris: 1844–1864
PRR	*Presbyterian & Reformed Review*
PTR	*Princeton Theological Review*
RD	Herman Bavinck, *Reformed Dogmatics*. 4 vols. Edited by John Bolt. Translated by John Vriend. Grand Rapids: Baker Academic, 2003–2008
SVTQ	*St Vladimir's Theological Quarterly*
WTJ	*Westminster Theological Journal*

1

INTRODUCTION

THE DOCTRINE OF GOD IN ECUMENICAL DIALOGUE

In a literal etymological sense, theology is the study of God. It is, therefore, unsurprising that the doctrine of God has been so central to the constructive endeavors of Christian theologians. The reconsideration of its significance in the twentieth century is owed mainly to renewed interest in the *Trinitarian* God. This revival, indebted to Karl Barth, awakened an interest in the doctrine of the Trinity, which since the Enlightenment had often been regarded as overburdened with philosophical speculations. Barth not only rearranged the doctrines by placing the Trinity "at the head of all dogmatics," but also attempted to present it as the controlling principle of all Christian theology.[1] The resurgence of Trinitarian interest was further stimulated by Roman Catholic theologian Karl Rahner, who—working from a different standpoint and drawing mainly from other sources—reconsidered the Triune God as "the transcendent primal ground of salvation history."[2] For their part, a number of Orthodox theologians noted that the liturgical practice, spirituality, and theology of the Christian East have always been marked by a Trinitarian structure, which serves as a helpful corrective to the alleged essentialism and unitarian inclinations of the West.[3]

1. Karl Barth, *Church Dogmatics* (hereafter *CD*), vol. 1, *The Doctrine of the Word of God*, Part 1, trans. Geoffrey W. Bromiley (Edinburgh: T&T Clark, 2004), 300.

2. Karl Rahner, "Der Dreifaltige Gott als transzendenter Urgrund der Heilsgeschichte," in *Mysterium Salutis: Grundriß heilsgeschichtlicher Dogmatik*, ed. Johannes Feiner and Magnus Löhrer (Einsiedeln: Benziger, 1967), 2:317–401.

3. Vladimir Lossky, *The Mystical Theology of the Eastern Church*, trans. Members of the Fellowship of St. Alban and St. Sergius (London: Clarke, 1968), 44–66; John Zizioulas, *Being as Communion: Studies in Personhood and the Church* (Crestwood, NY: St Vladimir's Seminary Press, 1997), 17–19, 27–49.

Subsequent developments of the doctrine of God included, among others, an emphasis on the relationality of God, which was developed as an alternative to substance metaphysics and implied that God's being does not precede relation and can be known only through personal communion and commitment; the articulation of eschatological ontology in which the futurity of God and his kingdom defines the nature of the present reality and is the goal and meaning of world history; a reexamination of classical theist doctrines such as immutability, impassibility, and timelessness; and the further reconsideration of the doctrine of God in view of the postmodern turn in philosophy.[4] New approaches to the doctrine of God have also been closely interrelated with developments in other areas. Special mention must be made of the renaissance of participatory language, which first became apparent in *nouvelle théologie* and in the retrieval of the Eastern notion of theosis, but which later extended to other traditions and movements, including the new Luther interpretation in the Finnish school, the reevaluation of the place of "union with Christ" in Calvin's theology, and the centrality of the notion of participation in the Anglo-Catholic Radical Orthodoxy movement.[5]

Most remarkable about all these theological shifts and developments is that they occurred in an atmosphere of dialogue between different traditions. The doctrine of God has been both an impetus for and a fruit of ecumenical dialogue. On the one hand, the affirmation of the Niceno-Constantinopolitan Creed with its Trinitarian doctrine testified to the fact that different Christian traditions share much in common (which may

4. The most important publications include Wolfhart Pannenberg, *Theology and the Kingdom of God*, ed. Richard John Neuhaus (Louisville: Westminster John Knox, 1969); Jürgen Moltmann, *The Crucified God: The Cross of Christ as the Foundation and Criticism of Christian Theology*, trans. Robert A. Wilson and John Bowden (London: SCM, 1974); Robert Jenson, *The Triune Identity: God according to the Gospel* (Philadelphia: Fortress, 1982); Catherine Mowry LaCugna, *God for Us: The Trinity and Christian Life* (San Francisco: HarperCollins, 1991); Clark H. Pinnock et al., *The Openness of God: A Biblical Challenge to the Traditional Understanding of God* (Downers Grove, IL: InterVarsity Press, 1994); Colin Gunton, *Father, Son and Holy Spirit: Toward a Fully Trinitarian Theology* (London: T&T Clark, 2003); John Zizioulas, *Communion and Otherness: Further Studies in Personhood and the Church* (New York: T&T Clark, 2006); David Bentley Hart, *The Hidden and the Manifest: Essays in Theology and Metaphysics* (Grand Rapids: Eerdmans, 2017).

5. For a helpful overview of the importance of the concept of deification in contemporary theology, see Michael J. Christensen and Jeffery A. Wittung, eds., *Partakers of the Divine Nature: The History and Development of Deification in the Christian Traditions* (Grand Rapids: Baker Academic, 2007).

be less obvious in the doctrines of Scripture, sin, salvation, church, and sacraments) and therefore stimulated dialogue and held out the promise of greater mutual understanding. On the other hand, the doctrine of God over the last fifty years has also been the *product* of a growing ecumenical awareness and exchange that has challenged all traditions and given rise to new ways of thinking. Engaging in dialogue, each tradition had the opportunity to learn from other theological heritages and be enriched without denying its own distinctive features.

The subject of the present book is not the doctrine of God in general, but a more specific issue—the relation between God's hiddenness and revelation.[6] This issue has also been discussed in ecumenical dialogue, drawing the attention of many theologians from different Christian traditions. Here too, the impulse toward new reflections was largely generated by Karl Barth, whose thought was permeated with the persistent dialectic of God's hiddenness and revealedness, of his veiling and unveiling. According to Barth, there is no *Deus absconditus* behind Christ; however, this does not exclude God's hiddenness *in* revelation itself. The one who loves us in freedom is both fully known and wholly unknowable within his revelation.[7]

Barth's concern to preserve the genuine character of God's self-giving and self-disclosure was echoed in Rahner's *Grundaxiom*, "the 'economic' Trinity is the 'immanent' Trinity and the 'immanent' Trinity is the 'economic' Trinity."[8] The main point of this dictum was relatively straightforward: the actual self-communication of God in revelation cannot be divorced from the internal constitution of the Trinity. What God is in his economy toward us, he is eternally in himself, and vice versa. To be sure, the precise character of the identity requires clarification, and many scholars from different traditions have insisted that the axiom must be qualified, especially in its second half, which, taken literally, may seem

6. The terms "hiddenness" and "revelation" may create the impression that I am dealing only with epistemological aspects of the doctrine of God. In this book, however, these terms are used more broadly as describing what God is in himself and what he is for us. By subsuming all God's activities concerning us under the term "revelation," I am not seeking to reduce their function to that of making God known.

7. *CD* II/1:199, 210, 341–44.

8. Karl Rahner, *The Trinity*, trans. Joseph Donceel (New York: Herder and Herder, 1970), 22.

to imply that the immanent Trinity is in the process of being constituted by salvation history.[9]

Rahner's axiom seemed to present a challenge for Orthodox theologians—not so much because of its potential implications for the doctrine of the *filioque* (which received little attention in the works of Rahner),[10] but because it seemed to establish a stronger identity between God *ad intra* and God *ad extra* than is implied in the traditional Eastern distinction between God's essence and energies. Since the axiom itself was susceptible to different interpretations, however, it has rarely been directly and systematically used to oppose the Palamite distinction.[11] The differentiation between God's essence and energies has remained the standard Orthodox approach to the relation between God's hiddenness and revelation (as I will show in more detail below). In certain aspects, this approach has even gained sympathy among some Catholic and Protestant theologians who linked the essence-energy distinction with a bold affirmation of divine transcendence and freedom and used the distinction to secure an ontological ground for the doctrine of theosis.

Due to the broadness of the topic and the wide variety of approaches to it, it is impossible to satisfactorily deal with all of them within the limits of the present book. I will focus, therefore, only on two traditions—Reformed and Eastern Orthodox.[12] Two main reasons informed this choice. The first is

9. For a brief overview of critiques of Rahner's axiom, see Dennis W. Jowers, *The Trinitarian Axiom of Karl Rahner: The Economic Trinity Is the Immanent Trinity and Vice Versa* (Lewiston, NY: Edwin Mellen, 2006), iii.

10. David Coffey, "Trinity," in *The Cambridge Companion to Karl Rahner*, ed. Declan Marmion (Cambridge: Cambridge University Press, 2005), 110.

11. The most notable attempt has been made by Duncan Reid in his book *Energies of the Spirit: Trinitarian Models in Eastern Orthodox and Western Theology* (Atlanta: Scholars Press, 1997), where he compares "the identity principle" of the West (with Barth and Rahner as key representatives) with "the doctrine of energies" of the East. Reid, however, does not put the two perspectives in a sharp contrast; rather, he seeks common ground between them and tries to find their "common intentions" (124–34).

12. Orthodoxy, of course, is no longer "Eastern," due to globalization and the growth, albeit insignificant, of the Orthodox population in several Western countries. The inadequacy of identifying Orthodoxy with the "East" is especially evident in the sphere of theology, because the majority of prominent contemporary Orthodox theologians have worked in Western ecclesiastical and secular institutions. One of the main goals of Orthodox theologians of the twentieth century was to present their tradition as genuinely catholic—true and accessible for everyone. In this study I mostly use the word "Orthodox," but in some cases (and in the title in particular) I found it necessary to add the word "Eastern" in order to make it clear which tradition I have in mind.

personal: the Reformed tradition had a decisive influence in my own theological formation, while the Orthodox tradition has been the predominant shaping influence of religious life in my home country of Ukraine. The second impetus for this choice is the lack of detailed, specialized studies that compare the approaches of these two traditions regarding the doctrine of God and, more specifically, regarding the hiddenness and revelation of God.[13] Despite some fruitful Orthodox-Reformed interactions, (which resulted, for example, in the adoption of the "Agreed Statement on the Holy Trinity"), and several contributions on the topic by individual authors, the dialogue between the Reformed and Orthodox traditions still leaves much to be desired.[14]

GOD'S HIDDENNESS AND REVELATION IN EASTERN ORTHODOX AND REFORMED TRADITIONS

Eberhard Jüngel once noted that if one compares how Martin Luther and Karl Rahner employ one and the same idea—the hiddenness of God—"it is as if two theological worlds encounter each other."[15] A similar impression

13. Joseph McLelland, who has represented the World Alliance of Reformed Churches in a dialogue with American Orthodox theologians, acknowledged that the essence-energy distinction was "a most difficult point to grasp" for the Reformed side. See McLelland, "Sailing to Byzantium," in *The New Man: An Orthodox and Reformed Dialogue*, ed. John Meyendorff and Joseph C. McLelland (New Brunswick, NJ: Agora, 1973), 18.

14. On fruitful interactions, see two volumes of Thomas F. Torrance, ed., *Theological Dialogue between Orthodox and Reformed Churches* (Edinburgh: Scottish Academic Press, 1985, 1993), and the aforementioned volume *The New Man: An Orthodox and Reformed Dialogue*. See the "Agreed Statement on the Holy Trinity," in Torrance, *Theological Dialogue*, 2:219–26. The most important publications of Reformed authors dealing with the Eastern distinction between essence and energies will be mentioned below. Orthodox theologians often take the Western tradition as a whole and do not discuss the peculiarities of Reformed theology. Gunton notes, "Christians in the Reformed tradition are often able to engage with Orthodox theology in ways not so readily available to the Catholic tradition. The reason is that John Calvin, despite his heavy dependence upon Augustine, was also a careful reader of the Eastern, including the Cappadocian, Fathers, especially in matters trinitarian" (*Father, Son and Holy Spirit*, 51). While it is true that in some respects Reformed and Orthodox traditions are closer to one another than either of them is to Roman Catholicism (see Thomas F. Torrance, "Memoranda on Orthodox/Reformed Relations," in Torrance, *Theological Dialogue*, 1:4), it is still doubtful that Reformed theologians have *actually* engaged with Eastern Orthodoxy with any frequency. Although Gunton speaks in this context of "a major historical conversation," this seems to be an exaggeration, given the insignificant number of serious theological encounters between the traditions in the past.

15. Eberhard Jüngel, "The Revelation of the Hiddenness of God: A Contribution to the Protestant Understanding of the Hiddenness of Divine Action," in *Theological Essays II*, trans. Arnold Neufeldt-Fast and John B. Webster (London: Bloomsbury T&T Clark, 2014), 122.

may arise when one compares Orthodox and Reformed perspectives on the relation between God's hiddenness and revelation. The understanding of this relationship in each of the two traditions forms part of a broader theological vision, which has its own history, vocabulary, motivation, and structure. The elucidation of concrete differences and similarities between the traditions will occupy us later. In this chapter I will limit myself to a brief introduction of the different approaches of the Orthodox and Reformed traditions, especially as they developed in the twentieth and twenty-first centuries.

God's Hiddenness and Revelation in the Orthodox Tradition

The renaissance of Orthodox theology in the twentieth century must be largely attributed to the work of Russian émigré theologians who were forced to leave their country after the Revolution of 1917. Many of these emigrants settled in Paris, which became the center for the emergence of two theological schools. The first, associated primarily with the name of Sergei Bulgakov, stood in direct succession to the religious philosophy of Vladimir Soloviev and paid special attention to the concept of *Sophia*.[16] Another school, associated primarily with the name of Georges Florovsky, has been called neo-patristic, because it was driven by the idea of a return to the fathers and the formation of a neo-patristic synthesis. Florovsky deplored what he called the "Western captivity" of Orthodoxy in the seventeenth to nineteenth centuries, when it was heavily influenced by Roman Catholic and Protestant scholastic theologies and later by German pietism and philosophy.[17] The idea that fidelity to the Eastern tradition can help in answering the challenges of the modern world found its expression in Florovsky's appeal of "*forward*, to the Fathers."[18]

16. See especially Bulgakov's books *Sophia, the Wisdom of God: An Outline of Sophiology*, trans. Patrick Thompson, O. Fielding Clarke, and Xenia Braikevitc (Hudson, NY: Lindisfarne Press, 1993), and *The Lamb of God*, trans. Boris Jakim (Grand Rapids: Eerdmans, 2008).

17. Georges Florovsky, "Western Influences in Russian Theology," in *The Collected Works of Georges Florovsky*, vol. 4, *Aspects of Church History*, ed. Richard S. Haugh (Belmont, MA: Nordland, 1975), 157–82.

18. Paul Gavrilyuk, *Georges Florovsky and the Russian Religious Renaissance* (Oxford: Oxford University Press, 2014), 183.

One of the doctrines rediscovered by Orthodox theologians was the distinction between God's essence and energies. This distinction was occasionally drawn by the early church fathers, but received its classical formulation in the works of Gregory Palamas (1296–1359). Seeking to give a theological account of the experience of monks who claimed to contemplate the uncreated divine light, Gregory postulated a distinction between God's essence, which always remains inaccessible and imparticipable, and God's uncreated energies, in which the saints do participate. For Palamas's contemporaries, this issue was anything but a speculative doctrine and provoked fierce polemics—perhaps unprecedented in the Greek world.[19] Synods held in 1341, 1347, and 1351 approved the doctrine of Gregory, and the Synod of 1368 declared him a doctor of the church. In late Byzantium, Palamas had many adherents, though most of them did not strictly follow his doctrine.[20] However, from the sixteenth to nineteenth centuries the Palamite distinction was rarely invoked and did not occupy a significant place in Orthodox theology and apologetics.[21] In the West, Palamas was little known and was thought to be dependent on a rather opaque metaphysic resembling Neoplatonist emanationism.

The situation changed dramatically in the twentieth century when Palamas became a significant voice for many Orthodox theologians and his distinction became a defining mark of Orthodox doctrine. Although the revival of Palamism may be traced to some works of Russian church historians at the end of the nineteenth century, to the movement of the so-called Name worshipers (Russian monks on Mount Athos who claimed to be followers of Palamas), and to leading émigré theologians who had

---

19. Norman Russell, "Theosis and Gregory Palamas: Continuity or Doctrinal Change?," *St Vladimir's Theological Quarterly* 50 (2006): 374.

20. See John A. Demetracopoulos, "Palamas Transformed: Palamite Interpretations of the Distinction between God's 'Essence' and 'Energies' in Late Byzantium," in *Greeks, Latins, and Intellectual History 1204–1500*, ed. Martin Hinterberger and Chris Schabel (Leuven: Peeters, 2011), 263–372.

21. In the words of Florovsky, "Palamite teaching on the divine ἐνέργειαι is hardly mentioned in most of our textbooks. The peculiarity of our Eastern tradition in the doctrine of God and His attributes has been forgotten and completely misunderstood." See Georges Florovsky, "Patristics and Modern Theology," in *Procès-verbaux du Premier Congrès de Théologie Orthodoxe à Athènes*, ed. Hamilcar S. Alivisatos (Athènes: Pyrsos, 1939), 239.

made remarks about Palamas's doctrine in the 1920s and '30s,[22] substantive scholarly discussion was sparked by two articles about Palamas and the Palamite controversy written in 1932 by the Catholic scholar Martin Jugie. According to Jugie, the Palamite distinction was a novelty in the history of Byzantine theology and could not adequately be proved from the fathers. He was convinced, moreover, that the essence-energy distinction destroys the absolute simplicity of the divine being, so that it is "not only a grave philosophical error, but, from the Catholic perspective, also a true heresy."[23] The first solid attempts from the Orthodox side to justify and revive Palamas's theology were made by Basil Krivoshein (1936), who emphasized its compatibility with the simplicity of God, and Dumitru Stăniloae (1938), whose monograph was, unfortunately, available only in Romanian and thus could hardly contribute to the disputes over Palamas in the Western academic world.[24]

The true founder of neo-Palamism was Vladimir Lossky, who, especially in his *Mystical Theology of the Eastern Church* (1944), presented the Palamite distinction as the essential interpretive framework for Orthodox theology and experience. First, Lossky contested the right of the sophiologists to appeal to Palamas: unlike Florovsky, who abstained from openly criticizing Bulgakov out of respect to his older colleague, Lossky sharply attacked

22. Writing in 1914 to Pavel Florensky, Sergei Bulgakov reported that he "was working on Palamas" and found it "necessary and timely" to publish his tracts. See *Perepiska svyashchennika Pavla Aleksandrovicha Florenskogo so svyashchennikom Sergiem Nikolaevichem Bulgakovym* [Correspondence of Rev. Pavel Aleksandrovich Florensky with Rev. Sergii Nikolaevich Bulgakov] (Tomsk: Vodolei, 2001), 78. In his major publication, *The Unfading Light* (1917), Bulgakov dedicates several pages to Palamas's doctrine, in which he apparently saw similarities to his own emerging views on *Sophia*. Florovsky, in his 1926 letter to Bulgakov, refers to the distinction between οὐσία and ἐνέργεια and tries to convince Bulgakov that *Sophia* could have a place in Orthodox theology only as a synonym for "energy" and "glory," but not as a creature. See "Pis'ma G. Florovskogo S. Bulgakovu i S. Tyshkevichu" [Letters of G. Florovsky to S. Bulgakov and S. Tyschkevich], *Simvol* 29 (1993): 206. Florovsky further elaborates on the topic in his work *Creature and Creaturehood* (1928). Vladimir Lossky briefly mentions Palamas's distinction in his first publications in 1929 and 1931 about negative theology and the notion of "analogy" in pseudo-Dionysius. Later he made clear that he was first introduced to Palamas through the lectures of Sorbonne professor Charles Diehl, who shared the disparaging attitude to Palamas typical for Western scholars of that time. See Rowan Williams, "The Theology of Vladimir Nikolaievich Lossky: An Exposition and Critique" (PhD diss., University of Oxford, 1975), 7.

23. Martin Jugie, "Palamas, Gregoire," in *Dictionnaire de théologie catholique*, ed. Jean Michel Alfred Vacant et al. (Paris: Librairie Letouzey et Ané, 1932), 11.2:1764.

24. For a helpful overview in English, see Adrian Agachi, *The Neo-Palamite Synthesis of Father Dumitru Stăniloae* (Newcastle upon Tyne: Cambridge Scholars, 2013).

Bulgakov—reproaching him for misinterpreting Palamas's doctrine and recommending that he "reread the writings of St Gregory Palamas in order to learn from him true theology, freed from any human philosophy."[25] Second, and more importantly, Lossky presented the essence-energy distinction as the main characteristic of Orthodox theology as distinct from the Western doctrinal system. The chief target of Lossky's criticism was Western essentialism, which identifies God with his essence and thus does not admit anything to be God that is not the very essence of God. According to Lossky, this identification compromises God's transcendence, because it implies some intellectual knowledge of the divine essence (so that even the beatific vision becomes just a *philosophical* beatitude). Simultaneously, it does not allow for real deification because it understands grace in terms of causality (so that grace is a created effect of the divine cause). Lossky contrasts the Orthodox faith in the living God of Abraham, Isaac, and Jacob with the Western view of God as one simple, static, and impersonal substance. Lossky believed that the Palamite distinction, by contrast, safeguards both true apophaticism and true experience. On the one hand, it honors God's transcendence by denying the communication and knowledge of the divine essence. On the other hand, it provides the dogmatic basis for real communion with God. In his energies, God personally encounters us and deifies us, so that by grace we become all that he is by nature, save only identity of nature.[26]

The works of Lossky determined the dogmatic character of the neo-Palamist movement that he initiated. Although they were original, provocative, and passionate, they did not, however, contain a scrupulous analysis of Palamas's theology and historical context. This gap was partially filled in 1959, when John Meyendorff published his study of Palamas's life and thought as well as his annotated translation of Palamas's *Triads*.[27] According to Jaroslav Pelikan, through these and other works, Meyendorff made "the most substantial contribution to the historical and theological appreciation

25. Vladimir Losskiy, "Spor o Sofii" [The Controversy over Sophia] in *Stat'i raznykh let* [Articles of Various Years] (Moscow: Svyato-Vladimirskoe Bratstvo, 1996), 23.

26. Lossky, *Mystical Theology*, 64–65, 69–72, 77, 87.

27. Jean Meyendorff, *Introduction à l'étude de Grégoire Palamas* (Paris: Éditions du Seuil, 1959). In the present study, the following English edition is used: John Meyendorff, *A Study of Gregory Palamas*, 2nd ed., trans. George Lawrence (1974; repr., Crestwood, NY: St Vladimir's Seminary Press, 1998).

of Gregory Palamas in the West."[28] In some respects, the study and especially its appendixes have lost their original significance, but this should be taken as a sign of Meyendorff's influence: he produced the explosion of unprecedented interest in Palamas's views, so that the number of publications dedicated to this topic has grown a hundredfold after the appearance of Meyendorff's book.[29] The distinction between essence and energies remains the most discussed aspect of Palamas's thought. Starting in the 1960s, the Palamite revival spread also to Greece, which resulted not only in a critical and more comprehensive edition of Palamas's works, but also in original contributions from such theologians as George Mantzaridis, John Romanides, and Christos Yannaras.[30] In the English-speaking world, the most renowned neo-Palamite theologian has been the retired Oxford professor Timothy (Kallistos) Ware.[31]

Among recent publications endorsing the Palamite distinction, two books deserve special mention.[32] In his study *Aristotle East and West*, as well as in several articles, David Bradshaw traces the usage of the term ἐνέργεια in Greek philosophy from Aristotle through Plotinus and then describes how it was received into and interpreted within the Christian tradition.[33] Bradshaw suggests that in the New Testament ἐνέργεια and related terms are used to designate both the divine transforming power and the activities of the Christian that are enabled and supported by this power. Thus, the vocabulary of ἐνέργεια underscores the necessity of cooperation between

---

28. Jaroslav Pelikan, preface to Palamas, *The Triads* (Mahwah, NJ: Paulist, 1983), xiii.

29. "OT redaktsii" [Editorial], in *Zhizn' i trudy svyatitelya Grigoriya Palamy: Vvedenie v izuchenie* [The Life and Works of St Gregory Palamas: Introduction], by Ioann Meyendorf (Saint Petersburg: Vizantinorossika, 1997).

30. See especially Christos Yannaras, "The Distinction between Essence and Energies and Its Importance for Theology," *SVTQ* 19 (1975): 232–45.

31. See especially Timothy (Kallistos) Ware, "God Hidden and Revealed: The Apophatic Way and the Essence-Energies Distinction," *Eastern Churches Review* 7 (1975): 125–36; Ware, "The Debate about Palamism," *ECR* 9 (1977): 45–63.

32. Other important titles include Georgi Kapriev, *Philosophie in Byzanz* (Würzburg: Königshausen und Neumann, 2005), 249–308; Jean-Claude Larchet, *La Théologie des énergies divines: Des origines à saint Jean Damascène* (Paris: Cerf, 2010), passim; Joost van Rossum, "Palamas and Aquinas," *SVTQ* 59 (2015): 29–41.

33. David Bradshaw, *Aristotle East and West: Metaphysics and the Division of Christendom* (Cambridge: Cambridge University Press, 2004). See also his articles "The Concept of the Divine Energies," *Philosophy and Theology* 18 (2006): 93–120; "The Divine Energies in the New Testament," *SVTQ* 50 (2006): 189–223; and "The Divine Glory and the Divine Energies," *Faith and Philosophy* 23 (2006): 279–98.

God and humanity without implying that such synergy is a symmetrical relation. The later Christian tradition drew on Plotinus's theory of two acts, according to which "the One" not only has the internal energy *of* the essence, but also the external energy *from* the essence. While Plotinus identified the external energy with "the Intellect," Christian theologians understood it as the free acts of God. Thus, the Cappadocians distinguished between the incommunicable divine essence and communicable divine energies. Bradshaw emphasizes that they understood the divine energies not simply as that which God *does*, but also that which God *is* in his relation to the world. In the Eastern tradition, the same idea was expressed by a number of other terms, including "processions" (πρόοδοι), "things around God" (τὰ περὶ Θεόν), and the λόγοι.[34] This tradition culminates in the doctrine of Gregory Palamas, who "synthesizes under the general heading of the divine energies a number of ideas that had developed more or less independently in earlier patristic thought."[35]

Bradshaw is at pains to demonstrate that such a doctrine of God has several advantages over the Western (Augustinian, Thomistic) concept. First, it is truly apophatic and preserves the unknowability of the divine essence, while Augustine and his followers believed that the blessed in heaven enjoy a direct intellectual apprehension of the divine essence. Second, the Eastern doctrine understands participation in the divine energies as dynamic and engaging the body as much as the soul, while the Western doctrine posits greater discontinuity between the present state and that of glory and does not assign any role to the human body in the beatific vision. Third, and most importantly, the Eastern concept can meaningfully affirm that God can *do* otherwise without *being* otherwise, because it differentiates between God's essence and his energies, some of which are contingent. In contrast, the Western identification of God's essence with his will leads to the conclusion that he cannot will differently without his essence being different. Such an identification means that God

34. To be sure, Bradshaw's explanation is more nuanced: in particular, he notes that although "the *logoi* in Maximus serve a role similar in many ways to that of the *energeiai* in the Cappadocians," Maximus "splits the Cappadocian conception of the divine *energeiai* into three: one part relating to creation (the *logoi*), another to God's eternal attributes (the 'things around God'), and the third to the activity and energy of God that can be shared by creatures (for which he tends to reserve the term *energeia*)" (*Aristotle East and West*, 206).

35. Bradshaw, *Aristotle East and West*, 241.

cannot respond to his creatures' acts because they would then be constitutive of the divine essence. In short, the Western account of divine simplicity, which identifies God's essence with his will, endangers both the freedom of God and the freedom of humanity. As Bradshaw puts it: "If one were to summarize the differences between the eastern and western traditions in a single word, that word would be 'synergy.'"[36] Bradshaw's book has provoked intensive scholarly discussions, which have resulted in the publication of *Divine Essence and Divine Energies*, in which Orthodox, Catholic, and Protestant contributors follow up on the subjects addressed by Bradshaw.[37]

Another recent, noteworthy publication is Torstein Tollefsen's *Activity and Participation in Late Antique and Early Christian Thought*.[38] Tollefsen pays less attention than Bradshaw to the genealogy of key ontological concepts in Greek philosophy and does not enter into a detailed polemic with the West. He focuses on the Eastern Christian tradition and seeks to prove that Palamas's doctrine was not innovative but rather well-established in the East. Tollefsen analyzes the thought of Gregory of Nyssa, Dionysius, and Maximus and maintains that all of them taught basically the same thing: God in himself is beyond comprehension, but he can be known through his external activities. (Tollefsen prefers this word to translate ἐνέργειαι.) Participation in God means that humankind receives more and more of God's activities into his being. The theology of Palamas does not merely have verbal similarities with the preceding mainstream tradition; it remains faithful to it and uses it to highlight a certain conception of spirituality.

Christoph Schneider, the editor of the aforementioned *Divine Essence and Divine Energies*, opens the volume with the following sentence: "For most contemporary Orthodox theologians the distinction between the divine essence and energies belongs to the very core of the Orthodox tradition and has no direct equivalent in the West."[39] Schneider does not elabo-

---

36. Ibid., 264–65.

37. Constantinos Athanasopoulos and Christoph Schneider, eds., *Divine Essence and Divine Energies: Ecumenical Reflections on the Presence of God in Eastern Orthodoxy* (Cambridge: Clarke, 2013).

38. Torstein Tollefsen, *Activity and Participation in Late Antique and Early Christian Thought* (Oxford: Oxford University Press, 2012). See also his book *The Christocentric Cosmology of St Maximus the Confessor* (Oxford: Oxford University Press, 2008).

39. Christoph Schneider, "Beyond Agnosticism and Pantheism," in Athanasopoulos and Schneider, *Divine Essence and Divine Energies*, 9.

rate further on this statement, but for our purposes it is important to dwell at more length on his two claims: the distinction is, first, *essential* to the Orthodox tradition, and, second, it is a *distinctive* mark of this tradition when compared to the West.

Concerning the place of the Palamite distinction in Orthodox theology, Florovsky's position is representative: "This basic distinction was formally accepted and elaborated at the Great Councils in Constantinople, 1341 and 1351. Those who would deny this distinction were anathematized and excommunicated. The anathemas of the council of 1351 were included in the rite for the Sunday of Orthodoxy, in the Tradition. Orthodox theologians are bound by this decision."[40] Although Florovsky rarely appealed to the distinction and did not attach the same importance to it as Lossky and Meyendorff, he nevertheless affirmed that the distinction attained normative status in Orthodoxy.[41] It may perhaps seem difficult to reconcile this status with the apparent neglect of the doctrine throughout the sixteenth to nineteenth centuries, but Orthodox theologians often explain this neglect by referring to the "Western captivity" of Orthodox theology.[42] Given the place of the liturgy in Orthodoxy and its indissoluble ties with dogmatics, the yearly commemoration of Palamas on the second Sunday of Lent (which was in fact observed even throughout that four-century period) acquires special significance. Ware goes so far as to suggest that the Palamite distinction should be regarded as "an indispensable part of the faith," and, indeed, a dogma, and compares its significance to that of the dogma of the Holy Trinity.[43]

---

40. Georges Florovsky, "St. Gregory Palamas and the Tradition of the Fathers," in *The Collected Works of Georges Florovsky* (Belmont, MA: Nordland, 1974–1989), 1:117.

41. Gavrilyuk, *Georges Florovsky*, 143, 218, 240. It is also remarkable that the Encyclical of the Holy and Great Council of the Orthodox Church (Crete, June 20–25, 2016), mentions the councils of 1341, 1351, and 1368 in the short list of the "councils of *universal* authority" (emphasis added), through which the conciliar work continues uninterruptedly in history.

42. Ware, "God Hidden and Revealed," 129. André de Halleux, however, is not convinced by this explanation and admits the possibility that the "neo-Palamites exaggerate the canonicity of Palamism." See de Halleux, "Palamisme et scolastique: Exclusivisme dogmatique ou pluriformite theologique?," *Revue theologique de Louvain* 4 (1973): 441–42.

43. Ware, "God Hidden and Revealed," 136. See further details on this issue in Anna Ngaire Williams, *The Ground of Union: Deification in Aquinas and Palamas* (Oxford: Oxford University Press, 1999), 148–51.

In neo-Palamite theology, the essence-energy distinction not only has been treasured as an essential part of the Eastern spiritual and doctrinal legacy, but has also served polemical purposes. The revival of Palamas in the twentieth century can be properly understood only in the context of the necessity to establish a distinctive Orthodox identity in the midst of the Western theological world. The essence-energy distinction, coupled with the alleged personalism of the Eastern tradition, became the heart of Orthodox self-understanding and a kind of shibboleth that distinguishes Orthodoxy from Roman Catholicism. As Bradshaw notes, the distinction has been "recognized as the most important philosophical tenet distinguishing eastern Christian thought from its western counterpart."[44] It was used as a universal explanation of various divergences between East and West and as an indicator of the deficient character of the Western tradition. According to Yannaras, "the acceptance and rejection of this distinction represents two fundamentally different visions of truth, two noncoinciding ontologies, ... two diametrically opposite ways of life, with concrete spiritual, historical and cultural consequences."[45] It has even been suggested that the distinction has replaced the *filioque* as the most serious obstacle standing in the way of union between the Orthodox and Roman Catholic churches.[46]

Although hardly any contemporary Orthodox theologian would openly and consistently deny the essence-energy distinction, some individuals prefer to work out the doctrine of God without appealing to it. For example, according to John Zizioulas, the Palamite distinction preserves God's otherness and his communion with creatures, but does this in a way that is insufficiently personalistic: in this schema, the key ontological concept responsible for bridging the divine and the human is *energy* (common to all the Trinity) rather than a concrete person. Zizioulas concedes that Palamas understood the energies as enhypostatic, which places him *essentially* in line with the approach Zizioulas himself advocates, but he warns that an

44. Bradshaw, *Aristotle East and West*, xi.

45. Yannaras, "Distinction between Essence," 241. See also his book *Orthodoxy and the West*, trans. Peter Chamberas and Norman Russell (Brookline, NY: Holy Cross Orthodox Press, 2006), 23, 35–36, 49, 86, 278.

46. David Coffey, "The Palamite Doctrine of God: A New Perspective," *SVTQ* 32 (1988): 329; "Orient et occident: Grégoire Palamas," *Istina* 3 (1974): 257.

overemphasis on the energies may potentially endanger the role of the *hypostasis* of the Logos in the God-man relationship.[47] Thus, Zizioulas does not criticize the Palamite distinction as such, but rather disagrees with some aspects of its reception among neo-Palamites, who, according to Zizioulas, "tend to exhaust God's soteriological work with the divine energies and undermine the involvement of the divine persons in salvation."[48] The key distinctive mark of Orthodoxy for Zizioulas is the priority of person over essence, not the essence-energy distinction.

Another prominent Orthodox theologian, David Bentley Hart, is skeptical about both personalism and the essence-energy distinction as distinctive marks of Orthodoxy. He doubts whether Palamas himself knew what he meant by the distinction and wonders whether the Thomistic and Palamite positions "are divided by anything much more profound than the acceptations of their preferred metaphors."[49] According to Hart, any talk about the knowability or unknowability of the divine essence is after all "pious nonsense," because the essence is not a discrete object, whether of knowledge or of ignorance.[50] Hart relativizes the differences between the West and East and regrets that the prevalence of neo-Palamism in modern Orthodox theology has led to a certain narrowing of the spectrum of what can be treated as central or legitimate.[51] Replying to Hart, Bradshaw insists on the substantial difference between the Greek fathers and Augustine, who collapses the distinction between essence and energies by applying terms such as "Truth" or "Being" to the divine essence and by allowing contemplation of "God in himself" in the beatific vision.[52] In

---

47. Zizioulas, *Communion and Otherness*, 26–30, 278.

48. Zizioulas, *Communion and Otherness*, 139.

49. David Bentley Hart, "The Hidden and the Manifest: Metaphysics after Nicaea," in *Orthodox Readings of Augustine*, ed. George E. Demacopoulos and Aristotle Papanikolaou (Crestwood, NY: St Vladimir's Seminary Press, 2008), 211.

50. Hart, "Hidden and the Manifest," 214.

51. David Bentley Hart Hart, "The Myth of Schism," in *Hidden and the Manifest*, 273. Elsewhere he even notes that "some Eastern theologians might be emboldened partly to abandon the Neo-Palamite theology that has become so dominant in their Church since the middle of the last century, and frankly acknowledge its incoherence." See Hart, "Foreword," in *Encounter between Eastern Orthodoxy and Radical Orthodoxy*, ed. Adrian Pabst and Christoph Schneider (Farnham, UK: Ashgate, 2009), xiii.

52. David Bradshaw, "Augustine the Metaphysician," in Demacopoulos and Papanikolaou, *Orthodox Readings of Augustine*, 247–48.

contemporary theology, it is especially Bradshaw's works that prove the abiding legacy of neo-Palamism. The neo-Palamite interpretation of the relation between God's hiddenness and revelation remains dominant in contemporary Orthodoxy.[53]

The Relation of God's Hiddenness and Revelation in the Reformed Tradition

The Reformed tradition has also tried to simultaneously accentuate God's hiddenness and revelation. This tradition has been characterized by a strong emphasis on the transcendence and majesty of God and at the same time on his all-embracing providence and accommodated revelation in, and to, the world. Some formulations by early Reformers reveal at least an outward affinity with Eastern thought: in an often-quoted statement, Calvin writes that God is manifested through his virtues, "by which he is shown to us not as he is in himself, but as he is towards us; so that this recognition of him consists more in living experience than in vain and high-flown speculation." In interpreting this statement, we must keep in mind that Calvin's intent here is not to demarcate what is and what is not communicated to us, but rather to preclude inquisitive searching into the essence of God and his secret counsel. God is to be more adored than investigated. Instead of attempting "with bold curiosity to penetrate to the investigation of his essence," Christians should "contemplate him in his works whereby he renders himself near and familiar to us, and in some manner communicates himself."[54] Dawn DeVries calls Calvin's approach "a pious agnosticism": "it is better to say, when necessary, that we do not know than to claim an overreaching insight into the divine nature."[55] This does

53. According to Aristotle Papanikolaou, "the essence-energies distinction is central to most contemporary Orthodox theologians ... with the exception of Bulgakov and Zizioulas." See Papanikolaou, "Sophia, Apophasis, and Communion: The Trinity in Contemporary Orthodox Theology," in *Cambridge Companion to the Trinity*, ed. Peter C. Phan (Cambridge: Cambridge University Press, 2011), 249, 256. See also Papanikolaou, *Being with God: Trinity, Apophaticism, and Divine-Human Communion* (Notre Dame, IN: Notre Dame University Press, 2006), 106.

54. John Calvin, *Institutes of the Christian Religion*, ed. John T. McNeill, trans. Ford Lewis Battles (Philadelphia: Westminster, 1960), I.10.2; I.5.9.

55. Dawn DeVries, "The Living God: The Problem of Divine Personality in Reformed Theology," in *Reformed Theology for the Third Christian Millennium*, ed. Brian Albert Gerrish (Louisville: Westminster John Knox, 2003), 72.

not mean, however, that Calvin believed that God's nature is not revealed: although an exhaustive knowledge of God is impossible for creatures, Calvin explains that God reveals his attributes to a certain extent. Calvin occasionally differentiates between God's nature and essence, and speaks more confidently about the knowability of the former than of the latter.[56] Nevertheless, even the essence of God is not completely beyond revelation, since in Christ, God has communicated himself to us *essentially*.[57]

In general, Calvin does not attempt to conceptualize the relation between God in himself and God for us. He instead emphasizes our dependence on God's revelation and the need to soberly use God's word. We must humbly and carefully listen to God's own testimony instead of producing our own ideas about God, because our mind is nothing but "a perpetual factory of idols."[58] "What Calvin is insistent upon," explains Fred Klooster, "is that we must not go beyond the bounds of revelation for our knowledge."[59] Calvin does, however, experience difficulties with a consistent application of this principle: for example, in substantiating the claim that God is free from emotions and changes, Calvin seemed to proceed from metaphysical presuppositions as much as from biblical revelation.[60]

The Reformed scholastics did not elaborate the dialectical nuances of Luther's *Deus absconditus* and often did not share Calvin's modesty in speaking of God. Rather, they turned to medieval scholastics and borrowed their methodological categories. In Reformed orthodoxy, the relation between God's hiddenness and revelation was normally expressed through various kinds of distinctions. Concrete examples of such distinctions will occupy

---

56. See Calvin's commentary on 2 Pet 1:4 in *Commentaries on the Catholic Epistles*, trans. and ed. John Owen (Grand Rapids: Baker, 1996), 371. Carl Mosser even suggests that Calvin's distinction between God's essence and his nature/quality has "functional similarity with the Orthodox essence-energies distinction." See Mosser, "The Greatest Possible Blessing: Calvin and Deification," *Scottish Journal of Theology* 55 (2002): 54. For other references to Calvin's works and a helpful overview of his implicit distinction between essence and nature, see Arnold Huijgen, *Divine Accommodation in John Calvin's Theology* (Göttingen: Vandenhoeck & Ruprecht, 2011), 284–87.

57. Huijgen, *Divine Accommodation*, 283–84; Richard Muller, *Post-Reformation Reformed Dogmatics* (Grand Rapids: Baker Academic, 2003), 3:210, 274.

58. Calvin, *Institutes* I.11.8.

59. Fred H. Klooster, *The Incomprehensibility of God in the Orthodox Presbyterian Conflict* (Franeker: Wever, 1951), 83.

60. Huijgen, *Divine Accommodation*, 276–79, 353–54.

us later.[61] For the present, suffice it to say that these distinctions were meant to indicate that God is simultaneously knowable and yet infinitely beyond human comprehension. The traditional Reformed formula *finitum non capax infiniti* was not only an important argument in the disputes with Lutherans over Christ's bodily ubiquity,[62] but also served to indicate the epistemological limitations of human beings. It emphasized the disproportion between divine things and their creaturely analogues, and excluded the univocal predication of the divine attributes and those of the finite order. According to the Reformed scholastics, predicates used in theology proper do not perfectly convey God as he is in himself. Some Reformed theologians, in a way reminiscent of Eastern fathers, even denied that God is nature or preferred to call God's essence *hyperousion* in view of its infinite difference from any creaturely essence. Nevertheless, the divine essence was conceived as knowable—if only to a certain extent—through knowledge of its attributes. This knowledge was believed to be acquired through attributing to God—"in the highest degree and measure, yea above all degree and measure" (Edward Leigh)—perfections revealed in the Bible and found in creatures.[63] Most Reformed scholastics shared Thomistic analogical reasoning and, while admitting that attributes in God are infinitely more perfect, they still asserted that these attributes have weak but reliable analogies in creation.

In the twentieth century, the influence of Barth's theology led to a reconsideration of the relation between God's hiddenness and revelation. Barth regretted that Christian theologians—with the exception, notable for our study, of the Dutch theologian Herman Bavinck—had lost the true sense and significance of divine hiddenness. Barth put much stress on the "irrevocable otherness" of God: if we are to know God, we must set aside all human concepts and turn to God's revelation. We can know God only "in utter dependence, in pure discipleship and gratitude." This total

---

61. See "The Relation of God's Hiddenness and His Revelation" (pages 119–37).

62. Lutheran theologians argued that Christ, by virtue of the communication of properties between his two natures, can be present bodily in many places at the same time. Reformed theologians, however, rejected a flow of attributes from one nature to another and insisted that the finitude of human nature cannot grasp the infinity of God. They believed that Christ's body retains its human characteristics and cannot be omnipresent. For further details, see Calvin, *Institutes* IV.17.16–31.

63. Muller, *Post-Reformation Reformed Dogmatics*, 3:199–202, 204–5, 214, 237.

dependence on God's revelation is crucial, according to Barth, also for our understanding of God's *hiddenness*. It is a mistake to derive the idea of God's hiddenness from human experience. "God's hiddenness is not the content of a last word of human self-knowledge; it is not the object of a last performance of human capacity."[64] God is not the projection of finite concepts, stripped of their limitations.[65] "Nothing can be more misleading," explains Barth, "than the opinion that the theological statement of the hiddenness of God says roughly the same thing as the Platonic or Kantian statement, according to which the supreme being is to be understood as a rational idea withdrawn from all perception and understanding." According to Barth, even if one chooses the negative way and describes in negative terms what God is not, such theologizing is still controlled by human concepts and must be rejected. God's hiddenness, therefore, is not a conclusion drawn from a general theory of human knowledge, nor an abstraction based on our categories of time and space, but "the content of a statement of faith." The knowledge of God's hiddenness is a part of our knowledge of God. As we know God only by faith, so we also know God's hiddenness only by faith. Barth avoids, therefore, the notion of God's hiddenness as something "before" revelation. If we say that God remains hidden until he reveals himself, then we define his hiddenness abstracted from revelation. Such thinking is wrong because, according to Barth, all God-talk, including that of the hiddenness of God, must only be defined in accordance with God's revelation.[66]

Barth argues that *in and of ourselves*, we do not resemble God and are not capable of conceiving of him; *in and of itself*, our language is unable to speak of God; *in and of itself*, our reason is unable to think of God. To be sure, this does not mean that we cannot use human words in theology. We must not *start*, however, with ourselves or our human words. As Bruce McCormack explains: "If we are going to use any words rightly, we must be taught by God how to do so."[67] For Barth, our words and concepts are

64. *CD* II/1:182, 186.

65. Bruce L. McCormack, *Karl Barth's Critically Realistic Dialectical Theology: Its Genesis and Development, 1909–1936* (Oxford: Clarendon, 1995), 247.

66. *CD* II/1:183–86, 192.

67. Bruce L. McCormack, *Orthodox and Modern: Studies in the Theology of Karl Barth* (Grand Rapids: Baker Academic, 2008), 171.

taken into the service of God's revelatory act. It is only God's grace that enables human language to describe God. Barth vehemently rejects any attempt to ascend from creatures to God based on a static analogy in creatures themselves.[68] He does not deny the possibility of analogy altogether, but insists that it is dynamically "created" in the act of revelation. "What makes the creature the *analogatum* of God is ... *not* something that is found 'in' the creature. It is found, rather, in the revelation-relation, in the correspondence established in that relation between God and the creature."[69] A real analogy between God and humanity can only be created by the work of God's grace and accepted by faith.[70]

Although in and of ourselves we are not capable of apprehending the truth of God, God enables us to know him. In his revelation God is apprehensible: "He is so in such a way that He makes Himself apprehensible to those who cannot apprehend Him of themselves." Knowledge of the true God entails real human perception, but this perception is made possible by God and does not therefore cancel out his hiddenness. Our knowledge of God, including his hiddenness, is always a divine gift and possible only by faith. Further, God's revelation is *self*-revelation; it is God himself who is revealed: "In the revelation of God there is no hidden God, *no Deus absconditus*, at the back of His revelation." Barth suggests that Luther's theology "in certain contexts" implies an existence of God behind his self-revelation.[71] But, according to the testimony of Scripture, by God's initiative and grace he reveals himself in person and does not merely reveal some truths about himself.[72] God's presence in his revelation is whole and complete. Any other position would be an underestimation of God's revelation in Jesus Christ.[73]

---

68. *CD* II/1:231.

69. McCormack, *Orthodox and Modern*, 177.

70. *CD* II/1:83; see also 75–82, 225–31.

71. *CD* II/1:192, 195, 197, 210.

72. In spite of his emphasis on the identity of God's being and act, Barth still made a distinction between God's essence and operations in a typical dialectical tension: "All we can know of God according to the witness of Scripture are His acts. All we can say of God, all the attributes we can assign to God, relate to these acts of His; not, then, to His essence as such. Though the work of God is the essence of God, it is necessary and important to distinguish His essence as such from His work, remembering that this work is grace, a free divine decision, and also remembering that we can know about God only because and to the extent that He gives Himself to us to be known" (*CD* I/1:371).

73. *CD* II/1:342.

Barth accentuates the hiddenness of God even in the very act of revelation. God's hiddenness is to be found not *alongside* or *behind* revelation but *in* it.

In more traditional Reformed circles, the relation between God's hiddenness and revelation came to the foreground of theological reflection in the 1940s during the so-called Clark-Van Til controversy in the Orthodox Presbyterian Church.[74] The fundamental assumption of Gordon Clark was that revelation is given in propositional form, with each proposition having the same meaning for God and humanity.[75] For example, man's knowledge of the statement that Christ died for our sins is qualitatively identical to God's knowledge of this statement. God's incomprehensibility points out the need for revelation: by their own unaided powers humans can never discover truth about God, and therefore God is incomprehensible if he is not revealed. But insofar as God reveals himself, he can be comprehended by humanity . To be sure, human knowledge of God and God's self-knowledge are still different, for several reasons: God knows himself intuitively, while humanity can know God only discursively; propositions are infinite in number, and God does not reveal all of them (and thus human knowledge always remains limited); and humanity is not able to know any given proposition with all its infinite relationships and implications. Cornelius Van Til and his followers, however, complained that Clark's method was rationalistic and did not honor the incomprehensibility and otherness of God.[76] Van Til employed the old distinction between apprehension and comprehension: based on God's revelation, humanity can truly know God, but, due to the infinite difference between God and creatures, humanity cannot know any truth about God *comprehensively*. Without revelation, God is *unknown*; but he remains *incomprehensible* even in the revealed truths. The main point of Van Til was the qualitative difference

74. For an overview of the controversy, see Klooster, *Incomprehensibility of God*, 13–41; John M. Frame, *The Doctrine of the Knowledge of God* (Phillipsburg, NJ: Presbyterian & Reformed, 1987), 21–40.

75. Gordon H. Clark, *God's Hammer: The Bible and Its Critics* (Jefferson, MD: Trinity Foundation), 27–38.

76. Clark's arguments are stated in Gordon H. Clark, "The Answer to a Complaint against Several Actions and Decisions of the Presbytery of Philadelphia Taken in a Special Meeting Held on July 7, 1944" (unpublished defense paper, Philadelphia Orthodox Presbyterian Church). Cornelius Van Til's position is expressed in "The Text of a Complaint against Actions of the Presbytery of Philadelphia in the Matter of the Licensure and Ordination of Dr. Gordon H. Clark" (unpublished complaint, Philadelphia Orthodox Presbyterian Church).

between God's knowledge and humanity's knowledge: what humanity can know is only a faint analogy of the knowledge God possesses. Divine knowledge differs not only in mode (intuitive versus discursive) and in number of known propositions and their implications, but also in kind.[77]

In the last quarter of the twentieth century, due to the dissemination of Orthodox theology in the West, Reformed scholars started to pay more explicit and close attention to the distinction between essence and energies. This tendency not only reflected greater openness to other traditions and a desire to give a more ecumenical and comprehensive account of the doctrine of God, but correlated with the growing attentiveness to the idea of theosis in Protestant circles. As Todd Billings indicates, Palamism has frequently been used as the paradigm by which all Christian theologies of deification are judged.[78] In reaction, some theologians tried to show that the affirmation of deification is not necessarily bound to the acceptance of the essence-energy distinction.

Thomas F. Torrance, who was, undoubtedly, the most active Reformed participant in the dialogue with Eastern Orthodoxy, discussed the Palamite distinction. Torrance's principal theological mentors were Athanasius and Karl Barth, from whom he borrowed his emphases on the consubstantiality of the divine persons and on the unity of God's being and act. According to Torrance, in every religion apart from Christianity, God remains unknowable in his inner life. It is only through Christ and in the Spirit that God reveals himself "as he is in himself, and not just in his external relations toward us or in some merely negative way."[79] The Nicene ὁμοούσιος means that Jesus Christ is one with the Father in act as well as in being (Torrance prefers the word "being" to the word "essence"): the incarnation falls within the life of God himself, and in Christ God reveals whom he really is in his very being.[80] The economic Trinity, therefore, is normative for our

---

77. Cornelius Van Til, *An Introduction to Systematic Theology: Prolegomena and the Doctrines of Revelation, Scripture, and God* (Phillipsburg, NJ: Presbyterian & Reformed, 2007), 260–309.

78. J. Todd Billings, "John Calvin: United to God through Christ," in *Partakers of the Divine Nature: The History and Development of Deification in the Christian Traditions*, ed. Michael J. Christensen and Jeffery A. Wittung (Grand Rapids: Baker Academic, 2008), 200, 208.

79. Thomas F. Torrance, *Trinitarian Perspectives: Toward Doctrinal Agreement* (Edinburgh: T&T Clark, 1994), 2, 86, 128.

80. Thomas F. Torrance, *Trinitarian Faith: The Evangelical Theology of the Ancient Catholic Church* (Edinburgh: T&T Clark, 1995), 74, 130, 303; Torrance, *Trinitarian Perspectives*, 81.

understanding of the ontological Trinity: the interrelations between the divine persons in the history of salvation can be traced back to the eternal relations in the divine being because the activity of the economic Trinity is grounded in and flows from the ontological Trinity.[81]

Torrance suggests that in Athanasius's theology God's energy is intrinsic to his very being: "His activity and his being are essentially and eternally one."[82] Otherwise, it would be impossible to relate what God is toward us to what he is in himself. "An entire different" conception, Torrance argues, appeared in later theology, which distinguished between God's energies and his essence.[83] Basil and his brother Gregory introduced "the rather dualist distinction ... between the transcendent Being of God which is quite unknowable and the uncreated energies of his self-revelation."[84] According to Torrance, the essence-energy distinction amounts to restricting human knowledge of God to his energies and ruling out any real access to God in himself.[85] The distinction, according to Torrance, is sharp, dangerous, and unsatisfactory, because it downplays the oneness between what God is in Christ and what he ever was antecedently in his intradivine life. It does not do justice to the Nicene ὁμοούσιος doctrine, according to which, "in the Holy Spirit, God communicates *himself* to us, not just something of himself in his uncreated energies—the divine Giver and the divine Gift

---

81. Thomas F. Torrance, *The Christian Doctrine of God: One Being, Three Persons* (Edinburgh: T&T Clark, 1996), 172, 198.

82. Torrance, *Trinitarian Faith*, 73.

83. Thomas F. Torrance, *Divine Meaning: Studies in Patristic Hermeneutics* (Edinburgh: T&T Clark, 1995), 188.

84. Torrance, *Christian Doctrine*, 177; see also Torrance, *Trinitarian Faith*, 317. Although Torrance admits that for Basil this distinction was not as important as it later became for Palamas (*Trinitarian Perspectives*, 38), he nonetheless refers to it as "the Basilian and Palamite distinction" (*Christian Doctrine*, 187), because he himself does not see significant differences between how these two theologians understood the distinction. By contrast, Torrance clearly differentiates between Basil and Gregory of Nazianzus in this respect (*Trinitarian Perspectives*, 38–39). The same holds true for another point on which Torrance disagreed with Basil: causality within the Godhead. Torrance suggests that Basil's belief in the monarchy of the Father as the cause of the Son and the Spirit implies a hierarchical ontology and reveals traces of Origenist subordinationism. At the same time, Gregory of Nazianzus, according to Torrance, rejected such hierarchical structure and insisted that the monarchy may not be limited to one divine person (*Trinitarian Perspectives*, 29–32, 138–39).

85. Torrance, *Christian Doctrine*, 187. See also Torrance, *Trinitarian Faith*, 336.

are one and the same."[86] In this regard, Torrance notes what he considers Basil's strange hesitancy to explicitly affirm the consubstantiality of the Holy Spirit.[87] The idea that we know only the things *around* God's nature, and not his nature itself, introduces an "economic reserve" and "seems to put a question mark before any doctrine of oneness between the Immanent or Ontological Trinity and the Economic Trinity."[88]

To be sure, Torrance's critical remarks about the essence-energy distinction were occasional and are scattered throughout his many publications.[89] Myk Habets rightly observes that Torrance "never ventured a full-scale critique of the distinction, perhaps on account of his close relations with the Eastern Orthodox Churches."[90] Nevertheless, Torrance's negative attitude to the distinction is obvious and consistent, coming to the fore even in his interpretation of the theology of Calvin. Writing for an ecumenical Orthodox-Reformed volume, Torrance admits to problems in Calvin's theology, "the most obvious" of which "relates to his doctrine of predestination with its apparent split in the doctrine of God, … a duality between the eternal God as he is in himself, and God as he manifests himself in his incarnate and redemptive form in Jesus Christ." Torrance further notes that Calvin "partly" inherited this "dualism in the doctrine of God" from Augustine, but, adds Torrance, "perhaps the decisive thing here is that he was influenced by the distinction begun by the Cappadocians between the eternal 'Being' of God and his 'Energies.'"[91] Thus, according to Torrance, Calvin's preoccupation with the Eastern fathers in this area led to unfortunate consequences.

Another Reformed theologian, Robert Letham, agrees, for the most part, with Torrance's assessment and approvingly cites his conclusion that the essence-energy distinction drives a wedge between the inner life of God

---

86. Torrance, *Christian Doctrine*, 188, emphasis original. See also Torrance, *Trinitarian Faith*, 210.

87. Torrance, *Trinitarian Faith*, 232.

88. Torrance, *Trinitarian Perspectives*, 40, 86, 38.

89. A more detailed overview can be found in Stoyan Tanev, "The Concept of Energy in T. F. Torrance and in Orthodox Theology," in *T. F. Torrance and Eastern Orthodoxy: Theology in Reconciliation*, ed. Matthew Baker and Todd Speidell (Eugene, OR: Wipf & Stock, 2015), 194–217.

90. Myk Habets, *Theosis in the Theology of Thomas Torrance* (Farnham, UK: Ashgate, 2009), 131.

91. Torrance, "Memoranda on Orthodox/Reformed Relations," 13–14.

and his saving activities.[92] Letham views the distinction as a major flaw in Orthodox theology and sharply criticizes its implications. The doctrine of Palamas introduces into God a division—"a radical cleavage"—rather than a distinction.[93] On the one hand, the total unknowability of the divine essence amounts to a form of "invincible" and "profound" agnosticism; on the other hand, the fullness of God's revelation in his energies means that "we can be masters of his revelation." The distinction, Letham argues, threatens not only our knowledge of God but also our trust in him, because it questions his faithfulness and reliability. Letham also concurs with theologians who maintain that the Palamite distinction depersonalizes revelation by substituting impersonal energies for the persons of the Son and the Spirit. The Palamite schema is ultimately self-contradictory: one must know something about God's essence in order to judge it unknowable. Letham even claims that Palamas "identified the two natures of Christ with energies," "appeared to regard the person of Christ as a divine energy," and seemed to reduce "the person of the Son to a divine attribute."[94] Such identifications—Christ's natures with energies and then the person of the Son with an energy or an attribute—would indeed signal a collapse of classical Trinitarianism and Christology. Letham, however, does not clearly specify textual evidence to support such conclusions, and it seems clear that at this point he does not accurately represent the Palamite schema.

Apart from employing a sharper rhetoric, Letham differs from Torrance in his understanding of the historical development of the essence-energy distinction. While he similarly contrasts Athanasius with the later Eastern tradition on this matter, unlike Torrance, Letham puts Basil on the side of Athanasius and does not see strict continuity between Basil and Palamas. Letham agrees that the distinction as such was introduced by Basil, but insists that, nonetheless, the theology of Palamas was not a development of Basil's distinction, but "a radical departure from the Cappadocians." In Letham's reconstruction, it was not Basil but rather John of Damascus who

92. Robert Letham, *Through Western Eyes: Eastern Orthodoxy, A Reformed Perspective* (Fearn, UK: Mentor, 2007), 234, 283.

93. Robert Letham, *The Holy Trinity: In Scripture, History, Theology, and Worship* (Phillipsburg, NJ: Presbyterian & Reformed, 2004), 348, see also 346; Letham, *Through Western Eyes*, 283.

94. Letham, *Holy Trinity*, 237, 247–49, 346–47, 354; Letham, *Through Western Eyes*, 234.

"introduced a deep agnosticism about our knowledge of God" by asserting that positive qualities such as goodness or wisdom denote not God's nature but the things around his nature. According to Letham, this dichotomy departs from earlier Eastern thought and eventually leads to the distortion and defeat of Trinitarian theology.[95]

A far more positive evaluation of the essence-energy distinction can be found in the works of Michael Horton. He does not investigate the historical vicissitudes of the distinction in Greek thought, but takes it as a concept consistently developed from the Cappadocians to contemporary neo-Palamists. Horton contends that the distinction has "close parallels" to the Reformed view that we know God in his works rather than in his essence, to the epistemological distinction between archetypal and ectypal theology, and even to the Reformers' contrast between a theology of glory and a theology of the cross.[96] In general, Horton is far from a naive and shallow understanding of ecumenical problems,[97] but in this particular case he considers the Reformed and Orthodox traditions as close to each other: "Whatever remaining differences between Eastern Orthodox and Reformed theologies—and they are not insignificant—the distinction between essence and energies itself may reflect a point of convergence." Moreover, according to Horton, the essence-energy distinction not only is acceptable to Reformed theology, but indeed indispensable to it. It was appropriated by Calvin and "provides the context for Calvin's (and broader Reformed) reflection on everything from how we know God to union with Christ to sacramental theology."[98] Thus, Horton contends that the essence-energy distinction is presupposed in Reformed thought, even if it is not explicitly invoked.

Horton himself extensively uses the distinction as the necessary metaphysical underpinning of many ideas and doctrines. He regrets that Western theologians have normally recognized only two categories, God's

95. Letham, *Holy Trinity*, 165, 238, 249; see also 209; Letham, *Through Western Eyes*, 90, 283.

96. Michael Horton, *Covenant and Salvation: Union with Christ* (Louisville: Westminster John Knox, 2007), 211–12, 281; Horton, *The Christian Faith: A Systematic Theology for Pilgrims on the Way* (Grand Rapids: Zondervan, 2011), 130, 131, 994.

97. In the volume *Three Views on Eastern Orthodoxy and Evangelicalism* (Grand Rapids: Zondervan, 2004), Horton represents the view that these two traditions are incompatible.

98. Horton, *Christian Faith*, 613, 817; see also Horton, *Covenant and Salvation*, 212, 214.

essence and creation, and understood their relation in terms of causality. This was one of the most important factors behind certain problems in Western theology. The West needs, therefore, to borrow the East's *tertium quid*—divine energies—and interpret them as God's acts. Fortunately, Horton argues, this concept has been present in Reformed theology, albeit implicitly and under different terms.[99] With this concept, we can maintain that God's act of creating the world was neither an emanation of God's essence nor a creaturely effect. Other divine acts, such as sustaining and redeeming, should also not be identified with the essence or its extension, but rather understood as powerful energies that achieve God's eternal purposes.[100] The divine acts of speaking also belong to his energies: unlike the incarnate Word (consubstantial with the Father and the Spirit), the spoken and written word is not God's essence. But it is also not merely a creaturely witness: it is the energy of God, "the energetic Word."[101] The notion of the divine energies as distinct from the immutable divine essence allows us to see God's interaction with his creatures as a story, in dynamic and personal terms. We participate not in the divine essence but in the divine *drama*; we encounter and worship not the divine essence but the divine *persons*.[102] The object of theology is not God in his hidden essence but God in his covenant with creatures. "The triune God is known in his works, not in his essence," Horton repeats time and again.[103] The quest for "whatness"—divine or even human—is for Horton inherently philosophical and speculative.[104]

Interestingly, Horton tries to combine the essence-energy distinction with Thomistic analogical reasoning. Moreover, the acceptance of the distinction is a *necessary* corollary of analogical God-talk: "If one is serious about the doctrine of analogy, it [i.e., the distinction] would seem to be the

---

99. Michael Horton, *People and Place: A Covenant Ecclesiology* (Louisville: Westminster John Knox, 2008), 136–37.

100. Horton, *Christian Faith*, 130, 159, 237, 612, 690; Horton, *People and Place*, 133.

101. Horton, *Christian Faith*, 130, 136, 154, 164, 166, 181, 574, 751, 753, 758; Horton, *People and Place*, 101, 136–37; Horton, *Covenant and Salvation*, 302.

102. Horton, *Christian Faith*, 44, 45, emphasis original; Michael Horton, *Lord and Servant: A Covenant Christology* (Louisville: Westminster John Knox, 2005), 10; Horton, *Covenant and Salvation*, 211.

103. Horton, *Lord and Servant*, 22; Michael Horton, *Covenant and Eschatology: The Divine Drama* (Louisville: Westminster John Knox, 2002), 81, 249; Horton, *Covenant and Salvation*, 302; Horton, *Christian Faith*, 52, 363, 612.

104. Horton, *Christian Faith*, 373, 378, 781; Horton, *Covenant and Eschatology*, 249.

only appropriate move."[105] Given Horton's emphasis on analogy, one might expect that in his theology God's energies and essence would be analogically related, so that the knowledge of God's energies would give us an imperfect but true knowledge of God's essence. For instance, from God's faithfulness, wisdom, and holiness as revealed in his covenantal relationships, one could conclude that this is also what God is in his essence—albeit, to a far superior degree that we cannot fully comprehend. Horton himself does not refrain from asserting that God is holy, omnipresent, gracious, and merciful "in his essence." He also speaks of many other "essential attributes" and affirms that they are identical with God's essence. However, according to Horton, analogical knowledge of *the attributes* of God's essence does not mean that we also know the essence itself: "God reveals his attributes (i.e., characteristics) rather than his hidden essence." The essence itself is never revealed or communicated: neither directly nor indirectly, neither fully nor in a limited way, neither in this life nor in the life to come.[106] Horton seems to believe that the essence is not simply a set of attributes, but a sort of interior substantiality that requires strictly univocal predication in order to be known. Since this is obviously impossible for human beings, we do not know the divine essence at all. Horton affirms the importance of the distinction between archetype and ectype, but he employs it to emphasize the impossibility of archetypal knowledge of God rather than to establish an analogical relation between God's self-knowledge and our knowledge of God based on his ectypal revelation.

Horton criticizes modern theologians such as Barth and his followers, who reject the distinction between God's essence and his revelation. The identification of God's being with his act confuses being with becoming, eternity with history. The divine essence is then subject to being affected by creatures and susceptible to changes and suffering. But with the essence-energy distinction, Horton contends, one can simultaneously confess the impassibility and immutability of God's essence and his genuine interaction with creatures, which does make an impact on his energies. Further, the distinction allows us to combine God's simplicity with the

105. Horton, *Covenant and Salvation*, 272.

106. Horton, *Christian Faith*, 131, 255, 265, 267, 603, 694, 698; Horton, *Covenant and Salvation*, 282.

diversity of his works, to affirm God's freedom, and to distinguish between begetting as a hypostatic act and creating as an energetic act.[107]

Horton argues that the inability of the West to recognize the importance of the essence-energy distinction made its mysticism and theology prone to denying the boundary between Creator and creatures: "Eliminating this distinction leads logically to pantheism or panentheism." The distinction is therefore especially important in relation to participation in God and union with Christ: it "helps us to avoid the tendency in the West either to undervalue the realism of this union or to collapse into pantheism."[108] Horton appreciates the Eastern account of theosis and claims that Calvin and the Reformed tradition were "more congenial" to it than "some of the recent (mainly Protestant) proposals that claim this heritage."[109] According to Horton, genuine participation in God is not participation in his essence. The source enabling participation with Christ is rather God's energies: "It is not the essence of the historical person of Christ, either his deity or humanity, that is communicated to us, but his energies."[110] The essence-energy distinction, therefore, is the ontological underpinning of "a covenantal account of participation," which avoids the false dilemma of choosing either "participation in essence or nonparticipation."[111] According to Horton, this distinction was also crucial to Calvin's views on Christ's presence in the Lord's Supper: it is Christ's energies that are communicated to us by the Spirit in the sacrament.[112] "Only with the Eastern category of God's energies, distinct from his essence and from created things, was Calvin able to affirm that Christ is an inexhaustible life-giving fountain communicated in the Supper."[113]

The views of Torrance, Letham, and Horton represent three Reformed attitudes to the Eastern essence-energy distinction, which differ in their general appraisals (negative in Torrance and Letham and rather

---

107. Horton, *Christian Faith*, 127, 181, 228, 234, 237, 244–45, 248, 332, 556.

108. Horton, *Christian Faith*, 237, 615.

109. Horton, *Covenant and Salvation*, 274. Horton seems to mean the Finnish school and Radical Orthodoxy. See also his comment that the "Reformed notion of divinization is more oriented to the essence-energy of the East" (289).

110. Horton, *Christian Faith*, 700. See also Horton, *People and Place*, 136–37.

111. Horton, *Covenant and Salvation*, 215.

112. Horton, *People and Place*, 133–36.

113. Horton, *Christian Faith*, 818; see also 825.

enthusiastic in Horton), in theological backgrounds (a Barthian one in Torrance and more traditional ones in Letham and Horton), in their historical reconstructions of the period from the Cappadocians to Palamas, and in their understanding of the compatibility of the distinction with Calvin and the later Reformed tradition. The contributions of other Reformed theologians who touch on this issue incidentally tend to correspond with one of these three attitudes.[114] Overall, the diversity of Reformed approaches to the relation between God's hiddenness and revelation is more pronounced than that found in Eastern Orthodoxy. This diversity is noticeable in the assessment of the essence-energy distinction and it is also evident in other areas related to the task of developing a Reformed ontological language in the doctrine of God. It is difficult, therefore, to speak of any dominant trend in Reformed theology on the matter.

METHOD AND OUTLINE

As indicated above, the present study compares Orthodox and Reformed approaches to the relation between God's hiddenness and revelation. Further, the study also includes an evaluation of the main emphases of both traditions. In short, it aims to answer the following question: *What are the similarities and the differences between the Reformed and the Eastern Orthodox traditions regarding the relation between God's hiddenness and his revelation, and how can these differences be evaluated?*

The structure of the study is dictated by the structure of the above questions. While any comparison depends on careful observation and analysis, the general overview of Orthodox and Reformed approaches presented above makes clear that a comprehensive discussion is impossible due to their richness and diversity. In order that the scope of this research may be clear and specific, I will focus only on two theologians: the Reformed theologian Herman Bavinck and the Eastern Orthodox theologian John

114. See McLelland, "Sailing to Byzantium," 15–19; Donald Fairbairn, *Eastern Orthodoxy through Western Eyes* (Louisville: Westminster John Knox, 2002), 54–55, 115–16; Colin Gunton, *Act and Being: Towards a Theology of the Divine Attributes* (London: SCM, 2002), 110–12; J. Todd Billings, *Calvin, Participation, and the Gift: The Activity of Believers in Union with Christ* (Oxford: Oxford University Press, 2007), passim; James R. Payton Jr., *Light from the Christian East: An Introduction to the Orthodox Tradition* (Downers Grove, IL: InterVarsity Press, 2010), 78–82; Roy Clouser, "Pancreation Lost: The Fall of Theology," in Athanasopoulos and Schneider, *Divine Essence and Divine Energies*, 68–95.

Meyendorff. Both tried to faithfully represent their own respective traditions and did not pursue originality for its own sake. At the same time, both Bavinck the neo-Calvinist and Meyendorff the neo-Palamite did more than echo timeworn theological formulas. Instead, they tried to revive old traditions through interacting with contemporary movements. Both valued their traditions but realized the need for a more modern presentation of the treasures rooted in these traditions. To be sure, Bavinck's perspective does not (and cannot) represent the entire Reformed tradition in its fullness, just as Meyendorff's perspective does not represent the entire Eastern Orthodox tradition. They are, nonetheless, prominent theologians within their respective traditions and in many ways are rather typical representatives, which makes them highly suitable for the present study. Under "Why Bavinck?" (pages 34–37) and "Why Meyendorff?" (pages 140–42) I elaborate on the reasons for choosing each to represent their traditions.

Chapters 2 and 3 examine the views of Bavinck and Meyendorff respectively. In these chapters I allow the theologians to speak in their own terms, without imposing on them issues with which they themselves did not wrestle. These two chapters are independent of each other and reflect the method, context, and terms of each theologian. They are descriptive in character and form the foundation of the subsequent comparison and evaluation presented in chapter 4.

In comparing Bavinck and Meyendorff, I will focus on several key issues related to the topic and will identify areas of agreement and disagreement between the theologians. I will also try to determine whether the differences render their approaches mutually exclusive or whether they are instead caused by different vocabulary and emphases. The goal, however, is not to overemphasize similarities and relativize differences, thereby artificially bringing the two theologians into agreement. Rather, I will seek to deepen understanding the discussion and come to better disagreements—that is, to delineate aspects of disagreement that are informed and nuanced by a proper understanding of the views and intentions of the respective theologian on each side of the dialogue.

My choice of evaluation criteria stems from the character of the discussions about the relation between God's hiddenness and revelation. Orthodox theologians often criticize Western (including Reformed) theologies either for compromising God's incomprehensibility or for underestimating the reality of union with God, or both. The first accusation is primarily directed at Thomistic epistemology, while the second is related to the prevalence of juridical categories in Roman Catholic and Protestant soteriology. In response, Western theologians usually defend their views by indicating that knowledge or vision of the God's essence does not necessarily endanger his incomprehensibility, and that the legal soteriological dimension can be combined with ontological, transformative images. Although, as we will see in chapter 4, the Orthodox and Reformed traditions may assign somewhat different meanings to the concepts of God's incomprehensibility and union with God, they agree that the relation between God's hiddenness and his revelation must be formulated in a way that is compatible with both concepts. Thus, my first two criteria are the preservation of God's incomprehensibility and the reality of union with God.

Reformed theologians, for their part, criticize Orthodox theology mostly for driving a wedge between God in himself and God for us. Orthodox theologians typically dismiss this charge and insist that the essence-energy distinction does not result in the recognition of two divine entities. Both sides, therefore, confess one God who is in himself the same as he is for us. Consequently, my third criterion is the oneness of God.

Before proceeding with the task at hand, some small technical details should be clarified. Most of the texts cited in the present study were written in English or have been translated into English. In such cases, available English texts are used and referred to. Where translations are unavailable, I offer my own translation with a reference to the original publication (in Dutch or Russian in most cases). For Russian sources, the transliteration system of the US Board on Geographic Names is used. The English Standard Version is used for biblical citations.

2

HERMAN BAVINCK ON KNOWING GOD AS A REVEALED MYSTERY

INTRODUCTION

Overview of Bavinck's Life and Thought

Herman Bavinck (1854–1921) was a Dutch Reformed theologian. His father, Jan Bavinck, was a minister of the so-called Secession (*Afscheiding*) churches, which separated from the national church in 1834 and were characterized by deep piety, theological orthodoxy, social passivity, and cultural asceticism. Herman Bavinck was a committed son of the Secession movement. Later in his career he confessed: "I am a child of the Secession and I hope always to remain one. … The best I have I am indebted to the Secession."[1] Modernity, however, also left a deep impression on this child. Bavinck decided to pursue his theological education not at the school of the Secession churches in Kampen (where he spent only a year) but at the University of Leiden, where he could immerse himself in an academic environment and study modern theology firsthand.

After graduating from Leiden, Bavinck served for two years as a pastor in a Secession congregation. In 1882, he was appointed professor of dogmatic theology in Kampen, where he stayed until 1902. This period was the most fruitful for Bavinck as a theologian. Between 1895 and 1901, he published the first edition of his magnum opus, *Reformed*

1. Cited by Willem J. de Wit, *On the Way to the Living God: A Cathartic Reading of Herman Bavinck and an Invitation to Overcome the Plausibility Crisis of Christianity* (Amsterdam: VU University Press, 2011), 20. According to C. Veenhof, Bavinck mentioned this in his 1902 farewell lecture to students in Kampen, before he moved to Amsterdam. See Veenhof, "Uit het leven van de Theologische Hogeschool 6," *De Reformatie* 30 (1955): 123–24.

Dogmatics (*Gereformeerde Dogmatiek*).[2] This monumental work was marked by a broad scope of theological reflection, a profound knowledge of the Reformed tradition, and continual interaction with other Christian traditions—mostly Roman Catholic, Lutheran, and Remonstrant, but also Methodist, Anabaptist, and Eastern Orthodox—and contemporary philosophical systems.

Together with his renowned older colleague, Abraham Kuyper, Bavinck was one of the intellectual leaders of neo-Calvinism, a broad worldview project that aimed to articulate Reformed principles amid the challenges of modernity. In the course of time, Bavinck more and more realized the necessity of interacting with a wide variety of sciences. Gradually, and especially after the completion of his *Reformed Dogmatics*, Bavinck's interests shifted from theology to philosophy, pedagogy, and psychology.[3] As John Bolt concludes, "Bavinck's life and thought reflect a serious effort to be pious, orthodox, and thoroughly contemporary."[4] Bavinck was a theologian faithful to his own tradition and an inquisitive thinker about the modern world.[5]

Why Bavinck?

Herman Bavinck's theology is particularly suitable for a comparative analysis with Orthodox thought. The first reason, quite simply, is that Bavinck was a great theologian who articulated the Reformed faith amid the challenges of modernity with rare breadth and depth. According to Cornelius Van Til, "Herman Bavinck has given to us the greatest and most comprehensive statement of Reformed systematic theology in modern times."[6] For this research it is also important that the doctrines of God and his revelation

---

2. The second, revised and expanded edition appeared between 1906 and 1911.

3. Bavinck himself mentions this change in his letter to H. E. Dosker: "As I grow older my mind turns more and more away from dogmatic to philosophical studies and from these to their application to the practical needs of the world about me." See Henry Elias Dosker, "Herman Bavinck," *Princeton Theological Review* 20 (1922): 457.

4. John Bolt, "Editor's Introduction," *RD* 1:21.

5. This does not necessarily imply the existence of "two Bavincks." James Eglinton convincingly demonstrates the weakness of the argument for two incompatible and mutually confronting strands in Bavinck's thought. See Eglinton, "How Many Herman Bavincks? De Gemeene Genade and the 'Two Bavincks' Hypothesis," in *The Kuyper Center Review*, vol. 2, *Revelation and Common Grace* (Grand Rapids: Eerdmans, 2011), 279–301.

6. Van Til, *Introduction to Systematic Theology*, 89.

occupy an important place in Bavinck's theology. For this reason, some refer to him as "een openbaringstheoloog" ("a theologian of revelation").[7]

Second, while Bavinck experienced doubts, internal struggles, and shifts in his academic priorities, he remained faithful to his own tradition. Already in his student years, Bavinck had demonstrated strong interest in the early Reformed tradition and Reformed scholasticism.[8] His later works consolidated his reputation as an expert in Reformed theology and as one committed to the Reformed tradition. This deep commitment actually encouraged dialogue with other Christian traditions rather than forming an obstacle to it. Indeed, as Arie Brouwer insightfully observes, "The ecumenical movement is best served by faithfulness to one's own tradition."[9]

Third, Bavinck's works are characterized by an unusually close integration of theology, history, and philosophy. In his review of the second volume of Bavinck's *Reformed Dogmatics*, Geerhardus Vos writes: "From a formal point of view the most striking feature of Dr. Bavinck's work is its combination of much material which is usually assigned to the department of the History of Doctrine with what belongs to Dogmatics proper."[10] As other authors put it, Bavinck's *Reformed Dogmatics* is "historically oriented," is "a history of dogmatics as well as a dogmatics itself," and bears "a Christian-historical and therefore a catholic character."[11] Bavinck showed real interest in history and held the common theological heritage of all Christians in high esteem. In his own characterization of his *Reformed Dogmatics*, Bavinck mentions its focus on tradition: "More attention is paid in this work to Patristic and Scholastic theology than is often the case in a Protestant dogmatics." For Bavinck, this "fellowship with generations

---

7. Rolf Hendrik Bremmer, *Herman Bavinck als Dogmaticus* (Kampen: Kok, 1961), 375.

8. Bavinck edited a revision of the Leiden *Synopsis Purioris Theologiae*, an authoritative work within Dutch Reformed academies. Bavinck's dissertation focused on the ethical thought of Reformer Ulrich Zwingli.

9. Arie Brouwer, *Ecumenical Testimony* (Grand Rapids: Eerdmans, 1991), 309. Reflecting on the unity of the church in Christ, Bavinck makes a similar remark: "This unity cannot be reached by force but can best be advanced if each person thinks through the faith of his own church and makes the most accurate presentation of it" (*RD* 1:85).

10. Geerhardus Vos, "Herman Bavinck. Gereformeerde Dogmatiek, Volume Two," *The Presbyterian and Reformed Review* 10 (1899): 694.

11. Jan van Gelderen and Willem Velema, *Concise Reformed Dogmatics* (Phillipsburg, NJ: Presbyterian & Reformed, 2008), 16; Dosker, "Herman Bavinck," 461; "Herman Bavinck," *PTR* 6 (1908): 541. Bremmer also notes that, from a formal or methodological point of view, the first feature of *Reformed Dogmatics* is its "historical character" (*Herman Bavinck als Dogmaticus*, 385).

past" was an expression of the communion of the saints.[12] The importance of this historical consciousness becomes clearer if we consider a helpful distinction made by the Orthodox theologian Georges Florovsky. Florovsky laments that his contemporaries focused on "ecumenism in space," which is "concerned with the adjustments of the existing denominations as they are at the present."[13] He believed that such ecumenism lacked historical depth and overlooked that all Christians share a common history. Florovsky called instead for an "ecumenism in time," which views "Christian history as one comprehensive whole."[14] Bavinck's sense of history enabled him to trace developments in Christian theology throughout the centuries and to realize the role of the entire shared tradition for contemporary debates.[15]

Fourth, Bavinck's modesty and academic integrity are important for facilitating ecumenical dialogue. He readily recognized the positive aspects in other traditions, religions, and philosophical systems.[16] "Tolerant, genial, irenic, he never caricatured an opponent or impugned his motives but tried to give him all the credit he deserved."[17] With respect to other Christian traditions, Bavinck expressed his openness in an irenic, generous orthodoxy. He has been described as "a catholic, ecumenical, and profoundly open person," whose theology manifests "a catholicity or ecumenical

12. Herman Bavinck, "Foreword to the First Edition (Volume 1) of the *Gereformeerde Dogmatiek*," trans. John Bolt, *Calvin Theological Journal* 45 (2010): 9.

13. Georges Florovsky, "The Quest for Christian Unity and the Orthodox Church," in *Collected Works*, 13:139.

14. Georges Florovsky, "Patristic Theology and the Ethos of the Orthodox Church," in *Collected Works*, 4:30.

15. As Bavinck comments, "The task of the dogmatician is not to draw the material for his dogmatics exclusively from the written confession of his own church but to view it in the total context of the unique faith and life of his church, and then again in the context of the history of the whole church of Christ" (*RD* 1:86).

16. "As is universally acknowledged, it is a hallmark of his theology that he always seeks the 'grain of truth' in other systems." See Brian Mattson, *Restored to Our Destiny: Eschatology and the Image of God in Herman Bavinck's Reformed Dogmatics* (Leiden: Brill, 2012), 50. Some have even censured Bavinck's openness as his greatest fault: "The first, pervasive error is Bavinck's theological conviction that there is something good, something true, in virtually all the philosophies, all the scientific theories, and all the cultural proposals of the ungodly, antichristian, and unbelieving movers and shakers of the world outside of Jesus Christ." See David J. Engelsma, "Bavinck: The Man and His Theology," *Protestant Reformed Theological Journal* 46 (2012): 26.

17. James D. Bratt, *Dutch Calvinism in Modern America: A History of a Conservative Subculture* (Grand Rapids: Eerdmans, 1984), 31.

sensibility."[18] His mind was captured by the beauty of catholicity.[19] Willem de Wit even proposes to stop calling Bavinck a Calvinist theologian and instead call him "a catholic Reformed theologian," while Wolter Huttinga, following Gerrit Berkouwer, notes that the word "catholicity" "perhaps best characterizes Bavinck's theology."[20] Bavinck was well-known for his opposition to separatism in his own denomination. George Harinck draws attention to an ironic observation made by historian George Puchinger: "The most ecumenical protestant dogmatics in the Netherlands was written in Kampen, where they did theology in the most isolationistic way!"[21] Although Bavinck's practical ecumenical efforts were confined to churches of the Reformed tradition, his entire theological stance was rooted in history and characterized by theological depth and openness, which made it reminiscent of a wider ecumenism in time. In the words of John Bolt, Bavinck's theology sprang from an "ecumenical (genuinely Catholic) Reformed vision, a vision known for its inclusiveness and irenic character as well as its Reformedness."[22] As such, Bavinck's catholic approach renders it eminently suitable for comparison to the Eastern Orthodox tradition.

UNDERLYING CHARACTERISTICS OF BAVINCK'S APPROACH

Bavinck and Modernity

Bavinck was nurtured in a religious environment, which tended to guard against the challenges of modernity by way of a steadfast commitment to theological orthodoxy and evidenced little concern for the surrounding

18. John Bolt, "A Pearl and a Leaven," *CTJ* 45 (2010): 7; Eduardo J. Echeverría, "The Reformed Objection to Natural Theology: A Catholic Response to Herman Bavinck," *CTJ* 45 (2010): 87. See also Cornelius Van Til's conclusion, based on Bremmer's *Herman Bavinck als dogmaticus*: "His was a truly ecumenical spirit." See Van Til, "Bavinck the Theologian: A Review Article," *Westminster Theological Journal* 24 (1961): 49.

19. Gerrit C. Berkouwer, *A Half Century of Theology: Movements and Motives*, trans. and ed. Lewis B. Smedes (Grand Rapids: Eerdmans, 1977), 12. See also Barend Kamphuis, "Herman Bavinck on Catholicity," *Mid-America Journal of Theology* 24 (2013): 97–104.

20. De Wit, *On the Way*, 42–47; Wolter Huttinga, *Participation and Communicability: Herman Bavinck and John Milbank on the Relation between God and the World* (Amsterdam: Buijten en Schipperheijn, 2014), 23.

21. George Harinck, "Herman Bavinck and Geerhardus Vos," *CTJ* 45 (2010): 28.

22. John Bolt, "Grand Rapids between Kampen and Amsterdam: Herman Bavinck's Reception and Influence in North America," *CTJ* 38 (2003): 264.

culture. Bavinck, however, was not content with this isolated and suspicious approach. Among other reasons, genuine interest in modernity and the pursuit of an academically excellent education led him to Leiden University, which was the leading intellectual center in the Netherlands and the seat of modern theology.[23] At Leiden, Bavinck expanded his knowledge of modern ideas and methods and faced an existential crisis, but he remained faithful to the historical Reformed tradition. The struggle with the modernist worldview permeated his entire theological career, from an article titled "The Modern Worldview" (1883) to his oration "Modernism and Orthodoxy" (1911).[24] Bavinck realized the need to engage with modern philosophical thought and admitted that old theological formulas, coined in an age when God's existence and authority were almost universally assumed, could not simply be repeated under the new conditions brought on by the Enlightenment. His articulation of the doctrine of God can only be properly understood against the background of the philosophical tendencies and challenges to which he responded, either explicitly or implicitly.

The Primacy of the Subject

According to Bavinck, the basic idea of modern rationalism can be presented as follows: "The origin of knowledge is to be found in the subject." In modernity, the human autonomous subject became the centerpiece of knowledge, "the absolute first principle." Bavinck traced the modern turn toward the subject to Descartes, with his "Cogito ergo sum" as the starting point from which certain knowledge must be derived. Even if the Cartesian thinking subject later gave way to the believing, feeling, or moral subject, the basic idea remained: *not* the external world or an outside authority, but the human subject itself is the epistemological point of departure.[25]

Bavinck was convinced that the idea of knowledge as construed and ordered by the human subject had significant consequences for theology and particularly for the doctrine of God. While during the Middle Ages and

23. A helpful analysis of Bavinck's motivation to study at Leiden can be found in de Wit, *On the Way*, 21–22.

24. Herman Bavinck, "De hedendaagsche wereldbeschouwing," *De Vrije Kerk* 9 (1883): 435–61; Bavinck, *Modernisme en Orthodoxie: Rede gehouden bij de overdracht van het rectoraat aan de Vrije Universiteit op 20 October 1911* (Kampen: Kok, 1911).

25. *RD* 1:66, 215, 265.

the Reformation it was assumed that human ideas about God are dependent on God's objective revelation, in modernity the very idea of God became a human construct. To be sure, this did not mean that belief in God's existence was immediately abandoned or that the idea of God became irrelevant. Bavinck realized that Kant, for example, did not deny that reality may extend beyond the reach of the human senses or mind. However, Kant maintained that we have no means of verifying the truthfulness of statements about supersensible things. In Kant's view, Bavinck explains, "our knowledge ... is restricted to the sphere of experience," which makes "any knowledge of the noumena" impossible for us. This means, Bavinck concludes, that Kant understood the supersensible and supernatural as unattainable and unknowable.[26]

Nevertheless, Kant did not take the denial of the knowability of God by pure reason to mean that all talk of God becomes impossible. Without claiming to cognize a supersensible being theoretically, Kant found it possible and indeed necessary to postulate the existence of God based on practical reason. As Bavinck puts it, Kant sought to regain "by practical reason what he had lost by theoretical reason." In Kant's philosophy, Bavinck emphasizes, the idea of God is important, because belief in God prompts us to recognize and fulfill the universal moral laws as divine imperatives. According to Bavinck, this means that morality is no longer defined by religion; rather, religion is a means to reinforce moral principles formulated apart from revelation. The implication is that for Kant, man becomes "his own end (*Selbstzweck*) and all else, God included, only a means." The idea of God is saved, but it is saved to serve the practical interests of humanity.[27]

Bavinck further asserts that Kant's postulation of the existence of God under warrant of the moral imperative results in a separation between knowledge and faith.[28] Kant famously writes that in theological matters he had to "abolish knowledge, to make room for belief."[29] This implies that he treated knowledge and faith as separate domains. Bavinck understood Kant's significance for theology as primarily consisting in his positing a

26. *RD* 1:35, 575; 2:42, 46.

27. *RD* 1:57, 164, 251; 2:44, 432.

28. *RD* 1:35.

29. Immanuel Kant, "Preface to the Second Edition," in *Critique of Pure Reason*, trans. John M. D. Meiklejohn (London: Bell & Sons, 1901), xxxv.

split and even a dualism between *phenomena* and *noumena*, between science and religion, and between theoretical and practical reason.[30] Kant's primacy of the subject, his recognition of the limitations of human knowledge, and his separation of knowledge and faith imply, according to Bavinck, that God cannot be known with certainty and that theology cannot be considered a science.

Theologies of Consciousness

According to Bavinck, ever since the modern turn to the subject, religious consciousness has become the source and standard of religious ideas. Human consciousness was regarded as a faculty for understanding reality, and Christian theology was regarded as a systematic reflection on *Christian* consciousness. As Bavinck puts it, "Theology has, since Kant's time, become theology of consciousness and experience."[31] While all theologies of consciousness accept the primacy of the subject, they differ in determining the actual location of religious consciousness. Bavinck classified them according to three human faculties (reason, feelings, and will): the first approach attributes primacy in religion to speculative reason, the second takes its starting point in human feelings, and the third defines religion in terms of moral attitudes.

The Primacy of Reason: Hegel. The Cartesian primacy of the rational subject found its fullest expression in idealism, whose greatest representative was G. W. F. Hegel. For Bavinck, idealism was "the heresy *par excellence* of the nineteenth century."[32] According to Hegel, all of history is a dynamic expression of the Spirit or Mind (*Geist*). God is identified with this absolute Spirit and comes to the full development and completeness of his Being only through a dialectical process in world history. In and of himself, God is purely abstract Being, and he arrives at self-consciousness through the course of history.

---

30. *RD* 1:540–41.

31. *RD* 1:78; Herman Bavinck, *The Philosophy of Revelation* (New York: Longmans & Green, 1909), 206. In his *Reformed Dogmatics*, Bavinck attributes this change to Schleiermacher: "Since Schleiermacher the whole of theology has changed, among orthodox as well as modern theologians, into a theology of consciousness" (*RD* 1:78, see also 522). This is not a contradiction: Schleiermacher was the first prominent representative of the new approach, whose foundations were laid by Kant.

32. Bavinck, "Hedendaagsche wereldbeschouwing," 443. See also *RD* 2:410.

In Bavinck's view, Hegel's metaphysics of the self-unfolding subject were incompatible with the Christian idea of God. "In Hegel God is indeed Reason, Thought, Mind, Subject, but not in the sense that he had a life of his own prior to and apart from the world."[33] God is dependent on the world, because in order to become a self-conscious personality he needs the world's assistance. In Hegel's words, "without the world God is not God."[34] Hegel applies the idea of becoming to God, because originally God is devoid of content and comes fully into being only through the historical process. In Hegel's thought, "God *is* not, but *becomes*." For Bavinck, this meant that the boundary between Creator and creature is obliterated. Hegel's idealism denies not only the aseity of God but also his otherness. God produces the world from within himself and is not different from it. Before the creation of the world, God is simply a logical abstraction; after creation, God is identified with the world. God is not a person in the sense of a self-conscious subject who stands in free relation to the world as essentially different from him. God is not above or beyond the things we observe in the world but exists *in* them. Bavinck maintained that this view contradicts biblical teaching, in which God's personhood implies that he is a self-existing being with life, consciousness, and a will of his own.[35]

With respect to God's hiddenness and revelation, Bavinck noted the distinctive character of Hegel's philosophy. While the notion of God's unknowability characterized much modern thought, Hegel took a different position. "Reason, in his opinion, raises itself step by step through several stages to the level of absolute knowledge, then looks at truth face to face and knows its essence to be Reason, Thought, the Idea itself." In the end, God is not hidden, because he can be known adequately through conceptual thought. His being is not different from the idea itself. In Hegel's thought, Bavinck argues, "our God-consciousness is nothing other than God's self-consciousness. God exists to the extent he is known by us, that is, to the extent he knows himself in us." God's self-revelation *constitutes* rather than discloses his being, because it is by revealing himself that

33. *RD* 2:115.

34. Georg Wilhelm Friedrich Hegel, *Lectures on the Philosophy of Religion* (London: Kegan Paul, Trench, Trübner, 1895), 1:200.

35. *RD* 1:349; 2:33, 155, emphasis original.

God achieves self-consciousness.[36] Therefore, according to Bavinck, the Hegelian understanding of revelation fundamentally differs from the conscious, personal revelation of God as it was understood in the Christian tradition.

Bavinck insisted that in Hegel's system, nothing is hidden in God beyond the world: his revelation is unreserved and unrestricted. Even God's knowledge of himself is exhausted by his revelation and dependent on it. Not only does humanity know God through his revelation, but, explains Bavinck, God also knows himself only through his own revelation.[37] In short, Hegel conflates *God in himself* with *God for us*. For Bavinck, such conceptualization of the relation between God's hiddenness and revelation is unacceptable.

The Primacy of Feeling: Schleiermacher. Another important theological approach of the nineteenth century was marked by the primacy of the feeling subject. Its founder and most famous proponent was Friedrich Schleiermacher. For him, the essence of religion—or rather of piety—consists in the feeling of absolute dependence, which bears a religious character and thus implies relationship with God. His theology seeks to describe devout states of consciousness rather than revealed truth. As Bavinck notes, in Schleiermacher's approach, God "cannot be the object of our knowing," and, therefore, Schleiermacher did not propose an elaborate doctrine of God.[38]

The main problem Bavinck saw in Schleiermacher's methodology was that the feeling of dependence is detached from the categories of truth and untruth. This methodology makes any statements about God in himself impossible: "The moment we try to bring the Absolute closer to us, it is finitized in our thinking and we begin to speak in images." Schleiermacher was skeptical about the concept of revelation as a means to bridge the gap between God in himself and our knowledge of him. Bavinck claims that for Schleiermacher theology "became anthropology, 'pisteology,' ecclesiology and ceased to be what it had always claimed to be: knowledge of God." Bavinck concludes that Schleiermacher viewed religion not as a matter

36. *RD* 2:43, 48, 292.

37. *RD* 1:255, 292; 2:48.

38. *RD* 1:67; 2:43; Bavinck, "Hedendaagsche wereldbeschouwing," 451.

of knowing but of feeling, while dogmatics degenerated into the mere description of pious states of mind.[39]

Bavinck argued that the subjective nature of Schleiermacher's approach was reflected in his consideration of the divine attributes. According to Schleiermacher, they "express neither God's essence (which is unknowable) nor his relations to the world"; rather, claims Bavinck, for Schleiermacher "they are simply subjective ideas without any objective basis." Bavinck suggested that although Schleiermacher's classification of God's attributes is based on the relation in which God stands to the world, this relation lacks an objective foundation and is described in strictly subjective terms. Thus, some of God's attributes correspond to the human feeling of dependence; other attributes presuppose the consciousness of the antithetical nature of sin; still other attributes are experienced when that antithesis has been overcome.[40] Bavinck contended that in Schleiermacher's theology the attributes that God has in himself are completely unknowable and unattainable, while the attributes of *God for us* emerge from a critical analysis of human consciousness.

Bavinck was convinced, therefore, that Schleiermacher's thought was marked by a consistent denial of the accessibility of God in himself. The acknowledgment of God's incomprehensibility led Schleiermacher to seek God in the human feeling of absolute dependence. According to Bavinck, due to this subjective turn to human feelings, the character of *God for us* becomes a subjective and unstable human construct. In sum, Schleiermacher's subjectivism implies for Bavinck that *Deus in se* is unknowable and separated from *Deus pro nobis*.

The Primacy of Will: Ritschl. Bavinck repeatedly observed that the end of the nineteenth century was the time of a pervasive neo-Kantian influence in philosophy and theology.[41] Bavinck's early evaluation of this influence was perhaps best demonstrated in an article written in 1888 about well-known neo-Kantian theologian Albrecht Ritschl.[42] Ritschl's epistemology

39. *RD* 1:267, 522, 524; 2:43.

40. *RD* 2:125, 132; see also 2:108.

41. *RD* 1:44, 69, 169, 541; Bavinck, *Philosophy of Revelation*, 34.

42. Interestingly, the original article was published in *Theologische Studiën*, a journal promoted by the ethical theologians who shared many of Ritschl's insights. See Herman Bavinck, "De theologie van Albrecht Ritschl," *Theologische Studiën* 6 (1888): 369–403.

rested on the Kantian claim about the absolute unknowability of the supersensible world. According to Ritschl, we can be certain only about the way things appear to us and about how they exist in relation to us, but we are not able to know a thing in itself. Furthermore, Bavinck adds, "Realities have nothing more than a formal unity with their perceptions [*verschijningen*]," so that we are never certain that a thing's appearance gives us a true and sure knowledge of the thing itself. In this approach, Bavinck contends, "things in themselves have no existence."[43]

Bavinck realized that Ritschl's general epistemological principles were of great significance also for his doctrine of God. Applied to the domain of theology, these principles lead to the conclusion that "theology is never concerned with the realities of Scripture, God, Christ, Holy Spirit, etc., in themselves, but only as they are for us." God in himself is never attainable; we can only know what he is *for us*. "There is nothing that may be predicated of God apart from his relation to us."[44] Thus, according to Ritschl, dogmatic theology should be purged of all metaphysics and all appeals to substance, essence, or being.

Bavinck's main and often repeated remark about this epistemology was that it robs theology of objective truth. Ritschl's position, Bavinck claims, means that "from beginning to end, theology becomes subjective. All that is objective is lost." Theological claims become merely value judgments based on one's moral consciousness: "Value judgments are something in us; they do presuppose a reality outside of us about which we do the valuing, but this reality remains completely hidden, an unknown X, a mystery." In short, Bavinck's critique of Ritschl boiled down to the following point: without objective revelation and truth, "God for me" becomes a subjective construct about which we can have no certainty, whereas "God in himself" becomes an absolutely hidden reality.[45]

In his *Reformed Dogmatics*, Bavinck presented a more nuanced description of Ritschl's theology, though the substance of his argument had not changed a great deal. Bavinck argues that in Ritschl's thought, "a thing completely coincides with and is exhaustively present in its appearance."

---

43. Herman Bavinck, "The Theology of Albrecht Ritschl," trans. John Bolt, *The Bavinck Review* 3 (2012): 131, 133; see also 134; *RD* 1:544.

44. Bavinck, "Theology of Albrecht Ritschl," 131, 133.

45. Bavinck, "Theology of Albrecht Ritschl," 134, 138–39.

(Bavinck means that in the end it does not make much difference whether one openly denies "things in themselves" or identifies them with the appearances. In either case, the reality of a thing is exhausted by its appearance and becomes dependent on the observing subject.)[46] For Bavinck, Ritschl's approach seems to be subjective in one sense ("a thing for me") and agnostic in another sense ("a thing in itself").

Thus, in dealing with theologies of consciousness, Bavinck criticized two positions. On the one hand, he rejected the *identification* of *God in himself* with *God in his revelation*, whereby ontologically the former becomes exhaustively present in the latter or is even determined by it. Bavinck rejected this approach mainly because he believed it blurs the distinction between Creator and creature and implies that epistemology logically precedes and determines ontology. On the other hand, Bavinck rejected the *separation* of *God in himself* from *God for us*, where *God in himself* is absolutely hidden and, according to Bavinck, disappears as such. Bavinck rejected this approach primarily because he was convinced that it robs theology of any certain knowledge about God and of objective truth.

Bavinck's Leitmotifs

In order to describe Bavinck's views on God's hiddenness and revelation in the context of his overall theological system, I will first examine four leitmotifs of his theology, related to the topic of the present study. These reveal the broader scope of Bavinck's theological concerns. However, the leitmotifs should not be regarded as philosophical principles on which Bavinck grounded his subsequent theological ideas. Although Bavinck was criticized for methodological inconsistency and a reliance on natural theology in the first volume of his *Reformed Dogmatics*,[47] one should note that even in his prolegomena he did not abandon his Christian presuppositions, nor did he build his theology on a philosophical foundation. In all of his theology, Bavinck considered God and the world from the standpoint of faith, not as a neutral observer. The actual inclusion of chapters about the

46. *RD* 1:541–44.

47. According to Malcolm B. Yarnell, "on the one hand, Bavinck firmly rejects the scholastic method of building theology on top of natural theology. ... On the other hand he constructs his theology in almost exactly the same manner that he criticizes." See Yarnell, *The Formation of Christian Doctrine* (Nashville: B&H, 2007), 50–51.

role of faith in his *prolegomena* (*RD* 1, chs. 15, 16) is remarkable and unusual for orthodox Protestant dogmatics. Hendrik van den Belt observes that "Bavinck is very clear that the prolegomena do not precede the dogmatic system."[48] Bavinck's focus on epistemological issues was indeed a sign of his dependency on the modern obsession with knowledge. Nevertheless, the four leitmotifs of his theology are not the foundation of his subsequent treatment of the doctrine of God. Rather, they anticipate the direction he takes when considering the relation between God's hiddenness and revelation.

A Sense of Mystery

In Bavinck's later years, he believed that contemporary society was increasingly characterized by a sense of mystery and by a sense of disillusionment with the power of natural science. He commented, "There appeared to be more and more enigmas of which science could not give an explanation." The rapid development of the sciences in the first half of the nineteenth century gave rise to the hope of a comprehensive explanation of the world. However, the subsequent pursuit of scientific research, according to Bavinck, "caused people to see that mysteries, both in the world and in man, did not vanish, but grew in numbers and in nature."[49] The deeper science investigates, the more mysteries it encounters.[50]

Bavinck observed that this change manifested itself not only in the natural sciences but also in the fields of literature, art, architecture, and especially philosophy. The German turn to Kant was soon replicated in the Netherlands, and philosophers again realized the limitations of human

---

48. Hendrik van den Belt, "Autopistia: The Self-Convincing Authority of Scripture in Reformed Theology" (PhD diss., Leiden University, 2006), 294. Compare: "His prolegomena are in themselves already fully theological" (Huttinga, *Participation and Communicability*, 86).

49. Herman Bavinck, *Mental, Religious and Social Forces in the Netherlands*, A General View of the Netherlands 17 (The Hague: Commercial Department of the Netherlands Ministry of Agriculture, Industry, and Commerce, 1915), 39. Bavinck makes a similar remark in his Stone Lectures: "The intelligibility of nature, which was so long believed in by science, is ... more and more giving place to the confession of its unknowableness" (*Philosophy of Revelation*, 104). Berkouwer notes that Bavinck "was especially intrigued by the expending knowledge of a world rapidly opening its secrets" (*Half Century of Theology*, 15). There is no doubt that Bavinck was in a sense charmed by modernity, but nonetheless he had many reservations about its claims and alleged achievements.

50. Bavinck, *Philosophy of Revelation*, 94; Herman Bavinck, "Modernism and Orthodoxy," trans. Bruce Pass, *BavRev* 7 (2016): 91.

reasoning. Bavinck found this philosophical recognition of humanity's finite mental capacities in the face of the world's mysteries to be right-minded and promising. When reflecting on Calvinism's ability to appreciate and appropriate positive elements of culture, Bavinck noted that many nineteenth-century philosophical ideas corresponded to Reformed theology: "Even the philosophic systems of this century contain many elements which Calvinism may turn to an apologetic use. The agnostic philosophy falls in with the Calvinistic doctrine of the incomprehensibility of God, of the impenetrableness of His counsel, of the hidden character of the *voluntas beneplaciti*, of the finiteness of the human faculty of knowing."[51] To be sure, in other works Bavinck sharply criticizes agnosticism.[52] Although he revered agnostics' emphasis on the incomprehensibility of God, he himself remained critical of their views as he did not regard God as a mere "inexpressible depth" or "eternal silence." Nevertheless, Bavinck thought that especially this philosophical restraint, this reluctance to speculate about God, is mirrored in Calvinism, and for that reason can be used in Calvinist apologetics. The theme of God's incomprehensibility, which, according to Bavinck, was neglected in most Christian circles, becomes an important Calvinist doctrine in Bavinck's theology, and a point of contact with the philosophical systems of his time. Indeed, in his *Philosophy of Revelation* Bavinck lauds the rediscovery of mystery in philosophy and science as a reason for "encouragement" and "rejoicing."[53]

Bavinck's biographers agree that he became more and more convinced of the limitations of human knowledge in his later years.[54] But even in his earlier works the concept of mystery often came to the fore. Bavinck did not apply the terms "unknowability" and "incomprehensibility" exclusively to God, but used them for a wide range of subjects: "Everywhere and in every area of life we finally run into mystery." For Bavinck, creation is "a miracle in the absolute sense of the word, full of mysteries and secrets."

51. Herman Bavinck, "The Future of Calvinism," trans. Geerhardus Vos, *PRR* 5 (1894): 22.

52. See especially Herman Bavinck, "Het dualisme in de Theologie," *De Vrije Kerk* 13 (1887): 11.

53. Bavinck, *Philosophy of Revelation*, 29; *RD* 2:41. Bavinck emphasizes the importance of the philosophical rediscovery of God's incomprehensibility even more clearly: "When this truth of the incomprehensibility of God had been almost totally forgotten by theology, philosophy rose up to remind us of it" (*RD* 2:41).

54. Bremmer, *Herman Bavinck als Dogmaticus*, 381.

The mystery of humankind's very existence is "incomprehensible." Within the entirety of creation, humanity is the most mysterious being: "Every human being is a mystery." Every stage and aspect of human life is full of hidden depths: the origin of life is a mystery; the origin of evil is a mystery and "will presumably remain a mystery"; sin, also, "proves to be an incomprehensible mystery"; while "death is a mystery in the full sense of the word."[55] The renewed creation will be even more mysterious and incomprehensible for humankind than creation as we know it.

The incomprehensibility of human beings also lies in the fact that we do not know the internal, subjective, personal side of humans. According to Bavinck, "our thinking is bound up with our senses," but they cannot help us to observe and comprehend the *soul* of human beings and spiritual matters.[56] Impenetrable motives spur our human affections and actions. "Love—even for one's country—always has a mysterious character. It comes up out of the depths and is fed by hidden springs."[57] Bavinck contends that the word "instinct" fails to explain our motives and serves only to name that which is mysterious and obscure.[58] In Bavinck's later career, when he was particularly interested in psychology, this sense of the enigmatic character of human personhood remained.

To be sure, for Bavinck, the mystery of God is unique. Nevertheless, it is important to keep in mind that the confession of God's incomprehensibility was not an isolated statement in Bavinck's theology. It corresponds to Bavinck's general epistemological principles, which were full of reverence for any kind of mystery. For Bavinck, to acknowledge the mysteriousness of God is to preclude identifying God in himself with God in his revelation. There is more to reality than the outward appearance, and there is infinitely more to God than we, with our creaturely limitations, can assess. The one who recognizes the mystery of creation will more readily recognize the mystery of God and more gratefully receive his revelation.

---

55. *RD* 2:106, 496; 3:28, 39, 69, 145, 184.

56. *RD* 2:106.

57. Herman Bavinck, "The Problem of War," trans. Stephen Voorwinde, *The Banner of Truth* (July–August 1977): 51.

58. See paragraph 10.C, "Het Instinct," in Herman Bavinck, *Beginselen der Psychologie* (Kampen: Bos, 1897).

A Quest for Certainty

Science's rediscovery of mystery, which Bavinck mostly appreciated, did, however, have implications that he deplored: the loss of trust and the predominance of uncertainty. This "disease," which infects not only the natural sciences, but also modern philosophy and theology, Bavinck regretted.[59] He regarded this loss as devastating, because certainty is the deepest need of the human soul, according to Bavinck. While Bavinck's "need for certainty," as Bratt observes, was not as acute as Kuyper's, the quest for irrefutable truth was a recurrent theme in Bavinck's thought.[60] He dedicated a short book to the subject titled *The Certainty of Faith*, in which he summarized his views on the nature of, and ground for, certainty.

Unsurprisingly, Bavinck began with the Reformation, which "was born out of a deeply felt need for the assurance of salvation." Despite challenging the authority of the "infallible" church, the Reformers actually restored certainty by binding it firmly to the only infallible foundation, the word of God. Luther had vainly sought certainty in good works, but found it instead in God's free grace. Bavinck states that "certainty was a characteristic of the faith of all the Reformers." The certainty found by the Reformers was the sure knowledge that "God *is* and that He is *our* God." For Bavinck, therefore, Christian certainty is twofold: it is the certainty of truth and the certainty of personal salvation. He further notes that "these two kinds of certainty, easily distinguished, cannot be separated. They are closely interrelated; the one does not exist without the other."[61] The Christian believer is certain of the existence of God and his promises, and he is certain that these promises belong to him.

---

59. Bavinck, *Philosophy of Revelation*, 298.

60. "Kuyper suffered from an acute need for certainty; Bavinck—perhaps from his parents' Seceder piety—seems to have been more patient amid the struggles of faith." See James D. Bratt, "The Context of Herman Bavinck's Stone Lectures: Culture and Politics in 1908," *BavRev* 1 (2010): 21. As Van den Belt observes about Bavinck, "the quest for certainty is one of the main forces of his theological thought" ("Autopistia," 258).

61. Herman Bavinck, *The Certainty of Faith*, trans. Harry der Nederlanden (St. Catharines, ON: Paideia, 1980), 13, 38, 84, emphasis original. Although in *The Certainty of Faith* Bavinck only once refers to Calvin, it is not because he thought that for Calvin certainty was less important than for Luther. Elsewhere Bavinck says: "More than with Zwingli and Luther, faith is with Calvin *unshaken conviction, firm assurance*." See Bavinck, "Calvin and Common Grace," trans. Geerhardus Vos, *PTR* 7 (1909): 449, 463, emphasis added. See also *RD* 1:574.

How can one obtain such certainty? Rational arguments and personal experience cannot provide it, Bavinck argues. Only faith can give us certainty regarding truth and salvation. Bavinck emphasizes that "faith is not hope and opinion, not guess and conjecture, not even knowledge and assent, but certain knowledge and firm trust." Faith entails and implies certainty by definition: "Faith *is* certainty and as such excludes all doubt."[62] But what is the ground for faith and its certainty? Bavinck insists that since truth and salvation are matters of absolute importance that determine our eternal state, "we need an infallible, divine certainty, one that transcends all human doubt."[63] Such certainty requires infallible, divine authority. God's word alone can be the ground and source of such certainty, Bavinck concludes.

To be sure, certainty is not the same as truth: "Truth always brings certainty, but certainty is no proof of truth." People can, of course, be certain of wrong ideas. Nevertheless, truth and certainty of faith are closely interrelated as faith recognizes "the objective, self-subsistent truth." Faith is not the source, norm, or ground for truth, but rather a means by which we appropriate objective truth.[64] Although Bavinck realized the limitations of Christian apologetics, he defended the *objective* truth of the Christian religion. Truth is not objective in the sense that it can be discovered through neutral or unbiased reason, but it is objective in that it corresponds with reality and is independent of the believing subject.

In his historical survey, Bavinck writes that during the Reformation era, "people were convinced they possessed the truth." They were certain of God and their salvation. However, over time this confidence eroded. As Bavinck puts it, "Doubt has now become the sickness of our century."

---

62. Bavinck, *Certainty of Faith*, 84–85, emphasis original. Compare: "Certainty is a characteristic of faith throughout Scripture" (*RD* 1:573). This does not imply that Christians cannot doubt: "Even in the most sanctified Christian, faith is often mixed with doubt; this doubt, however, does not originate in the new man, but in the old" (*Certainty of Faith*, 86). As Donald MacLeod summarizes Bavinck's view on this issue, "Faith is certain. Believers may doubt. Faith never doubts." See MacLeod, "Herman Bavinck and the Basis of Christian Certainty," *Scottish Bulletin of Evangelical Theology* 29 (2011): 93.

63. Bavinck, *Certainty of Faith*, 24.

64. Bavinck, *Certainty of Faith*, 33, 83. Bavinck used different images to convey this idea: "Faith ... is never like a fountain that from itself brings forth the living water but like a channel that conducts the water to us from another source" (*RD* 1:81); "Faith is the pail with which the believer draws the water of life from the wellspring of God's Word" (*Certainty of Faith*, 83).

Certainty was shaken to its foundations: theologically, sociologically, psychologically, and spiritually. Bavinck viewed the most damaging erosive force as springing from the new philosophical mood that emphasized the primacy of the subject and the limitations of human knowledge. As we have seen, Bavinck regretted that modern philosophy had deprived theology of objectivity and certainty. The denial of the certainty of truth inevitably leads to the denial of the certainty of salvation. Bavinck observes that in modernist movements "one can no longer speak of the certainty of truth and, *thus*, not of the certainty of salvation either."[65] The denial of the certainty of truth, therefore, has detrimental consequences for Christian life and faith.

Christians cannot be satisfied with faith in an unknown god or a god of human invention, Bavinck maintained. They cannot be certain of an object whose knowability is denied. They need a complete, unshakable, and ineradicable certainty, which is only possible if God has revealed himself truly and clearly. The certainty of faith presupposes the knowability, revelation, and truth of its object. Thus it also presupposes, and even demands, a correspondence between God's hiddenness and his revelation. A God who is completely hidden cannot in any sense be the source of certainty. As Bavinck's sense of mystery resisted the identification of *God in himself* with *God for us*, so his quest for certainty and objectivity did not allow the separation between *God in himself* and *God for us*.

Christian Realism

In *Reformed Dogmatics* as well as in his other works, Bavinck persistently criticized two mainstreams in modern epistemology: rationalism and empiricism. In criticizing rationalism, Bavinck concurred with the theory that the human intellect is not able to produce the knowledge of things out of its own resources. While the intellect is capable of pursuing knowledge, this capability is activated only by the sensible world. Bavinck therefore rejected rationalism on the grounds that it overestimates the power of the human intellect. Criticizing empiricism, Bavinck claims that "in its intellectual activity the human mind is never totally passive or even receptive but also always more or less active." Further, in logic and mathematics,

65. Bavinck, *Certainty of Faith*, 8, 34, emphasis added.

there is truth that *cannot* be deduced from experience; in fact, all the sciences proceed from certain presuppositions.[66] Whatever rationalism or empiricism might claim, Bavinck argued that we need neither rational proofs nor evidences in order to be immediately certain of many things. Such natural and immediate certainty was a crucial concept for Bavinck, and he emphasized its significance for our knowledge of the world and our knowledge of God.[67]

Rejecting both rationalism and empiricism, Bavinck offered an alternative: a Christianized version of realism nurtured in the tradition of Augustine and Aquinas and synthesized with the Kantian mediation between rationalism and empiricism. Bavinck agreed with empiricism that the starting point of all human knowledge is sensory perception. He added, however, that the data acquired from the outside world are not perceived by the senses but by the mind, which operates in its own way. "It is the human mind that sees through the eye and hears through the ear."[68] The external world then becomes the source of knowledge, and the human intellect an instrument for perceiving exterior phenomena.

One of the most pivotal epistemological issues for Bavinck was the relation between a thing and its representation. Bavinck was conscious of the fact that modern philosophy created an ever-growing gap between the two. The object of our perception was claimed to be "not the thing outside of us, but some impression or neural vibration within us." The result of this belief is that the objective world becomes unattainable to us. In contrast, Bavinck says, his realism "does not deny the distinction that exists between the representation and the thing but at the same time maintains the inseparable connection between the two." This enables him to claim that these mental representations faithfully reflect the objective reality outside us.[69]

Bavinck emphasized that the function of the human mind is not exhausted by its observation of phenomena. The second and even more

66. *RD* 1:220, 225.

67. Based on Bavinck's antievidentialist position concerning beliefs about God, Nicholas Wolterstorff calls him "a proto Reformed epistemologist." See Wolterstorff, "Herman Bavinck—Proto Reformed Epistemologist," *CTJ* 45 (2010): 146. On the centrality of natural certainty in Bavinck's epistemology, see Arvin Vos, "Knowledge according to Bavinck and Aquinas," *BavRev* 6 (2015): 11–13.

68. *RD* 1:228.

69. *RD* 1:224, 227–28.

important step is to infer the universal from the particular, that is, to form the *idea* of the things. It is not enough to ensure the general reliability of our perception; it is also important to ensure our ability to formulate proper *conceptions* from what we perceive. Here Bavinck appeals to the idea of the Logos: "It is the same Logos who created both the reality outside of us and the laws of thought within us and who produced an organic connection and correspondence between the two."[70] The logos implicit in other creatures corresponds with the internal logos of human beings as they both ultimately depend on one and the same divine Logos. While all that we observe is outside us, and these objects in their internal being can never be approached by us, we are nonetheless able to receive mental representations of them that correspond to reality and to convert these representations into accurate concepts.

Speaking about human knowledge, Bavinck discerned three principles, which were foundational to his thinking and determined the structure of the first volume of his *Reformed Dogmatics*. First, God is the principle of being (*principium essendi*); "present in his mind are the ideas of all things; all things are based on thoughts and are created by the word." All creation is obliged to God's being, thought, and will for its very existence. Second, the created world is "an embodiment of the thoughts of God" and thus "is the external foundation of knowledge (*principium cognoscendi externum*) for all science."[71] Having perfect knowledge of all things, God also revealed some knowledge of himself and the created world to human beings, whom he created in his image. Opposing idealism, Bavinck emphasized that ideas are not innate and that instead humanity perceives things by observing God's creation. Human knowledge is thus always indebted to revelation. Third, in order to understand God's revelation, humans also need the light of reason, which is the internal foundation of knowledge (*principium cognoscendi internum*). Human intellect springs from the Logos and recognizes the Logos in creation. It is the Logos who establishes the harmony and correspondence between the subject (human beings) and the object (the created world).

70. *RD* 1:229, 231.

71. *RD* 1:233.

In Bavinck's doctrine of God, these principles mean that God has perfect knowledge of himself and is the source of all knowledge. God's self-consciousness and self-knowledge is the *principium essendi* of theology. Further, God makes himself known throughout the entirety of the created world and centrally through Jesus Christ and Scripture.[72] Thus, Scripture is the theological *principium cognoscendi externum*. Finally, the *principium cognoscendi internum* of theology is the internal illumination of the Holy Spirit, who enables us to understand external revelation.[73] Humanity receives knowledge of God through faith.[74] In Bavinck's general epistemological approach "the intellect is an instrument, not a source."[75] Likewise, his theology presents faith as the instrument for acquiring knowledge from revelation rather than as the source of knowledge itself.

Bavinck wanted to demonstrate the uniqueness of theology while defending its value as a university discipline and science. In explaining the scientific character of theology, he made statements that are also important for his doctrine of God. According to Bavinck, all sciences must have a knowable object and an epistemic source, which can be presented in a systematic form: "If a given science has no object and no epistemic source of its own, then neither does it have any right to exist."[76] The object of theology,

---

72. *RD* 1:212, 587.

73. In his early Kampen speech, Bavinck does not mention *principium cognoscendi internum* and calls the Scripture the only *principium cognoscendi* and the only source of theology: "The *principium cognoscendi* from which we receive the knowledge of God is Holy Scripture alone." See Herman Bavinck, *De wetenschap der H. Godgeleerdheid: Rede ter aanvaarding van het leeraarsambt aan de Theologische School te Kampen, uitgesproken den 10 jan. 1883* (Kampen: G. Ph. Zalsman, 1883), 12. But Bavinck adds there that Scripture is to be read under the guidance of the Holy Spirit, which implies the *principium cognoscendi internum* (11). In his early theology, Bavinck's concentration on Scripture probably resulted from his discussions with ethical theologians. In his mature theology, however, Bavinck emphasized the significance of the *principium cognoscendi internum* even more than the *principium cognoscendi externum*. The internal word of God is the *principal* word, because it introduces the knowledge of God to human beings, whereas the external word is the *instrumental* word and by its nature is incidental and temporary (*RD* 1:213).

74. Bavinck did not describe the nature of the *principium cognoscendi internum* consistently. In some passages he identified it with the illumination of the Holy Spirit, the witness of the Holy Spirit, or the Holy Spirit himself, while in other passages he interpreted it as faith or the "Christian mind." Bavinck also distinguished between the *principium internum* of general revelation (which is the light of reason) and the *principium internum* of special revelation (the saving work of the Holy Spirit). For a helpful analysis of Bavinck's distinctions, see Van den Belt, "Autopistia," 286–95.

75. *RD* 1:217.

76. *RD* 1:91.

Bavinck insisted, is not merely church history, church dogmatics, or the history of religions, but the knowledge of God. The very definition of theology as a science, therefore, implies God's knowability, God's revelation (the epistemic source of theology), the authoritative and normative power of this revelation, and the possibility and the need of its systematization. If God were unknowable, theology would cease to be a science.[77]

Noteworthy among these epistemological constructions is Bavinck's effort to weave theology in with the other sciences, the knowledge of God with the knowledge of the world. We know God through the world and we know the world from a perspective informed by our knowledge of God. Christians "see God in everything and everything in God."[78] Not only is God hidden, but the world also is full of mysteries. God can be known only through revelation, and creation can be known only through God's revelatory agency.[79] Regarding the knowledge of God, the epistemological direction taken by Bavinck is not totally different from the one he takes in his general epistemology. In both cases Bavinck continually attempted to point to the correspondence between reality and our knowledge of reality. The knowledge of God is not a product of feeling or fantasy, but corresponds to the reality of God himself.

The Idea of Correspondence

Although the idea of correspondence has been previously mentioned, it holds such significance for Bavinck that it deserves a separate section. The concept of correspondence not only inspired his epistemology, but also permeated his entire thought structure. According to Bavinck, the world is the embodiment of God's thoughts, and since there is no internal

---

77. "The doctrine of the unknowability of God can lead to nothing but the removal of theology from the scientific disciplines and from the university." See Herman Bavinck, *Godsdienst en Godgeleerdheid: Rede gehouden bij de aanvaarding van het hoogleeraarsambt in de Theologie aan de Vrije Universiteit te Amsterdam op woensdag 17 december 1902* (Wageningen: Vada, 1902), 32.

78. *RD* 1:321. Bavinck even claims that the knowledge of God is not the peculiar domain of theology: "It is often represented as if only the special science of theology concerned itself with God and divine things, and as if all the other sciences, particularly the natural sciences, have nothing whatever to do with God. ... But such a dualism is impossible. God does not stand apart from the world, much less from man, and therefore the knowledge of him is not the peculiar domain of theology" (*Philosophy of Revelation*, 83).

79. *RD* 1:341.

conflict in God, his creation manifests order and integrity.[80] Nothing in the world appeared or exists by chance; everything reveals the divine glory and has its place and purpose. The characteristic feature of this order is unity in diversity: all things in the world are interconnected and form a certain system. "It is the unity of harmony, which includes riches, multiformity, differentiation."[81] Correspondence relates not only to similarity or suitability but also to being connected to and remaining in harmony with another thing.

This sense of the interconnectedness of the created world is felt in all aspects of Bavinck's worldview. He constantly rejected any division between knowing and believing, reason and faith, science and religion, head and heart, nature and grace, creation and re-creation, theology and piety, the natural and the supernatural, the secular and the spiritual, the profane and the sacred. For Bavinck, these pairs are not opposites. He tried to maintain the bond between them without obliterating the difference between them. He did not accept chaos, but neither did he consent to uniformity; he rejected separation, but also identification. In order to express this sense of correspondence, Bavinck often used the distinction between the organic and the mechanical. For Bavinck, the terms "organic connection" and "correspondence" convey the same idea. When he explains that God's self-consciousness and his world consciousness "are organically connected," he confronts the opposing tendencies either to identify or to separate them.[82]

In his doctrine of God, Bavinck used the idea of correspondence primarily for connecting divine revelation to its reception by human beings. In terms of Bavinck's *principia*, the idea describes the relation between the *principium cognoscendi externum* and the *principium cognoscendi internum*. Just as all cognition is based on the "reciprocal correspondence" or the "agreement" between object and subject, so too the human knowledge of God is based on the correspondence between God's objective revelation in the world and our subjective ability to grasp it.[83] At the same

80. *RD* 1:233.
81. Bavinck, *Philosophy of Revelation*, 139.
82. *RD* 1:231; 2:195.
83. *RD* 1:341, 348, 501, 505, 564; Bavinck, *Philosophy of Revelation*, 79.

time, Bavinck referred to the idea of correspondence when describing the relation between God's self-knowledge and his revelation (that is, between *principium essendi* and *principium cognoscendi*). God in his revelation corresponds to God in himself. The knowledge given in God's revelation corresponds to God's very being.[84]

GOD HIDDEN

The Place of God's Incomprehensibility

Bavinck's reflections on the role of mystery in the Christian religion form the transition between the first two volumes of his *Reformed Dogmatics*. In the first volume, he presents and defends dogmatic theology as a science, but puts forward some reservations about the explanatory potential of theology in the concluding pages of the volume. Bavinck repeats his thesis that theology strives to obtain knowledge but admits that it cannot attain comprehension. He readily acknowledges this, because incomprehensibility leaves room for admiration and wonder. Knowledge answers the "what" questions, while comprehension answers the "how" questions. According to Bavinck, there are very few things we comprehend; and even if we think we do understand, the developments of modern science prove that apparent comprehension may vanish into thin air when we delve deeper into a subject. Bavinck then proceeds to analyze the concepts of mystery and incomprehensibility in the Bible and church history and ends the first volume by stating that the aim of theology "is not just a knowing [*weten*], much less a comprehending [*begrijpen*]; it is better and more glorious than that: it is the knowledge [*kennis*] which is life, 'eternal life' (John 17:3)."[85] True knowledge of God is life, not comprehension.

Bavinck opens the second volume by expanding on his concluding remarks from the previous volume regarding God's incomprehensibility. Now he applies them specifically to the doctrine of God. Bavinck's decision to put the concept of God's incomprehensibility at the very beginning of the doctrine of God is remarkable and unusual for the tradition on

84. It is important to bear in mind, however, that the idea of correspondence does not appear only in theology proper, but characterizes Bavinck's theological system as a whole.

85. *RD* 1:619, 621.

which he constantly draws in articulating his account. Typically, Reformed orthodox theologians placed this concept among God's (incommunicable) attributes or merely inferred it from such attributes of God as infinity, omniscience, and wisdom.[86] Sometimes they also discussed it in their prolegomena, but they rarely, if ever, opened their doctrine of God with the confession of his incomprehensibility as a topic in its own right. The passing mention of God's incomprehensibility in the list of God's attributes was characteristic not only of dogmatic textbooks but also of the decisions of councils and confessional documents.[87] Medieval and post-Reformation scholasticism diligently attempted to work out the doctrine of God in all its details and nuances, which led to the overshadowing of God's incomprehensibility. Theologians were driven by a concern to show the rationality of the Christian faith and to present it in a philosophically sophisticated manner, rather than to emphasize the mysterious side of Christianity.

In contrast to this predominant tradition, Bavinck treated God's incomprehensibility independently of, and prior to, any consideration of his essence and attributes. This methodological and structural feature indicates Bavinck's desire to give due attention to the philosophical and overall intellectual climate of his time. It also reflects his profound reverence of the mystery of God. By organizing his material in such a way, Bavinck seemed to emphasize that God's incomprehensibility permeates the entire doctrine of God: it is not merely one of several incommunicable attributes; rather, it is essential to every divine attribute, be it incommunicable or communicable. God's hiddenness does not simply pave the way for the doctrine of God's revelation but is worthy of discussion in and of itself. As J. Todd Billings puts it, for Bavinck the incomprehensibility of God was "one of the key presuppositions of his entire doctrine of God" and "a key presupposition for properly interpreting scripture."[88]

---

86. Muller, *Post-Reformation Reformed Dogmatics*, 3:165; Dolf te Velde, *The Doctrine of God in Reformed Orthodoxy, Karl Barth, and the Utrecht School* (Leiden: Brill, 2013), 144–46.

87. "Already at the Fourth Lateran Council in 1215, incomprehensibility was listed as an attribute together with the eternity, immensity, immutability, omnipotence, and ineffability of God" (Klooster, *Incomprehensibility of God*, 79). Later, the same approach was adopted in the French Confession (1559, art. 1), Belgic Confession (1561, art. 1), Westminster Confession of Faith (1646, art. 2.1), and other Reformed confessions (Klooster, *Incomprehensibility of God*, 85; see also *CD* II/1:185).

88. J. Todd Billings, *Union with Christ: Reframing Theology and Ministry for the Church* (Grand Rapids: Baker Academic, 2011), 77.

Historical Overview

In his *Reformed Dogmatics*, Bavinck usually introduces new themes with a survey of the relevant biblical data (without delving deeply into exegesis). Then, he presents a historical overview of the theme and its development throughout church history. Finally, he offers his own exposition of the subject.[89] Bavinck's treatment of the idea of incomprehensibility in Christian theology (at the end of the first volume), and more particularly in the doctrine of God (at the beginning of the second volume), follows this pattern. For the purposes of the present study, however, it is pointless to reproduce Bavinck's division between the volumes and his threefold structure (Bible, history, and dogmatics). Rather, I will examine his insights presented in both volumes and where necessary refer to other parts of the *Reformed Dogmatics*, as well as to some of his other works. I will start with Bavinck's reconstruction of the historical development of this topic and look at how Karl Barth situates Bavinck's own position in the history of Christian dogma. Then I will discuss Bavinck's use of biblical passages and his elaboration of the doctrine. Since Bavinck almost never provided detailed exegesis, his remarks on the biblical passages can be naturally merged with the presentation of his own views on the subject.

Bavinck starts his historical overview of the idea of God's incomprehensibility with non-Christian religions. In evaluating them, he uses the modern language of God's absoluteness and personality. Bavinck believes that Eastern religions, many of "Muḥammad's followers," and Greek philosophers emphasize God's absoluteness at the expense of his personality, that is, his unknowability over his knowability. Among the Greeks, "Plotinus is the most radical of all," since he does not apply any positive predicates to God.[90] Whether or not Bavinck is entirely correct in every nuance of his survey lies outside the scope of the present study. Suffice it to say that Bavinck recognized the idea of God's incomprehensibility in all religions, but he found the expression of this concept in non-Christian theologies to be deficient and unbalanced.

89. See details in Nicolaas H. Gootjes, "De Struktuur van Bavincks Gereformeerde Dogmatiek," *Radix* 16 (1990): 136–57.

90. *RD* 2:34–35.

Christianity is different, Bavinck argues. The key feature of Christianity is the unity of the personality and absoluteness of God, the unity of his revealedness and hiddenness. Christianity affirms the possibility of true knowledge of God but denies that such knowledge can be exhaustive. However, even if God's hiddenness was not *one-sidedly* emphasized in Christian tradition, it nonetheless remained a prominent idea. Justin Martyr, Irenaeus, Clement of Alexandria, Origen, and others recognized that God transcends human comprehension and that no name can describe him perfectly. Bavinck suggests, however, that the early fathers' affirmation of God's incomprehensibility was not unproblematic: the most widespread deficiency in their writings was the antithesis between the unknowable Father and the Son who revealed him.[91]

Among later theologians, Bavinck paid special attention to Augustine of Hippo, John of Damascus, pseudo-Dionysius, and John Scotus Eriugena. Augustine admitted that God is inexpressible and inconceivable in his very being. Bavinck cites Augustine's famous words: "If you comprehend him it is not God you comprehend." Since no human concepts fit him adequately, Augustine believed that God is known better by not knowing. Bavinck points out that the advantages of such negative theology were further emphasized by John of Damascus. According to his theology, we can only know *that* God is, but "what he is in essence and nature is altogether incomprehensible and unknowable." "What we say positively concerning God does not refer to his nature but to 'the things regarding his nature.'" Bavinck goes on to state that John of Damascus was influenced by the works of pseudo-Dionysius, who most emphatically taught the unknowability of God's essence. According to pseudo-Dionysius, Bavinck observes, neither positive nor negative theology gives us any knowledge of God's very being, because "God surpasses both all negation and all affirmation." Bavinck points out that the same thoughts were repeated by Eriugena: we cannot know what God is. For Eriugena, "what we predicate of him is only true of him figuratively; in reality he is altogether different." God surpasses all human terms and ideas. Later in his *Reformed Dogmatics*, Bavinck summarizes the position of the early tradition as follows: "In the thinking of the

91. *RD* 2:34, 36. I will describe Bavinck's evaluation of this antithesis at more length under "The Trinity and the Principles of Dogmatic Theology" (pages 111–14).

church fathers God was both unknowable and knowable: unknowable in essence, yet knowable from revelation."[92]

Bavinck further says that although the scholastics "attached greater value to positive theology," they did not abandon the idea of the unknowability of God's essence. Even Aquinas's statements about the beatific vision do not imply that in the state of glory the saints receive comprehensive knowledge of God. However, the subsequent elaboration of the doctrine of God in scholasticism tended, according to Bavinck, to underestimate the notion of God's incomprehensibility and treated it as an ordinary attribute of God alongside the others. "Against Thomas, Duns Scotus asserted that there was indeed a quidditative, albeit imperfect, knowledge of God."[93] Bavinck observes that the position of Scotus was rejected by the nominalists. Ockham, in particular, claimed that we cannot know the divine essence. During the post-Reformation period, in Bavinck's view, Catholic theologians preferred Aquinas's position on the issue of God's incomprehensibility.

---

92. *RD* 2:37–38; 128–29.

93. *RD* 2:38–39. This citation implies that, according to Bavinck, Thomas did not believe in the possibility of a quidditative knowledge of God. (On the same page Bavinck also clearly writes that Thomas denied the possibility of a knowledge of God's "whatness" [*quidditas*], but there Bavinck speaks about Thomas's views about our knowledge on earth.) This passage demonstrates how difficult and ambiguous this terminology can be. According to Gregory Rocca, Thomas asserted, "While there is no knowledge of God's quiddity in this life (against the Augustinians), there will be such a knowledge in heaven (against Albert)." See Rocca, *Speaking the Incomprehensible God: Thomas Aquinas on the Interplay of Positive and Negative Theology* (Washington, DC: Catholic University of America Press, 2004), 40. Rocca argues that Thomas did not identify (as Albert did) quidditative and comprehensive knowledge. "Although a quidditative knowledge of God is possible in heaven due to God's grace, a comprehensive knowledge of God by the creature is never possible, not even by God's grace" (47). In his *Reformed Dogmatics*, Bavinck rarely uses the term "quidditative" (or "quiddity"), and in each of these rare passages he refers to the scholastics (Thomas: *RD* 1:230; Anselm: *RD* 2:38; Thomas, Scotus, and Ockham: *RD* 2:39; Scotus: *RD* 2:107). From these passages it appears that "quidditative knowledge" for Bavinck was synonymous with the "knowledge as to essence," which, as we will see, Bavinck identifies with a comprehensive knowledge of God. This brings his thought closer to Albert in this respect, although Bavinck does not seem to have been influenced directly by him.

Although in this citation Bavinck contrasts Scotus with the preceding tradition, he does not attach major significance to this discontinuity. Elsewhere, Bavinck also notes that Scotus "asserted that 'essence' can be equally and univocally attributed to God and to creatures" (*RD* 2:113)—an idea that in contemporary theology was interpreted as "the turning point in the destiny of the West." See John Milbank, *The Word Made Strange: Theology, Language, Culture* (Oxford: Blackwell, 1997), 44. Bavinck disagreed with Scotus on this point (*RD* 2:121) but did not consider it essential for subsequent theological and social developments in the West.

In his overview of the Reformation doctrine of God's hiddenness, Bavinck naturally starts with Luther. In his publications, Bavinck mentions Luther's *Deus absconditus* at least five times.[94] In general, Bavinck was quite positive about Luther's differentiation between the hidden and revealed God, between God in himself and the word of God. Bavinck also constantly emphasized that the object of theology is not the hidden God in himself but God in his revelation. As we will see, Bavinck also concurred with Luther that even God's revelation in Christ does not exhaust his mystery. Further, Bavinck certainly approved of Luther's early linking of God's hiddenness and revelation to the hiddenness and revelation of God's *will* and the doctrine of predestination. Bavinck regretted that later Lutheran theologians abandoned Luther's views on God's will and predestination.[95]

Nevertheless, Bavinck did not seem to appreciate that Luther gradually focused more and more on God's revealed promises and pushed the doctrine of predestination into the background.[96] Referring to Luther's later works, Bavinck complains that they proceeded from an anthropological rather than a cosmological principle and no longer boldly affirmed the doctrine of predestination.[97] Bavinck also bemoans the fact that Luther "silently watched Melanchthon's change with respect to this doctrine."[98] He disapproved of Luther's concentration on God's revelation *instead of* predestination (and, correspondingly, on God's universal promises *instead of* the particularity of grace). Bavinck even criticized Luther's *early* treatment of the distinction between God's hidden and revealed will. Unlike Luther, who readily accepted some tension between God's hidden and revealed will, Bavinck sought to avoid all paradoxical expressions. In particular, while Luther maintained that God does not desire the death of a sinner in his revealed will but rather desires this in his hidden (inscrutable) will, Bavinck's systematic mind demanded a more consistent view: he denies that God's hidden and revealed will oppose each other, "as though according to the former God willed sin, but according to the latter he did not; as

94. *RD* 2:40, 152, 242, 356; Herman Bavinck, "Calvinistisch en Gereformeerd," *De Vrije Kerk* 19 (1893): 56.

95. *RD* 2:40, 152, 242.

96. *RD* 2:356; Bavinck, "Calvinistisch en Gereformeerd," 56.

97. Herman Bavinck, *Het Christendom*, Groote Godsdiensten 2.7 (Baarn: Hollandia, 1912), 46.

98. *RD* 2:356.

though according to the former he does not will the salvation of all, but according to the latter he does."[99] Bavinck argued that God takes no pleasure in sin also according to his hidden will, and neither does he will the salvation of all people without exception according to his revealed will. In Bavinck's theology, God's hiddenness and revelation are never related to wrath and mercy, respectively. It is not that in his revelation God is more merciful than he is in himself; it is not that in God's revelation his grace is given more generously that in his hidden decree; it is not that the thought of the hidden God must evoke fear and despair, while the thought of the revealed God must evoke gratitude and love. As we will see in more detail below, Bavinck attempted to show that God in himself and God in his revelation are one and the same God—righteous and holy, as well as merciful, at the same time. Bavinck seemed to miss this emphasis on consistency in Luther's doctrine and considered his distinction between *Deus absconditus* and *Deus revelatus* to be "a very sharp" one. Bavinck did not specify the nature of this "sharpness," but apparently this evaluation stemmed from Luther's failure to harmonize God's hidden and revealed will.[100]

Turning to the treatment of God's incomprehensibility among Reformed theologians, Bavinck says that the proposition that "the finite cannot contain the infinite" was taken more seriously in the Reformed tradition than in any other tradition. For Calvin, Bavinck notes, the search for God's "whatness" was an idle speculation. Later Reformed theologians

99. Martin Luther, *The Bondage of the Will* (London: Bensley, 1823), 158; *RD* 2:245.

100. *RD* 2:242. When reflecting on Bavinck's evaluation of Luther, one must keep in mind that these two theologians approached the doctrine of God's hiddenness with different interests and within different contexts. Luther was undoubtedly driven by soteriological concerns: he "is interested not in God as he is in himself, but in how God encounters us in a saving way." See Roland E. Ziegler, "Luther and Calvin on God: Origins of Lutheran and Reformed Differences," *Concordia Theological Quarterly* 75 (2011): 64. "God in himself" was of no concern for Luther because "God in himself" is of no help for salvation here and now. Luther simply confessed the *Deus absconditus* and *Deus revelatus* without attempting to reconcile them. He easily admitted and even celebrated paradoxes and apparent contradictions if he believed they sprung from Scripture. Bavinck, however, was driven more by dogmatic concerns and tried to integrate all insights into a system of doctrine. His confession of God's hiddenness was less personal and disturbing, but more coherent, more theoretical, and better thought-out. God's hiddenness was, for him, not so much a religious as a theoretical problem, which he treats in the context of the limitations of human knowledge. Bavinck's perspective was broader: while Luther considered God's hiddenness in distinctively biblical terms, Bavinck argued that the recognition of God's hiddenness is more or less typical for all religions and philosophies and stems not only from the Bible, but also from the *sensus divinitatis* and the objective world outside us.

"spoke of the nonknowability of God's being in even stronger terms." They insisted that human names and definitions do not make God's essence known to us. In the course of time, however, the recognition of God's hiddenness took on a merely formal aspect and lost its significance for theology to the point that it was "almost totally forgotten."[101] This, in Bavinck's estimation, was a negative trend. He did not want the doctrine of God's incomprehensibility to become a mere abstraction and believed that it was vitally important to the Christian faith.

Bavinck's concern for the doctrine of God's incomprehensibility was noted by none other than Karl Barth. Barth himself wrote a separate paragraph about God's hiddenness in his *Church Dogmatics* (II/1.27.1), where he claims that God's hiddenness is a positive assertion and not merely a recognition of the limitations of humanity's cognitive capacities. According to Barth, God's hiddenness means that we can know God only because of his revelation and good pleasure. Barth regrets that in the early church the idea of the hiddenness of God was not easily distinguished from the basic philosophical idea of the inaccessibility of the supreme being. Even when, in the Middle Ages, God's hiddenness was formally recognized as one of his properties, and even when, in the times of the Reformation, it found a place in Protestant confessions, "the full reach and power of the statement *Deus est incomprehensibilis*" was unknown. The recognition of God's hiddenness as witnessed in the Bible never "occupied a basic and determinate position ... in relation to the whole doctrine of the knowledge of God."[102] Barth openly says that he himself desires to give such a position to God's hiddenness, and at this point he refers to Bavinck:

> In the newer dogmatic literature I know of only one, the Dutch theologian H. Bavinck, who seems to have perceived this (cf. the beginning of the 2nd vol. of his Gereformeerde Dogmatiek, 1918). The fact that this was not seen in the older theology seems to me to be explicable only on the grounds that in those times it was not finally clear whether they really wanted to understand the incomprehensibility of God from Plato and Plotinus, or from Ps. 139 and

101. *RD* 2:40–41.

102. *CD* II/1:185.

from Paul, and therefore as an article of faith confirming the revelation of God as such.[103]

Thus, Barth found in Bavinck the only recent dogmatician who realized the importance of God's incomprehensibility and its place in theology proper.[104] This reference is especially important and worth noticing in light of the fact that Barth rarely explicitly referred to Bavinck.[105] The

---

103. *CD* II/1:186.

104. It is less clear whether, in Barth's view, Bavinck differed from "the older theology" in distinguishing between the philosophical and biblical understanding of God's incomprehensibility. But the fact that Barth's appreciative appeal to Bavinck is followed immediately by the criticism of the older theology seems to imply that, according to Barth, Bavinck really differed from the older theology on this point. John Vissers takes this citation as clearly saying that, for Barth, Bavinck "was a theologian who believed ... in the incomprehensibility of God as an insight derived from the Word of God in Holy Scripture." See Vissers, "Karl Barth's Appreciative Use of Herman Bavinck's Reformed Dogmatics," *CTJ* 45 (2010): 86. If this is really so, Barth seemed to have considered Bavinck's position closer to his own than it actually was. While Barth did not link God's hiddenness with the human natural sense of a higher incomprehensible being, Bavinck, in order to explain the origin of the human sense of God's incomprehensibility, used not only Scripture, but also his concept of general revelation. Barth argued that the hiddenness of God is completely different from the hiddenness of ordinary things, whereas Bavinck was far more open to discerning parallels between the knowledge (and the hiddenness) of God and the world. Although he admitted the uniqueness of the knowledge of God, Bavinck sought to avoid separating theological epistemology from general epistemology. Further, while Barth's doctrine of God's incomprehensibility was built on the persistent dialectic of veiling and unveiling, Bavinck's concept of God's hiddenness was less dynamic and dialectic: at the outset, it also emphasized the need of revelation, but later, in the course of theological reflection, focused more on human finiteness.

It is also ironic that Bavinck was criticized precisely for his alleged *failure* to distinguish between philosophical and biblical understandings of God's incomprehensibility. According to Klooster, Bavinck "apparently puts Plato, Philo, Plotinus and the Gnostics on the same plane as the Church Fathers" (*Incomprehensibility of God*, 100). Later in his book (107), Klooster also cites Van Til, according to whom "Bavinck should have distinguished more clearly the incomprehensibility of God from the non-Christian notion of mystery. The Christian and the non-Christian notions of mystery are as the poles apart. ... Bavinck sometimes speaks as though the concept of the incomprehensibility of God entertained by Christian theology and that entertained by pagan philosophy were virtually the same. ... Bavinck still speaks as though the only difference between the Christian and the non-Christian notions of the incomprehensibility of God were a matter of degree." See Cornelius Van Til, "Common Grace: Part II. The Latest Debate about Common Grace," *WTJ* 8 (May 1946): 189–90.

105. McCormack notes that the phrase *Deus dixit* (which in Barth's Göttingen lectures is presented as a guiding definition of God's revelation) was taken by Barth from Bavinck (*Karl Barth's Critically Realistic Dialectical Theology*, 338). For Bavinck, *Deus dixit* is "the principle into which all theological dogmas are distilled" and "the foundational principle (*primum principium*) to which all dogmas, including the dogma of Scripture, can be traced" (*RD* 1:30, 590; see also 1:46, 582). Referring to Ursinus, Barth formulates the role of *Deus dixit* in almost

hiddenness of God is the only doctrine in the development of which Barth recognized the special role of Bavinck.[106]

God's Hiddenness without Revelation

"Mystery is the lifeblood of dogmatics." This phrase opens the second volume of Bavinck's *Reformed Dogmatics*. He states that theology encounters the incomprehensible One.[107] But what is the meaning of God's incomprehensibility? Citing Isaiah 45:15 ("Truly, you are a God who hides himself"), Blaise Pascal famously said that "any religion that does not say that God is hidden is not true, and any religion which does not explain why [this is so] does not instruct."[108] God's hiddenness does not simply denote that God is unknowable. Rather, it is a rich concept, which contains a host of assumptions and implications. God's hiddenness can be understood in different ways, and therefore, as Pascal says, we need an explanation of this concept. For the sake of order and clarity, I will present Bavinck's answer to this question in four sections, devoted to God's hiddenness without revelation, God's hiddenness from unbelievers, God's hiddenness in revealedness, and the hiddenness of God's will. In this section, I will focus on the first point.

It is axiomatic for Bavinck that without revelation, God is hidden from us. If God did not reveal himself, we would know nothing of Him: "If we are to know God he must reveal himself." We cannot speak of God except on the basis of his self-revelation. In explaining why God's revelation is indispensable to our knowledge of him, Bavinck did not hesitate to bring forth an analogy with human beings. In my analysis of the underlying

---

the same terms as Bavinck: "The principle behind every theological dogma is: *Deus dixit*." See Karl Barth, *The Göttingen Dogmatics: Instruction in the Christian Religion*, trans. Geoffrey W. Bromiley (Grand Rapids: Eerdmans, 1991), 10. The principle shows that it is God who is the speaking Subject in revelation.

Barth's other references to Bavinck are analyzed in Vissers, "Karl Barth's Appreciative Use," 79–86. It is also noteworthy that in discussing patristic evidence for God's hiddenness Barth refers to the same works as Bavinck does: Justin Martyr's *Apology* 1.61, Athanasius's *Against the Heathen* 2, and Augustine's *Sermon* 117.

106. "It is interesting that Barth praised Bavinck precisely for his insight into the incomprehensibility of God" (Berkouwer, *Half Century of Theology*, 148).

107. *RD* 2:29, 48.

108. Blaise Pascal, *Pensées*, trans. A. J. Krailscheimer (Harmondsworth, UK: Penguin Classics, 1966), 103, L242 (the L refers to the Lafuma number that is used for citing different editions of *Pensées*).

characteristics of Bavinck's theology, I noted that the mystery of God has much to do with the mystery of the world in general and of the human person in particular. Human beings also reveal themselves, and until they do so, they remain unknown. Bavinck argued that in a sense, a human being is the *principium essendi* of our knowledge concerning his personality. To be known, he must first "reveal himself, manifest himself by appearance, word, and act, so that we may somewhat learn to know him."[109] In the case of humans, the only way to acquire knowledge of our inner beings and personalities is similarly through self-revelation. Our knowledge of others depends largely on what they choose to disclose.[110] In this sense, humans are closer to God than to other creatures. According to Bavinck, it is meaningless to apply the word "revelation" to animals or plants; but it is absolutely reasonable and meaningful to speak of *human* revelation.[111] To be sure, for many reasons, divine self-revelation and human self-revelation are merely analogical: unlike God, humans cannot perfectly know even themselves; human revelation can be untruthful and deceptive; the need of explicit human revelation is less pressing since we can still understand much about other persons even if they are unwilling to reveal themselves. Still, the limitations of the analogy only prove the necessity of God's revelation: If we need the revelation of humans in order to know them, how much more do we need the revelation of God?[112] The emphasis on our utter dependence on God's revelation is so strong in Bavinck's dogmatics that Bremmer observes a certain similarity between Bavinck and Schleiermacher.[113] Just as for the latter the idea of human dependence was crucial for his entire theological project, so for the former the idea of human dependence was crucial in the context of God's revelation. Bavinck's interpretation of this dependence,

---

109. *RD* 1:212, 286, 341; see also 1:297.

110. See Herman Bavinck, *Our Reasonable Faith*, trans. Henry Zylstra (Grand Rapids: Baker Book House, 1977), 33.

111. *RD* 1:296.

112. Bavinck even claims that the forms of human and divine self-revelations are the same: "Other people only become knowable to us when they reveal themselves to us, i.e., manifest their presence, speak, or act. Appearance, word, and deed are the three revelational forms between one human and another. The same is true in the case of the Lord our God; his knowledge, too, flows to us only through the channel of his revelation. Furthermore, that revelation, too, can only be his appearance, his word, and his deed" (*RD* 1:212). See also Herman Bavinck, *Handleiding bij het onderwijs in den christelijken godsdienst* (Kampen: Kok, 1913), 49.

113. Bremmer, *Herman Bavinck als Dogmaticus*, 165.

however, was directed against Schleiermacher's insights, because reliance on revelation meant for him the rejection of the subjective methodology of theologies of consciousness.

By stressing the unknowability of God apart from revelation, Bavinck also rejected the theory of innate ideas.[114] We cannot produce any knowledge of God from within ourselves. Just as in general epistemology we are dependent on the objective world outside, so even more in theological epistemology we are dependent on the objective revelation of God. As Bavinck puts it, "All the truths of the Christian faith come to man from the outside. They are known to him only through revelation."[115] Bavinck even criticized Kuyper for his idea that humanity, before the fall, could draw the knowledge of God from within itself. Bavinck put this notion of Kuyper on the same level as rationalism or mysticism.[116] According to Bavinck, Reformed theology maintained that humanity "does not produce [the knowledge of God], but receives and reproduces."[117] Regarding knowledge of God, we can only think God's thoughts after him and not create our own. Bavinck's criticism of the theory of innate ideas formed a part of his general opposition to the theologies of consciousness, which derive religious truth from the subject. In contrast to this position, Bavinck emphasized the epistemic

114. Opposition to this theory was a constant motif in Bavinck's theology from his early Kampen speech on (Bavinck, *Wetenschap der H. Godgeleerdheid*, 19–20).

115. Bavinck, *Certainty of Faith*, 71. Note also his comment that "No one knows by nature that God is the Almighty, Creator of heaven and earth" (68). Although Bavinck rejected our ability to "deduce conscious, clear, and valid knowledge of God from the contents of our own minds" (*RD* 2:71), this does not mean that he rejected the idea of implanted knowledge of God. Bavinck accepted this idea in the sense of the inborn capacity and inclination to arrive at a firm and certain knowledge of God in the normal course of development and without external coercion and scientific proofs. As Steven J. Duby describes the position of Bavinck, "God gifts us with innate ability to receive and appropriate his revelation and leads us to an awareness of God without compulsion or argumentation." See Duby, "Working with the Grain of Nature: Epistemic Underpinnings for Christian Witness in the Theology of Herman Bavinck," *BavRev* 3 (2012): 79. Bavinck protested both rationalism (idealism) and empiricism. Against the former, Bavinck argued that the human mind is not a source of knowledge and that humans are not born with ready knowledge of God. Against the latter, he argued that "this revelation of God speaks so loudly and forcefully and meets with such resonance in everyone's heart that it can be called uniquely appropriate to, and increated in, humans" (*RD* 2:72).

116. "Kuyper says that man, in and of himself—apart from sin—is able to obtain knowledge of God entirely from within himself. In principle, this is rationalism and mysticism." (The original excerpt from Bavinck's lectures can be found in Bremmer, *Herman Bavinck als Dogmaticus*, 41; see also 45.)

117. Bremmer, *Herman Bavinck als Dogmaticus*, 41.

dependence of humankind. Here he also used an analogy with other spheres of life: just as in our daily lives we gain knowledge from without and are shaped by our environment, so also in religion we are not the epistemic source of truth but are dependent on the external world.[118]

Time and again Bavinck repeats that we can know God only through his revelation. But the idea of revelation is wide-ranging in Bavinck's theology: the entire world is God's revelation. In Bavinck's own words, "Every creature is a revelation of God," and, "The entire universe is a revelation of God." Strictly speaking, there is nothing "outside revelation" in this world. Further, it is obvious that human reason is also within the realm of creation and thus, in a sense, revelatory: "There is a revelation of God in all his works, not only outside of, but *especially within* humans," Bavinck asserts. Humanity constitutes not simply "*a* part," but "*the primary part* of the nature from which God is known."[119] Nicholas Wolterstorff correctly concludes that, according to Bavinck, "human beings are especially revelatory of God."[120]

Nevertheless, this broad scope of revelation does not imply that we can attain knowledge of God independently of him. First of all, according to Bavinck, God's revelation in creation should not be taken for granted: it was an expression of God's mercy to leave traces of himself in his creation and to structure it in such a way that it reveals his glory. That we are innately disposed to receive knowledge of God is also his gift. Further, as indicated above, Bavinck's point was that humans are not a source of divine revelation to themselves. They have a natural disposition to external revelation, but they do not have any knowledge of God in themselves. As Bavinck writes, "The form of reason, conscience, and the sense of divinity" leap into action only "as a result of stimuli from related phenomena in the outside world."[121] In the prelapsarian world, humans needed external, objective revelation. In the fallen world, humans continue to need external revelation, but now also additionally need restoration of their subjective capacity to understand God's revelation. In both cases their knowledge of

118. *RD* 2:70.

119. *RD* 2:72, 135 206, emphasis added.

120. Wolterstorff, "Herman Bavinck," 139.

121. *RD* 1:586.

God is not abstracted from the world around them. As we have seen in the sections "Christian Realism" (pages 51–55) and "The Idea of Correspondence" (pages 55–57), in explaining this mutual relation between object and subject, Bavinck extensively used the idea of correspondence and the notion of the mediating role of the Logos: the logos implicit in other creatures corresponds to the logos in humans. Last, although humans are innately predisposed to know God, they need his guidance to recognize his revelation in the world and even within themselves.[122] As Donald MacLeod writes, "This fact of the dependence of the *sensus deitatis* on God's own action in revelation is enormously important."[123] We cannot rely on the divine light within us because it does not work apart from God's constant activity from without.

"The knowledge of God can have its origin only in revelation," Bavinck asserts. "Only in revelation" does not mean that there are some things in the world that are revelatory and other things that are not, so that God can be known in the former but not in the latter. Rather, Bavinck is speaking about the source. The knowledge of God rooted "only in revelation" means that humans are always recipients of such knowledge and never the font thereof: "No knowledge of God is possible except that which proceeds from and by God (Matt 11:27; 1 Cor 2:10–11)." Thus, God's hiddenness implies the futility of human attempts to perceive him "from below." "He is knowable only because and insofar as he himself wants to be known," Bavinck states.[124] If we look vertically upward and endeavor to understand God from below, God is hidden to us; but if we look horizontally, at creation and Scripture as his revelatory gifts, God is revealed to us.[125]

---

122. "God has implanted in his creation thoughts and forces that human beings gradually learn to understand *under his guidance*" (*RD* 1:341, emphasis added).

123. Donald MacLeod, "Bavinck's Prolegomena: Fresh Light on Amsterdam, Old Princeton, and Cornelius van Til," *WTJ* 68 (2006): 266.

124. *RD* 1:212; 2:56.

125. "One sees and knows God, not when he rises above the creation or when he denies the created world, but instead when one enters into the creation. The creature does not see God by turning away from the creation; on the contrary, he turns to the creation to see what God is doing in his creation." See Eugene Heideman, *The Relation of Revelation and Reason in E. Brunner and H. Bavinck* (Assen: Van Gorcum, 1959), 160.

God's Hiddenness from Unbelievers

According to Bavinck, "if we are to know something about God, he must come forward out of his hiddenness, in some way make himself perceivable, and hence reveal himself." Elsewhere Bavinck argues that the idea of revelation "conveys that something that was hidden comes to light. In the area of religion, it indicates that God ... comes forward before the eyes of his rational creatures." God's revelation "was intended to make known something that was hidden."[126] God's revelation is not symbolic, illusive, or delusive; it genuinely discloses God to humans. What has been disclosed is no longer veiled; what has been opened up is no longer closed; what has been revealed is no longer hidden; what has been proclaimed is no longer untold.

Bavinck reinforced this point in his analysis of New Testament terms that express the concept of revelation. He paid special attention to the words ἀποκαλύπτω and φανερόω, which imply the idea of disclosing that which was hidden up to that point. In particular, "Ἀποκαλυπτειν designates the removal of a cover by which a given object was hidden, and φανερουν denotes making known a matter that was hidden or unknown before. ... Ἀποκαλυψις takes away the cause by which something was hidden; φανερωσις makes known the matter itself."[127] Thus, God's revelation really communicates that which was previously unknown.

However, this reality of God's revelation does not necessarily lead all humans to a genuine knowledge of God or to communion with him. Although God exerts "revelatory pressure" on humans, their sin prevents them from recognizing the riches of his revelation. Bavinck emphasizes that the darkened human mind cannot "rightly know and understand" even God's revelation in nature. "Only the eye of faith sees God in his creation." The necessity of faith manifests itself even more clearly when it comes to preaching the gospel.[128]

Bavinck emphasized this meaning of God's hiddenness while examining the biblical idea of mystery and the Greek word μυστήριον, which is commonly used to describe God's plan of salvation in Christ (Rom 16:25;

126. *RD* 1:286, 307, 381.

127. *RD* 1:325.

128. *RD* 1:304, 315, 321, 340; 2:73, 330; 4:44.

Eph 1:9; 3:3; Col 1:26–27; 2:2; 4:3) and the manner in which it is carried out (Rom 11:25; 1 Cor 15:51; 2 Thess 2:7; Rev 10:7). Bavinck notes that although in the New Testament a mystery signifies something hidden, it ceases to be hidden as soon as it is revealed and made known. The hiddenness of a mystery belongs to the past; in the present, for those who accept the gospel, it is no longer hidden. "The NT term μυστήριον, accordingly, does not denote an intellectually uncomprehended and incomprehensible truth of faith, but a matter that was formerly hidden in God, was then made known in the gospel, and is now understood by believers."[129] According to Jesus, some people have been granted to know the mysteries of the kingdom of heaven, while the rest have not been granted this knowledge (Matt 13:11; Mark 4:11; Luke 8:10).

Bavinck was convinced that in the course of history, this meaning of mystery became overshadowed by another concept that emphasized a mystery as something that far surpasses even the intellect of believers. Using this definition of mystery, truths of the faith such as the incarnation or the sacraments are incomprehensible and therefore "mysterious" to believers and nonbelievers alike. "In the case of Rome, the mysteries are incomprehensible, primarily because they belong to another, higher, supernatural order, which surpasses the human intellect as such," explains Bavinck. The Reformation, however, returned to the New Testament meaning of the term "mystery" and put the real contrast not between the natural and the supernatural orders, but between sin and grace. According to Bavinck, the Reformation "located the essence of mystery, not in the fact that it is incomprehensible to human beings as such but to the intellect of the 'natural' (that is, unspiritual) person."[130] The reason the mystery is unknowable lies not in the mystery itself, but rather in the blindness and stubbornness of humanity. The biblical mystery is hidden from unbelievers but plain to believers.

Despite these remarks about the New Testament idea of mystery and its rediscovery by the Reformers, in most passages where Bavinck refers to mystery in Christian theology, he means something intellectually incomprehensible rather than something previously unknown and now made

129. *RD* 1:619–21; 4:465.

130. *RD* 1:620; see also 4:465.

plain to believers.[131] He usually refers to mystery in the context of reflections about theoretical knowledge and its limitations. Primarily it was Bavinck's characteristically modern preoccupation with epistemological issues and his understanding of revelation as the self-revelation of God that prevented him from consistently using the term "mystery" in the sense that he himself considered to be biblical (see more on this issue in "The Content of God's Revelation," pages 86–87). While in the New Testament, as Bavinck himself observed, God reveals the mystery of salvation in Jesus Christ, which ceases to be hidden for those who accept the gospel, in Bavinck's theology God reveals the mystery of his very self—and *this* mystery always remains inexhaustible. Bavinck's theocentric concept of revelation correlates with his understanding of the task of dogmatics:

> The knowledge of God is the only dogma, the exclusive content, of the entire field of dogmatics. All the doctrines treated in dogmatics—whether they concern the universe, humanity, Christ, and so forth—are but the explication of the one central dogma of the knowledge of God. ... Dogmatics is always called upon to ponder and describe God and God alone.[132]

Such a definition of the task of dogmatics involves the realization of the limitations of human intellectual capacity and human language. For this reason, the motif of incomprehensibility so often comes to the fore in Bavinck's references to mysteries in theology.

---

131. *RD* 1:436, 442, 477, 478; 2:29, 49, 106, 334, 351, 459, 496, 506, 583, 608, 618; 3:69, 101, 145, 184, 301, 308; 4:484, 636. Therefore, it is difficult to agree with the conclusion of E. P. Heideman that Bavinck uses the word "mystery" as something hidden but now revealed also with respect to God, the dogma of the Trinity, the incarnation, and other topics (*Relation of Revelation and Reason*, 214). In the context of discussing the clarity of Scripture, Bavinck speaks precisely of the topics Heideman mentions. Bavinck comments here that Scripture deals "with the deepest mysteries, with God, the Trinity, the incarnation, predestination, and other truths" (*RD* 1:475). Although in this sentence he seems to describe the position of the Roman Catholic Church, later in the text he makes it clear that the sentence also reflects his own view (*RD* 1:477). Bavinck does not mean that the mentioned truths *were* mysterious until revealed; rather, he mentions them to qualify his doctrine of the Bible's perspicuity: the message about salvation is clear, but there also remain some mysteries that "far exceed the reach of the human intellect" (*RD* 1:477). Thus, even with regard to the topics mentioned by Heideman, Bavinck typically understood mystery as a truth that surpasses the limited cognitive abilities of all human beings. This also means that Bavinck was closer to the Roman Catholic approach than his criticism of it might have led one to expect.

132. *RD* 2:29.

Nevertheless, the biblical notion of mystery did provide another dimension to Bavinck's understanding of God's hiddenness. It helped him conclude that, for believers, God's mystery is not an enigma or a puzzle that must be solved, but rather a source of joy, comfort, and praise. In Berkouwer's words, "Bavinck was right when he branded the identification of mystery with enigma as a flattening out of the mystery of faith."[133] It is therefore quite natural that Bavinck concludes his reflections about mysteries in the Bible with doxology, gratitude, and admiration: "Believers do know those mysteries; ... they do not experience them as an oppressive burden but rather as intellectual liberation. Their faith turns into wonder; knowledge terminates in adoration; and their confession becomes a song of praise and thanksgiving."[134]

God's Hiddenness in Revealedness

Although those who accept God's revelation can truly know him, this does not mean, according to Bavinck, that God is no longer hidden from believers. In some ways, God remains hidden—or, rather, incomprehensible—even for those who believe. Having placed so much emphasis on the disclosing power of God's revelation, Bavinck was also aware of the limitations of those receiving it. He asserts that even "the knowledge that God has revealed of himself in nature and Scripture far surpasses human imagination and understanding." As mentioned above, he emphasizes that the doctrine of the perspicuity of Scripture "does not mean that the matters and subjects with which Scripture deals are not mysteries that far exceed the reach of the human intellect."[135] At least in this life, therefore, the saints cannot fully comprehend all that has already been disclosed in general and special revelation.

It is even more important to recognize that, according to Bavinck, the fullness of God's being is not communicated, and cannot be communicated, in revelation. Even if humans were able fully to comprehend God's revelation, this does not mean that they would fully comprehend God himself. His innermost being necessarily remains hidden even *in* his

133. Berkouwer, *Half Century of Theology*, 148.

134. *RD* 1:621.

135. *RD* 1:477; 2:29.

revelation, because of human finitude. "The name of God in Scripture does not describe God as he exists within himself." "There is no knowledge of God as he is in himself." "In himself God has no name," and "we cannot name him as he is within himself." "No creature can see or understand God as he is and as he speaks in himself."[136] Bavinck repeats such formulations throughout his *Reformed Dogmatics* and other works.[137] He also cites numerous passages from the Old Testament in which God's incomprehensibility and his superiority over the whole of creation are emphasized. God is exalted "beyond our understanding" (Job 36:26) and does great things "beyond our understanding" (Job 37:5). He is incomparable (Isa 40:18, 25; 46:5), nameless (Gen 32:29; Judg 13:18), and unattainable (Job 11:7). Bavinck further observes that in the New Testament we encounter the same incomprehensible and incomparable God. "No one has seen him or can see him (John 1:18; 6:46; 1 Tim 6:16). ... No one knows him except the Son and the Spirit (Matt 11:27; 1 Cor 2:11)."[138] In sum, revelation does not exclude God's hiddenness, because God as he is in himself remains hidden even in the midst of revelation.

As early as his rectoral oration at Kampen (1883), Bavinck emphasizes that the object of theology is "not God as he is in himself, in the entire depth of his impenetrable being, but ... as he willed to reveal himself in nature and grace."[139] Later Bavinck criticized Foppe Marten ten Hoor's

---

136. *RD* 1:310; 2:47, 99, 106, 137.

137. Bavinck also argues that Eunomius was incorrect "in saying that either we know God's being [*wezen*] or else we do not know God at all" (*RD* 2:51). Although Bavinck realizes that the problem with Eunomius's doctrine was his belief that the term "unbegotten" *properly* designates God's essence, here Bavinck seems to justify a third option: knowing God without knowing his being (essence).

138. *RD* 2:33–34. Despite multiple references, Bavinck's treatment of the biblical examples of God's hiddenness is disappointingly brief. As usual in his *Reformed Dogmatics*, he simply mentions biblical verses in passing without giving any substantial explanation. In the second edition of the *Reformed Dogmatics*, Bavinck considerably expands the biblical part in his chapter about God's incomprehensibility: instead of half a page in the first edition, he writes five pages in the second edition. However, almost none of the new biblical passages he cites contain information about God's incomprehensibility. Rather, they are related more to God's intimate relationship with Israel and the impotence and falsehood of "other gods" in the OT. The biblical references relevant to God's incomprehensibility are almost identical between the two editions. The only remarkable difference is that Bavinck cites Isa 45:15 ("Truly you are a hidden God") in the first edition (GD^1 2:2), but oddly deletes this reference in the second edition.

139. Bavinck, *Wetenschap der H. Godgeleerdheid*, 29.

separation of theology from other disciplines. According to Ten Hoor, the object of theology is God, while the object of other sciences is the world. Bavinck refused to draw such a sharp distinction, arguing that theology does not deal with God in himself, but rather with his "worldly" revelation. Accordingly, theology, as well as the other sciences, has to do with the creaturely realities through which God has revealed himself.[140] As Heideman concludes, for Bavinck the knowledge of God "is never a knowledge of God in his essence, but knowledge of God in his revelation."[141]

Does this mean that for Bavinck God in himself (that is, God in his essence) is totally inaccessible to us? Several times Bavinck indeed states that God's essence is unknowable and laments that Christian theologians tended to forget about "this truth."[142] It is important, however, to look more closely at two specific reasons that prompted him to use the language of unknowability. First, Bavinck denies the possibility of knowing God's essence because he interprets such knowledge as full and comprehensive (see "God's Revelation as Mediated," pages 99–103). God "cannot be known perfectly, that is, in his essence." In Bavinck's terminology, *visio per essentiam* is "absolutely equal" [*volkomen gelijk*] to *comprehensio*.[143] To know God's essence is to know God exhaustively, and this is obviously impossible for human beings. Such impossibility is due to the distance between Creator and creature: "the gulf between the Infinite and the finite, between eternity and time, between being and becoming, between the All and the nothing." God's being far exceeds the capacities of the human intellect. "God is infinitely exalted above time and space and every creature."[144] *Finitum*

---

140. Bavinck's letter to Ten Hoor, 9 December 1895, cited in Bremmer, *Herman Bavinck als Dogmaticus*, 53.

141. Heideman, *Relation of Revelation and Reason*, 160.

142. *RD* 2:41. The English translation mentions the "truth of the incomprehensibility of God" where Bavinck actually speaks about the "truth of the unknowability of the divine essence" ("[de] waarheid van de onkenbaarheid van het Goddelijk wezen," *GD*[4] 2:14).

143. *RD* [2:190.] See Bavinck's comment: "There is no name that makes his *essence* known to us. There is no concept that *fully* encompasses him. There is no description that *fully* defines him" (*RD* 2:36, emphasis added). Since these three sentences have the same meaning for Bavinck, it is noteworthy that in the first sentence Bavinck denies the knowability of the divine essence, while in the next two sentences he denies the possibility of the *full* knowledge of God. For Bavinck "fullness" is implied in the very concept of God's essence.

144. *RD* 2:30, 33, 36.

non est capax infiniti. In sum, to deny the knowability of God's essence is simply to deny that God can be known fully and adequately.[145]

Second, Bavinck denies the possibility of the knowledge of God in his essence when rejecting attempts to understand God apart from revelation. For example, he writes that Christians "do not speculate about God; they do not proceed from an abstract philosophical concept of God. ... They do not reason about God as he is in himself, for this knowledge is completely unattainable."[146] Bavinck characterizes the desire to reason about God in himself as idle speculation. Since for Bavinck the essence of God is identical with God's own self-knowledge, it follows that inquiring into God's essence would be tantamount to attempting to speak about God in a divine language while neglecting God's speech to us in human language.[147] To inquire into God's essence, therefore, is to disregard his revelation, which is the only possible way to obtain real knowledge of God. Geerhardus Vos correctly observes that Bavinck put the search for "a quiddative, essential knowledge of God" in line with "mystical contemplation" and "abstract thinking."[148] Therefore, to deny the knowability of God's essence in this second sense is simply to deny that God can be known "from below" or "from within ourselves." Elsewhere, having said that the divine essence is unknown to us, Bavinck goes on as follows: "That which lies behind revelation is completely unknowable. We cannot approach it either by our thought, our imagination, or our language."[149] Here again Bavinck empha-

145. Bavinck repeatedly denies the possibility of having an *adequaat* knowledge of God. (The translator of the *Reformed Dogmatics* typically renders this word as "fully adequate" and sometimes as simply "adequate.") To be sure, Bavinck did not intend to state that the knowledge supplied in revelation is faulty or unsatisfactory. Rather, he meant that our knowledge of God is not totally fitting or proportioned to the infinite divine being. Bavinck uses the term *adequaat* synonymously with the word "absolute" (*RD* 2:108) and contrasts it with the word "analogical" (*RD* 2:111). Such usage was typical for Reformed orthodoxy, where the Latin word *adaequatus* meant "identical." By denying that our knowledge of God is *adaequatus*, theologians indicated that this knowledge is not identical with God's self-knowledge. As Richard Muller explains, "In the case of God, such 'adequation' is impossible inasmuch as there can be no proportion between infinite God and the finite mind. Our thoughts cannot be adequated to the divine reality—they necessarily remain 'inadequate'" (*Post-Reformation Reformed Dogmatics*, 3:205).

146. *RD* 1:110–11.

147. "To think and speak divinely of God is beyond us" (*RD* 2:50).

148. Vos, "Herman Bavinck," 697. See also *RD* 2:107.

149. *RD* 2:36.

sizes the futility of human endeavors in defining that which is not revealed. Later in this volume Bavinck writes:

> It is the incontrovertible teaching of Scripture ... that in God's secret being he is unknowable and unnamable, and that all God's names presuppose his self-revelation, that is, his creation. Of God's being and life apart from creation we know nothing for the simple reason that we ourselves are creatures and therefore always bound to creation.[150]

In this passage, Bavinck first argues that "in God's secret being [*wezen*] he is unknowable" and then clarifies that we know nothing "of God's being [*zijn*] and life apart from creation." This seems to imply that God's being is unknowable through any human attempts to reach him that bypass his revelation, while he is genuinely knowable, to a certain degree, by way of his creaturely revelation. Similarly, when Bavinck writes that "there is no name that *fully* expresses his being [*wezen*]," he implicitly suggests that divine names partly express his being in some manner.[151]

Explaining why God remains incomprehensible despite his revelation, Bavinck maintains that it is simply impossible for God to reveal himself to human beings as he is in himself. God "cannot fully impart himself to creatures. For that to be possible they themselves would have to be divine."[152] This resulting hiddenness in revelation stems not from a desire on God's part to evade us, but from the adjustment of his revelation to our capacities. For Bavinck, the partial nature of God's revelation does not endanger the reality or truth of revelation, but rather makes genuinely *human* knowledge of God possible. God can be comprehended only by God.

According to Bavinck, a denial or underestimation of God's incomprehensibility in revelation would impoverish Christian faith and experience. God's incomprehensibility is a sign of his grace because it implies that something always remains in him to be discovered and enjoyed:

---

150. *RD* 2:133.

151. *RD* 2:47, emphasis added. It is not easy to reconcile this admission of a possibility of a partial expression of God's being with Bavinck's conviction that the knowledge of God's being amounts to a perfect knowledge of God, nor with his more categorical claim that "there is no name that makes his essence known to us" (*RD* 2:36). I will discuss Bavinck's consistency regarding this matter in "Comprehension and Knowledge" (pages 132–34).

152. *RD* 2:36.

"Comprehension excludes amazement and admiration." Bavinck emphasizes that Christians cannot fathom the mystery of God: "In that sense Christian theology always has to do with mysteries that it knows and marvels at but does not comprehend and fathom." Christian theology has always opposed a shallow rationalism that "considered a fully adequate knowledge of God a possibility."[153] The recognition of God's incomprehensibility leaves room for wonder and mystery.

Further, God's incomprehensibility is closely related to his lordship. Bavinck makes a noteworthy remark about comprehension and control: "There are few things we comprehend; actually we comprehend only the things that are totally in our power, the things we can make or break." If we comprehended God (that is, if God were not hidden from us in any sense), we would control him. But this is by no means the case, for it is God who exerts control over his revelation.[154]

Although, as we saw above, Bavinck speaks of the complete unknowability of "that which lies behind revelation," he pays little attention to that which remains completely outside God's revelation. In Bavinck's thought, that which is behind revelation refers to the absolute sense of what is revealed rather than to that which is not revealed at all. *In* revelation God gives relative knowledge of his absoluteness, which always remains *behind* revelation because it is irreducible to creaturely forms. As we will see in "Incommunicable and Communicable" (pages 121–24), Bavinck contends that all God's attributes are simultaneously communicable and incommunicable: in an absolute sense, each of God's attributes is incommunicable, while in a relative sense each of them is communicable. We will also see that, for Bavinck, the communication of attributes implies that God endows humans with the capacity to know his attributes. The communicability and incommunicability of all attributes, therefore, means that in an

153. *RD* 1:619; 2:48.

154. *RD* 1:619. On this point one might notice some similarity between Bavinck and Barth. Barth repeatedly emphasizes God's active concealment and his full control over his revelation and its reception. God always remains the Subject of his revelation and never becomes an object of investigation. Although in this respect Barth was hardly influenced by Bavinck, statements such as "we are masters of what we can apprehend" or "to apprehend certainly means to possess" (*CD* II/1:188) resemble the above-cited words of Bavinck that "we comprehend only the things that are totally in our power" (*RD* 1:619). To be sure, whatever similarities may be found between the two theologians in this respect, Barth's emphasis on God's dynamic sovereignty over revelation was more prominent than Bavinck's.

absolute sense each of them is behind revelation and unknowable, while in a relative sense each of them is revealed and knowable (albeit only on a creaturely level and thus in a somewhat hidden form).

The Hiddenness of God's Will

In the preceding sections, I have presented Bavinck's doctrine of God's hiddenness in ontological terms with special focus on God's being. This doctrine, however, has another important aspect, which has been intensely discussed by Reformed theologians and traditionally draws much attention from both sympathetic and unsympathetic interpreters of Calvinism: the hiddenness of God's *will*. As a Reformed theologian, Bavinck demonstrated a sustained interest in this theme, as he speaks not only of God's "secret being") but also of his "secret will," "secret counsel," and "secret plan."[155]

The theme of the hiddenness of God's will has most often been raised in the context of the doctrine of predestination. The importance of this theme often springs from the personal need for assurance of salvation rather than only from theoretical considerations. Accordingly, the point of departure in discussing the hiddenness of election and the problems arising from it has been a pastoral concern. Reformed theologians have typically claimed that we may not attempt to delve into the hiddenness of God's will apart from Jesus Christ. Calvin, following in the footsteps of Augustine, famously refers to Christ as the mirror of election.[156]

However, since this study does not focus on the doctrine of predestination per se, I will mostly restrict my attention to the implications of the hiddenness of God's will *for the doctrine of God*. Bavinck accepted and defended the distinction between God's hidden and revealed will, which had a long history in Western theology and was treated by Reformed theologians in minute detail.[157] God's hidden will (Bavinck called it also "the will of God's

---

155. *RD* 2:133, 242, 245, 344, 365; 4:228. Bavinck distinguishes between "God's counsel" and "God's plan." The former is "one with his being, as his eternally active will" (*RD* 2:373) and includes (but is not exhausted by) the latter. The latter, "though closely connected with God's being, may not be equated with that being" and "relates to God's being in the same way world-consciousness is related to God's self-consciousness" (*RD* 2:373). In other words, God's counsel is independent of (the existence of) the world; God's plan is related to the world.

156. Calvin, *Institutes* III.24.5.

157. *RD* 2:242–45; see the works Bavinck lists in *RD* 2:242.

good pleasure," "God's secret will," and "the decretive will") is, maintains Bavinck, "the ultimate ground for both the existence of the world and its being what it is."[158] Bavinck agreed with Reformed theologians who, in contrast to Roman Catholics, Lutherans, and Arminians, proceeded not from the revealed will but from the hidden will of God and viewed this will as "the actual and essential will of God." Everything happens according to the hidden will of God: "That will is always carried out, always effects its purpose." God's hidden will is eternal, efficacious, immutable, and identical with God's being.[159]

In contrast to God's hidden will, his revealed will (Bavinck called it also "the expressed will," "the signified will," and "the preceptive will") is regarded as *voluntas Dei* only in a metaphorical sense.[160] According to Bavinck, it is not the actual will of God. It seems that Bavinck applies the term "will" to this concept only with great reluctance. The revealed will of God is not intended to disclose his very being. It does not tell us what God does or wills; rather, it tells what God wants *us* to do. Here it is worth quoting Bavinck at some length:

> The "expressed" or "signified" will ... is God's precept, concretely stated in law and gospel, the precept that serves as the rule for our conduct. ... God's revealed (preceptive) will is not really his (ultimate) will but only the command he issues as the rule for our conduct. In his preceptive will he does not say what he is planning to do; it is not the rule for his conduct; it does not prescribe what *God* must do, but tells us what *we* must do. It is the rule for *our* conduct (Deut 29:29).[161]

As indicated above, Bavinck expresses his dissatisfaction with Luther's "very sharp" distinction between *Deus absconditus* and *Deus revelatus*. Bavinck's own account of the hiddenness of God's will, however, was not without similar tensions. For example, he states that Scripture "by its teaching of the revealed will of God underscores how and in what sense

158. Bavinck, "Calvin and Common Grace," 449.

159. *RD* 2:243, 244, 247.

160. *RD* 2:244.

161. *RD* 2:243–44, emphasis original.

God does not will sin" and then goes on to claim that God's revealed will tells us only what God desires of us.[162] It remains unclear, however, how the revealed will may underscore that *God* does not will sin if, according to Bavinck, this will is related only to *our* conduct. If God's revealed will only shows that God does not want *us* to sin, then it reveals nothing about *God's own* attitude to sin.

Bavinck realizes that the main objection against his approach is that it questions the correspondence between God's hidden will and his revealed will: "Against this view it is objected that the revealed will bears that name because it reveals what he really wills and hence that it must be in harmony with his secret will." Bavinck's response to this objection is disappointingly brief and dubious: "And this ... is indeed the case: the revealed will is an indication of what God wills that we will do."[163] The phrase "this is indeed the case" creates the impression that Bavinck agrees with the legitimacy of the objection. But he actually disagrees with it, because he simply repeats what he already claimed before: namely, that God's revealed will refers to our conduct and not to God's proper will and desires. Later he tries to show that the two wills do not oppose or contradict each other, but his argument does not show how God's revealed will is related to God's actual will. He only claims again that God's hidden will and his revealed will are related to two different things (God and our conduct respectively) and thus are not inconsistent.

Although the hidden will of God, according to Bavinck, results from God's good pleasure and thus is in a sense revelatory of it, Bavinck preferred to emphasize the mysteriousness of this will rather than its role in revelation. Bavinck argued that though we may observe what is happening around us, we cannot begin to presume why it is happening. That is, even though we see what is happening in the world around us and can thus surmise *what* God wills in his inner being, we can never understand *why* this or that is happening. As Bavinck puts it, everything happens according to the hidden will of God's good pleasure, but "the reason why God willed one thing and not another, chose some and rejected others, may be

162. *RD* 2:244.

163. *RD* 2:244.

totally unknown to us."[164] In the end, God's hidden will is inexplicable to us. Speaking about sin or reprobation, Bavinck is cautious and reserved, often citing "unknown reasons" or qualifying his statements with phrases such as "in a certain sense."[165]

When dealing specifically with the distinction between God's hidden and revealed will, Bavinck does not demonstrate how the latter reveals God's being. However, in other parts of his *Reformed Dogmatics* he tries to show that it is not altogether detached from God's character. First, he describes God's law (which is also God's revealed will) as "an expression of God's being."[166] In this way, he emphasizes that the law corresponds to God's own desires and is grounded in his nature. God's law does not consist of arbitrary precepts that have nothing to do with God's own pleasure. Rather, the law subtly discloses God's actual will. God does not prescribe that which he detests, and his own desires are inseparably linked with his character and very being. Second, as we saw in respect to God's being, Bavinck sought to establish a link between God's hidden being and his revelation. Based on this analogy between God in himself and God in his revelation, one would expect a similar analogy between God's hidden and revealed will, but instead Bavinck explains God's revealed will as unrelated to God's own being, character, and pleasure.[167]

---

164. *RD* 2:396.

165. Some typical passages read: "For good and wise reasons, though *these reasons are unknown to us*, God has *in a certain sense* willed sin" (*RD* 2:244, emphasis added); "The fall, sin, and eternal punishment are included in the divine decree and *in a sense* willed by God, but then always only *in a certain sense*" (*RD* 2:389, emphasis added); "The entrance of sin into the world was ... *in a sense* willed and determined by him" (*RD* 2:391, emphasis added); "*In a sense* it can be said that God willed sin, that is, he willed that there would be sin" (*RD* 3:62, emphasis added). Thus, God's willing sin is always nuanced and coupled with his "not-willing" sin. Berkouwer rightly observes that "Bavinck stumbles for words to articulate this inexpressible idea. ... Inevitably, 'in a certain sense' can only lead to the question: *In what sense?*" See Gerrit C. Berkouwer, *Sin*, trans. Philip C. Holtrop (Grand Rapids: Eerdmans, 1971), 53.

166. *RD* 4:455.

167. See the helpful analyses of Bavinck's views in Gerrit C. Berkouwer, *Divine Election*, trans. Hugo Bekker (Grand Rapids: Eerdmans, 1960), 115–18, Berkouwer, *Sin*, 56–58.

GOD REVEALED

The Necessity, Content, and Possibility of God's Revelation

The Necessity of God's Revelation

As indicated frequently above, Bavinck recognized only one source of our knowledge of God, namely, God himself. For our knowledge of God, we are wholly dependent on his revelation: "We come to the knowledge of God only by contemplating God's revelation in nature and Scripture."[168] The need for revelation springs from the human inability to penetrate divine realities from "below." This means that divine revelation has *always* been necessary. Bavinck has been criticized for the apparent contradiction between his definition of revelation and his idea that revelation is rooted in creation.[169] Bavinck offers the definition in question in the first edition of his *Reformed Dogmatics*: "Revelation is all that God does in order to recreate humanity according to his image and likeness."[170] As it stands, the definition seems to restrict revelation to soteriological goals and thereby questions or even explicitly denies the existence and necessity of revelation in the pre-fall world. In the second edition, however, Bavinck revised this section for clarity and removed this definition. Elsewhere he links the idea of re-creating humanity with God's *special* revelation: "Special revelation must strive to the end of re-creating the whole person after God's image and likeness." Bavinck's point is that revelation as such has *always* been necessary and present (including before the fall), while *special* revelation became necessary only after the fall.[171]

Bavinck's key formula expresses well the need for revelation: "God can be known only by God."[172] This well-known maxim, with its roots in Greek

---

168. *RD* 2:69; see also 2:124.

169. See Bremmer's account of the critique of J. Riemens Jr. in *Herman Bavinck als Dogmaticus*, 103.

170. *GD*[1] 1:219.

171. *RD* 1:342, 346. This does not mean, however, that Bavinck was always precise on this matter. For example, he defines general revelation as "that conscious and free act of God by which ... he makes himself known ... to *fallen* human beings" (*RD* 1:350, emphasis added).

172. This is another example of a similarity between Bavinck and Barth. Bavinck mentions this formula several times in his *Reformed Dogmatics* (1:287, 506, 587), while Barth reproduces

philosophical thought, has Platonic overtones: like can only be known by like. Bavinck used this maxim to show the need for objective (external) and, especially, subjective (internal) revelation. Without objective revelation, God cannot be known. Without subjective revelation, God's objective revelation cannot be received or understood. We know God because of his Spirit in us: "By that Spirit we receive a fitting organ for the reception of external revelation. God can be known only by God; the light can be seen only in his light."[173] In Bavinck's terms, "subjective revelation" refers to God's activity within us rather than to our own activity.

Bavinck states that God's existence, knowability, and revelation are presupposed in religion and theology.[174] The existence of God without the ability to know him would amount to practical atheism.[175] When Bavinck speaks of God's knowability, he means the possibility of a true and reliable knowledge of God. Thus, along with God's existence and revelation, one also has to assume a correspondence between them. Religion and theology are meaningful only if God's revelation really corresponds to his inner self.[176] Bavinck admits that such correspondence cannot be a conclusion of an elaborate argument grounded in objective or neutral principles. We cannot prove the correspondence by logic or establish it by evidence, but, having assumed it, we can show the reliability and viability of this idea.

Despite his focus on epistemology, Bavinck recognized that revelation is needed not only to know God, but also to serve and to love him. Even according to his definition from the first edition of the *Reformed Dogmatics*, revelation is not only about making *God* known, but rather comprises "all that God does" for human beings. Without revelation, God would not be loved by humans, for "what we cannot know at all we cannot love and serve."[177] Although Bavinck emphasizes the intelligibility of revelation,

---

it in his *Church Dogmatics* (II/1:179, 182, 204, 232). For both theologians this statement implies that God himself is the only possible origin of any knowledge of himself.

173. *RD* 1:279, 348, 506.

174. *RD* 1:33, 37–38, 285, 505.

175. Bavinck, *Philosophy of Revelation*, 160.

176. Only *that* religion can be true which "makes God known to us as he really is" (*RD* 1:241).

177. Bavinck, *Philosophy of Revelation*, 160. Compare the following statements: "To be unknown is to be unloved" (*RD* 1:268); "It is God's will that we should love him also with the mind and think of him in a manner worthy of him. To that end he gave his revelation" (*RD* 1:79); "God is known in proportion to the extent that He is loved" (Bavinck, *Our Reasonable Faith*, 30).

he does not treat knowledge as either the primary or the ultimate goal of revelation. Bavinck attempted to offer a broader perspective: the goal of revelation is not simply to teach or illuminate, but to evoke a love that is rooted in this knowledge. Revelation should bring human beings into communion with God and should redeem them and the entire world in its organic interconnectedness. Ultimately, God reveals himself in order to delight in the glorification of his own attributes.[178]

The Content of God's Revelation

In his historical overview of the idea of revelation, Bavinck observes that the scholastics and the Reformers paid little attention to this matter. Since nobody disputed the necessity and possibility of revelation, they were taken for granted. The situation changed in subsequent centuries, and in Bavinck's day the concept of revelation was vigorously discussed. Bavinck was convinced that, although many theologians use the old term "revelation," they interpret it differently, and as a result some blur its meaning. Against this, Bavinck contends that the term has a specific meaning. His epistemological concerns come to the fore when he defines revelation as "the communication or announcement of something that is still unknown." He clarifies that in religion, revelation "includes three elements: (1) The existence of a personal divine being who originates the announcement; (2) a truth, fact, or event that up until the time of its announcement was not yet known; (3) a human being to whom the announcement was made."[179] Bavinck notes that the revealed truth (the second element) is God himself: "Revelation is an act of God by which he *communicates himself* and makes *himself* known to human beings."[180] God is the author as well as the content of revelation.[181] In Bavinck's theology, "God is always the subject, the one

---

178. *RD* 1:346, 349.

179. *RD* 1:287–88, 295. This corresponds to (although it does not coincide with) Bavinck's three fundamental principles of theology: God as the essential foundation (*principium essendi*), Scripture as the external cognitive foundation (*principium cognoscendi externum*), and faith and the illumination of the Holy Spirit as the internal principle of knowing (*principium cognoscendi internum*; *RD* 1:207).

180. *RD* 1:296; emphasis added. Similar definitions can be found in other places: revelation is "that deliberate and free act of God by which he makes himself known to human beings in order that by it they may come to stand in the right relation to him" (*RD* 1:349). Revelation is "a conscious, voluntary, intentional disclosure of God to human beings" (*RD* 1:286).

181. *RD* 1:341–43.

revealing himself, and the object, the one whom the revelation reveals."[182] Bavinck's concept of revelation is markedly theocentric.

According to Bavinck, "all divine revelation is, in the nature of the case, self-revelation."[183] Emphasis on God's self in his revelation was typical also for the theologians of the Hegelian school. The modern understanding of "self-revelation" implied that it is not religious truths (doctrines or propositions) that are being communicated but rather God himself. Bavinck sought to confirm the idea that God is the content of revelation without underestimating the intellectual aspect of revelation and without completely identifying God with his revelation. Revelation discloses God himself, which is not to deny that it discloses certain facts about God. According to Bavinck, revelation consists both of a personal engagement with God and a communication of some sort of information. Although God in his revelation communicates *himself*, God and his revelation do not exhaustively coincide. The idea that God is not *fully* present in revelation, despite being its object, is confirmed by the fact that God is not *equally* present in his various revelatory deeds and words. For Bavinck, there is always a gradation of God's presence.

As mentioned previously, Bavinck resisted modern attempts to undermine the objectivity of revelation and subordinate its content and reality to the subjective experience of its human recipients. According to Bavinck, certain events, words, facts, or things are not simply interpreted by believers as though they reveal God, but in fact they objectively disclose him to humans. "God very definitely, consciously, and intentionally reveals himself in nature and history, in the heart and conscience of human beings." Bavinck affirmed the subjective element of revelation, which consists in its reception by humans, but insisted that this illumination only completes and responds to objective revelation.[184]

The Possibility of God's Revelation: The Communicability of God

As a theologian who sought to face the challenges posed by modernity, Bavinck could not avoid tackling the question about the very possibility

182. Duby, "Working with the Grain," 76.

183. *RD* 1:341.

184. *RD* 1:92, 340, 350.

of God's revelation. He points out that in modern philosophical circles the issue provoked "immense confusion," primarily because of ambiguity surrounding the concept of revelation.[185] The variety of modern positions compelled Bavinck to resist them on multiple fronts. He first mentions materialism, but since this system of thought empties revelation of all its traditional meaning, Bavinck does not pay much attention to it. The other two challengers—pantheism and deism—were more important for him.[186] Already at an early stage of his career, he described them as the two most common unsatisfactory answers to the question about how God relates to the world.[187] Pantheism presents revelation as an unconscious process. Although pantheism acknowledges "that the content of being does not coincide with its appearance and that there is a 'something' that lies behind the phenomena and is manifest to us in these phenomena," still, "pantheism does not know what that 'something' is that lies behind the phenomena." Even if pantheism admits that the being who is the object of revelation is greater than its revelation, pantheism does not know that being by name and therefore uses numerous different words ("nature," "substance," "reason," and others), which "can mean everything and nothing."[188] In the final analysis, pantheism offers a revelation that does not reveal anything.

Deism, in contrast, allows for the existence of a personal God and for natural revelation but disputes the possibility of supernatural revelation. Against this, Bavinck argues that if we accept the possibility of revelation in principle, we cannot limit God with regard to the forms and means of his revelation. In Bavinck's thinking, the very possibility of revelation and its truthfulness go hand in hand. Kant, as well as modern theologians since, did not necessarily deny the idea and possibility of revelation, but they did

185. *RD* 1:295.

186. Henry Jansen suggests that Bavinck's "polemic against pantheism appears to be stronger" than that against deism. See Jansen, "Relationality and the Concept of God" (PhD diss., Free University, 1995), 56. Bavinck did wrote more against pantheism than against deism, but not because he regarded pantheist ideas as more dangerous and destructive for the Christian faith than deist notions. Rather, for Bavinck pantheism seemed to be a more serious and relevant opponent. Although the following quotation of Bavinck has a very specific application, it well describes his attitude in general: "Deism is untenable; the only choice is between theism and pantheism" (*RD* 1:297). See also Huttinga, *Participation and Communicability*, 182.

187. Bavinck, "Hedendaagsche wereldbeschouwing," 455.

188. *RD* 1:296.

deny its objective truthfulness. On their view, the claims of revelation can be helpful for our morality and self-understanding, but one cannot maintain their objective validity and correspondence to God's inner self. For Bavinck, however, denying the possibility of objectively true revelation was a denial of the possibility of revelation as such. Revelation consists "in the communication of truth." Saying that revelation is possible is meaningless unless one also affirms the possibility of attaining true knowledge of God on the basis of that revelation.[189]

But how is revelation possible? Given the ontological difference between God and creation, how can God truly reveal himself to humanity? As usual, Bavinck gives the mysteriousness of the doctrine its full due. Belief in the possibility of God's revelation is "a recognition of an incomprehensible mystery." Indeed, "it is completely incomprehensible to us how God can reveal himself and to some extent make himself known in created beings. ... This mystery cannot be comprehended; it can only be gratefully acknowledged."[190] Bavinck was not satisfied, however, with paradoxical expressions and a mere recognition of mystery. Nor was trivial appeal to God's omnipotence (claiming that if God wants to be known, then he will really be known) a satisfactory answer for him. Bavinck sought to present a more reliable ground for the possibility of revelation. He believed that although the "mechanism" of revelation cannot be fathomed, it is still intelligible in some very real sense and measure.

Bavinck sought the ground for the possibility of revelation in the communicability of God.[191] This concept was one of Bavinck's principal weapons in his polemics against deism and pantheism, because it enabled him to show that God is immanently and consciously present in all creatures (against deism), but not commingled with them (against pantheism). In different formulations and contexts Bavinck repeats one and the same

---

189. *RD* 1:288, 297, 345, 559.

190. *RD* 2:49.

191. Barend Kamphuis calls the concept of God's communicability "the original contribution of Bavinck" and argues that it has not been sufficiently fleshed out in Reformed theology. See Kamphuis, "Chalcedon in Kampen," *Theologia Reformata* 48 (2005): 31. For the significance of the concept in Bavinck's theology, see also Kamphuis, "Alles in alles: Rehabilitatie van het panentheïsme?," *Theologia Reformata* 48 (2005): 194–206.

thought: God communicates (gives, imparts, conveys, grants, joins) himself to creatures.[192]

According to Bavinck, the communication of God begins within the Trinity itself. The Father's essence is communicated to the Son in generation and to the Spirit in procession (spiration). This communicability shows that God is an infinite source of blessed life. The description of God as "a plenitude of life, an ocean of being," reveals the fundamental difference between God as Bavinck understands him and the lifeless God of deism. The communication of God is not limited to the intra-Trinitarian relations. In addition to speaking of God's internal communicability (in the generation of the Son and the procession of the Spirit), Bavinck refers to God's external communicability (in the world). Contrary to Gnosticism, which knows only emanation (internal communication) and no creation (external communication), and contrary to Arianism, which knows only creation and no emanation, Christianity, according to Bavinck, knows divine emanation and the creation of the world *ex nihilo*—both internal and external communication of God. Gnostics and Arians posited a dualism between God and the world, while in Christianity the world is distinct, but not separated from, or set "over against."[193]

---

192. In addition to the aforementioned passages, the following statements are typical for Bavinck: God "imparts himself to us" (*RD* 1:345); "In the Holy Spirit he communicates himself to us" (*RD* 2:334); "Without losing himself, God can give himself" (*RD* 2:159); God's love "not only conveys certain benefits but God himself" (*RD* 2:215); God "gave himself to Israel and dwells among its people" (*RD* 2:220); "God not only elects and calls, but gives himself to his people; he joins himself to them" (*Philosophy of Revelation*, 197).

193. *RD* 2:151, 232, 240, 285, 2:308, 331, 420. Bavinck's emphasis on the fundamental difference between Creator and creation compels James Eglinton to suggest, "Ontologically, Bavinck posits a rigid separation between God and the cosmos." See Eglinton, "Bavinck's Organic Motif: Questions Seeking Answers," *CTJ* 45 (2010): 65. In his book *Trinity and Organism* (Edinburgh: T&T Clark, 2012), 70, Eglinton uses the word "separateness" instead of "separation" in the same context. Indeed, some of Bavinck's phrases would seem to lead to such a conclusion. In particular, Eglinton refers to two passages. The first passage reads: "The distance between God and us is the gulf between the Infinite and the finite, between eternity and time, between being and becoming, between the All and the nothing" (*RD* 2:30). It must be noted, however, that the original text does not contain the word "gulf" (which seems to be stronger than the term "distance"): "Er is tusschen Hem en ons een afstand als tusschen het oneindige en het eindige, tusschen eeuwigheid en tijd, tusschen het zijn en het worden, tusschen het al en het niet" (*GD*[4] 2:2). In the second passage, Bavinck writes that "a deep chasm separates God's being from that of all creatures" (*RD* 2:158–59). In the original text, however, the word "separates" is missing: "Er is een diepe klove tusschen het zijn Gods en het zijn van alle creatuur" (*GD*[4] 2:128–29). Here Bavinck rejects the existence of any intermediary between God and humanity, but immediately he adds that God dwells immanently in all created beings.

According to Bavinck, the doctrine of the Trinity is crucial with regard to the possibility of revelation, because it "tells us that God can reveal himself in an absolute sense to the Son and the Spirit, and hence, in a relative sense also to the world." If God were not triune, neither revelation nor creation would be possible.[194] Therefore, one who denies God's internal communication also denies his external communication and, consequently, the very possibility of communication and revelation to the world. If God is incommunicable, then the world is "separate from, outside of, and opposed to God." In that case "God is absolutely hidden, 'cosmic depths,' 'absolute silence,' 'the unconscious,' 'the groundless.' The world does not reveal him;

A similar terminological issue can be found in the *Magnalia Dei*. The English translation reads: "The separation between God and man is not a gradual difference but a deep gulf" (*Our Reasonable Faith*, 323), but the original text does not contain a Dutch counterpart to the word "separation": "Want tusschen mensch en God is geen geleidelijke overgang, maar een diepe klove." See Herman Bavinck, *Magnalia Dei: Onderwijzing in de christelijke religie naar gereformeerde belijdenis* (Kampen: Kok, 1909), 359. It is also remarkable that elsewhere Bavinck links the idea of a gulf between God and creatures with Plotinus and Gnosticism (*RD* 2:35; 3:253) and especially with deism, which "creates a vast gulf between God and his creatures" and "separates God and the world" (*RD* 2:331, 600, see also 603; 3:576).

To be sure, at least once Bavinck uses the word "separation" concerning the relationship between God and the world: in rejecting Philo's doctrine of intermediate beings, he speaks of the "the boundary that in the Old Testament always separates [*scheidt*] the creature from the Creator" (*RD* 2:267). This passage affirms the legitimacy of Eglinton's conclusion. Nevertheless, in general Bavinck preferred to speak of "a sharp *distinction* between the Creator and the creature" (*RD* 2:422, emphasis added) rather than "a separation" between them, because the latter term, according to Bavinck, may have negative (deistic) connotations. In resisting a deist picture of God, Bavinck maintains: "Though God is essentially distinct from his creatures, he is not separate from them" (*RD* 2:168). "God and humanity, though never separate, are nevertheless always distinct" (*RD* 3:62). As Bavinck says in one of his early articles, the Reformed church does not believe in "a separation between God and world" ("De hedendaagsche wereldbeschouwing," 455). A similar statement can be found in the *Magnalia Dei*: "The church confesses both: God is above the world, distinguished from it in essence, and yet He is with His whole being present in it and at no point in space or time separated from it" (Bavinck, *Our Reasonable Faith*, 159). Not our creatureliness, but our sin alone, separates us from him (*RD* 2:169–70; 3:172, 198).

194. *RD* 2:333, 420. It is a somewhat questionable statement, especially in view of the fact that several lines before, Bavinck himself mentions Arianism, which knows only creation without emanation (that is, external communication without internal communication). Bavinck's argument seems to assume that if God is "communicable" he must "fulfill" this communicability internally. God is either communicable internally or not communicable at all. In Christian theology, such ideas have sometimes been supported by God's freedom and love: God must be triune (love in himself) prior to creation because otherwise he *needs* to create in order to have an object of his love. Although Bavinck also emphasized God's aseity, he did not use it as an argument for the necessity of internal communication prior to external communication. (See also *RD* 2:331, where Bavinck expresses his skeptical attitude regarding the derivation of the Trinity from love.)

there is no possibility of knowing him."[195] In sum, God's internal communication demonstrates and secures the possibility of the creation of the world, and of revelation to and within it.

Bavinck emphasizes that, although the external communication of God toward his creatures is grounded in his internal communication, it substantially differs from it. In the case of the internal communication, the Father communicates his very essence: the fullness of his being. The generation of the Son occurs in the divine being itself and implies essential communication. The same holds true for the spiration of the Spirit, which "has to be conceived as the eternal communication of the same essence." External communication, however, is a communication to creatures of only "a weak and pale image of God."[196] In Bavinck's frequently used terms, the internal communication is absolute, whereas the external communication is only relative.

Bavinck speaks of God's external communication as related not only to the act of creation, but also to preserving, maintaining, and saving the world. "The communicability of God is not a static given"[197] but a dynamic and progressive process. It is not a "once-for-all" event that took place in the act of creation alone. Bavinck postulates that "preservation is even greater than creation," because the former involves "the progressive and ever increasing self-communication of God to his creatures." The act of creation is the first revelation of God, but it is supplemented by God's constant activity in the world.[198] All that happens and exists reveals God in some way.

In external as well as internal communication, God, having communicated himself to others, fully remains himself. Revelation does not alter God's being in any sense: it neither enriches nor impoverishes it. According to Bavinck, God's immutability is a necessary implication of his aseity: "If God were not immutable, he would not be God."[199] Both ideas, immutability and communicability, were simply beyond questioning for Bavinck.

195. *RD* 2:332–33. Here Bavinck deliberately uses gnostic terms that were popular in his day. See Mattson, *Restored to Our Destiny*, 29.

196. *RD* 2:313, 420.

197. Kamphuis, "Alles in alles," 205.

198. *RD* 1:307; 2:608.

199. *RD* 2:154.

Although Bavinck used the term "communicability" with more confidence than the term "participation," the two terms belong together. As Huttinga observed, Bavinck's account of the relation between God and the world was "full of participatory language and conceptuality."[200] In Bavinck's theology, the ideas of communicability and participation seem to indicate two sides of one and the same reality. For example, in terms of internal, absolute communication, Bavinck argues that "from all eternity God *communicated* himself in all his fullness" to the Son, while the Son "from all eternity ... *participated* in his [Father's] divine nature." Bavinck uses the same terminology regarding external, relative communication: in the Spirit, Christ *communicates* the divine nature to us, and we become "*partakers* of his divine nature." To say that God *communicates* himself in and to his creatures is for Bavinck the same as saying that "every creature ... *participates* in God's being."[201] Thus, God's communicability enables humans to resemble him in a relative sense.[202] The possibility of God's revelation, according to Bavinck, demands a degree of similarity between God and his creatures. If humans were totally different from God ontologically, he would not be able to reveal himself to them. The analogy of knowledge must be rooted in the analogy of being: humans can participate in God's self-knowledge only if they participate in God's being.

The Character of God's Revelation

The next step is to study Bavinck's elaboration of the *character* of revelation. For the sake of structural clarity, I wish to delineate eight important characteristics; in Bavinck's theology, God's revelation is understood as voluntary, accommodative, creaturely, mediated, analogical, limited, intelligible, and trustworthy. This selection, of course, is not incontestable. For example, one could legitimately argue that Bavinck paid ample attention

200. Huttinga, *Participation and Communicability*, 191.

201. *RD* 1:350, emphasis added; 2:274, emphasis added; 2:309, 312; 332, 420; see also 3:225, 304. It must be noted that in the cited passages from Bavinck's *Reformed Dogmatics*, the meaning of participation in the divine *nature* ("natuur") differs from the meaning of participation in God's *being* ("zijn"). The former is based on 2 Pet 1:4 and has a soteriological flavor, while the latter secures the ontological dependency of creatures on God. In general, however, Bavinck did not differentiate between "zijn," "wezen," and "natuur." Further, it can be argued, as Huttinga does (*Participation and Communicability*, 207–12), that Bavinck did not clearly demarcate the soteriological and ontological contexts of communicability/participation.

202. *RD* 2:561.

to the soteriological nature of revelation after the fall and to Jesus Christ as the core and culmination of revelation. Nevertheless, I am not including such characteristics as soteriological and christological, as I wanted to choose only those elements that apply to both general and special revelation and to both prelapsarian and postlapsarian conditions. This focus on universal characteristics stems primarily from the need to examine the relation between God's hiddenness and revelation in broad terms, without restricting the analysis to a certain epoch in biblical history. Bavinck typically considers this relation apart from hamartiological considerations; in explaining why revelation does not convey the totality of God's incomprehensible being, he appeals to the finiteness and creatureliness of people, rather than to their sinfulness.

God's Revelation as Voluntary

Contrary to pantheist tendencies of his time, Bavinck contends that the very idea of revelation implies a conscious and voluntary act.[203] The word "revelation" is not applicable to animals or plants, whose being can be known through an unconscious and involuntary manifestation. Such manifestation does not deserve to be called revelation, Bavinck insists. Revelation is always an intentional self-disclosure. God *chooses* to reveal himself; hence, revelation is always the product of God's will: "It is his good pleasure (εὐδοκια) to be known by human beings."[204] The belief in *creatio ex nihilo* precludes any hint of unconscious and necessary emanation.

Modern theology widely assumed that the revelation of God reaches humanity only if God discloses himself *in* humanity and not simply *to* humanity.[205] This notion led thinkers to identify God's revelation with

---

203. Even in speaking about *internal* communication, Bavinck emphasizes that it is not unconscious and does not occur apart from the *will* of the Father. To be sure, Bavinck readily affirmed the Nicene formulation according to which the Son is generated out of the essence of the Father, and he clearly did not want to break with the well-established tradition that distinguished between generation and creation as the acts of God's nature and will, respectively (*RD* 2:309). As mentioned above, Bavinck even describes God's internal communication as "emanation" (*RD* 2:420). Nevertheless, he explicitly clarifies that this emanation is not unconscious or unwilled (*RD* 2:310).

204. *RD* 1:212–13, 286, 296–97.

205. Wolfhart Pannenberg, *Systematic Theology*, trans. Geoffrey Bromiley (Grand Rapids: Eerdmans, 1991), 1:222–23; Quentin Lauer, *Hegel's Concept of God* (Albany, NY: State University of New York, 1982), 43–46.

nature or human consciousness and eventually led towards pantheistic conclusions. Bavinck, therefore, was eager to emphasize the personal character of God's revelation. Revelation implies a certain relation between the revealer and the recipients of revelation. The revealer is not simply a being, principle, or substance, but a personal God, who thinks, speaks, and acts. While affirming God's presence in all things, Bavinck always made very clear that this presence is a *conscious* presence.[206]

God's Revelation as Accommodative

Due to the finiteness of human beings and the inability of the finite to contain the infinite, God must accommodate his revelation to the capacities of the human heart and mind. Bavinck wholeheartedly accepted this traditional axiom. Consequently, God's revelation is necessarily finite, accommodative, and anthropomorphic. According to Bavinck, God cannot reveal himself as he is in his inner being, because his light is so dazzling that we would perceive nothing. We simply would not understand him if he spoke to us on his own divine level—the only level that reveals him exhaustively.[207] Even in the prelapsarian state, although sin had not yet darkened the human mind, the creatureliness of humans made it impossible for them to receive and understand God's revelation in its absolute divine form.

God's accommodation implies "an act of divine condescension (συγκαταβασις)." In this sense, Bavinck even speaks of divine grace as manifested not merely in reaction to sin, but already in the revelation of God irrespective of the fall: "Revelation ... is always an act of grace; in it God condescends to meet his creature, a creature made in his image." Since humanity cannot understand God as he is in himself, God adjusts the portrait of himself to human powers of comprehension. "All revelation is ... a kind of humanization of God." He conforms himself to us and hence expresses himself in our language. For this reason, Bavinck explains, Scripture attributes to God human emotions, actions, occupations, relationships, qualities, and physical organs. The entire description of God in Scripture is necessarily expressed in human fashion—in human categories and forms, so that "even the most abstract names—such

206. *RD* 2:169.

207. *RD* 1:310; 2:100.

as existence, substance, the Absolute, the One, the Spirit, Reason—are and remain anthropomorphisms."[208] Thus, not only certain phrases or images are anthropomorphic, but all of Scripture is anthropomorphic.

Since the accommodative character of revelation is not caused by sin but is grounded in the ontological difference between Creator and creature, it is also applicable to God's revelation in the state of glory. Referring to the beatific vision, Bavinck explicitly confirms that even in this state God's knowledge remains accommodative.[209] On this point, Billings contrasts Bavinck's views with those of Calvin, who hints that the beatific vision implies nonaccommodative knowledge.[210]

But can God's being be truly represented by this accommodated revelation? Does not this condescension distort the character that it is supposed to convey? Bavinck's answer is twofold. First, this anthropomorphic revelation is all that we have and, indeed, all that we could ever have: "If anthropomorphic, creaturely names violate God's being, we cannot and may not call him by any name and have to be totally silent. ... As humans we have only two alternatives: either absolute silence or human thought and speech about God; either agnosticism (that is, theoretical atheism) or anthropomorphism."[211] Second, as we will see in more detail in the next section, God prepared the world for his self-revelation from its very beginning. God himself cared about the world's capacity truly to reflect his being and created it in such a way that it would reveal his glory.

God's Revelation as Creaturely

As was typical for the whole Western tradition, Bavinck argued that nothing stands between God's essence and the created realm, and he denied

---

208. *RD* 2:190, 310; 2:99–101, 182, 185. God's revelation is accommodated not only to human cognitive capacities in general, but also to the specific cultural context of the people to whom the revelation is directed. Bavinck appreciated the modern recognition of the affinity between the Bible and the religious representations and customs of other peoples: "Israel stands in connection with the Semites, the Bible with Babel" (*Philosophy of Revelation*, 22). This observation reinforced Bavinck's conviction that revelation always takes place in history rather than in isolation (see also Bremmer, *Herman Bavinck als Dogmaticus*, 320).

209. *RD* 2:190.

210. Billings, *Union with Christ*, 80–86.

211. *RD* 2:105. "There is no third way between anthropomorphism and agnosticism" (Bavinck, "Modernism," 103).

that the Bible contains any allusions to mediating entities.[212] Given that God cannot reveal himself in a purely divine and unaccommodated fashion, and given that there is no category or entity between the Godhead and creation, God's revelation must be creaturely. God's speaking to humanity in a creaturely way means that he speaks *in* and *through* creatures. As we have seen, Bavinck emphasizes that all God's names "are derived from the world of creatures."[213] Creaturely revelation is the only way open to God to reveal himself and simultaneously the only way for us to understand him, because we are creatures bound to the created world in our lives and understanding.

Bavinck repeatedly asserts that there is no creature that does not in some way manifest God's perfections.[214] Not only is all revelation creaturely, but, conversely, all creation is also revelatory. Although nothing is excluded from God's revelation, it does not follow that all things are *equally* revelatory. Bavinck points out that not all creatures reveal God and reflect his perfections with the same clarity. Among all the creatures, it is human beings who display God's attributes most clearly and gloriously. God's names, therefore, are derived primarily from the realm of humanity, which "constitutes the primary part of the nature from which God is known." Even within the human race there is diversity: believers reveal more about God than unbelievers. The restoration of God's image in believers implies their transformation into a mirror of God's perfections.[215]

Bavinck's unapologetic recognition of the creaturely character of God's revelation was undoubtedly related to his positive view of creation. To affirm the goodness of creation is to affirm not only that it is valuable to us, but also that it is valuable to God as the embodiment of his thought. God created the world through the Logos, and thus God's thoughts are imprinted on all of creation. Although revelation may be called supernatural, for Bavinck this did not mean that it occurs outside the natural realm.

---

212. Bavinck comments that "in the Old Testament 'the word' and 'wisdom' are not intermediaries between God and the world but stand wholly on the side of God" (*RD* 2:267).

213. *RD* 2:106.

214. "All things are also a revelation, a word, a work of God" (*RD* 1:370). "There is not an atom of the world that does not reflect his deity" (*RD* 2:109). "The entire universe is a revelation of God" (*RD* 2:135). "Every creature is a revelation of God" (*RD* 2:206). "The entire world is a revelation of God, a mirror of his attributes and perfections" (*RD* 2:530).

215. *RD* 1:346; 2:72, 103, 169.

Rather, "according to Scripture, all revelation, also that in nature, is supernatural." Bavinck noted the ambiguity of the terms "natural" and "supernatural" and preferred to avoid this distinction, not least because of its use in Roman Catholic supernaturalism, which Bavinck criticized. According to Bavinck, revelation is supernatural primarily because it discloses God, who transcends nature. Revelation is also supernatural because God may use extraordinary means such as theophany, prophecy, and miracle.[216] But these qualifications do not nullify Bavinck's fundamental belief that revelation bears a creaturely character.

As emphasized above, Bavinck could not but acknowledge "an incomprehensible mystery" in the fact that the infinite God reveals himself in finite creatures. Although we cannot explain this mystery, Bavinck insisted we should by no means call it "a palpable absurdity."[217] Creatures can manifest God because they are grounded in him and were designed for God's self-disclosure.

God's Revelation as Analogical

According to Bavinck, divine revelation in creatures is meaningful because of the analogy between them and God. Bavinck ventures to suggest a parallel: "Just as there is resemblance between various parts of the world, making comparison between them a possibility, so also there is kinship between God and his creatures, a kinship that warrants the use of creaturely language in speaking of him." To be sure, Bavinck realized that the difference between the Creator and his creatures is more substantial than between any two given creatures. But he also wanted to avoid radical extrapolations that emphasize the otherness of God, making him totally unperceivable. God's otherness notwithstanding, "there is in his creatures an analogy to what is present in God himself."[218] If this analogy did not exist, all God's names and attributes would be untrue and unintelligible, and theology would be impossible.

Just as all creatures are not equally revelatory, so they are also not equally analogous to God: "In all creatures but especially in humanity

216. *RD* 1:307, 310.

217. *RD* 2:49.

218. *RD* 2:106, 128.

there is something analogous to the divine being."[219] Whatever similarities to God other creatures may possess, only human beings were created in God's image and likeness. Since ontologically humans are analogous to God to a much greater degree than other creatures, epistemologically God can be known primarily on account of this analogy with human beings.

The analogical character of God's revelation implies that God's perfections are predicated of him neither equivocally nor univocally but analogously. According to Bavinck, the analogy between God and his creatures (and especially between God and humans) enables us to apply one and the same predicate to both God and humanity, even though the meaning of that predicate is not identical. Contrary to advocates of univocal predication, Bavinck suggests that divine and human understanding cannot coincide at any single point. He shared the reservations of his Reformed predecessors that human categories may be applied to God only to a certain extent. This means that we cannot see God as he is, but only analogically and in proportion to our creatureliness. According to Bavinck, "Since we cannot know God's being as such, all our knowledge of God ... bears an analogical character."[220] God's revelation presents only a faint analogy to what God really is in himself and of what God really knows about himself. As J. Eglinton summarizes Bavinck's approach, "All that God reveals shows what he is *like*, rather than what he *is*."[221]

God's Revelation as Mediated

Bavinck believed that all our knowledge is mediated in the sense that we do not have direct access to things, especially not to spiritual realities.[222] However, when asserting the mediated character of God's revelation, Bavinck points out something more profound: revelation is mediated not because of the distinction between *noumenon* and *phenomenon* but because of the distinction between Creator and creature. Bavinck emphasizes that "the distance between the Creator and creature is much too great for human

219. *RD* 2:135.

220. *RD* 2:70, 130.

221. Eglinton, *Trinity and Organism*, 106, emphasis original.

222. *RD* 2:109. Bavinck writes that "the inner being of things, the thing as such, escapes our perception," but he quickly adds that we still infer the essence of things from the phenomena, although this knowledge is finite and limited (*RD* 2:106).

beings to perceive God directly." We perceive God in faith, which involves an indirect knowledge, but we never encounter, experience, or see God immediately.[223] Our knowledge of God is mediated in the sense that it is not identical to God's self-knowledge, but it is communicated to us and involves concepts that are derived from the creaturely world. Revelation itself is mediated in the sense that God does not appear to us in the fullness of his glory, but always uses creaturely means.[224]

Some of Bavinck's quotations, however, may give the impression that he conceded that immediate revelation is possible in the state of glory. In discussing our present realities, Bavinck says that "*on earth* we cannot obtain a direct, immediate knowledge of God," thereby leaving the possibility of such knowledge *in heaven*. In the first volume of his *Reformed Dogmatics*, Bavinck comments that "in this dispensation all revelation is mediate," adding that "whether in the state of glory there will be a vision of God in respect of his being (*visio Dei per essentiam*) is something we can only examine later." This "later" apparently refers to the section about God's invisibility in the second volume, where Bavinck treats the beatific vision explicitly and more extensively. In that section, he raises the question of "whether an immediate, face-to-face vision of God is possible. Can God, as scholasticism said he could, be seen 'as he is in himself, in substance or

---

223. *RD* 1:309–10; Bavinck, *Certainty of Faith*, 71.

224. *RD* 2:130. There are some passages that, at the first glance, seem to contradict this conclusion. For example, Bavinck comments that "the ways and forms in which God reveals himself may vary. … God can reveal himself *directly* and *immediately* [*onmiddellijk*] and in the process use ordinary or extraordinary means" (*RD* 1:297, emphasis added). Here, however, the words "immediate" and "direct" do not mean the absence of means; rather, by these words Bavinck simply refers to God's direct speech to humanity (as in his revelation to prophets or apostles in person), in contrast to God's indirect speech to us through his Scripture (see *RD* 1:309).

For English-speaking readers it may also be confusing that in Bavinck's works the word "increated" is sometimes used with respect to humans. For example, Bavinck speaks about "their increated freedom" (*RD* 3:121), "increated 'seed of religion'" (*RD* 1:275; see also 2:59), "increated knowledge" (*RD* 1:303), "increated righteousness," and increated moral law of the first man (*RD* 2:558, 609). But such phrases simply mean that human freedom, religious sense, and moral law are innate: they are parts of the very nature of human beings (see *RD* 1:303, where "increated knowledge" is used interchangeably with "innate knowledge"). So, in Bavinck's words, Christian theology used such terms as "the 'innateness' and 'increatedness' of our knowledge of God" in order to show that "a knowledge of God never needs to be instilled in people by coercion or violence, nor by logical argumentation or compelling proofs, but belongs to humans by their very nature and arises spontaneously and automatically" (*RD* 2:73). In the original, Bavinck uses the Dutch word "ingeschapen" ("increated," "created into"), which should not be confused with "ongeschapen" ("that which exists without having been created").

essence' (*ut est in se per essentiam, in substantia ve essentia*)?"[225] From this it seems to follow that Bavinck identified "an immediate, face-to-face vision of God" with the vision of God "as he is in himself, in substance or essence." The question about the possibility of immediate revelation in the state of glory, therefore, can be answered if we can first answer the question about the possibility of seeing God in his very essence.

It is clear that Bavinck supported the distinction between seeing God with respect to his glory and seeing God with respect to his essence. He emphasizes that early theologians denied the possibility of the latter, but he also points out that later theologians, under the influence of Neoplatonism, concluded that it is possible to contemplate God's essence. In particular, Bavinck mentions Gregory the Great, who said that "God will be seen not only in his glory but also in his nature," and Bernard, who claimed that "the Trinity will also be seen in itself." Bavinck summarizes this Neoplatonic trend as follows: "God no longer comes down to humans; instead, by a supernatural gift, humans are lifted up to God and divinized." Later, he describes this view in similar terms: "The human creature, having received a supernatural gift, by his own merits raises himself to a higher level and becomes like God." These two sentences and the context in which they appear reveal that Bavinck is uneasy with the following ideas: (1) the concept of grace as a supernatural gift by which human beings are raised above their own nature; (2) the concept of divinization and an elevation of the soul, which obscures the difference between God and creatures; (3) the concept of merits; and (4) a movement "from below" rather than "from above" in divine-human relations.[226]

In view of these alarming ideas, which Bavinck took as implications of the *visio Dei per essentiam*, Bavinck aligned himself with the majority of Reformed theologians who, Bavinck claimed, either attempted to avoid such speculations or even openly rejected the vision of God in his essence. Bavinck clearly asserts that "comprehensive knowledge of God" and "vision as to essence" are synonymous. "Vision as to essence" implies a perfect knowledge, but such knowledge is unattainable for humans. That is why Bavinck is insistent that vision as to essence is unattainable. God

225. *RD* 1:310; 2:69, emphasis added; 2:187.

226. *RD* 2:188–89. See also Bavinck, *Christendom*, 31–32.

"is infinite, and human beings are finite and remain so also in the state of glory. Humans, therefore, can never have more than a finite human vision of God." In short, Bavinck's argument is the following: (1) the immediate vision of God is synonymous with the vision of God as to essence; (2) the vision as to essence implies perfect knowledge of God; (3) such knowledge is impossible due to the finitude of humanity; and, therefore, (4) neither the immediate vision of God nor the vision of God as to essence is possible, not even in the state of glory.[227]

To be sure, Bavinck realized that scholastic theologians did not teach the possibility of perfect knowledge of God in the state of glory. They were cautious to add that "the vision of God does not amount to comprehension," Bavinck admits. They taught *both* the incomprehensibility of God and a vision of God with respect to his essence. For Bavinck, however, this seemed to be a self-contradiction, because "noncomprehensive knowledge as to essence" was an oxymoron to him. This means that the difference between the scholastics and Bavinck on the issue of God's incomprehensibility is a matter of terminology rather than of substance. Bavinck rejected a vision of God as to essence not because it *necessarily* leads to the denial of God's incomprehensibility. He realized that a vision of God as to essence can be (and actually had been) interpreted in such a way that it does not contradict God's incomprehensibility (although Bavinck himself did not support such interpretation). The most important reason why Bavinck rejected the scholastic doctrine was his belief that "a corollary of vision of God in his essence would be the deification of humanity and the erasure

---

227. *RD* 2:190. Nevertheless, Bavinck acknowledges that the distinction between mediate and immediate revelation has had different meanings in different periods (*RD* 1:309). Bavinck himself seems to depart from his usual use of these terms when he writes on the last pages of his *Reformed Dogmatics* that in the state of blessedness the redeemed will know God "directly, immediately [*rechtstreeks, onmiddellijk*], unambiguously, and purely" (*RD* 4:722). It is not easy to reconcile this statement with the fact that Bavinck based the impossibility of the direct knowledge of God on the Creator-creature distinction (which will not be obliterated in the state of blessedness) or with his conviction that the immediate vision of God implies a perfect knowledge of God (which will also be unattainable in the age to come). It is possible that Bavinck does not use the word "immediate" here in a strict sense, but emphasizes the provisional character of the mediating role of Scripture and nature. On the same page, he writes that in the state of blessedness, the knowledge and fellowship with God will not be "mediated by either Scripture or nature" (*RD* 4:722). Bavinck does not explain, however, what forms of mediation apart from Scripture and nature may exist in the age to come.

of the boundary between the Creator and the creature."[228] According to Bavinck, in Roman Catholic doctrine, the vision of God *per essentiam* implied "deiformity or deification, a participation in the divine nature that was not only moral but corporeal, a 'melting union' with God," and "a mystical fusion of the soul with God." Bavinck's point is clear: humans remain human even in the state of glory. The beatific vision "will always be such that finite and limited human nature is capable of it."[229] The state of glory is not supernatural in the sense that the saints attain a vision of God in his essence by transcending their nature.

God's Revelation as Limited

From the preceding argument it is clear that, in Bavinck's view, the revelation of God is limited. "Though God to some extent becomes manifest in his creatures, there remains in him an infinite fullness of power and life that is not revealed," Bavinck notes.[230] Many questions remain unanswered, and many things remain hidden in God.

According to Bavinck, the limited character of revelation is caused primarily by the ontological difference between Creator and creature. God's accommodation to finite human capacities necessarily implies a limitation of God's revelation. Such limitation allows God meaningfully to reveal himself but also to preserve the creature's otherness.[231] Nevertheless, the finite capacity of human intelligence is not the only limitation of God's revelation. Another limitation is the will of God: "What we know of God we know only of his revelation and therefore only *as much as he is pleased to make known to us* concerning himself and *as much as* finite humans can absorb."[232] God is free to reveal or conceal himself. We cannot know whether he has revealed all that we could have understood.[233]

---

228. *RD* 2:188–90. Bremmer rightly notes that what Bavinck firmly rejected in his consideration of the *visio Dei per essentiam* was Neoplatonic mysticism (*Herman Bavinck als Dogmaticus*, 192, 216, 217).

229. *RD* 2:191, 540, 542.

230. *RD* 2:56.

231. Billings, *Union with Christ*, 77.

232. *RD* 2:51, emphasis added.

233. As mentioned in the context of God's incomprehensibility, Bavinck asserts that we do not understand perfectly even those things that have been already revealed at our creaturely level. Even accommodated analogical revelation is "already so rich and profound that it can

Bavinck employed many terms to express the idea of the limitation of God's revelation: "partial," "finite," "nonexhaustive," "imperfect," "inadequate," and others. As he used these terms more or less synonymously, they do not require separate consideration. It is helpful, however, to discern two aspects of this limitation: qualitative and quantitative. The first aspect indicates that we know God in a different *way* than he knows himself, while the second indicates that we know God to a different *degree*. There seems to be only one passage where Bavinck mentions this distinction explicitly: "[God's] absoluteness consists not only in quantity but also in quality."[234] Nevertheless, in other passages Bavinck presupposed the two aspects without mentioning them. For example, he states that "there is a vast difference, *not only in scope but also in character and depth*, between God's knowledge and that of rational creatures."[235] Here Bavinck uses the word "scope" for the quantitative aspect, and the words "character and depth" for the qualitative aspect.

Both aspects are important for Bavinck's understanding of the relation between God's hiddenness and revelation. The quantitative aspect means that God does not reveal his being in all its divine richness. Creatures can grasp his boundless knowledge and being only in part. The qualitative aspect means that even that which is revealed is not identical to God's self-knowledge. God is not only *more* wise, holy, and glorious than human beings: his wisdom, holiness, and glory are of a different *kind* or *quality*. Bavinck argues that God "is wise and good and holy and glorious—but not in the way his creatures are." Similarly, "His being is of a different and higher kind than that of the world."[236] Another passage in which Bavinck emphasizes the qualitative aspect reads: "There is a world of difference between infinite and endless, between omnipotent and the sum of all

---

never be fully known by any human being. In so many respects we do not even understand the world of created things and are at every moment confronted in all directions by enigmas and mysteries. How then should we be able to understand God's revelation in all its riches and depths?" (*RD* 2:56).

234. *RD* 1:214. Bavinck uses the same words when discussing the difference between eternity and time: "Between eternity and time there is a distinction not only in quantity and degree but also in quality and essence" (*RD* 2:162).

235. *RD* 2:196, emphasis added. Similarly, Bavinck asserts that "God can never be known by creatures as God knows himself, either as it concerns content and scope or as it concerns its mode" (*RD* 2:195).

236. *RD* 2:130; Bavinck, *Philosophy of Revelation*, 22.

power, between eternity and the sum of all moments of time, and so forth."[237] The implication of the qualitative aspect is that revelation does not diminish divine incomprehensibility. God is not more or less incomprehensible, in proportion to the amount of knowledge gained of him. However much humans know about their Lord, God always remains unfathomable for them in the qualitative sense.

God's Revelation as Intelligible

Bavinck was convinced that God reveals himself in order to become truly known and to enable humans to worship and serve him. As indicated above, it was important for Bavinck that God so designed the world that he gave humans the subjective capacity for perceiving him. With this capacity, humans cannot produce the knowledge of God from within themselves, but they are able to recognize and accept God's objective revelation. Bavinck notes that "in his self-revelation God certainly had to reckon with the human capacity for receiving truth."[238] The idea of correspondence, mentioned above among the leitmotifs of Bavinck's theology, plays a crucial role in the relation between objective revelation and humankind's subjective ability to understand it.

According to Bavinck, what God communicates does not have a mystical or nebulous character, but takes on the concrete form of thoughts and words. Bavinck warns against a skeptical attitude toward the idea of verbal revelation—an attitude that was typical for many theologians and philosophers of his time. They allowed some kinds of communication of life, being, or power, but they rejected the traditional idea of verbal revelation. According to Bavinck, however, he who denies that God can communicate thoughts and words also denies that he can communicate life. In making himself known, God adapts to the fact that "the bearer of the ideal goods of humankind is language, and the σαρξ of language is the written word."[239] God expresses his being in human language and uses people to record this revelation in Scripture.

237. *RD* 2:49.

238. *RD* 2:320.

239. *RD* 1:349, 380.

Bavinck's insistence on the importance of the cognitive aspect of revelation led him into polemics with ethical theologians, who charged him with intellectualizing and dogmatizing the truth.[240] Ethical theologians argued that Christian theology with its center in Jesus Christ bears an existential rather than scientific character. As Berkouwer notes, their favorite slogan was "not dead doctrine, but the living Lord."[241] It expressed their belief that Christian experience is more important than dogmatic concepts, and faith more related to our hearts and wills than to our intellects. According to ethical theologians, in revelation we encounter God *himself* rather than a set of truths or doctrines.[242]

Bavinck agreed with ethical theologians that God reveals *himself*, but he insisted that this personal, existential, vivifying dimension of revelation is fully compatible with its intellectual dimension. To be sure, revelation does not convey a set of dry propositions about God but the personal and vital knowledge of God himself. Bavinck was sensitive to the dangers of dead orthodoxy and emphasized the intimate relation between knowledge and life. This can be clearly seen in his article "Kennis en Leven" ("Knowledge and Life"): "On the one hand, knowledge is the way to life. ... But on the other hand, it is equally certain that life leads to knowledge." The person who knows God lives, and the one who does not know him is dead.[243] Nonetheless, Bavinck did not just warn against dead orthodoxy. As was typical for Bavinck, he strove to find a middle position between two extremes: in this case, between intellectualism, which equates revelation with Scripture,[244] and spiritualism, which detaches revelation from Scripture. According to the first extreme, revelation consists in the communication of doctrine, while according to the second, revelation consists *only* in the communication of life. Bavinck insisted that both of these extremes insufficiently recognize the unity of knowledge and life. Furthermore, contrary to the ethical theologians, Bavinck maintained that believing is an

240. Bremmer, *Herman Bavinck als Dogmaticus*, 79–91.

241. Berkouwer, *Half Century of Theology*, 11. Note, the phrase rhymes in Dutch: "niet de leer maar de levende Heer."

242. Bremmer, *Herman Bavinck als Dogmaticus*, 86.

243. Herman Bavinck, "Kennis en Leven," in *Kennis en Leven: Opstellen en artikelen uit vroegere Jaren* (Kampen: Kok, 1922), 215–16, 226.

244. Bavinck calls it "a false intellectualism" and "orthodox intellectualism" (*RD* 1:345, 382).

act of the intellect. It is true that the human will and emotions should not be detached from faith, but "faith always and everywhere includes knowledge (*notitia*) and, in accordance with this knowledge, arouses a certain kind and degree of trust."[245] According to Bavinck, believers not only trust and experience God, but also know him intellectually and are able to conceptualize him.

God's Revelation as Trustworthy

One of the most often recurring statements of Bavinck about God's revelation is that, although it is accommodative, creaturely, analogical, and mediated, it is still not impure or untrue. Bavinck's main ground for this conviction is an objective one: since the world was created to display God's perfections, his revelation through this world can be true. This "can be" becomes "is" on the basis of a more subjective argument, which is related to God's character: revelation not only can be, but actually is true because God is trustworthy. All that God reveals is pure truth.[246]

Bavinck distinguished between three concepts of truth: ontological (metaphysical), ethical, and logical. "God is truth in a metaphysical sense, for he is the unity of thought and being," Bavinck states. Further, God is truth in a logical sense, for "he knows all things as they really are." For the relation between God's hiddenness and revelation, it is the second (ethical) concept of truth that is most important. Bavinck uses this concept to show a correspondence between God in himself and his revelation: "In the case of God, there is complete correspondence between his being and his revelation (Num 23:19; 1 Sam 15:29; Titus 1:2; Heb 6:18). It is impossible for God to lie or deny himself." "God is truth in an ethical sense, for he reveals himself, speaks, acts, and appears as he truly is and thinks."[247] We can be sure that God's revelation corresponds to his very being because God did not intend to deceive us when he revealed himself. God's revelation is not a substitute for God in himself; rather, it is a true, creaturely reflection of God in himself.

245. *RD* 1:75, 345.

246. *RD* 2:106–7, 130, 208.

247. *RD* 2:209.

Trinity and God's Revelation

The Ontological and Economic Trinity

It has been argued, with good reason, that Bavinck's theology is "deeply Trinitarian."[248] Bavinck himself was forceful in expressing the theological significance of the Trinity: "It is the core of the Christian faith, the root of all its dogmas, the basic content of the new covenant." In "The Possibility of God's Revelation: The Communicability of God" (pages 87–93), we already saw that the doctrine of the Trinity is essential to Bavinck's doctrine of revelation (and indeed to its very possibility). It is God's internal communication (in the generation of the Son and the spiration of the Spirit) that makes his external communication (that is, his revelation and creation) possible. According to Bavinck, only a Trinitarian God can reveal himself and create.[249] In this section I will focus on how, in Bavinck's view, the revealed (economic) Trinity is related to the immanent (ontological) Trinity.

Here again Bavinck's concept of God's communicability plays a crucial role. As the "fountain of deity," the Father communicates himself from eternity to the Son and the Spirit. Although Bavinck suggests that the generation of the Son "is to be conceived in divine terms" and discusses biblical material that discloses the internal relationships within the Trinity, his main intention seems to be to establish a link between the internal relations in God and their external manifestations. With respect to the sending of the Holy Spirit, Bavinck argues that it is "most intimately bound up with the eternal procession in the divine being."[250] Likewise, the incarnation in time is a reflection of the internal relationship and is grounded in the eternal generation of the Son.[251] Unsurprisingly, Bavinck resorts to his usual

248. Keith E. Johnson, *Rethinking the Trinity and Religious Pluralism: An Augustinian Assessment* (Downers Grove, IL: IVP Academic, 2011), 26. See also Eglinton, *Trinity and Organism*.

249. *RD* 2:308–9, 333, 420; 3:277.

250. *RD* 2:273, 309, 320–21. Bavinck, however, did not use this as an argument for the *filioque* (which he affirmed).

251. Scholars have identified a tension in Bavinck's views on the necessity of the incarnation. For a list of sources, see Hans Burger, *Being in Christ: A Biblical and Systematic Investigation in a Reformed Perspective* (Eugene, OR: Wipf & Stock, 2009), 93. See also Chul Won Suh, *The Creation-Mediatorship of Jesus Christ: A Study in the Relation of the Incarnation and the Creation* (Amsterdam: Rodopi, 1982), 298. On the one hand, Bavinck was at pains to maintain the anti-speculative intent of Reformed theology, which, based on Scripture, traditionally connected the incarnation with sin: "People were ... wrong in thinking that the incarnation of the Son of God would also have taken place without sin" (*RD* 3:278). On the other hand, in attempting

analogical approach, in which the incarnation of the Son and the outpouring of the Spirit are conceived to be analogies of the eternal processions in God's being: "The incarnation of the Word has its eternal archetype in the generation of the Son, and the outpouring of the Holy Spirit is a weak analogy of the procession from the Father and the Son."[252] The incarnation of the Son and the outpouring of the Spirit reflect immanent relations between the three persons and are grounded in these relations.

Bavinck argues that "the 'ontological' Trinity is mirrored in the 'economic' Trinity." The term "mirror" seems to reflect Bavinck's conviction that the ontological Trinity should not be fully identified with the economic Trinity. In Bavinck's system, they are related as archetype and ectype, and these two are never identical. This is not to say that the Triune God reveals himself *differently* from how he actually is; rather, it means that the Triune God does not reveal himself in the *absolute manner* in which he exists from eternity. In defending the reliability of revelation, Bavinck says that in God's self-disclosure we see nothing but "the order present between the persons in the ontological Trinity."[253] Revelation, therefore, is always a reliable, albeit inexhaustive, means to know God.

Bavinck's understanding of the relation between the economic and immanent Trinity can be considered from two different perspectives. Epistemologically, Bavinck emphasized the primacy of the economic Trinity: we derive what God is in himself from what he reveals. Bavinck affirms the traditional approach, which derives the immanent relations of

---

to emphasize the central place of the incarnation in history, Bavinck considers it as God's ultimate *telos* for creation from the very beginning: "If, however, Christ is the incarnate Word, then the incarnation is the central fact of the entire history of the world; then, too, it must have been prepared from before the ages and have its effects throughout eternity" (*RD* 3:274). It is noteworthy that, having described arguments of other theologians in support of the incarnation independent of sin, Bavinck admits that they "contain ... much truth" (*RD* 3:279). The two approaches are in tension, because the former makes the incarnation contingent and dependent on sin, while the latter makes it an inevitable occurrence quite independently of sin. Bavinck seems to have found a resolution of this tension in the unity of God's decree: since all historical events (including the fall) were included in God's counsel from eternity, the incarnation is not arbitrary, even if it is a reaction to sin (*RD* 3:279).

252. *RD* 2:320.

253. *RD* 2:318.

the persons of the Trinity from their manifested relations.[254] Ontologically, however, primacy belongs to the immanent Trinity: God in himself is antecedent to what he reveals to us. Revelation does not constitute God's being; it constitutes only our understanding of his being. From God's perspective, his being comes first, followed by his revelation, while from our perspective, we first understand God's revelation and then project our understanding onto God's being. The epistemological priority of the economic Trinity affirms the importance of revelation, while the ontological priority of the immanent Trinity safeguards God's aseity and freedom.

The doctrine of the Trinity, according to Bavinck, is indispensable for us if we are to understand God's being and character: "Only by the Trinity do we begin to understand that God as he is in himself—hence also, apart from the world—is the independent, eternal, omniscient, and all-benevolent One, love, holiness, and glory." Using this statement, Bavinck wanted to emphasize that God does not need anyone or anything in order to live, to love, to be productive, and to be glorified. The Trinitarian relations form the perfect community and the perfect diversity within God, who is totally independent of the world. Further, Bavinck's statement affirms a close link between the inner existence of God and his external revelation. Because of his unfailing focus on God's revelation, Bavinck rarely references our understanding of God "as he is in himself … apart from the world." As we have seen in "God's Hiddenness in Revealedness" (pages 74–80), Bavinck even claims that the knowledge of God in himself "is completely unattainable."[255] As I argued in that section, Bavinck denies the possibility of the knowledge of God in himself, because he typically interprets such knowledge as perfect and rejected the very hunger for such knowledge as implying the neglect of the revelation that God has already given. Nevertheless, the aforementioned statement shows that Bavinck

254. *RD* 2:321. Bavinck demonstrates such a strong desire to link the internal and the external aspects of God (the intratrinitarian relations and his works *ad extra*) that sometimes his phrases are dubious. One such complicated passage reads: "There has been an eternal procession of the Son and the Spirit from the Father in order that, through and in them, he himself should come to his people and finally be 'all in all'" (*RD* 2:322). In the first part of the sentence Bavinck mentions the internal relations within the Trinity, while in the second part he describes the goal of the Father to come to his people and finally be all in all. The word *opdat* ("in order that") between the two parts seems to imply that what is described in the first part is true strictly for the sake of what is described in the second part.

255. *RD* 1:110–11; 2:331; see 2:47, 106, 310.

did not reject out of hand the idea of knowing God in himself—*as long as* human limitations are recognized and revelation is not disparaged. In manifesting himself as the Trinity, God not only discloses what he is for us, but also reveals something about what he is "apart from the world."

The Trinity and the Principles of Dogmatic Theology

In "Historical Overview" (pages 59–66) I already made a cursory note about Bavinck's criticism of the Trinitarian theology of the early church. In this chapter, his critical observations deserve a more detailed treatment. Several times in his *Reformed Dogmatics*, Bavinck points to a false antithesis in the works of such theologians as Justin Martyr, Theophilus, Irenaeus, and Tertullian. He refers here to the antithesis between the completely unknown Father and the Son who has revealed him. According to Bavinck, theologians who shared this view proceeded from the basic idea that "the Father is hidden, inexpressible, transcending time and space."[256] The Father was believed to be invisible, unknowable, ineffable, and unnameable. These theologians, however, had to explain how God could appear to the patriarchs and prophets. They concluded, in the words of Tertullian, that "He must be a different Being who was seen, because of one who was seen it could not be predicated that He is invisible. It will therefore follow, that by Him who is invisible we must understand the Father in the fullness of His majesty, while we recognise the Son as visible."[257] All God's revelations and appearances, therefore, were ascribed to his Son, the Logos. The distinction between the Father and the Son was treated as the distinction between the invisible and the visible, between the unknowable and the knowable. Bavinck contends that such views implied a "separation and contrast" between the Father and the Son and notes with relief that the separation was overcome later by Athanasius and the three Cappadocians, who were convinced that "the Son was truly God and hence equally as invisible as the Father." Bavinck makes clear that he appreciates this correction and stands firmly in the tradition of Augustine, who stated that "the Son, being himself true God, is no less hidden and invisible than the Father and

256. *RD* 2:36, 262, 280–83, 423.

257. Tertullian, *Against Praxeas* 14, in *Ante-Nicene Fathers*, vol. 3 (Grand Rapids, MI: Eerdmans, 1980), 610.

is perfectly equal to the Father."[258] Thus, there is no difference between the Father and the Son as to their hiddenness and invisibility.

However, in one aspect of his theology, Bavinck seems at first glance to come close to the theological views he opposed. This aspect is related to Bavinck's formulation of three fundamental theological principles (the *principium essendi*, the *principium cognoscendi externum*, and the *principium cognoscendi internum*), which, as indicated under "Christian Realism" (pages 51–55), formed one of the key features of his epistemology. In seeking to express them in a Trinitarian way, he states that the three principles "are rooted in the Trinitarian being of God. It is the Father who, through the Son as Logos, imparts himself to his creatures in the Spirit."[259] It appears that Bavinck argues here not only that all three persons of the Trinity are involved in the communication of the knowledge of God to human beings, but also that the three persons each have unique roles in this process. Given the context of the comment, Bavinck seems to mean that God the Father somehow corresponds to the *principium essendi*, God the Son to the *principium cognoscendi externum*, and God the Holy Spirit to the *principium cognoscendi internum*.[260] If this reading of Bavinck is correct, it leads to the following

---

258. *RD* 2:262, 287.

259. *RD* 1:214. Bavinck uses similar Trinitarian expressions as the concluding formulas of another two chapters of his *Reformed Dogmatics* that are devoted to the theological *principia*: he ends ch. 7 of the first volume with the phrase "the Father who by the Son and in the Spirit reveals himself to us" (*RD* 1:233); and he ends ch. 8 of the same volume with the words, "It is the Father who reveals himself in the Son and by the Spirit" (*RD* 1:279).

260. Matthew P. W. Roberts suggests that Bavinck clearly links the principles with the divine persons. See Roberts, "Thinking Like a Christian: The Prolegomena of Herman Bavinck," *Ecclesia Reformanda* 1 (2009): 77; see also Van den Belt, "Autopistia," 267. Although this interpretation of Bavinck's thought is natural and almost inevitable, it must be stated that Bavinck himself stopped short of a clear identification of the Father with the *principium essendi*. Much later in the first volume, Bavinck reverts to the theological principles he discussed before, uses a Trinitarian formula, and associates the principles with the persons of the Trinity: "No one knows the Father except the Son and anyone to whom the Son chooses to reveal him [Matt 11:27], and no one can say 'Jesus is Lord' except by the Holy Spirit [1 Cor 12:3]. God himself, therefore, is the principle of existence (*principium essendi*) of religion and theology. Objective revelation in Christ, recorded in Scripture, is its external source of knowledge (*principium cognoscendi externum*). And the Holy Spirit, who has been poured out in the church, regenerates and leads it into the truth, is the internal source of knowledge (*principia cognoscendi internum*)" (*RD* 1:506). What is notable in this passage is that while the associations of the *principium cognoscendi externum* with the Son and the *principium cognoscendi internum* with the Spirit are stated clearly, the *principium essendi* is linked to *God* rather than *the Father*, which may mean that Bavinck saw some drawbacks to this schematization. See also Hans Burger, "Christologisch én pneumatologisch: Herman Bavinck en de relatie tussen schriftleer en christologie," in *Weergaloze kennis: Opstellen over Jezus Christus, Openbaring en*

question: in light of Bavinck's own formulation of the principles—namely, that the *principium essendi* denotes God's perfect self-knowledge, which is not attainable for humans, while the *principium cognoscendi externum* denotes the knowledge he has revealed—does not this schema look similar to the views of some of the early church fathers Bavinck criticized? If the Father is linked to God's perfect and absolute self-knowledge and the Son is linked to his revelation, does this really differ from the doctrine he criticized, namely, the identification of the hiddenness of God with the Father and divine revelation with the Son?

The apparent confusion can be resolved if one considers that Bavinck takes his Trinitarian descriptions as appropriations rather than as strict ontological identifications. The idea of appropriation implies that special properties or deeds common to the whole Trinity may be attributed specifically to one person of the Trinity rather than the other. The idea has been used in Christian theology to emphasize the distinctness of the three persons (at least in our creaturely thought). One of the most widespread examples of the use of this idea is the appropriation of creation to the Father, redemption to the Son, and sanctification to the Spirit. Bavinck uses this idea, but indicates that such attributions or appropriations are not absolute or entirely exclusive of the other persons: while the work of creation is associated with the Father, the Son and the Spirit are not excluded from it, because ultimately God's works *ad extra* are indivisible and common to the three persons.[261] The same principle is applicable to redemption and sanctification, which preeminently, rather than exclusively, belong to the Son and the Spirit, respectively.

In the same way, Bavinck uses another distinction, which is less common in Christian theology. He maintains that revelation "divides itself in two grand dispensations. When the economy of the Son, of objective revelation, is completed, that of the Spirit begins."[262] Although Bavinck does not mention theological principles here, the idea of differentiation between two dispensations of revelation ("objective" and, correspondingly, "subjective") brings to mind the distinction between the *principium*

Schrift, Katholiciteit en Kerk aangeboden aan prof. dr. Barend Kamphuis, ed. Ad de Bruijne, Hans Burger, and Dolf te Velde (Zoetermeer: Boekencentrum, 2015), 127.

261. *RD* 2:318–21.

262. *RD* 1:505; see also 2:320 about the economies of the Father, the Son, and the Spirit.

cognoscendi externum (attributed to the Son) and the *principium cognoscendi internum* (ascribed to the Spirit). Importantly, Bavinck does not mean that the dispensation of the Son was without the Spirit, or that objective revelation could be effective without subjective revelation, or vice versa. This differentiation must also be understood in the sense of nonexclusive appropriation.

When understood in the sense of appropriation, Bavinck's Trinitarian description of the theological principles is compatible with his criticism of the immature views of the early church. Bavinck did not contradict himself when he criticized the sharp contrast between the unknown Father and the knowable Son (which he found in the works of some church fathers), while at the same time associating his own theological *principia* with particular persons of the Trinity. Although one may question the necessity of such associations, Bavinck's schema is internally self-consistent, because for him appropriation is a matter of emphasis rather than a precise ontological description. The attributions of the *principium essendi* to the Father and of the *principium cognoscendi externum* to the Son do not imply that the Father is not revealed at all or that revelation contains the Son in his fullness.

Revelation in Jesus Christ

Although my focus is the doctrine of God, this cannot be entirely abstracted from Christology. After all, it is in Christ that God has revealed himself most clearly and fully. Within the limits of the present study, I will therefore pay some attention to several aspects of Bavinck's Christology that are helpful in understanding the relation between God's hiddenness and revelation.

The Son of God is the Word of God, which means that all our knowledge of God comes only through the Son.[263] In Christ, God reveals and imparts himself to creatures. In a representative passage, Bavinck writes: "Since God communicated himself to the Logos, the Logos could communicate himself to us. The Logos is the *absolute* revelation of God, for from all eternity God communicated himself in all his fullness to him."[264] In Bavinck's theology, the expression "the absolute revelation" immediately captures

263. Bavinck further claims that not only the knowledge of God, but any kind of knowledge is mediated by the Logos ("Kennis en Leven," 207).

264. *RD* 2:274, emphasis added.

the reader's attention. Although his elaboration of the distinction between absolute and relative knowledge will be discussed in some detail later, we have already seen that for Bavinck all revelation is limited and relative. In this context, "absolute revelation" becomes a contradiction in terms.

One may advance the hypothesis that this "absoluteness" of God's revelation should be linked to the ontological Trinity. In other passages, where Bavinck discusses the uniqueness of the Logos, he points to the intra-Trinitarian relations. When Bavinck states that "nothing in the being of the Father is hidden from the Son" or that God "totally expresses himself in the one person of the Logos," he has in mind the internal communication, which has no limitations and can properly be called "absolute," without qualification.[265] However, when Bavinck speaks of the Logos in the passage above as "the absolute revelation of God," he has in mind God's external communication. We know this not only because "revelation" is an inaccurate description of intra-Trinitarian relations, but also because he *grounds* this "absolute revelation" in God's eternal communication within the Godhead.

The same train of thought can be found in another passage: "The essence of Christianity—the absolute self-revelation of God in the person of Christ and the absolute self-communication of God in the Holy Spirit—could only be maintained ... if it had its foundation and first principle in the ontological Trinity." Here again Bavinck distinguishes between "the absolute self-revelation of God in the person of Christ" and "the ontological Trinity," making clear that "the absolute self-revelation of God" denotes the historical coming of the Son rather than his eternal generation. Likewise, Bavinck states that the Son "was *fully* able to reveal the Father because from all eternity he participated in his divine nature." Again, Bavinck differentiates between "full revelation" (in time) and participation in the divine nature (from eternity). Elsewhere Bavinck calls the Logos "the *full* and *complete* revelation of God (John 1:1; 18; 14:9; 17:6; Col 2:9)." In Christ, "God is *fully* revealed and *fully* given (Matt 11:27; John 1:14; 14:9; Col 1:15; 2:19)." The lists of biblical passages in parentheses in both citations indicate that Bavinck refers to the historical revelation in Jesus Christ. Similarly, he

265. Bavinck, *Our Reasonable Faith*, 207; *RD* 2:309.

maintains that in Christ "the *full* being of God is revealed," and unhesitatingly he speaks of the Son as "the *perfect* revelation of the Father."[266]

If, however, according to Bavinck, God's revelation is necessarily partial, inexhaustive, and imperfect, and at the same time he describes the revelation in Christ with such strong words as "absolute," "full," "complete," and "perfect" (*absoluut*, *vol*, *voltooid*, and *volkomen*), does it mean that God's revelation in Christ does not share the limiting characteristics that we observed in the previous sections of the present study? How can we understand all these superlative epithets if Bavinck himself, apparently approvingly, cites Luther's words that "the fullness of God's being was *not exhaustively* revealed in Christ," so that even after his revelation in Christ "there remained in God a dark and hidden background: 'God as he is in his own nature and majesty, God in his absoluteness'"? Moreover, Bavinck acknowledges the limitations of the knowledge of Christ as a man: "Even the Son of God in His human nature ... [has] a knowledge of God which is different in principle and essence from the self-knowledge of God."[267] To be sure, Bavinck mentions the old division of ectypal theology into three types: *theologia unionis* (theology of union), which is the knowledge of God granted to Christ as a man by virtue of the hypostatic union; *theologia visionis* (theology of vision), which is the knowledge of God peculiar to the angels and the saints in the state of glory; and *theologia viatorum* (theology of the pilgrims), which is the knowledge of God accessible to human beings on earth.[268] By using this distinction Bavinck emphasizes that Jesus has a unique knowledge of God, which is different from the knowledge that the saints either in heaven or on earth may possess. Still, all three types of ectypal knowledge have some limitations, and they do not differ among themselves as fundamentally as any one of them differs from the archetypal knowledge of God, which alone can be properly called

266. *RD* 1:329, 335; 2:274, 296; emphasis added; Bavinck, *Our Reasonable Faith*, 24, 28, emphasis added.

267. *RD* 2:40, emphasis added; Bavinck, *Our Reasonable Faith*, 35. See Bavinck's comment that "The human consciousness in him, though having the same subject as the divine consciousness, only to a small degree knew that subject, that 'I,' indeed knew it as a whole but not exhaustively. Just as behind our limited consciousness there also lies within us a world of being, so behind the human consciousness of Christ there lay the depths of God, which could only very gradually and to a limited degree shine through that human consciousness" (*RD* 3:312).

268. *RD* 1:214.

absolute and exhaustive.[269] How then can the revelation in Jesus Christ be absolute and full and perfect, if Jesus himself did not have full and absolute knowledge of God?

Bavinck's considerations about the human nature of Christ may shed light on his views concerning this matter. According to Bavinck, Christ's "human nature, certainly, was not a fully adequate organ for his deity. ... Still the fullness of the deity dwelt in Christ bodily." Although human nature is "not a fully adequate organ" for the deity, the fullness of the deity dwells in it. Unfortunately, Bavinck does not provide any exegetical explanation of Colossians 2:9. The numerous allusions to this verse in his *Reformed Dogmatics* are disappointingly brief and come to nothing more than a mere reiteration of its content.[270] For our purposes, the most remarkable allusion to Colossians 2:9 occurs in one of his articles. Referring to this verse, Bavinck maintains that Christ's humanity is "a pure and unpolluted faculty of the divine," and "the divine reveals itself *bodily* in a perfectly human way."[271] Human nature, therefore, is a "pure," albeit "not a fully adequate organ" for the deity. We encounter here the same idea that Bavinck puts forward in his doctrine of God: God's revelation is pure, true, and reliable in spite of its inevitable limitations due to the difference between the finite and the infinite. But whereas in his reflections on God's revelation in general Bavinck repeated this idea time and again, in his christological

---

269. Contrary to their Lutheran opponents, the Reformed scholastics denied that the archetypal knowledge of God was communicated to Christ's human nature. This divergence of opinions was part of the broad discussion between the Reformed and the Lutherans over the communication of properties (*communicatio idiomatum*). According to the Reformed doctrine, communication takes place at the level of the person and not between the two natures; hence, the archetypal knowledge of God was not and could not be communicated to finite human nature. See Willem J. van Asselt, "The Fundamental Meaning of Theology: Archetypal and Ectypal Theology in Seventeenth-Century Reformed Thought," *WTJ* 64 (2002): 331–32.

270. *RD* 1:335, 398; 2:34, 107, 165, 169; 3:275, 298, 424, 436. The contexts in which Bavinck cites Col 2:9, however, give some hints about what he intended to prove or demonstrate by this verse. Bavinck uses it when defending the deity of Christ (*RD* 3:298, 424, 434) and the abundant presence of the Spirit in him (*RD* 3:436). He also draws a parallel between God's dwelling in Christ, God's residence in the church, and his presence in believers, implying that Christ's humanity can be understood as a visible temple of his divinity, which is similar to God's presence in other people, but also exceeds it (*RD* 2:34, 165). Finally, Bavinck uses the imagery from Col 2:9 in his ontological reasoning about creatures' participation in God's being: "God dwells in all creatures through his being, but in no one other than Christ does the whole fullness of deity dwell bodily" (*RD* 2:169).

271. Herman Bavinck, "Het Rijk Gods, het hoogste goed," in *Kennis en Leven*, 39, emphasis original.

thought Bavinck preferred not to stress the limitations inherent in Christ's human nature. There should be nothing that would threaten the revelatory capacity of Jesus Christ.

Another biblical passage often mentioned by Bavinck in his discussion of the revelation in Christ is John 14:9. The lists of biblical citations above show that for Bavinck this is one of the clearest and most powerful pieces of evidence for the "fullness" of Christ's revelation. "Those who have seen him have seen the Father."[272] People looked at the man Jesus, but they also saw the Father. People met and looked at a creature, but in this encounter they met and saw God himself. To be sure, "this 'seeing' was not the way that God sees God, but an ectypal knowledge, a derivative knowledge accommodated to human capacity."[273] Nevertheless, it is God himself whom they saw in the man Jesus. "As Christ is, such is the Father," Bavinck contends. Although the human nature of Christ cannot reflect the Father exhaustively, it "was equipped by the Holy Spirit to make known to people the Father and his name."[274] There is no need to look behind the scenes: whoever wants to know the invisible Father must behold the visible Jesus.

It is also worth noting that Bavinck emphasizes the dual role of Christ as the subject and content of revelation. Christ "is the Logos in an utterly unique sense: Revealer and revelation at the same time."[275] The phrase "at the same time," however, does not necessarily mean "in one and the same respect." Unlike later theologians such as Pannenberg, who focused on establishing the complete identity of the revealer with his revelation,[276] Bavinck did not consider God's self-revelation in Christ in such a strict

---

272. *RD* 2:98; see also Bavinck, *Our Reasonable Faith*, 27, 317; Herman Bavinck, "De Huishouding Gods," in *Kennis en Leven*, 100.

273. Billings, *Union with Christ*, 78.

274. Bavinck, *Our Reasonable Faith*, 317, 28; *RD* 2:104.

275. *RD* 1:402; As Richard Muller notes, in Reformed orthodoxy one can find a distinction between the *Logos internus* and the *Logos externus*, "the former indicating the mind and self-knowledge of God and the latter being the explanation and interpretation of the eternal will of God toward his elect." See Muller, "Christ—the Revelation or the Revealer? Brunner and Reformed Orthodoxy on the Doctrine of the Word of God," *Journal of the Evangelical Theological Society* 26 (September 1983): 314. Although the idea of the Logos as the Revealer and the revelation is close to this distinction, and the language of the internal and external communication is very typical for Bavinck, he does not mention this distinction in his elaboration of Christology.

276. In a representative passage, Wolfhart Pannenberg writes: "The Revealer and what is revealed are identical." See Pannenberg, *Jesus: God and Man*, trans. Lewis L. Wilkins and Duane A. Priebe (London: SCM, 1968), 127.

sense. The revelation is one with God in the sense that it is true and reliable: as Christ is, such is the Father. But the Son of God in his divinity is more than he can reveal in his humanity: the Revealer does not completely coincide with the revelation. The humanity of Christ is a medium for the Logos as the agent of revelation: "The Logos, in becoming flesh … enters into human nature, prepares and shapes it by the Spirit into his own appropriate medium."[277] God in his revelation is not creaturely—he is divine, but he can be known by humans only in a creaturely way. God in himself and the subject of revelation are one and the same, but the divine subject of revelation transcends revelation itself. The Revealer and the revelation should not be separated, but neither should they be confused.

Returning to the question posed earlier about Bavinck's description of the revelation in Christ as absolute or perfect, two things must be said. First, in Bavinck's view, the revelation in Christ is indeed absolute, full, and perfect inasmuch as human nature allows it to be. Jesus Christ is a revelation to which nothing can be added, because that which exceeds this revelation also exceeds the capacities of human nature. In Christ, the most perfect and complete *creaturely* knowledge of God is accessible. Second, although Bavinck realized that even the revelation in Christ cannot exhaust the richness of God's being, he preferred not to stress this limitation in the same way as he did with revelation in general. Such terms as "absolute" or "perfect" must be taken as rhetorical adornments rather than precise formulations. In using such expressions, Bavinck tried to point to the unique place of the Logos as God's revelation. Jesus Christ is the ultimate evidence and confirmation that God reveals himself as he is.

THE RELATION OF GOD'S HIDDENNESS AND HIS REVELATION

Bavinck's Use of Scholastic Distinctions

Having described Bavinck's views on God's hiddenness and revelation, I will now proceed to show how they are interrelated in his theology. Although some preliminary remarks about this interrelation were necessary earlier, here I will discuss this in more detail. I will structure my presentation of

277. *RD* 1:432.

his views on the basis of Bavinck's application of scholastic distinctions. This methodological choice is primarily determined by Bavinck's extensive use of a wide variety of distinctions when analyzing the doctrine of God. Bavinck's writings are well-known for their catholic spirit, historical depth, and profound knowledge of his own Reformed tradition. When writing his doctrine of God, he used many insights from the early and medieval tradition (especially from Augustine and Aquinas), as well as from the reception and development of that tradition by Reformed thinkers. Although Bavinck freely drew on a great variety of opinions in Reformed orthodoxy, he relied particularly on the Thomistic line of thought,[278] which is evident in his treatment of ideas such as participation, communicability, and analogy. Although Bavinck profited from the Thomistic renewal in the second part of the nineteenth century and found in neo-Thomism an ally and source of promising insights in his dialogue with modernity, he appropriated Thomism mainly through his Reformed mentors rather than his Catholic contemporaries.[279]

Bavinck was familiar with the many distinctions employed in the doctrine of God in both medieval and post-Reformation scholasticism to indicate the difference between what can and cannot be known of God.

---

278. This can be demonstrated even statistically. In the second chapter of the second volume of *RD*, where Bavinck treats the doctrine of God (his essence, names, attributes, and his being as the Trinity), Bavinck mentions Augustine and Aquinas in the text and footnotes more than 170 times (compared with only 14 mentions of Calvin and 11 mentions of Vitringa, who are the main Reformed sources for Bavinck in the *RD* overall and are referred to more often than Augustine and Aquinas in the fourth volume). Also remarkable is that the most cited Reformed theologian in the chapter is Zanchi (36 times). In the entire *RD*, Zanchi is referred less often (122 times) than other Reformed theologians such as Calvin (398), Vitringa (249), Voetius (206), de Moor (196), Turretin (148), and Polanus (136), but for Bavinck's doctrine of God, Zanchi's *De Natura Dei* seems to be the primary Reformed source. More important than statistics, of course, is the *content* of Bavinck's doctrine, which reveals many similarities to the thought of Zanchi, who had a Thomistic training and was called "the best example of Calvinist Thomism." See John Patrick Donnelly, "Calvinist Thomism," *Viator* 7 (1976): 444; see also Harm Goris, "Thomism in Zanchi's Doctrine of God," in *Reformation and Scholasticism: An Ecumenical Enterprise*, ed. Willem J. van Asselt and Eef Dekker (Grand Rapids: Baker Academic, 2001), 130. Muller mentions Zanchi first in his list of "Platonizing Protestants." See Muller, "Not Scotist: Understandings of Being, Univocity, and Analogy in Early-Modern Reformed Thought," *Reformation and Renaissance Review* 14 (2012): 127–50.

279. See Jan Veenhof, "Bavinck en de Wijsbegeerte," in *Ontmoetingen met Bavinck*, ed. George Harinck and Gerrit Neven (Barneveld: De Vuurbaak, 2006), 220–23; David S. Sytsma, "Herman Bavinck's Thomistic Epistemology: The Argument and Sources of His *Principia* of Science," in *Five Studies in the Thought of Herman Bavinck*, ed. John Bolt (Lewiston, NY: Edwin Mellen, 2011), 23.

However, he thought they were limited in their capacity to express the difference between God's hiddenness and revelation. He used them with some hesitation and even openly expressed some dissatisfaction with them.[280] Bavinck frequently bent old distinctions in the service of his own theological intentions and adapted them in order to engage with contemporary problems. Below I will consider several such distinctions together with Bavinck's application of them.

Incommunicable and Communicable

It was the custom of Reformed dogmaticians to classify God's attributes. Bavinck admits that "it is extremely difficult to introduce order into the treatment" of God's attributes.[281] From the available options he chose the distinction between incommunicable and communicable attributes, which was the most widespread division in Reformed orthodoxy (or at least in high Reformed orthodoxy).[282] Although some Reformed orthodox theologians explicitly rejected this classification, for many others it proved to be useful, not least because it provided additional weight in the debate with Lutherans over the ubiquity of Christ's human nature.[283]

Bavinck's motivation in applying this distinction, however, had to do not so much with his desire to keep in line with the Reformed tradition as with his search for conceptual tools in the struggle with contemporary opponents. He explains his choice by saying that he prefers the distinction between incommunicable and communicable attributes because it "has the advantage in that it safeguards Christian theism against both the error of pantheism and that of Deism."[284] The incommunicability of God's attributes prevents a pantheistic identification of God with the world, while the communicability of God's attributes prevents a deistic separation between God and the world.

---

280. *RD* 2:133–135.

281. *RD* 2:135.

282. Te Velde, *Doctrine of God*, 134; Muller, *Post-Reformation Reformed Dogmatics*, 3:216, 225. Normally, scholars recognize a period of high orthodoxy (1640–1725) occurring within the larger era of Reformed orthodoxy (1565–1790). See Muller, *Post-Reformation Reformed Dogmatics*, 1:331.

283. Zanchi maintained that the distinction is untenable, "inasmuch as none of the divine *perfectiones essentiales* can be communicated to creatures" (Muller, *Post-Reformation Reformed Dogmatics*, 3:217). The proponents of the distinction, however, emphasized that what is communicated is neither the divine attribute itself nor the divine essence, but an analogy (223–26).

284. *RD* 2:136.

Nevertheless, Bavinck used this distinction with great reluctance. This is immediately clear from the fact that in the first edition of his *Reformed Dogmatics*, Bavinck's division of attributes is based on a different schema. Only in the second edition does he categorize God's attributes according to the distinction between incommunicable and communicable attributes. Still, even in the second edition, he expresses some reservations about the distinction. Why did Bavinck hesitate? The idea of communicability did not seem problematic to Bavinck, because Reformed theologians who used it in the past emphatically stated that God's attributes are communicated to creatures only analogously and not univocally. The idea of *in*communicability, however, seemed more ambiguous to Bavinck. According to Muller's definition, Reformed orthodoxy reserved the term "incommunicable" "for those attributes proper to God which have neither a similitude or analogy nor an image or vestige in God's creatures."[285] But if incommunicable attributes have no analogy in creatures, Bavinck pondered, how can they be known by creatures? This question possessed special urgency in the post-Kantian context, in which the defense of God's knowability became one of the most important tasks.

Besides the danger of wrongly interpreting God's incommunicability, Bavinck points out another defect of the distinction. Any classification of God's attributes appears to divide God's being into two halves. Thus, also the distinction between incommunicable and communicable attributes seems to imply that there are two sorts of attributes in God. Bavinck sought to avoid such a sharp contrast and proposed a more nuanced approach. On the one hand, he maintains that God is fundamentally different from humankind. We cannot exhaustively know him as he is in himself. Even the so-called communicable attributes are not present in humankind as they are in God and hence are "as incommunicable as the others." On the other hand, God truly reveals himself and makes himself known. Even those attributes that have traditionally been regarded as incommunicable (such as eternity or omnipresence) are explained to us in relation to our finite state, and we can grasp their meaning through some analogy in creation. The description of the incommunicable attributes of God in Scripture and theology is inevitably bound to human speech. Thus, all of

285. Muller, *Post-Reformation Reformed Dogmatics*, 3:225; *RD* 2:132.

the so-called incommunicable attributes are, in a sense, communicable. "If that were not the case, if they were totally incommunicable, they would also be totally unknowable and unnamable," Bavinck notes.[286] Bavinck concludes that "in one sense each of his [God's] attributes is incommunicable and in another communicable."[287]

Thus, although Bavinck admitted some advantages of the distinction between communicable and incommunicable attributes and even classified God's attributes according to it (in the second edition of his *Reformed Dogmatics*), he did not want to draw a sharp contrast between them. In his usage of the distinction, Bavinck implicitly acknowledged that, in different ways, all attributes are both communicable and incommunicable, and he rejected a strict division between communicable and incommunicable attributes. Bavinck argues that it is legitimate and reasonable to speak of incommunicable attributes only if "one consistently bears in mind that

---

286. *RD* 2:132–34. In his treatment of God's communicable and incommunicable attributes, Bavinck focuses on epistemology rather than ontology. He was primarily interested in the *knowledge* of God's being. Given his epistemological concern, his views are understandable: we do know something about God's being (and thus his attributes are communicable), but still our knowledge is not, and cannot be, perfect (and thus his attributes are incommunicable). Bavinck argued, for example, that God's eternity is in a sense communicable because we *understand* the nature of eternity from the nature of time. The communicability of incommunicable attributes is thus to be understood epistemologically, not ontologically. Historically, however, the distinction between communicable and incommunicable attributes was introduced and supported mainly for ontological reasons. (This is obvious even in the aforementioned discussion between the Reformed and the Lutherans about the ubiquity of Christ's body, which was not an epistemological but an ontological question.) In the ontological sense, it is not clear how such attributes as immutability, eternity without a beginning, simplicity, or aseity are communicable. No sliding scale or degree of possessing of these attributes seems possible. They can hardly be properly predicated of creatures, even partially or imperfectly. It seems that Bavinck experienced some problems formulating his views in this regard. On the one hand, he maintains that God's incommunicable attributes are in a sense communicable ontologically as well. For example, he found in all creatures an analogy (albeit "weak") of God's aseity (independence). This point helped him to confront pantheism, because a relative independence of each creature emphasizes that it "has a distinct existence of its own" (*RD* 2:152). In general, all God's perfections, according to Bavinck, are "reflected in his creatures" (*RD* 2:254). On the other hand, Bavinck openly acknowledges that such attributes as eternity and simplicity "after all are not found in creatures" (*RD* 2:250). According to Bavinck, these attributes belong to God "characteristically" and differ from other attributes that belong to him "preeminently." Bavinck continues that the difference between the two groups of attributes is grounded in the fact that "a faint reflection" of the latter attributes can be discerned in creatures (*RD* 2:250), which again implies that Bavinck did not see even a remote ontological reflection of the former attributes (eternity and simplicity) in creatures.

287. *RD* 2:135. "In a certain sense all of his attributes are such as cannot be shared, and in another sense they are such as can all be shared" (Bavinck, *Our Reasonable Faith*, 134). See also Bavinck, *Handleiding bij het onderwijs*, 53–54.

these perfections are in fact descriptions of the wholly unique, absolute, divine *manner* in which the other attributes—those of being, life, and spirit, of intellect and will, of love and righteousness, and so forth—exist in God."[288] The term "incommunicable" does not refer to a separate group of attributes but rather to the preeminent manner, in which all God's attributes (including communicable attributes) exist in God. Bavinck continues to speak of incommunicable and communicable *attributes* rather than about incommunicable and communicable *senses of all attributes* only because he needed a structure when treating each of God's attributes individually, and he preferred not to repeat about each of the attributes that it is simultaneously incommunicable and communicable. In Bavinck's interpretation and application, the distinction between communicable and incommunicable attributes indicates a distinction between God and humankind rather than any distinction within the Godhead.[289] This distinction does not create division within God, but points out how God's absoluteness cannot be communicated to humans.

Absolute and Relative

Bavinck treats the distinction between the so-called absolute and relative attributes in a similar manner. In Reformed orthodoxy, absolute attributes described God as he is in himself, while relative attributes described God in relation to creatures.[290] Bavinck disliked this classification because it sounded as if absolute attributes describe God as such, apart from any relation to creation, while only relative attributes are derived from his relation to the world. According to Bavinck, this distinction obscures the fact that any perception or knowledge of God apart from creation is impossible.

288. *RD* 2:136, emphasis added.

289. C. Ouwendorp describes Bavinck's views as follows: "There are attributes or properties and relevant biblical texts that convey God's absolute being as God is in himself (*ad intra*). There are also attributes or properties and relevant biblical texts that express God's relationship to reality. These two sorts of properties are named incommunicable and communicable properties, respectively." See Ouwendorp, (*Jeruzalem & Athene* (Delft: Eburon, 2012), 215. But this description hardly does justice to Bavinck's nuanced approach. Bavinck does not claim that some attributes or properties "convey God's absolute being as God is in himself." Bavinck's point is precisely opposite to this claim, because he contends that no attributes convey God's being in its absoluteness. Further, as demonstrated above, the difference between God's communicable and incommunicable properties in Bavinck's theology is not as stark as one would conclude from Ouwendorp's description.

290. Muller, *Post-Reformation Reformed Dogmatics*, 3:217.

Attributes are called absolute not because we know them apart from creation but because we do not find them within creation in their absolute form. Bavinck argues that the classification of attributes into absolute and relative has yet another deficiency: it sounds as if relative attributes (such as love) are not present in God in the same unreserved sense as his absolute attributes (such as infinity). Bavinck, therefore, preferred to speak not of absolute and relative *groups* of attributes, but of absolute and relative *senses* of *all* attributes. In Bavinck's own words, "All God's attributes are both absolute and relative. They are all absolute, yet only known first from his relation to his creatures."[291] Therefore, in a relative sense, all God's attributes are communicable and knowable. But in an absolute sense, all God's attributes are incommunicable and incomprehensible.

Bavinck emphasizes that the Christian idea of God as the absolute being should not be confused with "the Absolute" in the philosophical sense of the word. In philosophy, absoluteness was often equated with the indefinite, on the grounds that any description implies a limitation. By contrast, Bavinck argues that we achieve the concept of God's absoluteness not by denying him creaturely perfections but rather by attributing them to him in an absolute sense. The concept means, therefore, that God possesses, in an absolute sense, "all the perfections, a faint analogy of which can be discerned in his creatures." According to Bavinck, the description of God as Absolute being, as the fullness and totality of essence, must be preferred over the description of God as love and person, "because it encompasses all God's attributes in an absolute sense." This does not mean, however, that Bavinck preferred God's absoluteness over his relationality, because such terms as "the fullness and totality of essence" implied for him not only God's otherness and majesty, but also his abundance and fecundity—that is, that as an ocean of being, God is the source of all beings.[292]

291. *RD* 2:120, 133–35.

292. *RD* 2:123–24. While this chapter focuses on the distinctions that Bavinck used, it is also notable that Bavinck ignores some of the distinctions that were drawn in Reformed scholasticism. He omits the distinction between God's essence and God's life, which, at least at first sight, would be the closest parallel to the Eastern Orthodox distinction between God's essence and energies. (The distinction between God's essence and life was used by Voetius. See Andreas J. Beck, "Gisbertus Voetius (1589–1676): Basic Features of His Doctrine of God," in van Asselt and Dekker, *Reformation and Scholasticism*, 218; and several other Reformed orthodox theologians [Muller, *Post-Reformation Reformed Dogmatics*, 3:217–19], not to mention medieval scholastics.) It appears that for Bavinck this distinction was unsuitable because the

As we saw in our discussion of the limitations of God's revelation, this absoluteness consists both in quantity and quality. God is not only *much* wiser than any of his creatures; he is wise *in his own, incomprehensible way*. "Knowledge, wisdom, power, love, and righteousness are uniquely his, that is, in a divine manner." At the same time, Bavinck notes, "there should be a certain correspondence between the Divine and the human love, or else all of our thinking and speaking of the love of God were a hollow sound."[293] Here our human language shows its weakness: on the one hand, we must proclaim the otherness of God; on the other hand, we must proclaim an analogy between him and his creatures, bearing in mind that an analogy is by no means an identity. God is different, and he possesses his attributes differently than they appear in creation, but he is not *altogether* different.

Archetypal and Ectypal

The third distinction that needs to be analyzed at some length is the scholastic distinction between archetypal and ectypal theology. It originated in late medieval Scotism and was first thoroughly investigated in Reformed orthodoxy in 1594 by Franciscus Junius, after which it became a commonplace in Protestant thought.[294] Bavinck took up the distinction at the very beginning of his scientific career. "All our theology, in its entirety, is ectypal," he contends in one of his early speeches.[295] Archetypal knowl-

---

concept of God's life in this distinction may be understood as associated primarily or even exclusively with God's relationality and his external activities. Bavinck emphasizes instead that the concept of life is applicable also to God in himself (*RD* 2:150). God has a nature and infinite life of his own within himself and apart from the world (*RD* 2:111, 177). If God's essence is differentiated from God's life, it risks becoming an abstraction, an empty and lifeless concept. Bavinck maintains instead that there is "an eternal movement of life in the divine being itself" (*RD* 2:320). God is "an infinite abundance of life" (*RD* 2:300), "a plenitude of life" (*RD* 2:308; also 331) and "the absolute fullness of life" (*RD* 2:127; also 139).

293. *RD* 1:211, 214; Bavinck, *Our Reasonable Faith*, 138.

294. Van Asselt, "Fundamental Meaning," 319–35; Muller, *Post-Reformation Reformed Dogmatics*, 1:225–38; Carl R. Trueman, *John Owen: Reformed Catholic, Renaissance Man* (Aldershot, UK: Ashgate, 2007), 36; te Velde, *Doctrine of God*, 95; Van den Belt, "Autopistia," 266–73.

295. Bremmer compares Bavinck's two rectoral orations (in Kampen in 1883 and in Amsterdam in 1902) and says that in the latter oration "there is more in common with Kuyper, especially as to his encyclopedic schema. It is striking that now he does not call God the object of theology, but the *cognitio Dei ectypa revelata*, in which a conscious agreement with Kuyper's *Encyclopaedia* can be noted" (*Herman Bavinck als Dogmaticus*, 375; see also 151–52). Bavinck, however, does not mention the phrase *cognitio Dei ectypa revelata* (the revealed ectypal knowledge of God) or any other words with the root "ectyp-" in the 1902 oration. And, as Bremmer admits, Bavinck's 1883 oration made clear that the object of theology is not

edge denotes God's self-knowledge, whereas ectypal knowledge denotes knowledge of God given in revelation to creatures. The distinction shows that human knowledge of God "is possible only as a copy and imitation of the divine archetypal theology."[296] Only God's self-knowledge is archetypal, immediate, comprehensive, and perfect. In contrast, our knowledge of God is ectypal, mediated, limited, and imperfect.[297] The two types of knowledge differ both quantitatively and qualitatively.[298]

Bavinck uses this distinction to make clear that though God chooses to reveal himself through creatures, this does not imply that our knowledge of God originates from creatures. God's archetypal self-knowledge is antecedent to the existence of creatures and to our ectypal knowledge of God through them. On our creaturely level, we first discover perfections in creatures and then attribute them in an absolute sense to God: "In our

---

God in himself, but God as revealed in Jesus Christ. "Only that in which God reveals himself, and in so far as He reveals himself in it, can and may be the object of theological science" (Bavinck, *Wetenschap der H. Godgeleerdheid*, 27). For Bavinck in 1883, the idea that God is the object of theology and the idea of the ectypal character of theology stand side by side: "All our theology, in its entirety, is ectypal. Its glorious subject is God in Christ Jesus" (29). Thus, there is no substantial difference between the orations.

296. Pannenberg, *Systematic Theology*, 1:4.

297. Speaking of archetypal and ectypal knowledge, Bavinck typically rejects both separation and identification. On the one hand, the two types of knowledge may "never be separated and detached from each other" (*RD* 1:214). Bavinck even says "that materially they are one ... , for it is one identical, pure, and genuine knowledge of God, which he has of himself, communicates in revelation, and introduces into the human consciousness" (*RD* 1:214). The word "identical" (in the Dutch original—éénzelfde) does not imply, however, that ectypal knowledge is an exact copy of the original, divine knowledge. Bavinck constantly reiterated that God in himself and God in his revelation are "one and the same" (éénzelfde), but still there is not complete identity. Ectypal and archetypal knowledge, therefore, "need to be distinguished" (*RD* 1:214).

298. Although Bavinck consistently uses and applies the distinction throughout his *Reformed Dogmatics*, one of his critical remarks is dubious. (Bavinck does not specify the name of the theologian(s) in question, but presumably he means Bernhard de Moor, who is explicitly mentioned by Abraham Kuyper, when he offers a similar critique: *Encyclopaedie der Heilige Godgeleerdheid, Tweede Deel, Algemeen deel* [Kampen: Kok, 1909], 207. See also Bremmer, *Herman Bavinck als Dogmaticus*, 156–57, 193). Bavinck writes: "In earlier times ... the archetypal knowledge of God was occasionally restricted to the part of the self-knowledge of God that he had decided to communicate to creatures. But this distinction makes the revelation [*sic*] between archetypal and the ectypal knowledge of God into a mechanical one and ignores the fact that absoluteness consists not only in quantity but also in quality" (*RD* 1:214). Bavinck's remark seems somewhat strange. He complains that the old position made the relation between the archetypal and the ectypal knowledge of God into a mechanical one. But if the old position restricted the archetypal knowledge of God to the knowledge that is revealed (that is, if quantitatively archetypal knowledge is the same as ectypal knowledge), then how they differ is precisely qualitatively, and the relation between them then is far from being "mechanical."

perception and thought we advance from the visible to the invisible, from the world to God." When speaking of God, we use names whose meanings originate in the created realm. Nevertheless, Bavinck maintains, "materially they first apply to God and then to creatures. All perfections are first in God, then in creatures." Although we experience and come to know notions and concepts in creation before we recognize them in God, in fact they primarily exist in God: "He is the archetype [the original]; the creature is the ectype [the likeness]. In him everything is original, absolute, and perfect; in creatures everything is derived, relative, and limited."[299]

When God says that he is holy, wise, or glorious, he inevitably uses our human perspectives on holiness, wisdom, and glory. If he did not, we would not understand anything, insists Bavinck. However, our perspectives on God's holiness, wisdom, and glory do not determine what God's holiness, wisdom, and glory in actual fact *are*. The description of God's attributes is not derived from human imagination. Rather, human ideas and names are derived from the divine and were implanted in humans by God himself. "God, therefore, is not really named after things present in creatures, but creatures are named after that which exists in an absolute sense in God."[300] The ideas and names that we employ in our God-talk are ultimately God's own ideas and names, which he "prepared" beforehand for his self-disclosure.

Thus, the recognition of the ectypal character of our knowledge of God demonstrates modesty and humility. Our knowledge of God is not original but derived from the archetypal self-knowledge of God. Bavinck employs the dictum that states, "the imperative task of the dogmatician is to think God's thoughts after him." Our theology is no more than a mirror of divine theology. In fact, Bavinck's schema had three levels: our theology, God's revelation, and God's self-knowledge. Our theology is only a mirror of God's revelation, while God's revelation, in turn, is only a reflection of God's self-knowledge. Theology is "thinking afterwards" about that which is revealed by God.[301] The distinction between archetypal and ectypal theology demonstrates our dependency on God's revelation and God's terms.

299. *RD* 2:69, 107, 129.

300. *RD* 2:107, 2:129–30.

301. *RD* 1:44. "Dogmatics is never more than a faint image and a weak likeness of the Word of God; it is a fallible human attempt, in one's own independent way, to think and say

For Bavinck the recognition of the ectypal character of our knowledge of God also points toward certainty and trustworthiness. Our theology *is* a mirror, or an imprint of divine theology. It rests on the divine truth and participates in God's self-knowledge. It is not purely a symbol detached from the reality of God. Our knowledge of God is no more—but also no less—than an ectypal reflection of the divine archetype. According to Bavinck, "the knowledge we have of God is correct because we know that it is not exhaustive—not false and untrue, but analogical and ectypal."[302] Thus, the distinction helps us to see that although we do not have archetypal knowledge of God, our knowledge is still true and reliable.

Negative and Positive

The fourth important distinction widely discussed in scholasticism and appropriated by Bavinck is related to the way we know God. Many theologians preferred a threefold approach to knowing God: by causality, eminence, and negation (causality, implying that we know God from his world as we know a cause from its effects; eminence, implying that we ascribe to God in a preeminent sense what we observe in creatures; and negation, which means that imperfections found in creatures are ruled out in the case of God).[303] However, some Reformed theologians preferred a twofold approach, in which two of the three ways are merged.[304] Unsurprisingly, Bavinck concurs with this approach, as it perfectly fits his beloved twofold schema, according to which God is knowable and communicable in one sense, and unknowable and incommunicable in another. According to Bavinck, "the way of eminence and the way of causality are actually one and may together be posited as the way of affirmation over against the way of negation."[305]

---

after God what he in many and various ways spoke of old by the prophets and in these last days has spoken to us by the Son" (*RD* 1:55).

302. *RD* 2:134.

303. te Velde, *Doctrine of God*, 97. See also Muller, *Post-Reformation Reformed Dogmatics*, 3:166, 217.

304. Muller, *Post-Reformation Reformed Dogmatics*, 3:220.

305. *RD* 2:129. In this respect it is remarkable that pseudo-Dionysius also speaks about two ways (*Divine Names* 1.5–7; it is not clear, however, how the enumeration of biblical names [in *Divine Names* 1.8] must be classified: as a separate way or as a subdivision of the way of causality; for some details, see Rocca, *Speaking the Incomprehensible God*, 25, 53, 54). Pseudo-Dionysius, however, joined rather the ways of negation and eminence. For Bavinck, the recognition

The distinction between a negative and a positive way to the knowledge of God coincides with the distinction between apophatic and cataphatic approaches to theology.[306] It has been often claimed that Eastern Christianity prefers apophatic theology, while Western theologians are more inclined to cataphatic theology. Bavinck, however, states that both approaches are equally important and indeed presuppose one another: "They do not even run parallel; neither can we take the one without taking the other." Theology is not simply *both* cataphatic and apophatic; it is *simultaneously* cataphatic and apophatic. These two approaches are closely interwoven in the sense that one and the same thing can and must be predicated of God, both negatively and positively. "All attributes are simultaneously ascribed and denied to him," Bavinck emphasizes.[307] Both approaches, therefore, are valid and even necessary. Every affirmation implies a negation and vice versa. Knowledge of God is positive in the sense that we speak of God as a distinct and infinite being to whom, based on his revelation, we can apply some attributes and names from the realm of creation. Knowledge of God is negative in the sense that none of these names or attributes can be applied to God in the same way as they are applied to creatures. We can speak of a negative way not only when we say, "God is not a liar," but also when we say, "God is truth," implying that he is truth not in our creaturely sense but in an absolute sense, which is incomprehensible to us. Positive theology affirms that perfections found in creatures are present in God in an absolute sense; negative theology denies that creaturely limitations are also present in God.

We *affirm* God's absoluteness, although we realize that we cannot perceive or express it *positively*. According to Bavinck, "We have a positive appreciation of God as the Absolute Being, even if we cannot put this awareness in so many words." For example, God is good in an absolute

of God's preeminence is a part of affirmative theology, which signifies the rather positive orientation of Bavinck's theology; for pseudo-Dionysius, God's preeminence is evidence of God's radical otherness.

306. Strictly speaking, the "negative *way*" (*via negativa*) is a broader concept than "negative *theology*," because it implies not only a cognitive approach (as negative theology does), but also the ascetical, mystical, and spiritual life. Negative *theology* is a theoretical concept concerning the knowledge of God; the negative *way* is a way of life directed towards union with God. See Rocca, *Speaking the Incomprehensible God*, 4. Bavinck, however, constantly used the term "negative way" in a narrow "theological" sense.

307. *RD* 2:130.

sense. But what do we mean by "absolute sense"? We can explain it most easily through negation: absolute is "not relative," "not creaturely." We can define eternity as a negation of time. All positive names "denote something in God that exists in him absolutely, 'properly,' and hence also 'negatively,' that is, in another sense than it exists in creatures." God possesses all his attributes "in a way that infinitely surpassed our comprehension," Bavinck contends. Yet, if we describe God's absoluteness only through negation, we run the risk of ending up with an empty concept. If God's goodness is qualified with "but this goodness is absolutely different from ours," it becomes a pure abstraction with no real content. God's attributes, therefore, must also be explained positively, in the way of eminence, based on God's revelation in creation. "The positive names—such as 'good,' 'holy,' 'wise'—have some meaning to our mind, because we observe examples (ectypes) of them in creatures." Even the so-called negative attributes are "presented in Scripture in forms and expressions derived from the finite world." Bavinck points out that we must follow the Bible, which always describes God's perfections positively in terms of their relation to the world.[308]

J. Todd Billings correctly notes that "Bavinck gives a thorough and robust negative theology."[309] It must be added that in doing so, Bavinck refrains from denying obvious things. That is, he does not focus on denying material, corporeal, bodily realities of God (such as "God is not a creature" or "God is not a body"). His negative approach focuses on denying that God's perfections are to be understood in the same way as they are revealed in creatures. He uses the negative way not to describe emptiness in our concept of God but to exclude any form of limitation or impoverishment. The negative way is not keeping silence, an absence of words, or a confession of absolute unknowing. It deals with the content of revelation, not with a lack of revelation. Without revelation, we would not have anything to deny. Bavinck's negative theology does not deny conceptual or rational knowledge of God, and it does not move humans to a kind of mystical union as opposed to mental knowledge. Negative and positive approaches are closely interwoven. For Bavinck, negations are not opposites of affirmations; rather, they go beyond affirmations. Negations are

308. *RD* 2:100, 130, 134.

309. Billings, *Union with Christ*, 75.

used not with regard to the *reality* signified but with regard to the *mode* of signifying.[310] It is not denied that God is good or wise; it is denied that he is good or wise in a creaturely sense.[311]

Comprehension and Knowledge

In general, Bavinck's use of each of the four distinctions dealt with above comes to one and the same idea: God can be truly *known* based on his creaturely and analogical revelation, but he cannot be *comprehended* in his absoluteness. He is knowable and incomprehensible at the same time and with respect to the same predicates. In this connection, it is noteworthy that Bavinck also uses the old distinction between apprehension and comprehension, as well as the distinction between knowledge and comprehension.[312] Both distinctions allow us safely to say that we know God without comprehending him. The limited nature of our knowledge of God does not contradict its reality and truth. As Bavinck puts it, "What is known in part and seen in part is known and seen." If "to know" meant "to know perfectly," we could not say that we know even creaturely things. "Knowledge of God ... does not include but excludes comprehension."[313] Partial knowledge is still *knowledge*.

In his *Reformed Dogmatics*, however, Bavinck does not always consistently distinguish between knowledge and comprehension. He still

310. See Gregory Rocca, *Speaking the Incomprehensible God*, 61.

311. Although Bavinck stuck to his twofold schema (with the way of negation on the one hand and the ways of eminence and causality on the other hand), his theology can be legitimately described as a combination of two ways (negation and causality) that *results* in the way of eminence. E.g., God is wise (causality), but not in the sense we are (negation); thus, he is preeminently wise (eminence; provided that wise and preeminently wise are related analogically as ectype and archetype).

312. In fact, this distinction is even threefold, because Bavinck distinguishes between *weten* ("being acquainted with"), *kennen* ("knowing"), and *begrijpen* ("comprehending"). As he explains this, *weten* refers "to a thing's existence, the *that*," *kennen* "concerns a thing's quality, the *what*," and *begrijpen* "relates to its inner possibility, the *how* of a thing" (*RD* 1:619, emphasis original). All three terms have a meaning that renders a difference in degree and manner of knowledge rather than in principle. The aim of theology is "not just a knowing [*weten*], much less a comprehending [*begrijpen*]; it is better and more glorious than that: it is the knowledge [*kennis*] which is life, eternal life" (*RD* 1:621). Bavinck says that God "can be apprehended; he cannot be comprehended. There is some knowledge (γνωσις) but no thorough grasp (καταληψις) of God" (*RD* 2:47). For the use of the distinction in Reformed Orthodoxy, see Muller, *Post-Reformation Reformed Dogmatics*, 3:165.

313. *RD* 1:602; 2:51.

employs the language of unknowability regarding God's essence (not only in historical overviews, where he sticks to the terms in question, but also in the expositions of his own views) and uses the terms "unknowability" and "incomprehensibility" synonymously.[314] However, within the framework of his system, it would be more consistent to avoid applying the term "unknowable" to that which is revealed. Rather, God's essence is to be called "incomprehensible" yet still analogically "knowable" based on revelation. Bavinck's lack of consistency in his *Reformed Dogmatics* was noted by Fred H. Klooster in his study on the conflict over God's incomprehensibility in Presbyterian circles. Klooster correctly observes that Bavinck continually used the words "unknowable," "incomprehensible," and "hidden" interchangeably. "Bavinck combines incomprehensible and unknown," whereas Klooster advocates a more careful distinction between the terms. According to Klooster, theologians who were influenced by Bavinck did actually make a more pointed distinction between incomprehensibility and unknowability, though this distinction was not made by Bavinck himself.[315]

Klooster, however, focuses only on *Reformed Dogmatics* and does not consider one important passage from Bavinck's later work, where he makes a clearer distinction between the unknowability and incomprehensibility of God, and calls for caution with the use of the term "unknowability." In *Magnalia Dei* (1909), Bavinck argues that denial of the knowability of God can spring from two very different mindsets. On the one hand, God's knowability can be denied based on purely rationalistic arguments, which results in agnosticism and practical atheism. On the other hand, denial of the knowability of God can "spring from a deep sense of one's own littleness and nothingness and from a deep feeling, combined with that, of

---

314. "It is the incontrovertible teaching of Scripture ... that *in God's secret being [wezen] he is unknowable* and unnamable" (*RD* 2:133, emphasis added); "This theory of *the incomprehensibility* of God and of *the unknowability of his essence [wezen]* also became the starting point and fundamental idea of Christian theology" (*RD* 2:36; emphasis added); "To a considerable extent we can assent to and wholeheartedly affirm this *doctrine of the unknowability of God*" (*RD* 2:47, emphasis added); "We *cannot know* God's being as such [in zichzelf]" (*RD* 2:70, emphasis added). Bavinck also concurs with the teaching of the church fathers described as follows: "Though God is *unknowable in his essence*, he was revealed in Scripture as the Triune God" (*RD* 1:130, emphasis added), and laments that theologians tended to forget the "truth of the unknowability of the divine essence" ("[de] waarheid van de onkenbaarheid van het Goddelijk wezen," *GD*[4] 2:14).

315. Klooster, *Incomprehensibility of God*, 97, 100–101.

God's infinite greatness and overwhelming majesty."[316] The latter attitude, Bavinck observed, is characteristic of all the saints, many of whom preferred to say what God is not rather than what he is. Bavinck then continues with a long sentence, which deserves to be quoted in full:

> Although this humble confession of God's sublime majesty and of human littleness can, in a certain sense, be called a denial of the knowability of God, still it would seem that, in the interest of avoiding misunderstanding, and in accordance with Holy Scripture, we ought to make a distinction between God's knowableness and His fathomableness.[317]

Thus, Bavinck respected a pious confession of God's unknowability, but found it somewhat misleading and potentially confusing, especially in the context of the agnostic tendencies and vocabulary of his own time. Bavinck was aware that many Christian theologians regarded God as in some sense unknowable, and he sought to explain his doctrine of God in line with this tradition. After all, Bavinck could treat the idea of knowability as he treated communicability: he could say that God's attributes are unknowable in one sense and knowable in another (as they are incommunicable in one sense and communicable in another). However, under the pressure of contemporary challenges, Bavinck preferred to avoid this ambiguity by clarifying the idea of knowledge. That is why in *Magnalia Dei* he strove for greater consistency, and gave the distinction between knowability and comprehensibility its proper and due weight. God is incomprehensible but still knowable based on his revelation.[318]

Conclusion

Throughout his scientific career, Bavinck never abandoned a sense of mystery. God's hiddenness is an essential part of his doctrine of God: not only structurally but also in the sense that all his God-talk is permeated with an

316. Bavinck, *Our Reasonable Faith*, 131.

317. Bavinck, *Our Reasonable Faith*, 132. "Fathomableness" stands in this sentence for the Dutch word *begrijpelijkheid*, which for the sake of consistency can be translated here as "comprehensibility." In the *Gereformeerde Dogmatiek*, this word is not used, but its antonym (*onbegrijpelijkheid*) is used many times, and in the English edition of this work and in the present study it is translated as "incomprehensibility."

318. See also Bavinck, *Handleiding bij het onderwijs*, 49–51.

awareness of the mysterious character of the Lord. In Bavinck's dogmatics, God remains majestic in his condescension, absolute in his relations with creatures, and mysterious in his self-disclosure. Bavinck's emphasis on the doctrine of revelation, however, was no less pointed. Not only our knowledge of God but also our certainty, worship, faith, hope, and love are fully dependent on God's revelation.

For Bavinck, therefore, God is simultaneously hidden and revealed, transcendent and immanent, incommunicable and communicable, incomprehensible and knowable. Bavinck did not conceal that he, as well as all other theologians, experienced great difficulties in combining these two important truths: "We always especially face the problem of doing equal justice to the absoluteness and the personality of God, the incommunicable and the communicable attributes, God's absolute superiority over, and his communion with, the world." The relationship between God's hiddenness and revelation is itself a mystery that "cannot be comprehended."[319]

However, Bavinck did not stop at paradoxical expressions. He realized the need for a more positive analysis of the relation between God in himself and in his revelation. Bavinck sought to avoid the extremes of identification and separation, and he promoted instead a kind of a correspondence model, which means that God's revelation *corresponds* to his very being. This model rejects an exhaustive identification of God with his revelation. Such identification would demand revelation on a divine level, which is impossible because of the finitude of human beings. Absolute knowledge is never attainable for them: they can only possess relative knowledge of the absolute being. To know God as he knows himself, humans would have to be divine. God's hiddenness does not mean for Bavinck that we do not know anything at all about God or that God's hiddenness relates to his revelation in a paradoxical way only. Rather, God's hiddenness means that we do not have access to an immediate, complete, exhaustive, and uncreated knowledge of God.

Bavinck's correspondence model also rejects a separation between God and his revelation. Such separation would eradicate the objectivity of truth and eventually destroy all our certainty. Although God transcends his revelation, it gives us a knowledge of God that is "true, pure, and sufficient."

319. *RD* 2:49, 117.

Every revealed attribute "makes known the content of God's being."[320] God himself speaks, works, and is present in his revelation. The limited nature of the revelation of God does not deny the reality of the encounter with God. Communion between God and humanity does not imply absorbing humanity into the divine, but rather preserving the divinity of God and the humanity of humans.

The correspondence implied in the relation between God and his revelation is not an exact one-to-one correspondence. Although Bavinck once mentions that "there is complete correspondence [*volkomen overeenstemming*] between his being and his revelation," this is said in the context of a discussion of God's ethical truth. Bavinck maintains here that all that God reveals is true, though not necessarily exhaustive.[321] God's being is only disclosed to a certain extent—that is, to the extent that the creature can reflect the divine. Bavinck, therefore, speaks of "the full revelation and *to that extent the very being [Wezen] of God himself*."[322]

The concept of correspondence is close to that of analogy. As "correspondence" is a mediating term between "identification" and "separation," so "analogy" is a mediating term between univocity and equivocity. For Bavinck, to say that God's revelation *corresponds* to his being amounts to saying that God's revelation is *analogous* to his being. The correspondence between God in himself and his revelation rests on the analogy between God and creation, which from the very beginning was so arranged that it was able to reveal God's perfections.

The main point of Bavinck is clear: God in himself and God in his revelation are one and the same God. There are no parts or divisions in God. So, Bavinck states in his *Reformed Dogmatics* that he "considered God

---

320. *RD* 2:110, 136.

321. *RD* 2:209. See also the following comment: "The revelation of God in the Old Testament ... does not exhaustively coincide with his being [*valt ... niet zo met Zijn Wezen samen, dat dit daarin zou opgaan*]. It does indeed furnish true and reliable knowledge of God, but not a knowledge that exhaustively corresponds ['exhaustively corresponds' = *adekwaat*] to his being" (*RD* 2:33).

322. *RD* 2:99 emphasis added. Bavinck uses the phrase "to some extent" in other similar contexts: "God ... must reveal himself, and hence *to some extent* be knowable" (*RD* 1:285, emphasis added); "God can reveal himself and *to some extent* make himself known in created beings" (*RD* 2:49, emphasis added); "God *to some extent* becomes manifest in his creatures" (*RD* 2:56, emphasis added).

as—according to his self-revelation—he exists in himself."[323] This statement may appear overconfident or even pretentious. How can a theologian be sure that he considers God "as … he exists in himself"? But for Bavinck this is, rather, a statement of humble trust. He believed that God's revelation shows God in himself, simply because he trusted God. God's revelation is like a voice from the blinding glare, from "unapproachable light"; we cannot check whether his words are true, but we can rely on them through faith.

God's hiddenness and his revelation do not stand in opposition to each other, because the knowable revealed God *corresponds* to the incomprehensible hidden God. By God's revelation "we do have true and authentic knowledge of God's incomprehensible and adorable being," insists Bavinck.[324] In order to love, worship, and trust God, we must know him and speak of him. And this love, worship, and trust will be real and true only if we remember that God transcends our thoughts and words, and indeed his own revelation itself. In theology, therefore, there must always be room for both knowledge and mystery.

---

323. *RD* 2:342.

324. *RD* 2:137.

3

—

JOHN MEYENDORFF ON UNION WITH GOD AS THE UNKNOWN

INTRODUCTION

Overview of Meyendorff's Life and Thought

John Meyendorff (1926–1992) was an Orthodox theologian, historian, and priest. He was born in France to a family of Russian emigrants who left their country after the October Revolution of 1917. Meyendorff studied at the Sorbonne University and the Orthodox Theological Institute of Saint Sergius, located in Paris. Shortly after graduating, Meyendorff was invited to lecture on church history at the institute and worked there until 1959. In 1958, he received the doctoral degree from the Sorbonne for his thesis on Gregory Palamas.

Paris, which became the center of Orthodox scholarship after the establishment of the Institute, gave rise to two theological schools, mentioned in the introduction: the Russian religious school and the neo-patristic school. Meyendorff, undoubtedly, sympathized more with the second school and called himself a follower—"absolutely and almost unreservedly"—of Florovsky.[1] His own efforts to rehabilitate the theology of Palamas should be considered within the framework of the neo-patristic project. By Meyendorff's own confession, his "historical mindset" could not accept sophiology.[2]

---

1. Ioann Meyendorf, *Pravoslavie i sovremennyy mir* [Orthodoxy and the Contemporary World] (Minsk: Luchi Sofii, 1995), 53.

2. "Pravoslavnaya pozitsiya—beseda s prof. prot. Ioannom Meyendorfom: Vremya osmysleniya," [The Orthodox Position—A Conversation with Prof. Prot. John Meyendorff: Time for Deep Reflection], *Voronezhskiy eparhial'nyy vestnik* 8 (1992): 45.

"The 'Russian Paris' of the 1930s was a world unto itself," a microcosm of Russian prerevolutionary society that included intellectuals, dukes, and former statesmen.[3] This world, however, lived largely in isolation and was too narrow for Meyendorff's broad vision. At the end of the 1950s, the future of Orthodox Paris seemed bleak: "If Orthodoxy really is the true faith, then can we allow its destiny to be bound up with the inevitable dying out of the Russian émigré community?"[4] In search of better opportunities for Orthodox witness in the contemporary world, Meyendorff moved to America in 1959 after his ordination to the priesthood.

In America, Meyendorff taught church history and patrology at Saint Vladimir's Orthodox Theological Seminary and later became its dean, in 1984. In addition to his responsibilities in the seminary, Meyendorff lectured at Harvard, Fordham, and Columbia Universities, as well as at Union Theological Seminary in New York. He was president of the Orthodox Theological Society of America and of the American Patristics Association. Meyendorff deeply involved himself in the life of Orthodox communities in America and actively participated in ecumenical dialogue, representing the Orthodox Church in many meetings organized by the World Council of Churches. From 1967 to 1975, he held the position of moderator of the World Council of Churches' Commission on Faith and Order.

Why Meyendorff?

During the last century, a significant number of reputable Orthodox thinkers left their mark on contemporary theology. From among that group, Meyendorff does not necessarily stand out as the obvious choice to represent Orthodox theology for the present work. So it is important first to consider why I selected his theology to represent Orthodoxy.

First of all, as a dogmatician, church historian, Byzantinist, and patrologist, Meyendorff is widely recognized as one of the foremost Orthodox theologians of the twentieth century. Theologians from different traditions have described him as "perhaps the greatest contemporary Orthodox theologian in America," "one of the most important thinkers on contemporary

3. John Meyendorff, "A Life Worth Living," in *Liturgy and Tradition: Theological Reflections of Alexander Schmemann*, ed. Thomas Fisch (Crestwood, NY: St Vladimir's Seminary Press, 1990), 145.

4. "Pravoslavnaya pozitsiya," 45.

Orthodox history and ecclesiology," and "one of the outstanding ecumenists of our time." It would not be an exaggeration to say that Meyendorff became one of the most authoritative interpreters of Orthodoxy for many Christians.

Second, Meyendorff represented "mainstream" Orthodox theology and was involved in the work of the two main centers for Orthodox theology in the twentieth century in the West (Paris and New York). He belonged to a group of theologians who paid special attention to the ideas of Gregory Palamas in their attempt to reinterpret the theology of the Eastern fathers for their contemporaries, and to establish a specifically Orthodox identity in the midst of the Western world.[5] Just as the neo-patristic movement has been the main current in Orthodox theology since the early 1930s, so the neo-Palamite movement has been the main current in neo-patristics—to the point that the two terms, "neo-Palamism" and "neo-patristics," have often been used almost interchangeably.[6]

Third, and most importantly for the present study, Meyendorff's most famous work—his Sorbonne thesis—is directly related to the topic of God's hiddenness and revelation. This work has been called "pioneering," "classic," "definitive," "groundbreaking," "brilliant," and "revolutionary" because it challenged prevalent assumptions about Palamas in the West.[7] According to Kallistos Ware, Meyendorff's thesis ushered in "a new era for the study of Palamism in the West."[8] The work secured for Meyendorff a

---

5. Jason Robert Radcliff posits a clear distinction between Meyendorff and the neo-Palamites. See Radcliff, *Thomas F. Torrance and the Church Fathers: A Reformed, Evangelical, and Ecumenical Reconstruction of the Patristic Tradition* (Cambridge: Clarke, 2015), 10, esp. n. 56. Yet, given the influence of Meyendorff's early study about Gregory Palamas and his other books on the development (or perhaps even the emergence) of neo-Palamism, such a postulation seems to be unwarranted. Meyendorff is not to be considered as an outsider, but as one of the most important figures within the movement. In the words of Marcus Plested, "Meyendorff is undoubtedly the foremost apostle of neo-Palamism in the twentieth century." See Plested, "Gregory Palamas," in *Wiley Blackwell Companion to Patristics*, ed. Ken Parry (Oxford: Wiley and Sons, 2015), 300.

6. Andrew Louth, *Modern Orthodox Thinkers: From the Philokalia to the Present* (Downers Grove, IL: InterVarsity Press, 2015), 178.

7. Tollefsen, *Activity and Participation*, 201, 211; Marcus Plested, *Orthodox Readings of Aquinas* (Oxford: Oxford University Press, 2012), 31; Plested, "Gregory Palamas," 300; Norman Russell, "The Reception of Palamas in the West Today," Θεολογία 83 (2012): 9; James Buchanan Wallace, *Snatched Into Paradise (2 Cor 12:1–10): Paul's Heavenly Journey in the Context of Early Christian Experience* (Berlin: de Gruyter, 2011), 321; Rowan Williams, "The Philosophical Structures of Palamism," *ECR* 9 (1977): 29; Patrick W. Carey and Joseph T. Lienhard, *Biographical Dictionary of Christian Theologians* (Westport, CT: Greenwood, 2000), 362.

8. Ware, "Debate about Palamism," 45.

reputation as "the finest twentieth-century student of Palamas" and "the most renowned Palamite scholar."[9]

Meyendorff's openness to other Christians and his willingness to dialogue with other traditions is another trait that makes his theology suitable for comparison with the views of a Reformed theologian. Among other contributions to the ecumenical movement, Meyendorff coedited volumes devoted to dialogue between Orthodox and Reformed theologians as well as between Orthodox and Lutheran theologians.[10] To be sure, Meyendorff's readiness to listen to other Christians was accompanied by a strong conviction in the truthfulness of Orthodox Christianity.[11] However, as I noted when defending the choice of Bavinck, faithfulness to one's own tradition is more likely to be a guarantee of, rather than an obstacle to, the earnestness of the dialogue.

Fifth, Meyendorff's personal and scholarly characteristics are worth exploring. A prolific author and a gifted lecturer, Meyendorff exerted profound academic, as well as personal, influence on many students and priests in the Orthodox world, and found admirers far beyond his tradition. Unlike Lossky, whose style was controversial and harsh, Meyendorff has been widely recognized as a moderate theologian with pastoral sensitivity.[12] Scholars have praised his "exceptional intellectual honesty," the "exactness of his scholarship and of his theology," and the clarity of his thought.[13] These characteristics combine to make Meyendorff an eminently suitable dialogue partner.

---

9. Plested, *Orthodox Readings of Aquinas*, 31; Agachi, *Neo-Palamite Synthesis*, 23.

10. John Meyendorff and Joseph McLelland, eds., *The New Man: An Orthodox and Reformed Dialogue* (New Brunswick, NJ: Agora, 1973); Meyendorff and Robert Tobias, eds., *Salvation in Christ: A Lutheran-Orthodox Dialogue* (Minneapolis: Augsburg, 1992).

11. In the words of the Ecumenical Patriarch of Constantinople Bartholomew I, Meyendorff "was a devoted son of the Church, a sterling churchman." See "Pastoral Reflections," in *New Perspectives on Historical Theology: Essays in Memory of John Meyendorff*, ed. Bradley Nassif (Grand Rapids: Eerdmans, 1996), 3.

12. "In his interpretation of the Orthodox faith he was always a 'moderate'" ("Pastoral Reflections," 4). See also Henry Chadwick, foreword to Nassif, *New Perspectives*, ix; Bradley Nassif, introduction to Nassif, *New Perspectives*, xii.

13. John Meyendorff, *The Orthodox Church: Its Past and Its Role in the World Today* (New York: Pantheon, 1962), 211; Lewis Shaw, "John Meyendorff and the Russian Theological Tradition," in Nassif, *New Perspectives*, 26; Joost van Rossum, "Otets Ioann Meyendorf: Zhizn', posvyashchennaya nauke i sluzheniyu Tserkvi," [Father John Meyendorff: A Life Dedicated to Science and Ministry to the Church], in *Paskhal'naya tayna: Stat'i po bogosloviyu* [Paschal Mystery: Theological Articles], by Ioann Meyendorf (Moscow: Eksmo, 2013), vii, xvii. Jaroslav

UNDERLYING CHARACTERISTICS OF MEYENDORFF'S APPROACH

As in the previous chapter, I will not start off directly with Meyendorff's treatment of God's hiddenness and revelation but with a number of characteristics underlying his theology. Speaking of the doctrine of Gregory Palamas, Meyendorff admitted that it had usually meant the distinction between God's essence and his energies, but he cautioned that the main impetus for the formulation of this distinction was Palamas's persuasion of the reality of union with God.[14] It was the real experience of God's grace that was the driving force for the development of the theological language related to God. That is, the doctrine of God was construed in light of a specific anthropology and in a way that safeguards the experience of true union with God, made possible through Jesus Christ. It is quite natural, then, that in the most systematic of Meyendorff's books, *Byzantine Theology: Historical Trends and Doctrinal Themes*, his "doctrinal themes" begin with "Creation" and "Man," continue with Christology, and only then commence a systematic treatment of the Triune God. Meyendorff's historical mindset, and his realization of the importance of anthropology and Christology to the doctrine of God, could hardly permit a different order. In the present chapter, I will follow Meyendorff's order, starting with his theocentric anthropology.[15]

Pelikan notes Meyendorff's "fairness, objectivity and sympathy" as a scholar ("In Memory of John Meyendorff," in Nassif, *New Perspectives*, 8).

14. John Meyendorff, "The Holy Trinity in Palamite Theology," in *Trinitarian Theology East and West: St Thomas Aquinas–St Gregory Palamas*, ed. M. A. Fahey and J. Meyendorff (Brookline, MA: Holy Cross Orthodox Press, 1977), 30; Meyendorff, "Two Visions of the Church: East and West on the Eve of Modern Times," in *Rome, Constantinople, Moscow: Historical and Theological Studies* (Crestwood, NY: St Vladimir's Seminary Press, 1996), 41. For the subsequent analysis, it is important to note that Meyendorff uses the words "nature" and "essence" interchangeably. It is somewhat strange, therefore, that Thomas Hopko differentiates between Meyendorff's "cataphatic affirmations about God's uncreated divine *nature*" and his "apophatic declarations about God's incomprehensible divine *essence*." See Hopko, "John Meyendorff," in *A New Handbook of Christian Theologians*, ed. Donald W. Musser and Joseph L. Price (Nashville: Abingdon, 1996), 302, emphasis added.

15. Van Rossum reports Meyendorff saying that the only reservation he had about Lossky's famous book on mystical theology was that Lossky started it not with the Incarnation, but with apophatic theology ("Otets Ioann Meyendorf," x).

Theocentric Anthropology

While examining the "basic affirmations" of the patristic legacy, Meyendorff mentions theocentric anthropology as the first of them.[16] The theocentricity of humans primarily means that they were created for real participation in the life of God. For Meyendorff, the "autonomy" of humanity is a deficiency and a consequence of sin, while the authentic existence implies the life "in God."[17] In Meyendorff's works, the idea of theocentric anthropology involves multiple aspects and implications, but I will briefly focus on only five topics: the essential presence of the Holy Spirit, the relation between nature and grace, the image and likeness of God in humanity , the openness of humanity to the divine, and the personal character of deification.

According to Meyendorff, humanity participates in God through the Holy Spirit, who belongs to both God and humanity. The main principle of theocentric anthropology is, therefore, that the Holy Spirit inherently belongs to human nature.[18] In the Eastern tradition, the breath of God's life from Genesis 2:7 was understood literally and identified with the Holy Spirit.[19] When expounding theocentric anthropology, Meyendorff usually made special mention of Irenaeus, who "described man as possessing the Holy Spirit of God, as the most essential and highest element of his natural being."[20] Irenaeus's trichotomism meant that humanity is composed of body, soul, and *the Holy Spirit*.[21] In this regard, Meyendorff emphasized that the Pauline use of the same word for the human spirit and the Spirit of God never provoked any problems or debates in the East.[22]

---

16. John Meyendorff, "Theological Education in the Patristic and Byzantine Eras and Its Lessons for Today," *SVTQ* 31 (1987): 205.

17. John Meyendorff, *Byzantine Theology: Historical Trends and Doctrinal Themes* (Fordham, NY: Fordham University Press, 1987), 139; Meyendorff, "Philosophy, Theology, Palamism and Secular Christianity [Reply to P. Sherwood]," *SVTQ* 10 (1966): 205.

18. Ioann Meyendorf, *Vvedenie v svyatootecheskoe bogoslovie* [Introduction to Patristic Theology], 4th ed. (Kiev: Khram prp. Agapita Pecherskogo, 2002), 34. Later in this paragraph Meyendorff even claims that without the Spirit man becomes an animal.

19. Meyendorff, *Byzantine Theology*, 169.

20. Meyendorff, "Theological Education," 205.

21. Meyendorff, *Byzantine Theology*, 138.

22. John Meyendorff, "The Unity of the Church and the Unity of Mankind," in *Living Tradition: Orthodox Witness in the Contemporary World* (Crestwood, NY: St Vladimir's Seminary Press, 1978), 134. See also "Palamas (Grégoire), théologien byzantin, auteur spirituel, archevêque de Thessalonique, 1296-1359," *Dictionnaire de Spiritualité* 12 (1984): 95.

Existence in God means the existence in grace. Meyendorff did not conceive grace as God's reaction to sin, nor as a created gift "given as a *donum superadditum* to an otherwise perfect and immortal being."[23] Rather, grace is part of original human nature; it is the divine life given to humanity or even God himself given to humanity. "The normal human existence as created by God presupposes 'grace.'"[24] Meyendorff was eager to demonstrate what he believed to be a significant difference between West and East: since Augustine, Western theology had been characterized by a dichotomy of nature and grace.[25] This resulted in the concept of humanity as autonomous, whereas in Eastern theology humanity's participation in God's grace was conceived of as natural. To be in God or in grace is the *natural* state of humanity: grace is what "gives man his 'natural' development" and makes him "fully man."[26]

Divine life in humanity is not only a gift but also a *task*: "man is called to *grow* in divine life."[27] Meyendorff did not mind expressing this as the relation between "image" and "likeness," although elsewhere he rightly observed that there was no *consensus patrum* for an exegesis of Genesis 1:26–27 and an understanding of "image" and "likeness."[28] According to Meyendorff, whatever the relation may be, the image and likeness are not to be found in humans *themselves*, nor in their particular qualities, but rather in their entire outward orientation beyond themselves. Since participation in God's grace is not static, but implies further progress toward

---

23. John Meyendorff, "The Significance of the Reformation in the History of Christendom," *Ecumenical Review* 14 (1964): 169.

24. John Meyendorff, "New Life in Christ: Salvation in Orthodox Theology," *Theological Studies* 50 (1989): 488.

25. John Meyendorff, "Orthodox Theology Today," in *Living Tradition*, 169. "The terms 'nature' and 'grace,' when used by Byzantine authors, have a meaning quite different from the Western usage; rather than being in direct opposition, the terms 'nature' and 'grace' express a dynamic, living, and necessary relationship between God and man" (Meyendorff, *Byzantine Theology*, 138). "This does not imply, however, that Palamas understands deification in Augustinian terms, implying a strict opposition between 'nature' and 'grace.'" See John Meyendorff, "The 'Defense of the Holy Hesychasts' by St Gregory Palamas," in *The Byzantine Legacy in the Orthodox Church* (Crestwood, NY: St Vladimir's Seminary Press, 1982), 188. See also Meyendorff, *Byzantine Theology*, 2.

26. Meyendorff, *Byzantine Theology*, 138, 139.

27. Meyendorff, *Byzantine Theology*, 139, emphasis original.

28. John Meyendorff, *Christ in Eastern Christian Thought* (Crestwood, NY: St Vladimir's Seminary Press, 1975), 114.

godlikeness, humans are "open beings"—open in an *upward* direction, where their fullness and destiny lies.

The idea of openness is crucial for Meyendorff's doctrines of humanity, Christ, and God. In anthropology it is related to the dynamic character of participation in God and to the capability of human beings to transcend themselves. This capability is a sign of "anthropological theocentrism" and enables humanity "to reach outside of the created level."[29] Without it, Meyendorff argued, an encounter between God and humanity would be impossible.[30] Humanity's destination in God transcends the created world; the understanding of humanity as the image of God implies that humans are similar to the Creator and are called to create and govern over the world in cooperation with God.

According to Meyendorff, the ability to transcend nature is personalistic.[31] Just as the divine *person* can "go beyond" divine nature and become that which he was not before, so also the human *person* can transcend the limitations of human nature and become divine.[32] Commenting on the words of Palamas that the apostle Paul "was only a creature, ... [but] he became uncreated by Grace," Meyendorff notes: "it is the life of Paul, *as a person*, that acquires an uncreated character, by receiving grace or a Divine energy, which is nothing else as [*sic*] the life of God."[33] Deification, therefore, is always "a personal, or hypostatic, possibility," when a human being

---

29. Ioann Meyendorf, "Svyatoy Grigoriy Palama i ego mesto v Predanii Tserkvi" [Saint Gregory Palamas and His Place in Church Tradition], in *Pravoslavie v sovremennom mire* [Orthodoxy in the Modern World] (Moscow: Put', 1997), 162; Meyendorff, *Byzantine Theology*, 13. Man is "called to overcome constantly his own created limitations" (4) and "possesses the natural property of transcending himself and of reaching the divine" (140). See also Meyendorff, "'Defense of the Holy Hesychasts,'" 183; Meyendorff, "New Life," 497; Meyendorff, "Palamas (Grégoire)," 92.

30. Meyendorff, *Byzantine Theology*, 13.

31. Meyendorff, "'Defense of the Holy Hesychasts,'" 184.

32. John Meyendorff, "Reply to Jürgen Moltmann's 'The Unity of the Triune God,'" *SVTQ* 28 (1984): 188. Although Meyendorff presents the incarnation of the Son and the divinization of humankind as analogous with respect to the relation between person and nature, they still have important differences. The incarnation implies that the divine Person assumes another (human) nature without ceasing to be divine and without changing his divine nature. If the divinization of humankind were really analogous or even symmetrical, it would imply that the human person assumes another (divine) nature without ceasing to be human and without changing his human nature. Meyendorff, of course, would not approve of this reading.

33. John Meyendorff, "Doctrine of Grace in St. Gregory Palamas," *SVTQ* 2 (1954): 24, emphasis added.

"transcends natural limitations and communes in divine life."[34] Humans become divine *as persons*, reaching *beyond* their human nature, because they are not strictly contained in it.[35]

Deification in Jesus Christ

As indicated above, the ability of humans to transcend themselves is a condition of their meeting with God. Meyendorff ascribed the same condition to God: to encounter his creatures, he must come out of his divine nature. An encounter is possible, therefore, because of two *ecstatic* movements: God steps out of his unapproachable essence, and humans step out of their limited nature. The encounter is fully realized in the person of Jesus Christ. "In His divine hypostasis the gulf created by the Fall between God and man has been bridged forever."[36] Although Meyendorff here links Christ's mediating office with the consequences of sin, elsewhere he emphasizes that the reason for the gulf is deeper than the fall. The gulf between God and humanity is that between Creator and creature and *necessarily* separates them.[37]

34. Meyendorff, "New Life," 497. See also Meyendorff, "'Defense of the Holy Hesychasts,'" 183.

35. "Each human person, as person, becomes able to transcend the limitations of created human nature." See John Meyendorff, "Continuities and Discontinuities in Byzantine Religious Thought," *Dumbarton Oaks Papers* 47 (1993): 75. It is difficult to escape the impression that some tension exists in Meyendorff's constructions. Trying to maintain faithfulness to his tradition, Meyendorff speaks of "natural deification" (*Christ in Eastern Christian Thought*, 150) and "deified human nature" (86, 160). Moreover, human nature was created to participate in God's uncreated life (79), and in the hypostatic union of Christ it acquired divinity and uncreatedness so that, being in Christ, we also acquire uncreated nature (*Vvedenie v svyatootecheskoe bogoslovie*, 329). But attempting to strengthen the existential emphasis in Eastern theology, Meyendorff presents the deification of humanity as the deification of human *persons* that overcome the limitations of human *nature*. In deification, human persons reach to God "*beyond human nature*" ("Continuities and Discontinuities," 75). Meyendorff's personalism, therefore, makes *natural* deification unnecessary. Why does humankind require a deification of their *nature*, if as *persons* they can transcend it? More pointedly: if deification *demands* such transcendence, it implies that deification of human nature is not only unnecessary, but impossible. Meyendorff's conviction that human nature was originally created with the possibility of overcoming itself and that this is even the *telos* of human nature does not sufficiently resolve the tension.

36. Meyendorff, "Significance of the Reformation," 171.

37. Meyendorff speaks of "l'abîme qui sépare nécéssairement le Créateur et les creatures." See Jean Meyendorff, "Le dogme eucharistique dans les controverses théologiques du XIVe siècle," Γρηγόροις ὁ Παλαμᾶς 42 (1959): 93.

Christ has bridged the gulf by assuming human nature and deifying it. In the incarnation, the hypostasis of the Son of God, in addition to his divine attributes, assumed the attributes of human nature but not a human person. Meyendorff emphasized that Christ does not possess a human hypostasis: his humanity is en-hypostatized in the divine Logos.[38] It is the divine *hypostasis* that is the source of divine life and deification. Human nature is restored, glorified, and made imperishable only on account of the hypostatic union with the Logos. However, deification did not occur in the incarnation itself: Meyendorff protested (without explicitly mentioning Bulgakov but probably having his theology in mind) against the view that "the Incarnation was simply the manifestation of a pre-existing God-manhood of the Logos."[39] Deification in Christ was neither automatic nor mechanical, but included struggle and was achieved only through the death and resurrection of Jesus.

According to Meyendorff, Christ did not assume merely an abstract nature, but a sinful and mortal nature corrupted by the fall. Neither was it an individual human nature, but rather humanity in its fullness, incorporating all human beings without exception.[40] Not all people, however, are deified. For us, deification is only accessible in the humanity of Christ, which, having been penetrated with divine life through the hypostatic union, becomes *itself* the source of divine life and light and communicates this life to those who are "in Christ."[41] We can share in Christ's glorified humanity by way of a free personal decision and through participation in the sacraments.[42]

Meyendorff carefully distinguished between the deification of Christ's humanity and our deification. Christ's humanity is deified by virtue of the hypostatic union with the divine Logos, and such hypostatic deification is by definition inaccessible for people, who are *human* hypostases. However, while humans cannot be deified through the hypostatic union, they can

38. Meyendorff, *Byzantine Theology*, 159, 163.

39. Meyendorff, "New Life," 495.

40. John Meyendorff, "Christ's Humanity: The Paschal Mystery," *SVTQ* 31 (1987): 37.

41. Meyendorff, *Christ in Eastern Christian Thought*, 78. See also Meyendorff, "'Defense of the Holy Hesychasts,'" 190.

42. Meyendorff, "New Life," 492.

be deified by grace, or by participation.[43] We are united to God neither by nature (because then we would be equal to the three persons of the Trinity), nor by hypostasis (because only "the man Jesus is God hypostatically"), but by grace.[44] Although Meyendorff thought it necessary to add certain qualifications to the anthropological maximalism of Maximus and Palamas (who state that the saints become "uncreated" and "are by God made gods without beginning or end"), he accepted the basic concept that underpins such phrases: "God became man so that man might become God," and "what God is by nature, we become by grace."[45] "In Jesus Christ, God and man are *one*."[46]

One with God

Meyendorff maintained that the Christian gospel as understood in the Greek patristic tradition is a message of deification—a message about the inclusion of people into the very life of God.[47] Life in God does not simply mean that humanity's life is directed by God, transformed by him, and conformed to his will; rather, it means—quite realistically—that "the life of God becomes his life, and God's existence his existence."[48] "It is the divine way ["*la vie*," "life"] itself, infinite and uncreated, which appears to us, and *really becomes ours*."[49]

The significance and beauty of this ontological union are so great that Meyendorff *contrasted* it with ethical discipleship, reflective practice, and

43. Meyendorff, *Christ in Eastern Christian Thought*, 78.

44. Meyendorff, *Byzantine Theology*, 164; Meyendorf, "Svyatoy Grigoriy Palama," 166.

45. Meyendorff, *Study of Gregory Palamas*, 177; Meyendorff, "Significance of the Reformation," 171. Meyendorff comments that "to be 'uncreated' does not mean that one ceases to be a creature, but that one is transported into a different state, and that one gratuitously acquires a condition fundamentally foreign to that of nature, and that condition is the divine life" (*Study of Gregory Palamas*, 178). By using the words "without beginning," Maximus and Palamas, according to Meyendorff, "simply wanted to express the full reality of salvation and deification accomplished in Christ" (178).

46. Meyendorff, *Byzantine Theology*, 152; emphasis in original.

47. John Meyendorff, "Mount Athos in the Fourteenth Century: Spiritual and Intellectual Legacy," *Dumbarton Oaks Papers* 42 (1988): 163.

48. Meyendorff, *Study of Gregory Palamas*, 175.

49. Meyendorff, *Study of Gregory Palamas*, emphasis original. French original: Meyendorff, *Introduction* à l'étude, 244.

forensic justification.[50] Becoming one with God is far superior to any moral, cognitive, or juridical aspects of salvation. Meyendorff also contrasts Old Testament legalism and autonomy with the New Testament "identification between Christ and the community."[51] Only "after the coming of Christ ... God enters into immediate communion with humanity."[52] According to Meyendorff, in the old dispensation, Israel and God were two "autonomous" parties of the covenant instituted by God and conditioned by Israel's obedience. In the new dispensation, however, there are no longer two parties that are "external" to each other. Rather, the union between God and humanity in Christ replaces the old categories that were mere shadows of the realities to come.[53] God no longer exists somewhere "out there"; instead, he is *within* us, so that we should seek God's Spirit, light, and kingdom within our bodies, sanctified by the sacraments.[54]

The central role of participation in God evidences itself not only in soteriology but also in epistemology. A key premise of Orthodox theology and Meyendorff as its representative is the belief that one cannot know God without participating in him, without having communion with him, without joining with him, and without *becoming one with him*. This means that the knowing subject does not remain exterior to the object known: rather, the two become fully united.[55] This knowledge not only *includes* experience, it *is* experience. Meyendorff emphasized that the term "theology" was used in the early church in the sense of contemplation of the

50. Meyendorff, *Byzantine Theology*, 164; Meyendorff, "Christian Theology," 66; John Meyendorff, "Humanity: 'Old' and 'New' - Anthropological Considerations," in Meyendorff and Tobias, *Salvation in Christ*, 62.

51. John Meyendorff, "Historical Relativism and Authority in Christian Dogma," in *Living Tradition*, 31.

52. Meyendorff, "'Defense of the Holy Hesychasts,'" 193.

53. "In both the Pauline and Johannine understanding of the New Covenant there is in Jesus Christ personal and direct encounter between God and man, ... an encounter which transcends and replaces the legal and external categories of 'commandment-obedience-faithfulness' of the Law. ... God is not simply *speaking* to the community any more, while remaining essentially external to it. He is *present* through the Spirit in the community" (Meyendorff, "Historical Relativism and Authority," 30, emphasis original).

54. Meyendorff, *Study of Gregory Palamas*, 175. See also John Meyendorff, *St Gregory Palamas and Orthodox Spirituality*, trans. Adele Fiske (Crestwood, NY: St Vladimir's Seminary Press, 1998), 107.

55. Meyendorff, *Gregory Palamas*, 116.

Holy Trinity rather than intellectual reasoning about it.[56] It was "a vision experienced by the saints" rather than "a rational deduction from 'revealed' premises."[57]

Meyendorff's epistemology was rooted in the old distinction between two modes of cognition and two corresponding cognitive faculties. Intellectual cognition with its faculty, the διάνοια, refers to the discursive reason that enables men to know *about* things and analyze them logically by formulating concepts. This cognition is rational, natural, and creaturely. Fundamentally different, however, is mystical cognition with its faculty, the νοῦς. This cognition is experiential, spiritual, immediate, and intuitive. Although the νοῦς is the faculty of mystical knowledge, it does not "produce" this knowledge itself, but only enables humans to receive this knowledge as a gift of deifying grace. The νοῦς signifies man's *capacity* for self-transcendence, and only through such self-transcendence can man receive mystical cognition.[58]

The vision of God attained via deification therefore transcends intellection and sense perception. Meyendorff warned against identifying it with any form of *natural* vision, even those bearing a mystical character.[59] "Vision and communion are not forms of natural created knowledge, but they are 'life in Christ.'"[60] The contemplation of God is impossible without transcending the limitations of human nature: the goal of our salvation is

56. Meyendorff, *Byzantine Theology*, 180; John Meyendorff, "Byzantium as Center of Theological Thought in the Christian East," in *Schools of Thought in the Christian Tradition*, ed. P. Henry (Philadelphia: Fortress, 1984), 68. At the same time, Meyendorff notes that Palamas contrasted "theology" with "vision" (and with "contemplation") and understood the former as "talking about God" and the latter as "a meeting with God" (*Study of Gregory Palamas*, 168).

57. Meyendorff, *Byzantine Theology*, 8–9.

58. In his work on Palamas, Meyendorff admits that this notion was borrowed by the fathers from Plato: "Palamas takes up again the Platonic doctrine that the mind (νοῦς) is the part of the composite human being which is naturally able to surpass itself" (*Study of Gregory Palamas*, 165). In Meyendorff's own interpretation, however, the νοῦς "is not so much a 'part' of man as the ability which man possesses to transcend himself in order to participate in God" (*Byzantine Theology*, 142). The desire to avoid identifying the νοῦς with any *part* of human nature is a sign of the more personalistic approach of Meyendorff. No wonder he continues with a characteristic citation from Vladimir Lossky: "The spirit (*nous*) in human nature corresponds most nearly to the *person*" (142).

59. In discussing Palamas's theology, Meyendorff observes that he was "particularly concerned with one possible misunderstanding: the identification of the Christian experience with either intellectual knowledge, or any form of physical, or mystical—but natural—vision" ("'Defense of the Holy Hesychasts,'" 187).

60. Meyendorff, "Byzantium as Center," 70.

"to make us contemplate God, *that is to say* to surpass ourselves."[61] Elsewhere, Meyendorff maintains that the vision of God implies that humanity transcends its creaturely existence.[62]

Meyendorff admitted that some knowledge of God may be acquired through the created realm. But such "natural" knowledge is merely an indirect knowledge of God's *manifestations* and *works* in nature rather than a direct knowledge of God *himself*.[63] In order to see and know God *himself*, the human senses must be transformed and the human intellect must be illuminated. Meyendorff even argues that "God Himself united Himself to man, communicating to him *the knowledge he has of Himself*." While creaturely knowledge presupposes a distance between the knower and the known, mystical knowledge is immediate and surpasses all distance.[64] Being filled with God's light, the saint becomes, himself, God's light and contemplates God in his transformed self. The old maxim "God can be seen only by God" here means that one must become God to see God. "No creaturely being has ever seen God," but the deified saints become *un*created, become Spirit, and thus in Spirit they see God.[65]

In Palamite theology, this oneness bore a material or corporeal character and often pointed to the Eucharist, in which Christ "becomes one single body with us."[66] As Meyendorff puts it, "The hesychasts do not seek God outside of themselves, ... but they find him in themselves, in their own bodies," which are one with Christ's body by virtue of the Eucharist.[67] Seeking God in himself, therefore, the saint does not seek his own "I," but Christ. This affirmation of matter played a major role in the hesychast spirituality and was approved by Meyendorff as a sort of "Christian materialism."[68] Since hesychasm did not ignore or disparage the body but rather

61. Meyendorff, *Study of Gregory Palamas*, 165, emphasis added.

62. "'The vision of God' presupposes ... a going-out from creaturely existience itself" (Meyendorf, "Svyatoy Grigoriy Palama," 162).

63. Meyendorf, "Svyatoy Grigoriy Palama," 160.

64. Meyendorff, *Gregory Palamas*, 116, emphasis added.

65. Meyendorff, "Doctrine of Grace," 24.

66. Meyendorff, *Study of Gregory Palamas*, 151.

67. Jean Meyendorff, "Le thème du 'retour en soi' dans la doctrine palamite du XIVe siècle," in *Byzantine Hesychasm: Historical, Theological and Social Problems* (London: Variorum Reprints, 1974), 200. "Ever since the incarnation, there has been no need to seek God outside of ourselves as He dwells within us" (Meyendorf, *Vvedenie v svyatootecheskoe bogoslovie*, 326).

68. Meyendorff, *Study of Gregory Palamas*, 156.

affirmed the goodness of the material, it was, Meyendorff contended, fundamentally different from Platonic spiritualism.

Meyendorff was also eager to show that Eastern spirituality (including hesychasm) excluded any form of esotericism, subjectivism, or elitism. Christ is present in Christians objectively and sacramentally and is common to all of them. Meyendorff agreed that Eastern theology may be called mystical, provided this mysticism is understood as associated not with "emotional individualism" but with "a continuous communion with the Spirit who dwells in the whole Church."[69] Although it does require a radical spiritual conversion, the mystical vision of God is not an exceptional gift intended only for individual monks but an experience open to all Christians. The most important point for Palamas's defense of hesychasm and for Meyendorff's defense of Palamism is that union with God is not only *possible* but *real* and *objective*.[70] The unity of God and humanity by grace is as real as the unity of the divinity and humanity in the person of Christ.

Trying to emphasize the fundamental difference between the knowledge of God and other kinds of knowledge, Meyendorff—following pseudo-Dionysius and Palamas's reception of him—speaks of "joining with the Unknowable," "communion with the Unknowable," and, in more personalistic terms, "a positive meeting with the Unknown." Encounter and union with God implies a contemplation that is "greater than knowledge," or maybe something that is not even knowledge at all.[71] Such formulations do not merely mean that God is beyond knowledge *in his essence*, because in his essence he is also beyond communion, contemplation, and meeting.[72] Rather, they point to the uniqueness of the knowledge of God and to the primacy of ontological (and, especially in Meyendorff's case,

69. Meyendorff, *Byzantine Theology*, 14.

70. Meyendorff, *Christ in Eastern Christian Thought*, 128.

71. Meyendorf, "Svyatoy Grigoriy Palama," 163; Meyendorff, "'Defense of the Holy Hesychasts,'" 184; Meyendorff, *Byzantine Theology*, 13; Meyendorff, *Study of Gregory Palamas*, 168.

72. To be sure, sometimes Meyendorff uses similar formulations, but implies the distinction between God's essence and energy. Referring to Simeon the New Theologian, for instance, he writes that the essence of Christian experience is "communion with the Incommunicable One and the knowledge of the Unknowable One, made possible by the Incarnation of the Word" (*Gregory Palamas*, 48).

existential) categories in the Orthodox understanding of humanity's relation to God. "The knowledge of the incommunicable God" would be nonsense for Meyendorff, while "communion with the unknowable God" is postulated by him without hesitation. God is ultimately unknown to reason, but he is accessible through participation.[73]

Taking all this into consideration, one is tempted to ask: If in mystical union humanity is one with God to such an extent that God's life becomes his life, God's existence his existence, God's light his light, God's spirit his spirit, and that humanity becomes "uncreated" and "unoriginated"—does this not imply a blurring of the distinction between the human and the divine and an absorption of humanity into God? Remarkably, Meyendorff himself raised a similar question, but avoided giving a direct answer.[74] However, the careful reader may discern his answer from other writings, in which Meyendorff tries to show that Orthodox doctrine does not lead to such conclusions. First, he insists that "communion with God does not diminish or destroy humanity, but makes it fully human."[75] As we have seen, the central idea of theocentric anthropology is that human destiny is to become God. Becoming God is to be considered as the fulfillment of humanity rather than its abrogation. Being deified, humans receive an uncreated mode of existence without ceasing to be created. Second, although in deification humanity really becomes God, it becomes God by grace. What God is by nature, humanity becomes by grace. But is not "what God is by nature" the same as his very nature? No, it is not. For Meyendorff "what God is by nature" is rather his *life*, which—by grace—is fully shared

---

73. It is worth noting how Meyendorff describes the views of pseudo-Dionysius: "Dionysius specifically rejects Origen's notion of the knowledge of God 'by essence,' since *there cannot be 'knowledge' of God*. For knowledge can apply only to 'beings,' and God is above being and superior to all opposition between being and non-being. With God, *there can be a 'union,'* however: the supreme end of human existence; but *this union is 'ignorance' rather than knowledge*, for it presupposes detachment from all activity of the senses or of the intellect, since the intellect is applicable only to created existence" (*Byzantine Theology*, 27, emphasis added). Such description of pseudo-Dionysius's views resonates with the views of Meyendorff himself. It is not surprising that Meyendorff finishes the paragraph about pseudo-Dionysius with the words that "the God of Dionysius is again the living God of the Bible," and "Dionysius will provide the basis for further positive developments of Christian thought" (28).

74. Meyendorff, *Introduction* à l'étude, 252. The paragraph in question is not available in the English edition.

75. Meyendorff, *Byzantine Theology*, 39.

with human beings.[76] Finally, and most importantly, God and humanity are united without intermingling because God's essence remains inaccessible. Humanity is called to participate in God without "confusion between his nature and that of God."[77] God is communicable, but he is not communicable as to his essence. In Meyendorff's view, it is primarily this idea that protects Orthodoxy from the accusation of having pantheistic tendencies.[78]

GOD HIDDEN

God's Absolute Transcendence

Meyendorff believed in the existence of a coherent theological tradition consisting of the Cappadocians (whom Meyendorff normally presented as a single voice), John Chrysostom, pseudo-Dionysius, Maximus, and—reaching its zenith—Palamas. Noting that the entire doctrine of God in Greek patristics "is based upon the notion of the absolute transcendence of divine nature," Meyendorff adds that "there is an absolute unanimity in patristic tradition for the affirmation of this absolute transcendence."[79] Meyendorff contrasted this consistent tradition with the alleged vestiges of Neoplatonism in the East and with essentialism (also based on Neoplatonism) in the West.

The word "absolute" in combination with "transcendence" may seem redundant, but it is not difficult to understand why Meyendorff needed it. As we saw above, he extensively used the word "transcendence" and its paronyms in his explanations of the union between God and humanity . This union is possible when humans transcend their nature and God, on his part, also transcends his nature. Thus, the capacity of self-transcendence allows

76. Meyendorff, "Significance of the Reformation," 171. "Of course, human participation ... in the life of the Trinity does not mean pantheism. The gulf between the Creator and the creatures remains. It is being bridged by *divine* love (or 'grace,' or 'energy'), not by human 'created' achievement or natural merit." See John Meyendorff, "Theosis in the Eastern Christian Tradition," in *Christian Spirituality: Post-Reformation and Modern*, ed. Louis Dupré and Don E. Saliers (New York: Crossroad, 1989), 476.

77. Meyendorff, *Christ in Eastern Christian Thought*, 126. See also Meyendorff, *Study of Gregory Palamas*, 183–84.

78. Thanks to this idea, "the extreme realism of Palamas in his doctrine concerning deification does not lead him to assert a more or less pantheistic fusion of the human and the divine" (Meyendorff, *Study of Gregory Palamas*, 218).

79. Meyendorff, "Christian Theology," 61–62.

God and humanity to meet personally outside their natures. "*Absolute* transcendence," however, refers only to the divine nature and means that it always remains unapproachable and unparticipable. Whatever capacity for self-transcendence humanity may have, it does not allow it to reach the divine essence, because it is *absolutely* transcendent.

Explaining the meaning and significance of the absolute transcendence of God's essence, Meyendorff often alluded to two controversies in the early church. First, he liked to contrast Origen's and Athanasius's doctrines of creation.[80] In Origen's system, God is the Creator *by his nature*: he creates "necessarily" and thus neither is independent of creation nor transcends it. Since it belongs to his nature to create and this nature is unchanging, God has always been creating: creation is coeternal with God, and its eternity is ontologically indistinguishable from his eternity. Creation is a necessary expression and "continuation" of God's very essence. These views of Origen, Meyendorff explains, were rejected by Athanasius, who differentiated between God's nature and his will. By nature, God is not Creator but Father: he generates the Son and the Spirit by his *nature*, while creation is an act of his *will*. God is not dependent on creation and could have chosen not to create it. This allowed Athanasius to preserve God's aseity, as well as his transcendence and superiority over creation. It is in this context that Meyendorff also emphasizes that God cannot be reduced to his nature: "Because *God is what He is*, He is not determined or in any way limited in what He *does*, not even by His own essence and being."[81] Creation as an act of God's will shows that God can transcend his inaccessible nature and come out of it.

Discussing "the inaccessibility of the essence of God," Meyendorff states that its affirmation "is only another way of saying that He is the Creator *ex nihilo*: anything which exists outside of God exists only through His 'will' or 'energy,' and can participate in His life only as a result of His will or 'grace.'"[82] Elsewhere he says that "God's transcendence is a logical

---

80. See, *inter alia*, Meyendorff, *Byzantine Theology*, 128–30; Meyendorf, *Vvedenie v svyatootecheskoe bogoslovie*, 96–99, 115–17; Meyendorff, "Christ's Humanity," 9; Meyendorff, "New Life," 489–90.

81. Meyendorff, *Byzantine Theology*, 130, emphasis original.

82. Meyendorff, *Byzantine Theology*, 77.

consequence of the Biblical account of creation *ex nihilo*."[83] Meyendorff, however, did not find it necessary to offer any arguments as to why the doctrine of creation *requires* the inaccessibility of the essence of God. That is, he did not explain why God could not create—by his will—in such a way that his creation could participate in the divine essence; much as it participates in the divine life, according to Meyendorff. Meyendorff's schema allowed only two options: either creation originates from God's nature and would therefore be indistinguishable from God (pantheism), or it originates from God's will and is therefore totally separated from God's nature. "Divine essence and human nature can *never* mix or be confounded or be participated by each other."[84] Having described the distinction between God's will and nature as demonstrated in the act of creation, Meyendorff concludes: "Divine 'nature' and created 'nature' are, therefore, separate and totally dissimilar modes of existence."[85]

Another historical controversy, which received much attention in Meyendorff's explanations of God's absolute transcendence, is the Cappadocians' polemics against Eunomius's epistemology.[86] According to Eunomius, the human mind has a divine origin and, having been purified and exalted, is capable of direct knowledge of God. Eunomius further claimed that the most suitable term for designating God's essence is "unbegottenness." By way of this term, God's essence can be known by people, because the term refers to God as he really is.[87] The Cappadocians rejected this "rationalistic optimism"[88] and, according to Meyendorff, claimed instead that God's essence is totally unknowable and inaccessible to the human mind. This inaccessibility is a result of the abyss between God's nature and creatures rather than a consequence of sin or imperfection. It

83. Meyendorff, *Orthodox Church*, 176. Also: "the notion of the absolute transcendence of divine nature … is implied by the doctrine of creation *ex nihilo*, from nothing" (Meyendorff, "Christian Theology," 61).

84. Meyendorff, "Significance of the Reformation," 169, emphasis original.

85. Meyendorff, *Byzantine Theology*, 130.

86. See, *inter alia*, Meyendorff, *Byzantine Theology*, 11, 77, 185, 225; Meyendorf, *Vvedenie v svyatootecheskoe bogoslovie*, 145–49, 162–68; Meyendorff, *Christ in Eastern Christian Thought*, 93–94; Meyendorff, "Christian Theology," 61–62.

87. John Behr, *The Nicene Faith*, part 2 (Crestwood, NY: St Vladimir's Seminary Press, 2004), 273.

88. Meyendorf, *Vvedenie v svyatootecheskoe bogoslovie*, 162.

implies "an *absolute* transcendence of the divine essence" and reflects "the unknowability of God *himself*, who is absolutely transcendent because he is Sovereign and Creator."[89]

The Cappadocians, Meyendorff added, excluded the possibility of identifying God's essence with any human concept. Such identification would be nothing short of idolatry because it would equate God with a creaturely reality.[90] Describing the reaction of the Cappadocians to Eunomius's doctrine, Meyendorff asserts that "any positive definition of God implies his identification with something." Thus, it is clear that since identification of God's essence with anything creaturely is impossible and even blasphemous, a positive definition of God's essence is also impossible. God's knowability would lead to God's impoverishment and limitedness: "A known God is necessarily limited," Meyendorff contends.[91] Here again Meyendorff recognized only two alternatives: either God's nature is *fully* accessible and *identified* with a creaturely reality, or it is *totally* unknowable, inexpressible, and incommunicable.

Opposing Forces: Neoplatonism and Western Essentialism

Though Meyendorff put special emphasis on Origen and Eunomius in his historical and dogmatic deliberations on the doctrine of God's unknowability, he also pointed to broader philosophical traditions that stood in opposition to the Orthodox one. As noted above, Meyendorff contrasted the tradition of Athanasius, the Cappadocians, and later Eastern theologians with what he called Neoplatonism and essentialism. The choice of these terms and the meaning Meyendorff assigned to them will be clearer if one takes into consideration his general theological interests. First, Meyendorff was eager to demonstrate that the Orthodox tradition, having adopted some terms and ideas from Greek philosophy, nevertheless preserved its uniqueness and faithfulness to the apostolic faith. Although the Greek fathers selectively employed the philosophical concepts of that time, seeking to make the Christian gospel relevant to their contemporaries,

89. Meyendorff, *Christ in Eastern Christian Thought*, 93–94, emphasis original.

90. Meyendorf, "Svyatoy Grigoriy Palama," 161.

91. Meyendorff, *Christ in Eastern Christian Thought*, 93.

they did not take up these concepts uncritically, but radically transformed them by endowing them with new content derived from the biblical witness.[92] Consequently, in his treatment of God's transcendence Meyendorff sought to emphasize points that, in his view, highlighted crucial differences between Greek philosophy (in particular, Neoplatonism) and Orthodoxy.

Second, Meyendorff shared the age-old tendency of Orthodox theologians to focus on the distinctiveness and superiority of their tradition in comparison to the Western one.[93] This tendency increased during and after the Reformation, when Orthodoxy struggled against Western influences, but it especially came to the fore in the twentieth century, when Orthodox émigré theologians felt the necessity to prove to the Western world that their faith was not "Catholicism without a pope" but rather a rich and unique tradition with its own history, identity, and theological emphases.[94] If Meyendorff's account of Augustine, Aquinas, or Reformation theologians seems to suffer from oversimplification, schematization, and even tendentiousness, this should not be attributed to a lack of proper understanding or the desire to misconstrue Western theology but rather to his attempts to emphasize—as strongly as possible—the differences between East and West.

The two polemical motifs came together when Meyendorff claimed that it was Western, and not Eastern, theology that—mainly through Augustine—came under the significant influence of Greek philosophy. In

92. Meyendorff constantly criticized "dead traditionalism" and "formal conservatism," which repeat old formulas without attempting to be relevant or to express the true faith in new cultural conditions. He called instead for the creative development of Orthodox theology and emphasized that even Christ himself, as well as the apostles and the fathers, developed their theology in "dialoguing with outsiders" ("Orthodox Theology," 185). The fathers' example, therefore, was important for Meyendorff's own theological aspirations: it helped him to demonstrate that engagement with contemporary philosophy and culture does not necessarily harm the Christian message. See also the observations about Meyendorff's attitude to tradition in Timothy (Kallistos) Ware, "'Following the Holy Fathers': Is There a Future for Patristic Studies?," in *A Celebration of Living Theology: A Festschrift in Honour of Andrew Louth*, ed. Justin Mihoc and Leonard Aldea (New York: Bloomsbury, 2014), 221–22.

93. Vera Shevzov, "The Burdens of Tradition: Orthodox Constructions of the West in Russia (Late Nineteenth-Early Twentieth cc.)," in *Orthodox Constructions of the West*, ed. George E. Demacopoulos and Aristotle Papanikolaou (Fordham, NY: Fordham University Press, 2013), 83–101.

94. John Behr, "Calling upon God the Father: Augustine and the Legacy of Nicea," in Demacopoulos and Papanikolaou, *Orthodox Readings of Augustine*, 153–54.

Meyendorff's view, Augustine, unlike the Cappadocians, could not discard his philosophical assumptions, and his reasoning was "always based on Neoplatonism."[95] As for theology originating in the East and West at a later date, Meyendorff observed the same contrast: the Byzantine tradition "took a much more negative stand toward Greek philosophy than the West ever did," while Western Christianity quite uncritically accepted Augustine's philosophical views.[96]

Meyendorff's interpretation of the Neoplatonic views of God's incomprehensibility is already evident in his early work on Gregory Palamas, where he draws a distinction between two currents in Eastern apophatic theology. "The first, directly dependent on Neo-Platonism, conceives the transcendence and unknowability of God as a consequence of the *limitations of the created mind*," and affirms the possibility of knowledge of the divine being if one detaches oneself from created things. By contrast, the second current, "while keeping the universally accepted Neo-Platonic vocabulary, asserts divine transcendence as a *property of God*," denies all human possibility of reaching it.[97] The second position, according to Meyendorff, was characteristic of Palamas and the entire tradition he

95. John Meyendorff, "Greek Philosophy and Christian Theology in the Early Church," in *Catholicity and the Church* (Crestwood, NY: St Vladimir's Seminary Press, 1983), 36. The contrast Meyendorff drew between the Cappadocians and Augustine was sometimes very straightforward and even somewhat naive: "In his system, Augustine proceeds from the premises of Greek philosophy, which was basically essentialist—in contrast to the Eastern fathers, for whom the starting point of all theologizing has always been the Truth of revelation." See Ioann Meyendorf, "U istokov spora o Filioque" [The Origins of the Filioque Controversy], in *Paskhal'naya tayna*, 307.

96. Meyendorff, *Byzantine Theology*, 64; Meyendorff, "Greek Philosophy and Christian Theology," 38. Meyendorff's interpretation finds some support also in Reformed circles: "Paradoxically, John Meyendorff could possibly be proved right when he charges that it has been Western Christianity, not the East (despite general opinion to the contrary), that has been more influenced by Platonism precisely due to this inattentiveness to sources such as Augustine. Meyendorff argues that the church fathers were more 'consistently aware of the incompatibility between ancient Greek philosophy and the gospel' due to their closeness to it." See Julie Canlis, *Calvin's Ladder: A Spiritual Theology of Ascent and Ascension* (Grand Rapids: Eerdmans, 2010), 36. For an alternative reading of Augustine's Trinitarian theology, which rejects a decisive influence of Neoplatonism on Augustine and places him instead in the context of Latin theology of the late fourth and early fifth centuries that strove to express the Nicene faith, see esp. Michel René Barnes, "Rereading Augustine's Theology of the Trinity," in *The Trinity: An Interdisciplinary Symposium on Trinity*, ed. Stephen T. Davis, Daniel Kendall, SJ, and Gerald O'Collins, SJ (Oxford: Oxford University Press, 1999), 145–76.

97. Meyendorff, *Study of Gregory Palamas*, 203, emphasis original.

represented, whereas all of his adversaries—each in his own way—represented the first current of thought.[98]

In his later works Meyendorff repeats variations of this thesis in other words. The Neoplatonic negative method only leads to the concept of God's simplicity, whereas the Orthodox position affirms God's "absolute transcendence." The latter implies that no negative or positive statements whatsoever can be applied to God's nature.[99] In Neoplatonism, God's essence "is accessible for spiritual contemplation." The Neoplatonic God is "not incomprehensible *per se*, but due to our fallen nature. His transcendence is relative."[100] More specifically, God's incomprehensibility is "the result of the fallen character of the soul and, in particular, of its union with a material body."[101] According to Neoplatonism as Meyendorff depicts it, once humanity purifies itself and rids itself of its "fallenness," it will be able to contemplate the essence of God and to be united with it. In Orthodox theology, on the contrary, even "redeemed, purified, deified humanity is unable to perceive God's essence."[102] Meyendorff owed this interpretation of Neoplatonism to Lossky, who tried to draw "a line of demarcation between Christian mysticism and the mystical philosophy of the neoplatonists" and, more specifically, to prove that despite the same vocabulary, resemblances between pseudo-Dionysius and Plotinus are only superficial.[103] According to Lossky and Meyendorff, by confessing the absolute

98. It is proper to ask, however, what the real difference is between God's unknowability as a property of God and as a consequence of creaturely limitations. Is it not the same, just expressed from the divine and human perspectives respectively? R. Williams correctly argues that those who deny the statement that God's unknowability is caused by the limitations of our finite minds confuse this statement with the idea (not seriously defended by any Christian theologian) that this unknowability is due to only accidental limitations of creaturely minds ("Philosophical Structures," 41). In any case, it seems to be clear what Meyendorff intended to achieve by drawing this distinction: he sought to clearly secure the transcendence and unknowability of the divine essence even when human persons overcome the limitations of their created nature.

99. Meyendorf, "Svyatoy Grigoriy Palama," 161–62.

100. Meyendorf, *Vvedenie v svyatootecheskoe bogoslovie*, 99, 274; see also 162.

101. Meyendorff, *Byzantine Theology*, 12.

102. Meyendorf, *Vvedenie v svyatootecheskoe bogoslovie*, 274.

103. Lossky, *Mystical Theology*, 30. Lossky comes to the conclusion, which is later repeated by Meyendorff, that "the God of Plotinus is not incomprehensible by nature" (30). See Meyendorf, "Svyatoy Grigoriy Palama," 161. To be sure, in general, Meyendorff was far less influenced by the *Corpus Areopagiticum* than Lossky, and his reception of pseudo-Dionysius was also far less positive and deferential. Meyendorff believed that pseudo-Dionysius had

transcendence of the divine nature, pseudo-Dionysius radically diverged from Neoplatonism.[104] Whether or not Meyendorff was right in his interpretation of Neoplatonism, his complaints are clear: Neoplatonism failed to recognize that God's essence is absolutely transcendent, inaccessible, and ineffable.[105]

Meyendorff's discussion of Western theology reveals he was dissatisfied with it for the same reasons that he was dissatisfied with Neoplatonism. In his article devoted to the Reformation, Meyendorff sets forth the Orthodox understanding of God's transcendence and contrasts it with Augustine's theology:

---

adequately overcome the Neoplatonic influence in his doctrine of God, but in his cosmology, ecclesiology, and Christology he was still captivated by the hierarchical constructions of Neoplatonism in which higher elements served as intermediaries for the lower ones (*Christ in Eastern Christian Thought*, 91, 94, 99; *Vvedenie v svyatootecheskoe bogoslovie*, 276–81). According to Meyendorff, the insights of pseudo-Dionysius had to be Christianized and corrected by later theologians, especially Maximus and Palamas. Meyendorff's views on pseudo-Dionysius will be explored in more detail under "Energies as Light" (pages 208–12). For a good analysis and comparison of the interpretations of pseudo-Dionysius in the theologies of Lossky and Meyendorff, see Paul Gavrilyuk, "The Reception of Dionysius in Twentieth-Century Eastern Orthodoxy," in *Re-thinking Dionysius the Areopagite*, ed. Sarah Coakley and Charles Stang (Oxford: Wiley and Sons, 2011), 182–90.

104. In one of his reviews, Meyendorff notes that "the affirmation of an absolute divine transcendence ... is the single element which distinguishes the philosophy of Dionysius from the Neoplatonists." See John Meyendorff, "Review of *Biblical and Liturgical Symbols within the Pseudo-Dionysius Synthesis* by Paul Rorem," *SVTQ* 29 (1985): 365. Apart from this concept, the view of pseudo-Dionysius on the movement of divine procession downward is "practically indistinguishable ... from that of Iamblichus and other Neoplatonists" (365). Elsewhere Meyendorff noted another point of divergence: while Plotinus maintained that in the process of divine emanation humans receive only drops from an overfilled vessel, pseudo-Dionysius argued that God is not susceptible to diminishing and that divine emanations communicate the fullness of the Godhead (Meyendorf, *Vvedenie v svyatootecheskoe bogoslovie*, 274).

105. Although some scholars accept this presentation of Neoplatonism uncritically (see, for instance, Jennifer A. Herrick, *Does God Change? Reconciling the Immutable God with the God of Love* [Parkland, FL: Universal, 2003], 38, where Meyendorff's "two currents" schema is reproduced almost literally), it hardly does justice to the Neoplatonic view of God. According to Plotinus, the One is not only "beyond *human mind*," but "beyond *being*." No categories of human existence or language are applicable to it. Even the term "One" is not to be understood in any positive sense, because it contains nothing more than a denial of multiplicity. See Eric D. Perl, *Theophany: The Neoplatonic Philosophy of Dionysius the Areopagite* (Albany: State University of New York Press, 2012), 12. In fact, negative definitions are also rejected, because negation implies a kind of affirmation, while the One ultimately exceeds all concepts. According to Plotinus, therefore, the One absolutely transcends human beings. As Tollefsen observes, "to use Meyendorff's term, transcendence is a property of God and not something that created minds can overcome" (*Activity and Participation*, 209). See also the critical remarks about Meyendorff's description of Neoplatonism in Gavrilyuk, "Reception of Dionysius," 187.

> God is absolutely transcendent in this essence, which can never be known or seen even in the life to come. The divine transcendence is not due, *as in Augustine*, to the limitations of our fallen state or to the imperfections of our bodily existence, disappearing when our soul is liberated from material bonds: God, in His very being, is above creature.[106]

In another paragraph of the same article Meyendorff claims that for Augustine God's transcendence was "relative to the deficiency of the creature, especially that of the fallen creature." According to Meyendorff's reading of Augustine, humanity does not intrinsically possess the necessary capacities to know and comprehend God, but, with the help of God's grace, it "is able to develop a natural capability to know God." As a result of this capability, humanity may "know the essence of God, once the soul is liberated from its present dependence upon the body."[107] All these formulations are almost identical to Meyendorff's reproaches of Neoplatonism. It is not surprising that, in his view, Augustine's theory of knowledge was "based on neoplatonic notions." Meyendorff further asserts that in his early writings Augustine even acknowledged "that the biblical doctrine of the Creator is the same as 'what Plato and Plotinus have said about God.'"[108]

What seems to be most important for Meyendorff is that Augustine's rejection of "God's absolute transcendence" was not an isolated problem but rather an integral part of his "essentialism." The core problem is that Augustine identified God "with a rationally conceivable essence, that of the Supreme Good."[109] Greek philosophy, which so profoundly influ-

---

106. Meyendorff, "Significance of the Reformation," 169, emphasis added.

107. Meyendorff, "Significance of the Reformation," 165, 169 . See also "grace ... can first forgive, then restore man to the natural capability of his soul to contemplate God's essence" (165). Elsewhere Meyendorff says that Augustine filled "the ontological gap between God and man by having recourse to a Platonic anthropology, attributing to the *sensus mentis* a particular ability to know God" ("Orthodox Theology," 169).

108. Meyendorff, "Greek Philosophy and Christian Theology," 37. It must be noted, however, that the formulation of Augustine, to which Meyendorff refers, is more cautious. Having been asked whether it is enough to know God as Plato and Plotinus knew him, Augustine replies: "It does not necessarily follow that, even if those things which they said are true, they knew them to be so" (*Soliloquies* 1.4.9).

109. Meyendorff, "Significance of the Reformation," 165.

enced Augustine, was an "essentialist"[110] one. A natural consequence of the Augustinian identification of God with his essence was that he can be participated and known only in his essence.[111] And if God is somehow participated or known in his essence, then, according to Meyendorff, his absolute transcendence is compromised. In order to be faithful to biblical revelation, therefore, the West must not simply restate God's absolute transcendence, but also renounce that which contradicts it: namely, the identification of God with his essence. God is not imprisoned in his essence, and the West must admit the reality of the "going out of God from his transcendent essence," which in Orthodox theology is called "the will of God or His uncreated energies."[112]

In Meyendorff's view, the problems with Western essentialism are not restricted to the fact that it is unable to properly distinguish between God's essence and his deeds (will, grace, or energies). Western Trinitarianism suffers also from another deficiency: "the absolute priority of the Unique Essence over the personal or Trinitarian aspect of the divine being."[113] Meyendorff believed that, from the Cappadocians and Augustine onward, the Eastern and Western doctrines of God took separate paths, leading to two distinct traditions, whose main representatives were Palamas and Aquinas, respectively. Meyendorff came to this belief under the influence of Théodore de Régnon's famous paradigm, which Meyendorff summarized thus: "Latin philosophy considers the nature in itself first and proceeds to the agent; Greek philosophy considers the agent first and passes through it to find the nature."[114] This paradigm became popular in Orthodox émigré circles for the reason indicated above: it helped Orthodox theologians emphasize the distinctiveness of their tradition.[115] Unsurprisingly, Meyendorff interpreted the paradigm as referring to geographical rather

110. Meyendorf, "U istokov," 307; Meyendorff, *Study of Gregory Palamas*, 222; Meyendorff, "'Defense of the Holy Hesychasts,'" 192.

111. Meyendorff, "Significance of the Reformation," 173.

112. Meyendorff, "Christian Theology," 63.

113. Meyendorff, "Greek Philosophy and Christian Theology," 37.

114. Théodore de Régnon, *Etudes de théologie positive sur la Sainte Trinité* (Paris: Victor Retaux, 1892), 1:433, cited in Meyendorff, *Byzantine Theology*, 181.

115. In the words of David Bentley Hart, the distinction of de Régnon "has served little purpose in recent years but to feed Eastern polemic and Western insecurity." See Hart, *The Beauty of the Infinite: The Aesthetics of Christian Truth* (Grand Rapids: Eerdmans, 2004), 170.

than chronological differences without paying much attention to the nuances of de Régnon's use of the words "Greek" and "Latin." While de Régnon juxtaposed the *patristic* (including Western fathers) and *scholastic* epochs,[116] Meyendorff, following many other scholars of his time, used it to describe the differences between the *Eastern* (Orthodox) and *Western* (Roman Catholic and Protestant) approaches to the Trinity. Whether de Régnon's paradigm is historically accurate lies outside the scope of the present work. I will not attempt even to sketch its diverse reception in modern scholarship. Suffice it to say that Meyendorff was convinced of the correctness of the paradigm and suggested that its main point was unanimously accepted among his contemporaries.[117] For both constructive and polemical purposes, he employed the paradigm, even without explicit references to it, whenever he spoke about the primacy of the persons in relation to the essence.[118]

---

116. See Michel René Barnes, "De Régnon Reconsidered," *Augustinian Studies* 26 (1995): 54; D. Glenn Butner Jr., "For and against de Régnon: Trinitarianism East and West," *International Journal of Systematic Theology* 17 (2015): 401.

117. "Historians of Christian thought, as well as theologians of all confessional backgrounds concerned with problems of Christian unity, *unanimously recognize* that already in the fourth century the formulation of the Trinitarian doctrine, which can be defined a [*sic*] 'Cappadocian' and the Western 'Augustinian' presentation of the Trinity, are two distinct systems of thought which determined the later development of theology in the East and the West" (Meyendorff, "Holy Trinity," 25, emphasis added). Similarly: "Indeed, as all scholars today would agree the real difference between the Latin—Augustinian—view of the Trinity, as a single Essence, with personal characters understood as relations, and the Greek scheme, inherited from the Cappadocian Fathers, which considered the single divine Essence as totally transcendent, and the Persons, or *hypostaseis*—each with unique and unchangeable characteristics—as revealing in themselves the Tri-personal divine life, was the real issue behind the debates on the Filioque." See John Meyendorff, "The Mediterranean World in the Thirteenth Century Theology: East and West," in *The Seventeenth International Byzantine Congress: Major Papers* (New Rochelle, NY: Aristide D. Caratzas, 1986), 678. As Plested notes, in the revised version of the paper (John Meyendorff, "Theology in the Thirteenth Century: Methodological Contrasts," in *Rome, Constantinople, Moscow*, 73–86), "all scholars" was amended to "most" (Plested, "Gregory Palamas," 300). Although de Régnon's thesis was widely embraced to the point that it became an axiom for many scholars, in Meyendorff's time it was already coming under criticism, especially by French Augustinians (see some titles in Barnes, "De Régnon," 55).

118. See Meyendorff, *Study of Gregory Palamas*, 228, 230; Meyendorff, *Orthodox Church*, 178; Meyendorff, "Greek Philosophy and Christian Theology," 37; Meyendorff, "Christ's Humanity," 11; John Meyendorff, "The Theology of the Holy Spirit," in *Catholicity and the Church*, 16; Meyendorff, "The Nicene Creed: Uniting or Dividing Confession?," in *Faith to Creed: Ecumenical Perspectives on the Affirmation of the Apostolic Faith in the Fourth Century*, ed. S. M. Heim (Grand Rapids: Eerdmans, 1991), 11.

The Meaning of God's Absolute Transcendence

As noted above, Meyendorff maintained that the entire patristic doctrine of God is based on the notion of the absolute transcendence of the divine nature. In the early church, and later in Byzantine theology, "the total transcendence and inaccessibility of the essence of God becomes ... a matter of Christian faith fundamental for spiritual life."[119] Although Meyendorff did not treat this topic systematically, he used it extensively in his writings to underscore some aspects of his theology. I will try to trace his theological concerns as expounded in his various books and articles.

First of all, the notion of God's absolute transcendence (or unknowability) demonstrates the futility of all human attempts to perceive God "from below." "Even if I am the greatest ascetic and mystic in the world God is not truly known to me if He Himself does not come out of His transcendence to condescend to reveal Himself to me."[120] The explanation for God's unknowability is not to be found in human frailty or sinfulness. There is no ladder that would allow even the worthiest human beings to climb up into God's presence by their own initiative, because they are totally dependent on God's self-disclosure.

The unknowability of God's essence, therefore, is also a necessary background for understanding revelation as "a free and sovereign act of God, by which the Transcendent comes down from his transcendence and the Unknowable makes himself known." A creature's knowledge of God is neither guaranteed nor something that can be assumed. In Christianity, God *chose* to reveal himself. As Meyendorff puts it, "The God of the Bible is a 'hidden God' who only reveals himself when he so desires and on conditions which he himself fixes."[121]

One of the things Meyendorff most frequently repeated with regard to God's absolute transcendence is that it prevents people from thinking that they can somehow possess God. It is because of the transcendence of God's essence that "all participation in his being remains ... a gift, a grace," and the human response can never be a sense of "possession."[122] In receiving

119. Meyendorff, *Byzantine Theology*, 72.

120. Meyendorff, "Christian Theology," 62, 63.

121. Meyendorff, *Study of Gregory Palamas*, 203, 209. See also Meyendorff, *Gregory Palamas*, 119.

122. Meyendorff, *Christ in Eastern Christian Thought*, 207.

God's life, "man does not 'possess God.'"[123] To be sure, Meyendorff did not reject the idea of possession completely, since it has been well established in the Eastern tradition that the saints somehow possess God: Gregory of Nyssa said that "to possess God in oneself"[124] is the blessed condition, and Meyendorff himself cited Palamas maintaining that one who purifies oneself through virtue and transcends oneself can "possess God in oneself."[125] In repudiating the idea of possessing God, Meyendorff meant that humanity cannot be the master of God, and its participation in God never bears a meritorious or automatic character or implies a mixture with the divine nature. God is always free in relation to the world, and "nothing created can either possess Him or see Him."[126]

Such considerations would hardly provoke major objections from theologians of other Christian traditions. However, Meyendorff's point, of course, is not merely that God *would be* unknown if he *had not* revealed himself. His point is that God, even in revealing and communicating himself, *remains* "totally inaccessible in His essence, both in this life and in the future."[127] The ultimate reason for the unknowability (inaccessibility, incommunicability) of God's essence lies in Meyendorff's high view of humanity's union with God. As we saw in previous sections, in this union humanity becomes one with God: God's life becomes its life, God's way its way, God's existence its existence, God's light its light. Meyendorff's unexpressed premise apparently is: "whatever God shares with man, is shared fully." If God were identified with his essence and his essence were knowable or communicable, it would be knowable and communicable *fully*, which, in turn, would undermine any difference between Creator

123. Meyendorff, "Significance of the Reformation," 171. "Vision of God and communion with God can never imply *possession*" (Meyendorff, "Byzantium as Center," 70, emphasis original). See also *Study of Gregory Palamas*, 174. Elsewhere, referring to Gregory of Nyssa, Meyendorff states that any vision or understanding is a form of "at least partial possession" (*Vvedenie v svyatootecheskoe bogoslovie*, 186). Thus, if one believes that humanity cannot possess God in any sense, one must also admit that humanity cannot see or understand God.

124. "The Lord does not say that knowing something about God is blessed, but to possess God in oneself." See Gregory of Nyssa, *On the Beatitudes*, in Hubertus R. Drobner and Alberto Viciano, eds., *Gregory of Nyssa: Homilies on the Beatitudes* (Leiden: Brill, 2000), 69–70.

125. Meyendorff, *Byzantine Theology*, 140.

126. Meyendorff, "Significance of the Reformation," 169.

127. Meyendorff, *Byzantine Theology*, 77; Meyendorff, "'Defense of the Holy Hesychasts,'" 184; Meyendorff, *Study of Gregory Palamas*, 183–84; Meyendorff, "Palamas (Grégoire)," 92.

and creature.[128] The identification of God with his essence leads to pantheism; and vice versa: the rejection of pantheism requires the rejection of such identification. As Meyendorff writes, the result of the identification of God with his essence would be "the impossibility of any 'participation' of man in God's life, of any 'deification' of humanity."[129] Thus, the most important implication of the absolute transcendence of God's essence is that it makes deification possible without degenerating into pantheist unity. While Meyendorff admits that the Orthodox emphasis on participation of humanity in God "may be understood as implying a kind of pantheism," he immediately adds: "It is important, therefore, to maintain that the divine, transcendent divine nature will always remain distinct and transcendent."[130]

Given the breadth and depth of the mystical union between God and humanity, therefore, the confession of the absolute transcendence of God's essence is necessary to preserve the fundamental difference between God and human beings, which is so clearly taught in Scripture and Christian tradition. "We cannot see God ... because God is God. ... This transcendence of God is a characteristic of the nature of God Himself."[131] God in his essence is unapproachable not only for humans but for all creatures including angels. If Origen were right in claiming that we are capable of uniting with God's essence, the line between the Creator and his creatures would not only be blurred; it would be totally eliminated. "Origen's God ceases to be the absolute Other, the God of Abraham, of Isaac, and of Jacob, and becomes the god of the philosophers."[132] Meyendorff constantly assumed that revelation and participation belonged together and resulted in such a close union that all differences between the content of revelation and its recipients are obliterated. Thus, to safeguard the transcendence and otherness of God against pantheism, we must discern something in him that is not revealed or participated in any way, and this something is

---

128. It would also mean that creatures "possess" God: "To know the divine essence would be to possess God" (Meyendorff, *Gregory Palamas*, 119).

129. John Meyendorff, "Review of *Symvolai eis ten peri Nestoriou erevran (Contributions to the Study of Nestorius)*, by G. S. Bebis," *SVTQ* 10 (1966): 215.

130. Meyendorff, "Reply to Jürgen Moltmann's," 187.

131. Meyendorff, "Christian Theology," 62.

132. Meyendorff, *Byzantine Theology*, 12.

God's essence. As Meyendorff puts it, "even when He manifests Himself, He remains unknowable in His essence, for a revelation of the divine essence would bring God down to the level of creatures and make man a 'God by nature.'"[133] All in all, essence is a concept that refers to that which is *not* shared in the mystical union.[134]

In Meyendorff's view, only the absolute transcendence of God's essence can preserve the reality of the created order. The absolute separation between the divine and creaturely natures enables humans to maintain their creaturely status. While the destiny of humanity is deification, it "does not consist of an absorption into God's essence." Although in union with God man becomes divine, he "remains totally himself in his *nature*."[135] Meyendorff believed that if human nature participated in the divine nature, it would be immersed in the divinity and dissolved within it. Explaining the significance of God's "essential transcendence" for Palamas, Meyendorff comments that it was indispensable for avoiding "the identification of God with creatures" that would eventually lead to "a pantheist blending of them and a disappearance of the creature as such into the depths of the divine being."[136] Again, Meyendorff's premise is that whatever God shares with the saints and communicates to them becomes one with them. Thus, to escape the pantheistic implications, there must be something in God that is absolutely incommunicable, unattainable, and unknowable, and remains such even as God communicates and reveals himself.

Finally, Meyendorff's apologetic activities and his openness to people with other worldviews led him to identify God's absolute transcendence as a starting point for dialogue between Christians, atheists, and agnostics. According to Meyendorff, "we are all necessarily involved" in this dialogue, which makes the doctrine "extremely relevant" in the modern world.[137] Atheists refuse to believe in a primitive god: an old man with a white beard sitting in heaven. But if we agree that "God is totally incomprehensible, indefinable, and inaccessible [to] the human mind," the

133. Meyendorff, *Gregory Palamas*, 118.

134. Meyendorff, *Byzantine Theology*, 130.

135. Meyendorff, *Byzantine Theology*, 72, emphasis added.

136. Meyendorf, "Svyatoy Grigoriy Palama," 165.

137. Meyendorff, "Christian Theology," 63.

conversation shifts to another level, Meyendorff observes.[138] Thus, Meyendorff proposed, "there is a vast area of collegiality between us Christians and the atheists and agnostics in fighting idols and false ideas about God or simply our own anthropomorphic ideas about God."[139] Meyendorff took the matter further by stating that an "atheist is closer to God than a philosopher who seeks to prove God's existence and knowability." The doctrine of God's absolute transcendence, Meyendorff concludes, is important not only within Christian theology, but also "for the preaching and defense of Christian doctrine."[140]

Apophatic Theology

Along with the extensive exploitation of de Régnon's paradigm, Orthodox émigré theologians, seeking to underscore the fundamental difference between West and East, also stressed the dissimilarity of their theological approaches: Western theology was regarded as prevailingly cataphatic, while Eastern theology was presented as apophatic. On this view, the Western approach uses positive statements based on drawing analogies between God and creation, while the Eastern approach moves all human categories aside and is directed instead toward a the mystical encounter with the unknown God. Western theology focuses on intellectual understanding, while Eastern theology strives for experiential union. Even when Orthodox theologians recognized traces of apophaticism in Western theologians, they did not consider them to be sufficiently apophatic, while the Eastern theological tradition, on the contrary, was described as being characterized by "radical apophaticism" that induces the mind to acknowledge the utter otherness of God.[141] In particular, Meyendorff argued that "the whole of Byzantine theology ... would be completely misunderstood if one forgets its other pole of reference: apophatic, or negative, theology." According to Meyendorff, apophatic theology had already "fully developed" in the writings of the Cappadocian fathers. Against Eunomius, they

---

138. Meyendorf, *Vvedenie v svyatootecheskoe bogoslovie*, 170.

139. Meyendorff, "Christian Theology," 63.

140. Meyendorf, *Vvedenie v svyatootecheskoe bogoslovie*, 170.

141. Lossky, *Mystical Theology*, 37. On traces of apophaticism in Western theologians, see, e.g., Vladimir Lossky, "Elements of 'Negative Theology' in the Thought of St. Augustine," *SVTQ* 21 (1977): 67–75.

asserted the absolute transcendence of God and the necessity of eliminating all human concepts for a true encounter with God. "By saying what God *is not*, the theologian is really speaking the Truth, for no human word or thought is capable of comprehending what God *is*."[142]

Some of Meyendorff's statements seem to imply that a negative approach may be employed in the absence of revelation.[143] He claims that apophatic theology belongs to the realm of natural thought: "It is by contemplating beings that one perceives their relativity and arrives at the conception of an Absolute and of a Creator." As earlier noted, Meyendorff argued that Greek philosophers underestimated God's absolute transcendence, but he admits that they too "had been aware of apophatic theology."[144] For Palamas, Meyendorff maintains, apophatic theology as such "is available without revelation" and contains "nothing specifically Christian."[145]

Given the emphasis on the *absolute* unknowability of God's essence, one could expect that Meyendorff would deny the legitimacy of *both* cataphatic and apophatic approaches with respect to the divine essence. For if we can know nothing about the essence, neither positive nor negative discourse is applicable to it. Meyendorff, however, endorsed the use of apophatic language in regard to God's essence. He argues that "the essence of God is absolutely transcendent and can be adequately expressed only by negatives: humanity can only know what God *is not*, not what God is."[146] Outlining the Orthodox doctrine in a simple manner, Meyendorff writes:

> God, in his essence, is totally transcendent and unknowable. In this understanding, God can only be designated by negative attributes: it is possible to say what God is not, but it is impossible to say what God is. A purely negative, or "apophatic" theology ... [is] the only one applicable to the essence of God in the Orthodox view.[147]

142. Meyendorff, *Byzantine Theology*, 11, emphasis original.

143. Meyendorff, *Orthodox Church*, 176.

144. Meyendorff, *Study of Gregory Palamas*, 206; see also Meyendorff, *Byzantine Theology*, 13.

145. Meyendorff, "Doctrine of Grace," 19.

146. Meyendorff, "Theosis in the Eastern Christian Tradition," 476, emphasis original.

147. John Meyendorff, "Eastern Orthodoxy," accessed February 27, 2017, https://www.britannica.com/topic/Eastern-Orthodoxy.

Meyendorff did not mean to say, however, that we advance via negative formulations to some positive knowledge of the essence. Denying what God's essence *is not* by no means reveals what it *is*. Denying that God is material does not mean that he is spiritual; denying that God is evil does not mean that he is good, and so forth. This negative approach does not deny a single thing that requires affirmation of the contrary. Rather, *all* human concepts, words, and ideas are equally inapplicable to God's essence. "No single concept, conceivable by the human mind, can express the essence of God."[148] Such an approach could be called *pan*-apophaticism: it demonstrates the inadequacy of all creaturely tools in describing God. Any other form of apophaticism would not be sufficiently apophatic, for God ultimately transcends negations as well as affirmations.

In tracing the historical roots of radical apophaticism, Meyendorff usually appealed to pseudo-Dionysius and Palamas. One of their key ideas was that God transcends not only positive concepts but also negations. Since God surpasses all human concepts, he also exceeds theological concepts such as being or essence. For pseudo-Dionysius, God is nonbeing: not because God lacks existence but because he is beyond any existence. Similarly, God transcends even essence, which prompted pseudo-Dionysius to use such terms as "superessential," "supereminent," and "superluminous." God is "neither the One, nor Unity"; he is neither goodness, nor divinity, nor spirit.[149] Meyendorff appreciatively describes the views of Palamas along the same lines. God is the source of all being, but he himself is nonbeing because the same category cannot be applied to both him and to creaturely realities. Even "such concepts as 'the essence' or 'God' ... lose their meaning, for the God of the Bible is 'superessential' ... and 'more-than-God.'" That is, the Transcendent not only is a God who surpasses beings, but surpasses God himself: it transcends affirmations and negations, knowledge and unknowing.[150] Whatever other beings are, the Transcendent is not; whatever it is, other beings are not.

The apophatic approach, therefore, is bound up primarily with the cerebral sphere: the saints detach their minds from all created things,

148. Meyendorf, "Svyatoy Grigoriy Palama," 161.

149. Meyendorff, *Byzantine Theology*, 12; Meyendorf, "Svyatoy Grigoriy Palama," 161.

150. Meyendorff, *Study of Gregory Palamas*, 206–7, 210; Meyendorff, "'Defense of the Holy Hesychasts,'" 183.

acknowledge the absolute otherness of God, and abandon any attempt to perceive God through intellectual inquiry. Meyendorff, however, describes the approach as not only mental but also ethical: it implies "a spiritual purification (*katharsis*) which discards all forms of identifying God with that which is not God."[151] By freeing its mind from human categories, humanity cleans the space, as it were, and prepares for it to be filled with the true revelation of God, leading to the transfiguration of humanity by the Holy Spirit. "The negations of apophatic theology signify only the inability of reaching God without such a transfiguration by the Spirit."[152]

Neither for Palamas nor for Meyendorff, therefore, is negation the last word. Rather, it is only "a preliminary step," "a necessary stage in the knowledge of God."[153] The negations do not present the true vision of God, but rather prepare the way for it. This vision implies a higher state of cognition, when the saints are united with God and transformed—in soul and body—by his grace. It is a vision "from inside": humanity does not contemplate God as an external object, but participates and lives in him. Apophatic theology "describes a state, beyond the conceptual process, where God reveals himself positively to the 'spiritual senses.'"[154] This state—*ecstasis* or self-transcendence—is irreducible to any mental activities or emotions and surpasses all creaturely capacities. It is accessible only to the "spiritual senses" formed by God as a part of the complete renovation of humanity. This is where, according to Meyendorff, biblical apophaticism differs from the apophaticism of the philosophers: the latter is purely formal, negative, and intellectual, whereas the former leads to a positive encounter with the living God.[155] Therefore, apophaticism in Meyendorff's theology is nei-

151. Meyendorff, *Byzantine Theology*, 12.

152. Meyendorff, "'Defense of the Holy Hesychasts,'" 183.

153. Meyendorff, "'Defense of the Holy Hesychasts,'" 183; Meyendorff, *Byzantine Theology*, 12.

154. Meyendorff, "'Defense of the Holy Hesychasts,'" 184.

155. Meyendorff, *Byzantine Theology*, 13. Meyendorff argued that the "negative" aspect implied no substantial difference between the Christian and philosophical apophaticism. As he describes the views of Palamas, "'Apophatic theology' springs from the natural mind and is available without Revelation. There is nothing specifically Christian in it, and pagan philosophers were able to enunciate its principles" ("Doctrine of Grace," 19; see also Meyendorff, *Study of Gregory Palamas*, 206). The difference is that Christian apophaticism does not stop at mere negations, but paves the way to a living communion with God and a mystical contemplation of his incomprehensibility.

It remains obscure, however, whether Christian apophaticism for Meyendorff *includes* mystical union or simply *leads* toward this union. In one of the citations above he has clearly

ther restrained to negations nor exhausted by them. The mystical vision it describes constitutes a *positive* experience of the saints, presupposes a *positive* revelation of God, and involves a *positive* and personal encounter with him. Meyendorff repeatedly emphasized the *positivity* of this vision—presumably in order to reject the conclusion that the incomprehensible nature of this experience makes it devoid of all content.[156]

Still, however positive this vision and experience may be, it "does not allow man to know God, except as the Unknowable and Incomprehensible."[157] Although, as we saw, negations are "a necessary stage in the *knowledge of God*," and the mystical experience—the next and final stage—grants this *knowledge*, it is nothing but a knowledge of God's unknowability. The positive meeting is a meeting "with the Unknown," and the positive experience is "communion with the Unknowable." It is "a contemplation greater than knowledge."[158] Following pseudo-Dionysius and Palamas, Meyendorff did not hesitate to call this mystical knowledge "darkness" and "ignorance," adding that it is superior to the "merely intellectual knowledge" of philosophers. This knowledge should be "received in loving silence," and it "exceeds negative as well as positive description."[159] Meyendorff calls this knowledge "the experience of God's otherness [and] ... of His transcendence": this was what Moses experienced "when he entered the cloud on the top of Mount Sinai and perceived the presence of God in the darkness of unknowing."[160]

To be sure, Meyendorff argues that the approach he advocated does not mean agnosticism and anticipates that, after the preliminary stage of negations, God may freely make himself known. Meyendorff maintains

---

stated that apophatic theology "describes" this state, so that mystical union seems to be included in the apophatic approach. But elsewhere Meyendorff comments that the union and the experience thereof "went beyond conceptual apophaticism," which seems to mean that the union is not part of apophaticism itself (Meyendorff, "Byzantium as Center," 69–70).

156. Meyendorff, *Byzantine Theology*, 13; Meyendorff, "'Defense of the Holy Hesychasts,'" 184; Meyendorff, "Holy Trinity," 31; Meyendorff, *Study of Gregory Palamas*, 207; Meyendorf, "Svyatoy Grigoriy Palama," 163.

157. Meyendorff, *Byzantine Theology*, 12.

158. Meyendorff, *Byzantine Theology*, 13; Meyendorff, "'Defense of the Holy Hesychasts,'" 184.

159. Meyendorff, *Byzantine Theology*, 117, 134.

160. Meyendorff, "Holy Trinity," 31; Meyendorff, "'Defense of the Holy Hesychasts,'" 183.

that "the darkness of the cloud surrounding God is not an empty darkness."[161] However, the saints obtain true knowledge when they are plunged into a dark and mysterious abyss, where God can only be positively "experienced," but not positively known or described. Thus, true knowledge is a supernatural knowledge and is incompatible with "intellectual knowledge."[162] The saint is endowed with true knowledge only when he realizes his ignorance; he achieves true vision only when he ceases to see.[163]

Meyendorff contends that true experiential knowledge and therefore "true theology" is a "positive experience of divine transcendence, or a 'knowledge through ignorance.'" He also states that his understanding of divine transcendence presupposes "the experiential nature of theology."[164] One may ask, however, how much knowledge is left in this experiential knowledge, if it is freed from all concepts and descriptions, and how much ϑεολογία is left in this experiential theology, if no λόγοι may be attributed to God. But Meyendorff made it plain that he used the term "experiential theology" only with reference to a mystical experience rather than words, ideas, or expressions. Moreover, Meyendorff notes that Palamas refused to even apply the term "apophatic *theology*" to an experience of the Transcendent, "because, in his time, 'theology' had come necessarily to mean expression and conceptualization." In the same context, Meyendorff states that the true vision of God "does not express itself in terms of a *positive* or cataphatic *theology*; it constitutes an encounter with a God who is by nature transcendent."[165] It is doubtful, however, that what is decisive here is the transcendence of God's essence, because this essence is inaccessible not

161. Meyendorff, "'Defense of the Holy Hesychasts,'" 183.

162. Meyendorff, *Study of Gregory Palamas*, 204; Meyendorff, "'Defense of the Holy Hesychasts,'" 187; Meyendorff, *Gregory*, 84; Meyendorf, *Vvedenie v svyatootecheskoe bogoslovie*, 312. According to Meyendorff, Palamism "maintains the possibility of a real and not merely an intellectual communion with God." See "O vizantiyskom isikhazme i ego roli v kul'turnom i istoricheskom razvitii Vostochnoy Evropy v XIV v" [Byzantine Hesychasm and its role in the cultural and historical development of Eastern Europe in the fourteenth century], in *Trudy otdela drevnerusskoy literatury* [Works of the Department of Old Russian Literature] (Leningrad: Nauka, 1974), 294. An intellectual communion (or intellectual knowledge) is not real, because "real" communion requires an "ecstasy" beyond any creaturely function of intellect or sight.

163. Meyendorff, "'Defense of the Holy Hesychasts,'" 184.

164. Meyendorff, "Byzantium as Center," 70.

165. Meyendorff, *Study of Gregory Palamas*, 207, emphasis original. For Palamas, the mystical experience "is incomparably higher than negative theology" (*Triads*, 65).

only in terms of positive knowledge but also in terms of positive encounter. More significant in this regard is that knowledge, for Meyendorff, is incompatible with uncreated realities and always has creaturely, natural connotations. Thus, even when revealing himself in his uncreated energies, God becomes accessible for a positive encounter, but remains beyond all positive descriptions and thoughts.

Impassibility and Immutability

As noted above, on the one hand, Meyendorff approved the use of negative predicates regarding God's essence and even claimed that it can be "adequately expressed" by them, yet, on the other hand, he maintained that the divine essence ultimately exceeds both affirmations and negations. Thus each negative predicate concerning God's essence should not be understood as a tacit affirmation of the opposite. But how does this actually function? Following established Christian tradition, Meyendorff often ascribed impassibility and immutability (or unchangeability) to the divine nature. Meyendorff *contrasted* the impassibility and immutability of the divine nature with the passibility and mutability of the human nature. So, "in contrast with the divine nature," human nature is dynamic and capable of suffering.[166]

It is remarkable how divine impassibility and immutability function in Meyendorff's dogmatic constructions concerning the relation between the divine essence and persons. If God by nature is immutable, how could he *become* Creator? And how could the Son of God have *become* man? If God is by nature impassible, how could the Son of God have suffered? If God is by nature immortal (another essential characteristic of the divine nature,)[167] how could the Son have died? These questions, Meyendorff states, can only be answered by admitting the distinction between essence (*ousia*, nature) and person (hypostasis, subject). A subject—divine as well as human—"is able to transcend, or go beyond, the limits of the nature it possesses."[168] A person remains independent of the characteristics of their own nature

166. Meyendorff, *Christ in Eastern Christian Thought*, 160.

167. Meyendorff, *Byzantine Theology*, 155.

168. Meyendorff, "New Life," 497.

and can be liberated from them.[169] In particular, "the characteristics of the divine essence—impassibility, immutability, etc.—are not absolutely binding upon the *personal*, or hypostatic, existence of God."[170] Thus, according to Meyendorff, the Orthodox position defines the divine nature as "the unchangeable, impassible, transcendent, creative essence, common to the Father, the Son, and the Spirit," whereas the term "hypostasis" denotes a personal existence with the openness "to existential change."[171]

The hypostasis of the Logos, therefore, could really suffer while his divine nature remained impervious to passions and sufferings. In Meyendorff's view, the Logos accepted the kenosis on the level of his personhood, while his nature was not affected by it. The Son could suffer hypostatically, because within his hypostasis he assumed a passible, human nature, and what is asserted of this nature can be asserted of the hypostasis.[172] Meyendorff pursues the same argumentation concerning divine immutability: "the hypostasis 'becomes,' whereas 'nature' is absolutely unchangeable."[173] Since God is not confined to his nature, he can become what he was not. "The divine nature would remain immutable and impassible, but the *hypostasis* would be open to 'change' and passibility."[174] The Son could become flesh, assume human nature, be born as a man, grow in wisdom, and so forth only if his divine person, in contrast to his divine nature, "was capable of real *change*."[175] Likewise, if God were *only* nature, he would be immutable and unable to *begin* to create. But since he is also energy, he is able to create in time without his nature changing. In sum, Meyendorff argued that by refusing to identify God with his essence we can understand how the God of the Bible can be *both* impassible and passible, immutable and mutable.[176]

Meyendorff realized that the idea of impassibility has deep roots in the Greek philosophical tradition, in which suffering was considered a

169. Meyendorff, *Christ in Eastern Christian Thought*, 159.

170. Meyendorff, *Byzantine Theology*, 155–56.

171. Meyendorff, "Christ's Humanity," 13.

172. Meyendorff, *Christ in Eastern Christian Thought*, 70, 77; Meyendorff, "Holy Trinity," 33; Meyendorff, *Byzantine Theology*, 155.

173. Meyendorff, "New Life," 496.

174. Meyendorff, "Continuities and Discontinuities," 75.

175. Meyendorff, "Reply to Jürgen Moltmann's," 188, emphasis original.

176. Meyendorff, *Study of Gregory Palamas*, 223.

sign of deficiency and was denied of God primarily for this reason. As with other topics, Meyendorff strove to demonstrate that the Orthodox tradition fundamentally differed from the philosophers, in spite of having common terms and lines of thought. But when he solemnly states that "the notion of the impassible, changeless Absolute of Platonism is ... useless in Christian theology," he immediately adds that "this does not mean ... that the idea of divine transcendence is abandoned. Quite the contrary."[177] Later, Meyendorff explains that the absolute transcendence of the divine *essence* has been, and must be, preserved in Christian theology, but with equal emphasis given to God's personal existence and his energies, which allow him to go beyond his essence. What Meyendorff actually discards then is the impassibility of *God*, but not the impassibility of God's *essence*.[178]

An analysis of Meyendorff's view on the relation between person and essence must be postponed to a later chapter. In the context of the present work it is also impossible to present even a superficial overview of how the notions of God's impassibility and immutability were interpreted, challenged, and criticized in recent theology. I will restrict myself to the observation that when Meyendorff deals with these notions—whether he contrasts divine and human natures, ascribes one attribute to the divine nature and another to the divine person, or explains how they are interrelated within the godhead—it is difficult to escape the conclusion that "apophatic" characteristics such as impassibility and immutability function as opposites of corresponding positive attributes rather than as notions pointing to realities that surpass all creaturely concepts and words. Divine

177. Meyendorff, "Greek Philosophy and Christian Theology," 42.

178. Although Meyendorff notices that "our time becomes increasingly estranged from a theology which considers God and man as two distinct, philosophically definable entities, with incompatible characteristics, such as passibility and impassibility, capacity for change and changelessness, composition and simplicity," it is difficult to see how his own approach differed from such theology if "God" and "man" from this sentence were interpreted as "divine *nature*" and "human *nature*." See John Meyendorff, "Justinian, the Empire and the Church," *Dumbarton Oaks Papers* 22 (1968): 60. Meyendorff's point is that in the hypostasis of the Logos God "ceases to remain 'in heaven,' bound by philosophical notions, a prisoner of His own transcendency, becomes fully 'compatible' with suffering humanity, and makes it His own" (60). But his *nature* remains "incompatible" with human sufferings, being philosophically defined as the opposite of human nature with respect to impassibility and changelessness. If categories such as impassibility, changelessness, and simplicity are indeed burdened with philosophical speculation, then Meyendorff seemed to release only God's personality from the boundaries of philosophical theology and left God's *nature* in philosophical captivity.

impassibility and immutability are hardly located beyond the dialectic of passibility and impassibility, mutability and immutability. Rather, they are the opposites of passibility and mutability and thus receive, *nolens volens*, a kind of a positive meaning, which casts doubt on the consistency of Meyendorff's use of negatives.

Participation in the Divine Nature

As we saw in previous sections, Meyendorff advocated the view that "divine essence and human nature can *never* ... be participated by each other."[179] They are separate and totally dissimilar.[180] The divine essence remains completely unknowable, totally unparticipable, incommunicable, transcendent, unattainable, and inaccessible both now and in the life to come.[181] Although humanity is called to participate in *God*, "there cannot be any participation in *divine essence* by man."[182] "Even in Christ, creatures cannot share God's essence."[183]

At the same time, Meyendorff makes some bold statements that seem to contradict the aforementioned principles. He says that in Jesus Christ "we have again access to the Father and become *participants in the divine nature*."[184] Elsewhere he says that the "divine and the human natures, while always remaining distinct, are not mutually incompatible, but, on the contrary,

---

179. Meyendorff, "Significance of the Reformation," 169, emphasis original.

180. Meyendorff, *Byzantine Theology*, 130.

181. Meyendorff, *Byzantine Theology*, 77, 181, 186; Meyendorff, "'Defense of the Holy Hesychasts,'" 184; Meyendorff, "Significance of the Reformation," 169; Meyendorff, "Reply to Jürgen Moltmann's," 187; Meyendorff, *Study of Gregory Palamas*, 183–84; Meyendorff, *Gregory Palamas*, 119, 122; Meyendorff, "Orthodox Theology," 184; Meyendorff, "Holy Trinity," 31; Meyendorff, *Christ in Eastern Christian Thought*, 144; Meyendorff, "Le dogme," 98; Meyendorf, *Vvedenie v svyatootecheskoe bogoslovie*, 274; Meyendorf, "Svyatoy Grigoriy Palama," 160; John Meyendorff, "An Early Medieval Bridge-Builder: Remarks on Eastern Patristic Thought in John Scot Eriugena," in *Rome, Constantinople, Moscow*, 67; Meyendorf, "Istoricheskoe znachenie ucheniya sv. Grigoriya Palamy" [The historical significance of the teaching of St. Gregory Palamas] *Vestnik Russkogo Studencheskogo Khristianskogo Dvizheniya [Bulletin of the Russian Student Christian Movement]* 46 (1957): 5.

182. Meyendorff, *Byzantine Theology*, 164, emphasis added. See also Meyendorff, *Christ in Eastern Christian Thought*, 126.

183. Meyendorff, "Holy Trinity," 34.

184. Meyendorff, "Significance of the Reformation," 171, emphasis added. See also Meyendorff, *Christ in Eastern Christian Thought*, 144. It is remarkable that in the same essay Meyendorff criticizes Western theology, which, proclaiming the identification of God with his essence, does not allow any other participation in God than participation in the divine essence (173).

are *open to communion*."[185] He also maintains that "deified human nature" is a "human nature *having come into communion with the divine nature*." It is remarkable that Meyendorff approvingly cites a passage from John of Damascus where he says that people (unlike angels, who partake only in grace but not in the divine nature) "*participate* ... [and] are *in communion with the divine nature*"—particularly concerning those who participate in the Eucharist: they have communion with Christ's body and blood, which are hypostatically united to the divine nature.[186] Is there a plausible account that would reconcile these statements with the alleged absolute transcendence and inaccessibility of the divine nature? The issue obviously needs some terminological and conceptual clarification.

In dealing with this matter, Meyendorff largely drew on the works of Gregory Palamas, who also, in his day, had to explain how the saints participate in God in one sense and do not participate in God in another. Palamas and his adversaries had to propose solutions to the antinomy caused by two seemingly competing and contradictory beliefs: on the one hand, 2 Peter 1:4 clearly states that the saints participate "in the divine nature"; on the other hand, there existed a "*consensus patrum* on the imparticipability of the divine essence."[187] Palamas's opponents held the opinion that the only uncreated reality is God's nature, and, seeking to avoid the notion of participation in the very nature of God, they either interpreted such participation in a nominal and symbolical sense or made several qualifications.[188] By contrast, Palamas did not equate the uncreated with God's essence, but believed that God exists in his essence *and*—also completely and entirely—in his energies. God, therefore, is wholly inaccessible and imparticipable in his essence and at the same time wholly accessible and participable in his energies. The Eucharist does not imply participation in the divine *nature*; rather, it is a participation in the deified humanity of

185. Meyendorff, "Christ's Humanity," 26, emphasis original.

186. Meyendorff, *Christ in Eastern Christian Thought*, 86, emphasis added.

187. Meyendorff, "Le dogme," 95.

188. Meyendorff, *Study of Gregory Palamas*, 205. See also Norman Russell, "'Partakers of the Divine Nature' (2 Peter 1:4) in the Byzantine Tradition," in *Kathegetria: Essays Presented to Joan Hussey on Her Eightieth Birthday*, ed. Julian Chrysostomides (Camberley, UK: Porphyrogenitus, 1988), 61. Akindynos clarified that participation in God's essence through the Eucharist is "relative, invisible, insensible, and in a sense naturally imparticipable" (Meyendorff, "Le dogme," 95).

Christ permeated by divine *energies*.[189] But since this solution insufficiently corresponded to 2 Peter 1:4 (which clearly speaks about the participation in divine *nature*), Palamas resorted to the distinction between two different meanings of the term "nature." In Meyendorff's words,

> Palamas rightly answers that there is no question of identifying the word "nature" (φύσις) as used in the New Testament with the Patristic conception of "nature"; all that the Apostle wished to express was the *reality* of our participation in the *very* life of God; ... therefore by "nature" he means sanctifying and deifying grace.[190]

Later Meyendorff cites Palamas himself, who says that theologians "have been accustomed to use the words 'nature' and 'essence' not only of that anonymous superessentiality which passes beyond all names, but also of the productive power of essence and of all the natural properties of God."[191] In the former sense, therefore, essence (or nature) means the unapproachable, impenetrable, unknowable divine "superessentiality." Participation in the divine nature in this sense is inadmissible and would obliterate the distinction between God and creatures. In the latter sense (as in 2 Pet 1:4), essence (or nature) means the "productive power" of essence. Participation in the divine nature in this sense is not only admissible but is the highest destiny of humanity. As indicated above, Meyendorff never made a distinction between the words "essence" and "nature." However, it is clear from his works that he tried to consistently use the word "essence" in the former sense (given its technical meaning as something distinct from "energy") and allowed more flexibility with the word "nature."

Giving the term "nature" two different meanings is not the only solution Palamas and Meyendorff contrived. They also suggested an approach that notionally is very close to the first one, but focuses on what may be called the "mode" of participation in the divine nature rather than on the

189. See Meyendorff, "Le dogme," 96–98.

190. Meyendorff, *Study of Gregory Palamas*, 178, emphasis original. In the French original, Meyendorff says that φύσις as used in the NT should not be identified with the patristic conception of οὐσία (which in the cited English translation was rendered also as "nature"). This does not mean, however, that Meyendorff differentiated between these two Greek terms. Rather, he used the words "nature" and "essence" interchangeably (Meyendorff, *Study of Gregory Palamas*, 184; Meyendorff, *Gregory Palamas*, 119).

191. Meyendorff, *Study of Gregory Palamas*, 178.

terms themselves. Although between the inaccessible essence and the accessible energies there is a real distinction, they are not to be separated. In this sense, while participating in the divine energy, the saints participate—indirectly—in the divine essence. Participation in the divine essence is a participation in what flows from the essence, but not in the essence itself. In a representative passage, Palamas states: "If we say that we participate in the divine nature through such an energy but not in the divine nature in itself, we remain within the bounds of orthodoxy."[192] Meyendorff continues this line of thought when, immediately after stating that we "become participants in the divine nature," he adds: "What He is by nature, we become by grace."[193] By grace (or energy), we share with God what he possesses by nature. Consequently, the difference between God and the deified saints consists not in the "what-ness," but in the "how-ness": they do not differ in *what they are*, but rather in *how they are* what they are. As we will see in "Ways to Unify" (pages 240–48), however, Meyendorff's thinking was ambiguous on this point, as he elsewhere denied that the energies manifest the divine nature, a notion that calls into question the very idea of an indirect manifestation of the nature or an indirect participation in it by grace.[194] Typically, Meyendorff maintained that grace is that which the saints participate in rather than a mode or channel of participating in the divine nature.

GOD REVEALED

In the previous two chapters I broadly covered two subjects: mystical union with God (with its anthropological and soteriological premises) and the absolute transcendence of the divine nature. In brief, these two subjects mean that Christians really experience God and participate in him, but at the same time the divine nature remains hidden and beyond participation. According to Meyendorff, these two considerations are foremost in the Orthodox understanding of true communion with God. The possibility and indeed reality of mystical union is deduced from the experience

192. PG 150:937D, cited in Russell, "'Partakers of the Divine Nature,'" 62.

193. Meyendorff, "Significance of the Reformation," 171.

194. Meyendorff, *Byzantine Theology*, 27, 130.

of the saints and precedes any "conceptual system."[195] Meyendorff asserts that the absolute transcendence of the divine nature is a basic assumption of Eastern theology,[196] but we can also understand it as being derived from the necessity to safeguard Orthodox theology against the pantheist implications, which arise given the breadth and depth of the union.

These key avowals bring us to "the main problem: *how to combine* the two affirmations, that we humans know God and that God is by nature unknowable."[197] This is the traditional Orthodox formulation of the task common to all Christian theologians: how to combine God's hiddenness with his revelation, God's transcendence with his immanence, and God's incommunicability with his communicability.[198] Meyendorff believed Western theology incapable of solving this issue. For him, in spite of all its seeming diversity, Western theology is inherently "essentialist," while "it is obvious that these two truths cannot be reconciled in the framework of an essentialist philosophy."[199] In such a framework, the allegation is, theology either ends up with the beatific vision of the divine nature (as in scholasticism), which denies the unknowability and transcendence of God, or with the radical otherness of God and eventually deism (as in Protestantism), which denies any real participation in God.[200]

The Orthodox solution is well known: it distinguishes between God's essence and energies. As a leading Palamas scholar of his time, Meyendorff, of course, often referred to the distinction and called it "the very basic palamite concept" and the "focal point of Palamite theology."[201] Together with other Orthodox theologians, Meyendorff argued that the concept allows the transcendence of God and communion with him to be affirmed and integrated. In what follows I will explore this distinction and other closely

195. Meyendorf, "Svyatoy Grigoriy Palama," 161, 165. See also Meyendorff, *Byzantine Theology*, 77.

196. "The absolutely unattainable nature of the divine essence" is one of "the basic axioms of Greek patristics" (Meyendorff, *Gregory Palamas*, 122).

197. Timothy (Kallistos) Ware, *The Orthodox Church: An Introduction to Eastern Christianity* (London: Penguin, 1993), 77, emphasis added.

198. Meyendorff, "Mount Athos in the Fourteenth Century," 163–64.

199. Meyendorff, *Gregory Palamas*, 119.

200. Meyendorff, "Significance of the Reformation," 173; Meyendorff, "Mount Athos in the Fourteenth Century," 164.

201. Meyendorff, "Holy Trinity," 31; Meyendorff, "'Defense of the Holy Hesychasts,'" 191.

related issues in detail. The discussion in this chapter, however, will start not with the essence-energies distinction but with a more general subject. More than most other Orthodox theologians, Meyendorff insisted that the concept of energies can only be understood from within the framework of a personalistic understanding of God. Only theological personalism provides the key to perceiving the doctrine of the divine energies, while all other interpretations are "bound to lead into a dead end."[202] Meyendorff mentioned "personalistic Trinitarianism" along with the essence-energies distinction as the two motives that enable Eastern Orthodoxy to maintain both the transcendence of the divine essence and the reality of humanity's communion with God.[203] Thus, before treating Meyendorff's view on the divine energies, we need to pay attention to his *personalistic* approach to the Trinity.

"Christian Personalism"

Philosophical and Theological Context

For Meyendorff, the task of the theologian is nothing other than explaining the Christian faith in terms and categories that are acceptable and familiar to their own generation. He was convinced that the church fathers were neither innovators nor formal conservatives: rather, they listened to their contemporaries and employed concepts available that could really reach them. This is what all Orthodox theologians are supposed to do: "Our task today consists not simply in repeating patristic formulae, but in developing a Christian Trinitarianism also *consistent* with that Tradition while confronting the challenges of our time."[204] Although Meyendorff did not write specifically on philosophical issues, he was sensitive to the philosophical mood and ideas of his contemporaries.

Meyendorff and other Orthodox theologians recognized that the middle decades of the twentieth century were marked by the predominance of existentialism in Western philosophy. In an atmosphere of anxiety, uncertainty, and alienation, philosophers rediscovered such nineteenth-century

---

202. Meyendorff, *Study of Gregory Palamas*, 212–13; Meyendorff, "Holy Trinity," 31.

203. Meyendorff, "Theosis in the Eastern Christian Tradition," 476.

204. Meyendorff, "Holy Trinity," 42, emphasis original.

thinkers as Søren Kierkegaard and Fyodor Dostoevsky with their emphases on an individual's quest for truth and freedom, subjective experience, and the paradoxical nature of Christianity. Martin Buber's distinction between the I–Thou relationship and the I–It relationship led to a reconsideration of the importance of a personal encounter with God; Nikolai Berdyaev's insistence on the centrality of the human personality induced others to likewise focus on this concept in theology; Martin Heidegger's interpretation of the disclosure of truth as something that "happens" strengthened the idea of the free and personal revelation of God as an event. Most importantly, Jean-Paul Sartre's view of existence as preceding essence meant that a person first exists and then "chooses" their essence. The person is not bound to their nature; they are able to transcend it.

For a better understanding of the reaction of Orthodox theologians to existentialism, it is important to realize that they also depended on some Catholic thinkers who argued that "true existentialism" is to be found in the Christian tradition. Few Catholics went as far as Gabriel Marcel, who considered himself a "Christian existentialist," but many found at least similarities between existentialist concerns and the insights of such theologians as Augustine and Aquinas. Jacques Maritain called Thomism "existential philosophy," adding that it does not give primacy to existence by suppressing essence.[205] It was another theologian from the neo-Thomist movement, Étienne Gilson, who especially criticized essentialism on the one hand and atheistic existentialism on the other, and who presented Thomism as the authentic existentialism: "Thomism is not *another* existential philosophy, it is *the only one*."[206]

Orthodox theologians, mainly by way of Lossky, who wrote his dissertation under the direction of Gilson, took up these philosophical themes and borrowed heavily from this Catholic strategy. However, their thinking turned it in another direction. In their schema, Roman Catholic theology, if not Western theology in general, had been essentialist at least since Augustine, whose dependence on Neoplatonic—essentialist—thinking was

205. Jacques Maritain, *A Preface to Metaphysics: Seven Lectures on Being* (New York: Sheed & Ward, 1958), 24, emphasis original.

206. Étienne Gilson, *Thomism: The Philosophy of Thomas Aquinas*, 6th ed., trans. Laurence K. Shook and Armand A. Maurer (Toronto: Pontifical Institute of Mediaeval Studies, 2002), 417.

taken for granted.[207] This unfortunate synthesis of Greek philosophy and the Christian faith culminated in scholasticism and Thomism, in particular. By contrast, Eastern theology remained faithful to biblical revelation and approached the doctrine of God in a more personalistic way.[208] The culmination of this tradition was Palamism—a truly "existential" theology. Therefore, Palamas, not Aquinas, was a promising source for those wishing to respond to the problems of contemporary philosophy. Neo-Palamism, not neo-Thomism, was able to offer a genuine Christian alternative to secular existentialism and present the gospel in a creative fashion that could be readily accepted. Using this strategy, Orthodox theologians not only tried to achieve their abiding task of proving the distinctiveness of Eastern theology, but they also hoped to impress their contemporaries with a theological way of thinking that supposedly had striking parallels with the leading philosophical movement of the time. The contribution of yet another Catholic theologian, de Régnon, was also crucial for Orthodox theologians, because their reading of his paradigm (discussed above) perfectly served their goals.

Meyendorff, especially in his early works, openly followed this argumentation strategy. Even the chapter titles from his books reveal how ingenuously he tried to express Orthodox doctrine in existential terms. The chapter of his dissertation (1959), about Palamas's famous distinction, is titled "An Existential Theology: Essence and Energy."[209] Another book published the same year, *St Gregory Palamas and Orthodox Spirituality*, contains a chapter devoted to the essence-energy distinction called "A Christian Existentialism."[210] Already in the introduction to his famous study about Palamas, Meyendorff recommends him as "a theologian who, in some respects, is more in tune than others with the preoccupations of modern thought"—and it is obvious which preoccupations Meyendorff

207. Meyendorff, *Study of Gregory Palamas*, 228; Meyendorff, "Greek Philosophy and Christian Theology," 45.

208. Meyendorff, *Study of Gregory Palamas*, 212–13, 215, 232; Meyendorff, *Orthodox Church*, 177–78.

209. Meyendorff, *Study of Gregory Palamas*, 202–27.

210. Meyendorff, *Gregory Palamas*, 115–26. In another publication, Meyendorff identifies Palamism as "Christian existentialism" and claims that the distinction between essence and energy is "a suitable theological formula for the expression of a kind of Christian existentialism" ("Istoricheskoe znachenie," 5).

has in mind.[211] Palamas's case is described further in the book as an "existential" one over and against the "essentialist" position of his opponents.[212] For Palamas, the image of God in humanity is an "existential" reality and the divine operations are "existential"; what diverted Palamas from purely abstract thinking and allowed him to start from actual historical data was again his "existentialism."[213] In his article about Palamas's doctrine of grace (1954), Meyendorff argues that Palamas adopted an "existential attitude" in his concept of God, and his doctrine of energies had "existential and dynamic aspects." He finishes the article with the hope that his contemporaries will recognize and welcome the "existential" side of the Orthodox tradition: "Our epoch, which is regaining a more 'existential' attitude towards God and the world, will be perhaps more able to appreciate this particular aspect of the Orthodox theology than was possible in the past."[214]

Meyendorff's early works on Palamas were mostly well received. Not only his main conclusions but also his terms were taken up by others. Some Orthodox theologians, however, were more skeptical of Meyendorff's persistent attempts to bring Orthodox doctrine into the modern context. One reviewer accused him of modernizing Palamas's teaching through the irksome repetition of a modern philosophical vocabulary.[215] In the course of time, Meyendorff himself became less enthusiastic about the term "existentialism" (though he did not abandon it altogether) and began to prefer the term "personalism" with the same meaning.[216] He used both terms in different theological loci to characterize a variety of theological motifs and concerns in Eastern theological thought. In spite of the diversity of issues,

---

211. Meyendorff, *Study of Gregory Palamas*, 6.

212. Meyendorff, *Study of Gregory Palamas*, 211. In trying to translate the essence of the Palamite controversy into terms that are common to the Western philosophical tradition, Meyendorff, curiously enough, claimed that Barlaam was both a nominalist and a Platonist. Romanides sharply criticized Meyendorff's choice of terms, arguing that nominalist and Platonist views are mutually exclusive. See John Romanides, "Notes on the Palamite Controversy and Related Topics. Part 1," *The Greek Orthodox Theological Review* 6 (1960–1961): 187–88.

213. Meyendorff, *Study of Gregory Palamas*, 120, 130, 210.

214. Meyendorff, *Study of Gregory Palamas*, 24–25.

215. Basil Krivoshein, "Svyatoy Grigoriy Palama. Lichnost' i uchenie po nedavno opublikovannym materialam" [Saint Gregory Palamas: His life and teaching according to recently published materials], *Vestnik Russkogo Zapadno-evropeyskogo Patriarshego Ekzarkhata* [Bulletin of the Russian West-European Patriarchal Exarchate] 33–34 (1960): 101–2.

216. Meyendorf, "Svyatoy Grigoriy Palama," 165; Meyendorff, "Christian Theology," 67.

the main function of this alleged Orthodox "existentialism" or "personalism" is to indicate a specific approach in the doctrine of God: namely, a certain priority of the divine personal existence over the divine essence (nature).

The Priority of Person over Essence

In dealing with Meyendorff's explanation of God's absolute transcendence, I have already drawn attention to his belief in a consistent theological tradition from the Cappadocians (and even earlier theologians including the authors of the Bible) to Palamas. The same holds true for the alleged personalism of the Eastern tradition. According to Meyendorff, personalism has been characteristic of theology in the East from at least the Cappadocians onward, though it was already anticipated and grounded in the biblical doctrine of the living God. Like the doctrine of the unknowability of God's essence, the personalistic emphasis in Eastern theology is another point where its fundamental difference from Greek philosophy and Western theology becomes manifest. Meyendorff maintained that the Cappadocians did not simply borrow such terms as ὑπόστασις and φύσις from Greek philosophy but produced a revolution in Greek ontology by totally reinterpreting them.[217] Aristotle could hardly have been able to understand Basil, because the latter used the same terms with a different meaning.[218] In particular, "the Cappadocians ... refined the meaning of *hypostasis* in the direction of personalism."[219] Meyendorff explains this refinement in greater detail elsewhere: "neither in Aristotelianism nor in Neoplatonism was the term intended to designate a person in the Christian (and modern) sense, an agent, 'possessing' his own nature and 'acting' accordingly, a unique subject, whose absolute identity can in no way be duplicated."[220] It is the Cappadocians, therefore, who first imparted to the term "hypostasis" (person) the connotations of agency, uniqueness, and subjectivity. Meyendorff, in fact, identified "the Christian" (or Cappadocian) sense of

217. Meyendorff, *Vvedenie v svyatootecheskoe bogoslovie*, 164.

218. Meyendorff, "Historical Relativism and Authority," 42. "This new meaning was certainly scripturally inspired, but it was also foreign to Greek philosophical thought" (Meyendorff, "Christ's Humanity," 11).

219. Meyendorff, "Christ's Humanity," 11.

220. Meyendorff, *Byzantine Theology*, 182, emphasis original.

person with the "modern" sense, which, of course, reveals his "existential" concerns. He seemed to recognize a clear continuity and evolution not only from the Cappadocians up to Palamas but even beyond, toward the modern philosophers. The modern notion of person originates then, not with Descartes, Locke, or Kant but with Basil and the Gregories.[221]

In one form or another, Meyendorff repeated the idea of the priority of person over essence, although he never gave it its own systematic treatment. While not confined to a single book chapter or lengthy article, various elements of this idea are scattered throughout his numerous publications. Apart from the peculiarities of Meyendorff's style, this can be explained by the fact that he considered this priority not as a specific doctrine but as a general perspective, which sets the proper tone for the discussion of various theological matters. For the sake of order and clarity, however, I will outline several aspects of this prioritization as it appears in Meyendorff's writings and treat them sequentially, even if this entails a higher level of systematization than Meyendorff himself aspired to.

The Methodological Aspect. I will start from an aspect that has arguably drawn the most attention of scholars. It may be called methodological, as it concerns the order in which the doctrine of God is approached and taught. This aspect is prominent in many of Meyendorff's writings, especially his historical overviews. He argued that the Cappadocians began with the three divine persons, whereas Augustine preferred to begin with the essential unity of God. As noted above, Meyendorff followed de Régnon's paradigm, as popularly received, in claiming that these two approaches later led to the establishment of the "Eastern" and "Western" schools of Trinitarian theology.[222] What is noteworthy, however, is that Meyendorff urged that

---

221. The point of the Cappadocians' linguistic and philosophical "revolution" was explained in more detail by Zizioulas, who argued that by dissociating ὑπόστασις from οὐσία and giving primacy to ὑπόστασις, the Cappadocians broke off with ancient Greek philosophical thought and brought about a "great innovation," which had immense consequences for the development of European philosophy and remains relevant for contemporary (existential) thought. See John Zizioulas, "The Doctrine of the Holy Trinity: The Significance of the Cappadocian Contribution," in *Trinitarian Theology Today*, ed. Christoph Schwöbel (Edinburgh: T&T Clark, 1995), 49–54.

222. Meyendorff, *Orthodox Church*, 178. Meyendorff argues that the Cappadocians' personalism was further developed in the East by Maximus, who had "a personalistic concept of the hypostasis" (*Christ in Eastern Christian Thought*, 145), which for him was "a central notion in both theology and anthropology" (*Byzantine Theology*, 142). Maximus, in particular, affirmed that hypostasis is the source and not the product of the nature. The centrality of the notion of

this difference not be overplayed. He believed that the two approaches as such were not at odds, but could rather complement and enrich each other. In an article for an ecumenical volume, Meyendorff writes that "the contrast between the two traditions must not, of course, be exaggerated. It is indeed legitimate to contemplate the mystery of the One and of the Three, starting with one end of it or with the other."[223] Elsewhere he states that the Trinitarian approach of the Eastern fathers "distinguished them—without opposing them, however—to the way in which their Latin brothers preferred to think of God first as a unique essence, and then only as a Trinity."[224] Meyendorff used to describe the difference between the two approaches as merely a "difference of emphasis" and, at first sight, he found them equally acceptable and helpful.[225]

---

hypostasis also played a major role in the eighth century, when disputes over icons reached fever pitch. According to Meyendorff, "it is only the personalism of patristic theology that makes it possible to overcome the essential dilemma of the iconoclastic controversy and provides a solid basis for the veneration of images" (*Christ in Eastern Christian Thought*, 188–89). This is because the iconoclast Christology failed to recognize the implications of the hypostatic union, which allows the preservation of the characteristics of divine and human natures within a single hypostasis. In later centuries, Meyendorff claims, the Greeks "continued to defend the primacy of the hypostases in relation to the essence" (*Study of Gregory Palamas*, 228) in their polemics with the Latins and thus "remained faithful to the old 'personalism' of the Greek Fathers" (*Orthodox Church*, 178). The Eastern personalism reached its zenith in the theology of Palamas: it was "a personal existentialism" (Meyendorff, *Gregory Palamas*, 123) and his "completely personalist" (Meyendorff, *Study of Gregory Palamas*, 230) thought that helped Palamas to confront "essentialist" challenges of his time, be they "philosophical" or "Western." Meyendorff emphasized that Palamas did not discover the distinction between essence and energy or the priority of person over essence; rather, he shaped them into a more concrete form.

223. Meyendorff, "Theosis in the Eastern Christian Tradition," 475.

224. Meyendorff, *Orthodox Church*, 178.

225. Meyendorff, *Byzantine Theology*, 181; see also Meyendorff, *Orthodox Church*, 178. To be sure, Eastern theologians also used to start with the Father to confirm *both* the diversity and unity in God. In particular, as Beeley says, Gregory of Nazianzus "repeatedly locates the divine unity not in the common Divinity, ... but in the monarchy of the Father." See Christopher A. Beeley, *Gregory of Nazianzus on the Trinity and the Knowledge of God: In Your Light We Shall See Light* (Oxford: Oxford University Press, 2008), 207. In other words, God is one not because the three persons share one and the same nature but because there is only one source and principle of the Trinity: God the Father. However, the choice of the Father as a starting point did not imply the priority of person over essence, because in the early tradition the *person* of the Father was not as detached from the *essence* as he was in Meyendorff's theology (see pages 195–99). In any case, Meyendorff understands the priority of person over essence as the "priority of trinitarianism over the notion of divine unity," that is, the priority of diversity over unity ("Theology of the Holy Spirit," 16; see also John Meyendorff, "The Holy Spirit, as God," in *Byzantine Legacy*, 154).

Despite such generous ecumenical remarks, Meyendorff adopted a critical attitude toward the "Western" position in a number of ways. First, he argued that the responsibility for the failure of the complementary development of the two approaches is to be placed on the West. For it is the West that, by adding the *filioque* clause, turned into dogma what would otherwise have been only methodological or pedagogical in nature.[226] Meyendorff held that the *filioque* is no accidental element in Western theology but a natural consequence of Western Trinitarianism. While formally recognizing the legitimacy of the Western approach, Meyendorff adds, however, that in a theology in which the persons are considered as the simple inner relations of the Godhead, the doctrine of the *filioque* "becomes a logical, dogmatic necessity."[227] So, according to Meyendorff, Photius was right to recognize that behind the *filioque* dispute lay two differing concepts of the Trinity: "the Greek personalistic concept," which starts with the Father, the Son, and the Spirit, and the Latin concept, which starts with God as simple essence.[228] To make the *filioque* justifiable, Meyendorff contends, one needs to postulate that the origin of the Spirit is the essence rather than the person.[229]

Second, Meyendorff pointed to the detrimental effects of prioritizing the unity of essence for the whole structure of Western theological thinking. The *filioque* is the most (in)famous, but not the most deplorable, consequence of the Western Trinitarian approach. Having described the different Trinitarian starting points in West and East, Meyendorff comments: "These two tendencies are at the origin of the *filioque* dispute, but they are also of great relevance for the present."[230] In the quoted passage he does not specify the relevancy, but in other works he explains that the Western focus on the divine essence led to neglect of the doctrine of the Trinity. Meyendorff regretted that Western theology and spirituality often dealt

226. Meyendorff, *Byzantine Theology*, 181; see also Meyendorf, *Vvedenie v svyatootecheskoe bogoslovie*, 305–6.

227. Meyendorff, *Orthodox Church*, 178; see also Meyendorff, "Reply to Jürgen Moltmann's," 183; Meyendorff, *Byzantine Theology*, 188.

228. Meyendorff, *Byzantine Theology*, 61.

229. Meyendorff, "Christ's Humanity," 16; Meyendorff, "Two Visions," 47.

230. Meyendorff, "Orthodox Theology," 184.

with the Trinity only as an afterthought.[231] As a result, the average Western Christian (especially the Protestant Christian!) believes in a God-in-general, while the belief in the Father, the Son, and the Spirit is an outdated complexity and an unnecessary appendage.[232] Meyendorff went so far as to outline a relatively straightforward evolution from the Augustinian emphasis on the unity of God to modern deism. Ultimately, the Western approach to the Trinity is abstract, theoretical, and philosophical, whereas the Eastern approach is "truly Christian, that is, biblical and experiential."[233]

The Experiential Aspect. It has often been argued that one of the most significant features of Eastern theology as compared with the Christian West lies in its experiential nature. In the East, theology supposedly implies mystical contemplation, communion with the Spirit, and personal involvement, while in the West it is a matter of intellectual exercise rather than religious experience. Meyendorff shared these sentiments, and for him this was another example of the uniqueness of Eastern theology and spirituality. To his credit, he was not satisfied with general observations, but tried to demonstrate how this difference manifests itself in various theological issues. The doctrine of God is particularly revealing in this sense, because, according to Meyendorff, the more experiential orientation of Eastern theology has direct implications for the priority of person over essence.

Since Meyendorff was not a theologian whose works were saturated with biblical references, every Bible verse cited by him with any regularity naturally attracts our attention. When Meyendorff dealt with the relation between the divine persons and the essence, he referred to Matthew 16:16 with surprising frequency. In this verse, Peter confesses Jesus as the Christ and the Son of the living God.[234] Meyendorff took this verse as paradigmatic and a proof that God's revelation always bears a *personal* character.

---

231. Meyendorff, "Theosis in the Eastern Christian Tradition," 475.

232. Meyendorf, *Vvedenie v svyatootecheskoe bogoslovie*, 166. To substantiate this criticism, Meyendorff, unsurprisingly, referred to such Catholic theologians as de Régnon and Karl Rahner, who also lamented the decline of Trinitarian thought in Western theology (Meyendorff, *Byzantine Theology*, 181).

233. Meyendorf, *Vvedenie v svyatootecheskoe bogoslovie*, 166, 230; see also 305.

234. Meyendorff, "Holy Spirit, as God," 154; Meyendorff, "Theology of the Holy Spirit," 17; Meyendorff, "Theosis in the Eastern Christian Tradition," 475; Meyendorff, "Reply to Jürgen Moltmann's," 186; Meyendorff, "Christ's Humanity," 11; Meyendorf, *Vvedenie v svyatootecheskoe bogoslovie*, 305.

He argued that the Cappadocians' starting point (three persons instead of one essence) sprang from the fact that Christian faith, as illustrated in this verse, starts with the confession of *one* of the divine persons—namely, the Son of God.[235] As our experience begins with Jesus Christ, so also our approach to the Trinity in theology should start from the three persons instead of the one essence.

In a similar vein, but without appealing to a central Scripture verse, Meyendorff tried to prove the priority of person over essence based on the personal revelation of the Holy Spirit. It was the *person* of the Spirit who spoke to individual Christians and the church (Acts 8:29; 10:19; 13:2), entered into fellowship with human persons, and comforted them.[236] Although the three persons are inseparable from one another, the divine personal presence of the Spirit is distinct from the divine personal revelation of the Son. "Each divine Person is met or encountered in a unique, personal way."[237]

"The primarily personal revelation of God" is further found by Meyendorff in the baptismal formula of Matthew 28:19, the benediction of 2 Corinthians 13:14, and other passages.[238] Meyendorff deduces from such passages that Christian experience does not have to do with the abstract essence of God but with the living God in three persons. Christianity is all about the encounter of humanity and God. Salvation consists not in the participation of human nature in the divine nature, but in the restoration of an interpersonal relationship—when "human persons enter into the loving circle of the Three Divine Persons."[239] A theology in which the focal or starting point is the essential unity of God does not do justice to this experiential primacy of the divine *persons*, Meyendorff contended. "There is no meeting with an impersonal Divinity, or divine essence," and if our theology corresponds to our experience, it is natural that it also gives a certain priority to the *persons*.[240]

---

235. Meyendorf, *Vvedenie v svyatootecheskoe bogoslovie*, 305; Meyendorff, "Reply to Jürgen Moltmann's," 186.

236. Meyendorff, "Holy Spirit, as God," 154–55; Meyendorff, "Theology of the Holy Spirit," 17–19; Meyendorff, "Theosis in the Eastern Christian Tradition," 475; Meyendorf, *Vvedenie v svyatootecheskoe bogoslovie*, 330.

237. Meyendorff, "Christ's Humanity," 11–12.

238. Meyendorff, "Holy Spirit, as God," 154–55.

239. Meyendorff, "Reply to Jürgen Moltmann's," 187.

240. Meyendorff, "Christ's Humanity," 11.

As was typical for Meyendorff, he contrasted the Eastern tradition with Greek philosophy and Western Christianity. The emphasis on the personal encounter with the *three* divine persons indicates a profound difference between Eastern theology and Neoplatonism, which focused on communion with the *One*.[241] Neoplatonic notions later played a crucial role in shaping Augustine's theological thought, which in its turn played a crucial role in the development of Western theology as a whole.[242] According to Meyendorff's description, the West was captivated by essentialist thinking and did not recognize the primacy of the divine persons in Christian experience.[243] By contrast, Eastern theologians took the personalistic emphasis of the New Testament more seriously.[244] As a result, they "insisted on a certain experiential primacy of the personal—and trinitarian—existence of God, over His essential or 'natural' unity."[245]

Meyendorff did not clearly differentiate this experiential priority of the divine persons over the common essence in *our perception of* God from the *objective* God's existence.[246] The *filioque* clause may again be a case in point. Meyendorff asserts that the *filioque* dispute "was not a discussion on words" but on the issue of "whether tri-personality or consubstantiality was the first and basic content of *Christian religious experience*."[247] Thus, the Eastern rejection of the *filioque* is fundamentally caused by the experiential primacy of tri-personality in the Eastern perception of God, while the Western addition of the *filioque* clause follows on from its experiential focus on the unity of God. It appears then that the dispute over the eternal procession of the Spirit is dependent on our religious experience. When it comes to the relation between person and essence, Meyendorff moved rather quickly and easily from how we experience God to what is in God. This is particularly remarkable when one considers that Orthodox theologians normally carefully distinguish between the eternal procession of the Spirit and the temporal sending of the Spirit, and deny that the

241. Meyendorff, "Theosis in the Eastern Christian Tradition," 475.
242. Meyendorff, "Greek Philosophy and Christian Theology," 36–37.
243. Meyendorff, "Orthodox Theology," 180.
244. Meyendorff, "Theosis in the Eastern Christian Tradition," 475.
245. Meyendorff, "Christ's Humanity," 11.
246. Meyendorff, "Reply to Jürgen Moltmann's," 186.
247. Meyendorff, *Byzantine Theology*, 94, emphasis added.

economic necessarily coincides with the ontological.[248] Meyendorff, however, supposed that the key to solving the *filioque* issue lay in analysis of the Christian *experience*.

The (Onto)logical Aspect. In speaking about the "experiential primacy of the personal ... existence of God over His essential or 'natural' unity" in the theology of the Cappadocians, Meyendorff immediately adds that "this primacy was neither chronological, nor, certainly, ontological."[249] While the meaning of the chronological priority is obvious, it is less clear what Meyendorff means by denying "ontological" primacy. He may have wanted to exclude the connotation of qualitative superiority, which could be associated with the word "primacy," or, perhaps, to differentiate between aspects of the primacy of person over essence, restricting himself in this particular passage to the experiential one. Whatever his intentions are in this rather obscure sentence, it is evident that in explaining the priority of the divine persons over the one essence Meyendorff tried to eschew the terms "logical" or "ontological." To be sure, he once contrasts the Eastern preference of "personal diversity over essential unity" with the Western recognition of "the *ontological* primacy of essential unity over personal diversity in God."[250] But even here the word "ontological" describes the position of the West, not the East. Thus, before analyzing what I have called the (onto)logical aspect, I must acknowledge that Meyendorff himself might have had some reservations, perhaps even objections, about such terminology.[251] The following analysis, however, will hopefully make clear that Meyendorff's language

---

248. Meyendorff himself notes that the usual argument of the Orthodox side in the *filioque* dispute consisted in distinguishing between the "procession of the 'Spirit' from or through the Son ... *in time*" and "the *eternal* procession of the Spirit from the hypostasis of the Father" (*Byzantine Theology*, 93). In this way, Orthodox theologians can deny the *filioque* clause on the eternal ontological level and simultaneously admit the procession "from both" on the economic level (189). It must be added, however, that Meyendorff preferred another strategy in dealing with the *filioque*, which will be described below in the section about God's internal energies.

249. Meyendorff, "Christ's Humanity," 11.

250. Meyendorff, *Byzantine Theology*, 184, emphasis added.

251. The reluctance to speak of an "ontological priority" is typical also for other Orthodox theologians. Zizioulas, to mention only one, maintains the priority of the persons with respect to essence and even develops it further by using his favorite relational categories, but he also refuses to accept that such priority can be called ontological. Thus, having explained that the nature of God is communion, Zizioulas goes on to say: "This does not mean that the persons have an ontological priority over the one substance of God" (*Being as Communion*, 134). Elsewhere, however, Zizioulas admits such priority, claiming that by "stressing that it is the person of the Father and not divine substance that is the source and cause of the

and ideas *suggested* the terms "logical" and "ontological" or at least failed to provide convincing reasons why they should be avoided.

As a theologian who sought to faithfully represent the Eastern tradition, Meyendorff stated his adherence to the monarchy (μοναρχία, singleness of source) of the Father—an idea that has been firmly established in the East since the Cappadocians. Basil and the two Gregories might have had somewhat different purposes for establishing this idea, but they unanimously held that the ὑπόστασις should not be conceived independently of the οὐσία and the οὐσία independently of the ὑπόστασις. The Father, as the single source of the Trinity, is never *only* hypostasis but hypostasis *and* essence.[252] Meyendorff, however, sought more clarity and precision with respect to the ontological terms. Referring to the Cappadocians and Maximus, in the section titled "Personalism," he states that the Son of God receives "the divine nature from the hypostasis of the Father." Remarkably, Meyendorff explains here the monarchy of the Father as having to do with the *hypostasis* of the Father and the *nature* of the Son. The hypostasis is the nature's "possessor": who gives it (in the case of the Father) and receives it (in the case of the Son). Later in this section, Meyendorff identifies this idea with "theological personalism" and calls it "the fundamental feature" of the Eastern tradition.[253] Elsewhere, again appealing to the Cappadocians, Meyendorff claims that the monarchy of the Father has a "personalistic emphasis," for it is the hypostasis of the Father that is the cause and principle "of the divine nature, which is in the Son and in the Spirit."[254] By focusing on the priority of the *hypostasis* of the Father over the *nature* of the Son and the Spirit, Meyendorff shifts the emphasis from relations between the Father, the Son, and the Spirit to the relation between two categories—person and nature.[255]

Trinity," the Cappadocians "gave to the person ontological priority" ("Doctrine of the Holy Trinity," 52, 54–55, see also 53).

252. Torrance, *Christian Doctrine*, 141. See also Beeley, *Gregory of Nazianzus*, 216.

253. Meyendorff, *Study of Gregory Palamas*, 212–13.

254. Meyendorff, *Byzantine Theology*, 183.

255. As Beeley observes about Meyendorff's interpretation of Gregory of Nazianzus: "By artificially separating the categories of *hypostasis* and nature from one another, Meyendorff grossly misrepresents Gregory's doctrine. For Gregory, the first principle of the Trinity is neither 'personhood' nor the divine essence per se, but God the Father, who, as unbegotten

The demands of logic and ontological interests (the prioritization of person over essence) urged Meyendorff to take yet another step. Since the divine nature is one, it is logical that the hypostasis of the Father is also the cause and source of his own nature. Meyendorff appeals to Palamas to support his own view that "the origin of the divine Essence is the *hypostasis* of the Father." If that were not the case, Meyendorff continues, "Christian personalism would give place to the essentialism of the Greek philosophers."[256] Here, Meyendorff no longer attempts to differentiate between how the divine essence subsists in different persons, but states that the hypostasis of the Father is the origin of the divine essence. In this way, Meyendorff again adjusts the Cappadocians' belief in the monarchy of the Father to conform to his polemical interests in the personalist-essentialist (Eastern-Western) debate.[257]

In other writings, Meyendorff argued that the hypostasis of the Father is the origin of all divine existence.[258] Although here he speaks of existence rather than essence, the contexts of these statements do not imply a major difference between the two terms in this passage. The most

Divinity, is both *hypostasis and* divine essence" (*Gregory of Nazianzus*, 212).

Obviously, Meyendorff was uneasy with the pronouncement of the Nicene Creed (325) about the generation of the Son from the *essence* of the Father. Unlike the Creed of Constantinople (381), which simply stated that the Son proceeds from the Father, this older pronouncement was more precise. However, in Meyendorff's view it contained a wrong term. Meyendorff's solution is straightforward and consists in replacing the word "essence" with the desired word "hypostasis": "When Nicaea said that the Son proceeded 'from the essence' (ἐκ τῆς οὐσίας) of the Father, it meant to say that he comes 'from the *hypostasis*' of the Father and that the person or *hypostasis* of the Father is the 'origin of the Godhead.' This personalistic approach to Trinitarian theology was to be developed by the Cappadocian Fathers" ("Nicene Creed," 11). For more recent opposing assessments of the alteration made by the Council of Constantinople, see esp. Zizioulas, *Communion and Otherness*, 120; Zizioulas, "Doctrine of the Holy Trinity," 51–52; Torrance, *Trinitarian Perspectives*, 113; Torrance, *Christian Doctrine*, 141, 186; Torrance, *Trinitarian Faith*, 319.

256. Meyendorff, *Study of Gregory Palamas*, 215. Demetracopoulos contests this reading of Palamas and concludes that in the passage to which Meyendorff refers, Palamas *rejects* as a mere "prattle" the view that Meyendorff ascribes to him. See John A. Demetracopoulos, *Is Gregory Palamas an Existentialist? The Restoration of the True Meaning of His Comment on Exodus 3,14: "Ἐγώ εἰμι ὁ ὤν"* (Athens: Parousia, 1996), 19–25.

257. Compare: "The claim that God the Father 'as a person' is above or prior to His existence would be meaningless for the patristic mind. ... Monarchy is not the monarchy of the 'person of the Father' above or beyond the common nature." See Chrysostom Koutloumousianos, *The One and the Three: Nature, Person and Triadic Monarchy in the Greek and Irish Patristic Tradition* (Cambridge: Clarke, 2015), 20–21.

258. Meyendorff, "Theology of the Holy Spirit," 18; Meyendorff, "Christ's Humanity," 16.

characteristic statement is found in Meyendorff's study on Palamas: "The Greeks continued to defend the primacy of the hypostases in relation to the essence and, particularly, to assert that the Father, as hypostasis, is the Source of all Divinity."[259] The monarchy of the Father is presented here as just a particular example of the general ontological rule about the primacy of the hypostases in relation to the essence. Thus, Meyendorff makes another move: the priority in relation to the essence belongs not only to the one hypostasis (of the Father), but to the *hypostases* (note the plural ending in the quote). Remarkably, when Meyendorff makes the statement (which he claims follows on from the Cappadocians and Maximus) that the divine person "is source and not product of nature," he is talking about the person of the Logos and not that of the Father. In Meyendorff's view, the relation between the hypostases and the essence is not that of identity (where the essence and the person relate as the general to the particular), but rather of causality and ownership (where the persons "possess" the essence).[260]

Meyendorff experienced difficulties in demonstrating such (onto)logical priority of the divine person(s) from the Bible. The only passage to which he regularly referred in such contexts was Exodus 3:14, where God reveals himself to Moses as "I am who I am." Meyendorff, however, did not delve into the exegetical details but confined himself to reproducing Palamas's deeply ontological interpretation of this text. His approach has striking parallels with that of Gilson: just as Gilson tried to demonstrate that Exodus 3:14 allowed Aquinas to understand God as *esse ipsum subsistens*, so also Meyendorff tried to demonstrate that the same verse allowed Palamas to articulate the priority of hypostasis over essence (or more specifically, the derivation of essence from the person).[261] Nevertheless, Meyendorff's interpretation of Palamas was sharply criticized by a number of Orthodox theologians, which, given the weighty character of

---

259. Meyendorff, *Study of Gregory Palamas*, 228.

260. Meyendorff, *Study of Gregory Palamas*, 212; Meyendorff, *Christ in Eastern Christian Thought*, 77.

261. Meyendorff bases his conclusion on Palamas's words, which he translates as follows: "God, when he was speaking with Moses, did not say: 'I am the essence,' but 'I am that I am' (Ex. 3:14). It is not therefore He-that-is who comes from the essence, but it is the essence which comes from He-that-is" (Meyendorff, *Study of Gregory Palamas*, 213; see also Meyendorff, *Gregory Palamas*, 118; Meyendorff, *Byzantine Theology*, 188; Meyendorff, "'Defense of the Holy Hesychasts,'" 192; Meyendorf, *Vvedenie v svyatootecheskoe bogoslovie*, 330; Meyendorff, "Palamas [Grégoire]," 98).

the criticism, suggests that even Palamas can hardly be enlisted in support of Meyendorff's idea.[262]

The Existential Aspect. As noted above, Meyendorff attributed not only a clearer distinction between the terms ὑπόστασις and οὐσία to the Cappadocians but also the priority of ὑπόστασις over οὐσία. Meyendorff adds that the subsequent "refinement" of theological terminology in the Eastern tradition after the Cappadocians was tied to the idea of "openness to existential change." Seeking to explain how the divine Logos could undergo natural growth, suffering, and death, Eastern theologians made an even sharper distinction between hypostasis and essence and defined hypostasis as a subject that can transcend his essence and assume another essence.[263] Meyendorff ascribed a key role in the evolution of the concept of person to Leontius of Byzantium, who worked out the Cappadocian "personalistic emphasis" in Christology.[264] Meyendorff believed that Leontius's major contribution to Christian theology consisted in interpreting the term ἐνυπόστατον as implying existence within a hypostasis. In Leontius's theology, Meyendorff argued, hypostasis denotes an existence "by itself": it is not derived from nature but indicates that in which nature exists.[265]

According to Meyendorff, the person's capacity to transcend his essence means that a person is not bound to, or determined by, his essence but

---

262. Demetracopoulos suggests that Meyendorff wrongly translated the text, took it out of context, and attributed to it an ontological meaning which was foreign to Palamas. Demetracopoulos demonstrates that the Palamite distinction between "he who is" and "essence" does not have anything to do with the distinction between "God as person" and "God as nature," but should rather be interpreted in the light of a similar statement of pseudo-Dionysius, in which this distinction means the distinction between the transcendence (superessentiality) of God and the beings of his creatures. In the final analysis, in the passage in question Palamas "states nothing more than the trivial Christian doctrine that it is creation that is derived from God and not, of course, God that is derived from creation" (Demetracopoulos, *Is Gregory Palamas an Existentialist?*, 33). Demetracopoulos's verdict is rather severe: "My view is that Meyendorff's interpretation of Palamas's thought is altogether unjustified and totally misleading" (12). See also John Romanides, "Notes on the Palamite Controversy and Related Topics. Part 2," *The Greek Orthodox Theological Review* 9 (1963–64): 269–70; Koutloumousianos, *One and the Three*, 20.

263. Meyendorff, "Christ's Humanity," 11, 13, 18; Meyendorff, "Continuities and Discontinuities," 75.

264. For Meyendorff, hypostasis has the same meaning in theology proper and Christology.

265. Meyendorff, *Christ in Eastern Christian Thought*, 62, 65.

also exists outside it. The personal existence of God "reaches out of" his nature and "goes beyond it."[266] As noted in previous chapters, an encounter between God and humanity is possible only as a result of two ecstatic movements: when the divine person comes out of his transcendent essence and the human person comes out of his limited nature.[267] The divine persons, therefore, *possess* their common nature but are neither *identified* with it nor *reducible* to it. In this regard, Meyendorff referred to the act of creation: although God is essentially unchangeable, he became the Creator, which means that changeability can be "seen as a real attribute of the divine" without being an attribute of his nature.[268]

Since hypostasis is more than a particular nature, it is logical that it can assume and possess other natures. "The hypostasis remains in some way independent of the characteristics of its own nature; it can be liberated from it assuming the characteristics" of another nature.[269] The person is, so to speak, a reservoir or container of nature(s).[270] God is not a prisoner of his transcendent divine nature; instead, he is able to personally assume another nature. As Meyendorff puts it, "Only a personal and a trinitarian God can *become* that which He was not before."[271]

According to Meyendorff, this existential primacy of the person is far from being a purely theoretical concept, because it makes two important doctrines possible.[272] The first is the incarnation. Only the person's "openness to the existential change," Meyendorff contends, can explain how the divine person could be the subject not only of his own divine nature but also of the fullness of humanity.[273] If the person could not go beyond his divine nature, the Son of God would not be able to assume human nature. In that case, the Chalcedonian formula would be unfeasible, and the

266. Meyendorff, "Christ's Humanity," 18; Meyendorff, "Reply to Jürgen Moltmann's," 188. See also Meyendorff, "Continuities and Discontinuities," 75.

267. Meyendorff, *Christ in Eastern Christian Thought*, 97; Meyendorff, "New Life," 497; Meyendorff, "Justinian, the Empire," 60. In fact, the language of ecstasis is not even necessary, because in Meyendorff's thought nature does not constrain the person from the outset.

268. Meyendorff, *Byzantine Theology*, 225.

269. Meyendorff, *Christ in Eastern Christian Thought*, 159.

270. Meyendorff, *Study of Gregory Palamas*, 214.

271. Meyendorff, "Reply to Jürgen Moltmann's," 188, emphasis original.

272. Meyendorff, *Christ in Eastern Christian Thought*, 77.

273. Meyendorff, "Christ's Humanity," 13.

confession of the real humanity of the Son would demand the existence of a human hypostasis in Christ. But since the hypostasis of the Son is not bound by his nature, he can acquire the properties of human nature *in addition* to his natural divine properties. Humanity is en-hypostatized in the Logos, so that Jesus Christ can be understood as fully human even without having a human hypostasis.[274] Furthermore, only such an ontology, according to Meyendorff, preserves the unchangeability of the divine nature. If the person were not more than the nature, then all the deeds of the person would also influence the nature, but since the hypostasis of the Son is not bound by his nature, the Son can become man without jeopardizing the unchangeability of his nature. Thus, Orthodox Christology implies "the inaccessibility and absolute transcendence of divine nature, as well as the openness and existential changeability of the hypostasis."[275]

Another doctrine made possible by this approach is no less important for Meyendorff because it relates to the very possibility of revelation and salvation. If God's person were identical to his essence, then, given the unknowability and unapproachability of this essence, God could not have revealed himself. But since the divine persons can exist and act both *in* and *outside* their nature, a revelation of the divine persons becomes a real possibility. The second doctrine, therefore, is that of God's energies: God can personally reveal himself in his energies while remaining absolutely unknowable in his essence. Meyendorff argued that without this personalistic concept of God, the distinction between essence and energy in God would be impossible.[276] "It is only because God is personal that His existence is not limited to the essence but is really present in creation through his energies, or acts." The existential primacy of the person in the concept of God allows "the possibility of divine acts outside of the

274. Meyendorff, "Holy Trinity," 38. To be sure, "in becoming man, the Son of God does not assume an abstract humanity, but becomes a human individual, Jesus of Nazareth." See John Meyendorff, "The Time of Holy Saturday," in *Orthodox Synthesis: The Unity of Theological Thought*, ed. J. Allen (Crestwood, NY: St Vladimir's Seminary Press, 1981), 51. But this human individual life was en-hypostatized in the hypostasis of the Logos (Meyendorff, *Byzantine Theology*, 154, 159).

275. Meyendorff, "New Life," 491.

276. Meyendorff, "Holy Trinity," 33.

nature."[277] Meyendorff considers this possibility as "the real significance of what is called 'Palamism.'"[278]

Divine Energies

In the introduction to this chapter, I noted that according to Meyendorff it is theological personalism that provides the key to perceiving the doctrine of the divine energies.[279] Without using this key, it would be difficult to progress further into Meyendorff's explanation of the divine energies. Having now analyzed the central notion of theological personalism (namely, the priority of person over essence), I can further elaborate on the doctrine of God's energies.

The Greek term ἐνέργεια was coined by Aristotle and has a long and exciting history in philosophy and theology. David Bradshaw's book *Aristotle East and West* provides the most nuanced account of the concept's development. In Bradshaw's reconstruction, the idea of divine energy in the Eastern theological tradition has been used in two interrelated ways: energies as God's activities and energies as God himself.[280] In the first sense, energies indicate that which God *does*; in the second sense, energies indicate that which God *is*. This is indeed a convenient and historically accurate approach, which makes one realize that in Orthodox theology energies both *manifest* God (as he is capable of being revealed to human beings) and *are* God (as he is capable of being participated in by human beings).

Bradshaw willingly admits his indebtedness to his predecessors and mentions that a clearer and more correct understanding of the idea of energy, as well as of the distinction between essence and energy, developed thanks to the investigations of several twentieth-century theologians, including Meyendorff.[281] It is therefore tempting to make use of Bradshaw's twofold approach in outlining Meyendorff's views on the divine energies, especially because Meyendorff himself did not offer any schema

277. Meyendorff, *Christ in Eastern Christian Thought*, 77.

278. Meyendorff, *Study of Gregory Palamas*, 213. See also Meyendorff, "Palamas (Grégoire)," 81.

279. Meyendorff, *Study of Gregory Palamas*, 212–13.

280. Bradshaw, *Aristotle East and West*, 165, 167, 170, 181, 209.

281. Bradshaw notes that his work rests, among others, on that of "Eastern Orthodox scholars such as Lossky and Meyendorff" (*Aristotle East and West*, 264; see also p. x).

for structuring this rich concept. Such an approach, however, would also reveal some shortcomings. The main problem is that it is hardly possible to make a clear distinction between energies as acts of God and energies as God and then structure other concepts related to energies according to this distinction. This problem becomes apparent when one considers four concepts that Meyendorff often used in context of the divine energies: light, grace, life, and property. Light is the illuminating *power* enabling the saints to contemplate God, but it is also the *object* of their vision; grace is what God *does* for and in human beings, but simultaneously it is what God *is*; energies *bring* the saints into the divine life and *are* themselves the life and presence of God communicated to creatures; properties, such as goodness or immortality, are the divine *works*, but at the same time they also *describe* God and are participated in by creatures.[282] Thus, energy is that which *effects* union with God and God *himself* as he is participated in and experienced in this union.

In view of these considerations, I will treat Meyendorff's views in a different order. First, although the distinction between essence and energy is sometimes taken to mean that the latter refers only to God's works and presence *ad extra*, I will differentiate between the internal and external dimensions of the divine energy and will try to discern what Meyendorff understood by God's energies *ad intra*. Second, I will examine his treatment of God's energies *ad extra* more thoroughly, investigating the richness of their meaning by making use of the four aforementioned concepts: light, grace, life, and property.

The Internal Energies

Like the concept of the unknowability of the divine essence and the priority of person over essence, the history of the Orthodox doctrine concerning the divine energies was presented by Meyendorff as a consistent development without any serious discontinuities or fundamental innovations. Meyendorff, of course, did not deny the role of Palamas in systematizing the doctrine, but he argued that his role consisted simply in the fuller and clearer explanation of a doctrine that had already been taught

282. See Bradshaw, *Aristotle East and West*, 94, 147.

by the Cappadocians, pseudo-Dionysius, and Maximus.[283] It is actually more remarkable how Meyendorff evaluated the transition of the doctrine from Greek philosophy to Christian theology. As noted previously, the Christian understanding of God's unknowability and personality marked, according to Meyendorff, a decisive break with Greek philosophy (namely, with the "essentialistic" Neoplatonism). With respect to ἐνέργεια, however, Meyendorff's disapproval of Greek philosophy in all its varieties was less categorical. He noted that the Aristotelian dyad, nature-energy, was insufficient for Christian theologians, because it did not allow them to emphasize that God's energies are *personal*. In order to describe God's personal being more adequately, they had to transform the Aristotelian dyad into the triad: essence-hypostasis-energy.[284] However, this is the only reservation that Meyendorff mentioned. He did not reject what he understood to be Aristotle's fundamental principles: every essence is manifested through its energy, essence is the cause of its energy, and without energy essence does not exist.[285]

Although the last of these principles (without energy essence does not exist) had primarily an economic meaning for Meyendorff (i.e., without energy God would not exist *for us*), he also seemed to agree with its ontological validity independent of the world: God possesses internal energy independently of the creation of the world. In this regard, Meyendorff pointed out the significance of the Aristotelian dyad for Maximus's defense of the two energies in Christ against the monoenergists. The presupposition of Maximus in this polemic was that "without an energy every nature, whether divine or human, does not possess a real existence."[286] If energy is denied of God, it not only renders his existence *for us* abstract, but also deprives *God* of his existence. Meyendorff also relied on Palamas to

283. John Meyendorff, "Theological Thought in the Christian East," in *Rome, Constantinople, Moscow*, 34; Meyendorff, *Gregory Palamas*, 122.

284. Meyendorff, "Holy Trinity," 31; Meyendorff, *Byzantine Theology*, 185.

285. Meyendorff, *Study of Gregory Palamas*, 216; Meyendorf, *Vvedenie v svyatootecheskoe bogoslovie*, 329.

286. Meyendorff, *Study of Gregory Palamas*, 211. There is "no nature without movement, without energy, without existence; without movement, it is not nature" (Meyendorff, *Christ in Eastern Christian Thought*, 146). "Created nature would lose its very existence if it were deprived of its proper energy" (Meyendorff, *Byzantine Theology*, 133; see also Meyendorff, *Study of Gregory Palamas*, 212).

postulate the reality of the internal energy of God, for Palamas affirmed the Aristotelian ontological rule ("every essence must possess natural energies") and made a distinction between energies that have a beginning and those that do not.[287]

But it is far easier to acknowledge the existence of the divine internal energies than to determine their meaning and function. In his recent work on the concept of ἐνέργεια, Tollefsen suggests that Eastern Orthodox thought understood the generation of the Son and the procession of the Spirit as the Father's essential activities (ἐνέργεια in the Aristotelian sense). In his own words, "There has to be a certain *energeia* at play in the structuring of the three-hypostatic being of God. What else could generation and procession be?"[288] Meyendorff, however, was more skeptical about speaking of energies in this context, primarily because, following Palamas, he deployed the difference between generation and creation to justify the distinction between essence and energy. He mentions what he calls the patristic "axiom": "to beget is the property of nature, and to create that of energy."[289] This axiom was introduced by Cyril of Alexandria and proceeded from two ideas: creation as the expression of God's will (a notion promoted by Athanasius), and the divine energy as identical with the divine will (which became especially important later during the mon*oenergism* and mono*theletism* controversies).[290] The begetting of the Son and the procession of the Spirit are described, therefore, as essential acts of the Father *in contrast to* the acts of God's energy. Meyendorff faced some difficulties here because, in any case, generation is an *act*, while for him "to act" was basically synonymous with possessing and using energies.[291] A nonenergetic act is an oxymoron in his theology. Furthermore, it seems

287. Palamas, *Triads*, 95, 104.

288. Tollefsen, *Activity and Participation*, 48, 58, 65.

289. Meyendorff, *Study of Gregory Palamas*, 221. Although Meyendorff refers here only to Cyril of Alexandria and John of Damascus, his original source seems to be Palamas, who said: "If, in God, the energy does not differ from the essence, then in Him generating will be the same thing as creating. There will be no difference between the Son and the Holy Spirit, on the one hand, and creatures on the other." See Palamas, *Capita physica, theologica, moralia et practica*, 96–97 (PG 150:1189).

290. Meyendorff defines the divine energy as "a free act of the Divine will" ("Doctrine of Grace," 25).

291. "God acts, that is to say possesses energies" (Meyendorff, *Study of Gregory Palamas*, 214). See also Meyendorff, "Holy Trinity," 37, where he explains the word "active" as "energetic."

that the formulation as Meyendorff used it is exclusivistic and works in both directions: just as creation comes from God's energy alone (and not from nature), so generation also comes from God's nature alone (and not from energy); just as nature is the source of generation alone (and not of creation), so energy is the source of creation alone (and not of generation). Such a strong coupling of energies to creation questions the very idea of internal energy. Another difficulty for Meyendorff is that such an approach weakens his personalistic pathos. It is not easy to combine the idea of generation as an act of essence *in contrast to* that of energy and will with the idea of generation as a personal act of the hypostasis of the Father.[292] In defending the distinction between generation and creation as acts of God's nature/essence and will/energy respectively, Meyendorff blamed Palamas's opponents for violating Nicene orthodoxy, according to which the Son proceeds from the *essence* of the Father (although, as indicated in "The (Onto)logical Aspect" [pages 195–99], Meyendorff himself had characterized the pronouncement of Nicaea as a sign of underdeveloped Trinitarian theology).[293]

Since Meyendorff refrained from considering eternal generation as an act of the energies, one needs to look in other directions to determine the concrete meaning of God's internal energy in his theology. In this regard, it is worthwhile mentioning Meyendorff's analysis of Orthodox attitudes to the *filioque* clause.[294] He discerned two strategies employed by the Byzantine fathers in response to Latin theologians. According to the first approach, represented by Photius, the *eternal* procession of the Spirit from the Father alone must be carefully distinguished from the *temporal* sending of the Spirit, which is indeed from the Son. In this approach, any eternal procession of the Spirit from the Son was inadmissible. Meyendorff observed that Photius's views were not questioned in the East until the thirteenth century, when Gregory of Cyprus proposed an alternative, which was later taken up by Palamas. According to this alternative, the Spirit does indeed proceed eternally from the Father and the Son (or through the

292. See Romanides, "Notes on the Palamite Controversy and Related Topics. Part 2," 268; Williams, "Philosophical Structures," 33.

293. Meyendorff, *Study of Gregory Palamas*, 222.

294. Meyendorff, *Study of Gregory Palamas*, 13–15, 229–32; Meyendorff, *Byzantine Theology*, 93–94.

Son), but only as power and energy and not as hypostasis.[295] This natural procession (or rather illumination) is different from the hypostatic procession and is manifested in time to human beings, who receive the Spirit as energy and not as hypostasis. Although Meyendorff described Photius's approach as legitimate and traditional, he also found it "insufficiently convincing" and clearly preferred the second approach—not only because it seemed to be more promising in ecumenical dialogue, but also because it emphasized the distinction between essence and energy.[296]

This does not mean, however, that Meyendorff was very clear about this eternal illumination of the Spirit. Although it would seem to naturally follow that such illumination could be called "energetical" and "internal," Meyendorff remained indecisive, because the illumination is known only via the economic order, which cannot be easily projected into the internal Trinitarian relations. In this context, Meyendorff even claims that "the essential order ... does not involve the action of the energies of God"—a statement that totally undermines the possibility of internal energy. Meyendorff found a way forward in Palamas's passage in which the Spirit is likened to the reciprocal love between the Father and the Son.[297] Such an analogy, of course, sounds very Augustinian, but in Palamas (and Meyendorff) it is applied to the Spirit as energy and not as hypostasis. In later articles, Meyendorff confirmed the idea of the eternal procession of the Spirit and immediately connected it with the mutual love of the Father and the Son.[298] But here he also considered this idea more broadly and seemed to be more inclined to identify the eternal energies with the love that unites the divine persons, so that the Spirit is no longer love

295. Here Meyendorff's personalism can express itself in full: "that which comes by nature is the energy, not the hypostasis" (*Study of Gregory Palamas*, 231), although this statement does not perfectly correspond with the "axiom" he mentioned several pages before: "to beget is the property of nature" (221).

296. Meyendorff, *Byzantine Theology*, 61, 189; Meyendorff, *Study of Gregory Palamas*, 232; Meyendorf, *Vvedenie v svyatootecheskoe bogoslovie*, 307. According to Basil Lourié, in his last years Meyendorff admitted that the first to introduce the new approach was Gregory of Cyprus's teacher Nicephorus Blemmyda, but he did not find the opportunity to explain this in print. See Lourié, "Kommentarii" [Commentaries], in Meyendorf, *Zhizn' i trudy*, 444, 446. Lourié also reports that in a letter to himself, Meyendorff acknowledged that he contrasted Photius with Palamas "somewhat artificially" (447). In any case, Meyendorff's preferences are clear, and historical precision is not decisive here.

297. Meyendorff, *Study of Gregory Palamas*, 232.

298. Meyendorff, "Holy Trinity," 40; Meyendorff, "Theology of the Holy Spirit," 19–20.

itself (which might perhaps make him in a sense less of a person), but one of the three subjects and objects of the eternal circle of love within the Godhead. Manifestation of love to creatures would be impossible without the reciprocal manifestation of love in the internal life of God. "Therefore," Meyendorff concludes, "the doctrine of the uncreated energies is not only a manifestation of the personal being of God *ad extra*."[299]

The External Energies

Meyendorff's indecisiveness and ambiguity regarding God's internal energy is explained primarily by the fact that he almost exclusively focused on the *external* divine energies. When mentioning divine energy, Meyendorff normally meant the divine energy *ad extra*. In his theology, it is a very broad concept encompassing all that God does and is for us. Simply put, external divine energy is that which enables communion with God: it is the act, the means, and the content of God's revelation. Given the impressive many-sidedness of this concept in Meyendorff's theology, I will discuss it under the following four heads: light, grace, life, and property. Meyendorff used each of the four terms synonymously with the term "energy," but it would be more accurate to say that they are *subsumed* under the general term "energy" in his theology. The choice of the four concepts has some textual basis in Meyendorff's writings, but its chief rationale lies in their explanatory capacity: although all the terms signify a single reality, each of them conveys the broad meaning of energy in its own particular way so that we do not overlook any of its important aspects.[300]

Energies as Light. Since Meyendorff has been known primarily as a Palamas scholar, it is natural to start with a concept that occupied an important place in the Palamite disputes. The hesychast monks claimed that in contemplative prayer they beheld a light, which they identified

---

299. Meyendorff, "Holy Trinity," 35, 41.

300. The closest parallel can be found in the following passage: "Whatever name one gives them—grace, divine life, light, illumination—the energies or divine acts belong to the existence of God himself" (Meyendorff, *Study of Gregory Palamas*, 217). The term "illumination" is not included in my list, because its meaning coincides with that of light. I decided to include the term "property" instead—not only because Meyendorff uses it as a synonym of "energy," but also because this term focuses on two themes that are significant for the present study: God's attributes/names and the mechanism of the *communicatio idiomatum*. There are many other passages where Meyendorff uses two or one of the chosen four terms interchangeably or side by side with the word "energy."

with the uncreated light of Thabor radiating from the body of Christ at his transfiguration. Palamas maintained the distinction between essence and energy in order to theologically vindicate and defend their experience. Although the point of the distinction was to justify two important notions (the inaccessibility of God's essence and the reality of the union with God in his energies), the first notion was not disputed by Palamas's principal opponent, Barlaam, who emphasized it even more strongly than Palamas.[301] Thus, unlike the Cappadocians, who introduced the distinction between essence and energy (whatever it may have meant to them) into Christian theology to safeguard the incomprehensibility of God and oppose the epistemological optimism of Eunomius, Palamas focused on the positive side of the distinction and opposed what Meyendorff calls the "agnosticism" of Barlaam.[302]

A vision of the light, Meyendorff stated, is not accessible to the created intellect or senses and has nothing to do with the natural contemplation of God in creation.[303] Since the light is divine, uncreated, and supernatural, a vision of this light also requires divine, uncreated, and supernatural power. The contemplation of the light of Christ's transfiguration, therefore, implies a transfiguration of humanity as a whole: the divinization of

301. Meyendorff observed that the unknowability of God was fundamental for Barlaam's ecumenical efforts: if we cannot prove anything about the intratrinitarian relations, then the *filioque* becomes an irrelevant, speculative doctrine that should be no obstacle to church unity.

302. Meyendorff, *Study of Gregory Palamas*, 43–44, 203, 210; Meyendorff, "Doctrine of Grace," 19; Jean Meyendorff, "Les débuts de la controverse hésyhaste," in *Byzantine Hesychasm*, 109, 117–18; Jean Meyendorff, "Notes sur l'influence dionysienne en Orient," in *Byzantine Hesychasm*, 550. In his recent essay, Vladimir Kharlamov convincingly demonstrates that, contrary to the claims of Bradshaw and earlier proponents of neo-Palamism (including Meyendorff), the Cappadocians' views cannot be regarded as precursors of the distinction between essence and energy in its Palamite sense. See Kharlamov, "Basil of Caesarea and the Cappadocians on the Distinction between Essence and Energies in God and Its Relevance to the Deification Theme," in *Theōsis: Deification in Christian Theology*, ed. Vladimir Kharlamov (Cambridge: Clarke, 2012), 2:100–145. Kharlamov shows that "the Cappadocian testimony to this distinction, at the very least, is inconclusive, and more likely *accidental*" (110, emphasis original).

303. Meyendorff, *Study of Gregory Palamas*, 168. Meyendorff does not altogether reject the revelatory capacity of the created world, and he speaks about divine revelation "through" (*Gregory Palamas*, 115) and "in" (*Vvedenie v svyatootecheskoe bogoslovie*, 186) creatures. At the same time, he preferred to consider revelation in experiential and existential terms and identified it with the *uncreated* energies. "All revelation ... is a divine energy" that surpasses all creaturely things and concepts (*Gregory Palamas*, 118–19). Ultimately, God reveals himself not through creatures but rather through *the deification of* creatures. See Jean Meyendorff, "Une théologie mystique," *Christus: La spiritualité de l'Orient chrétien* 39.155 (1992): 291.

body and soul, the overcoming of the limitations of created faculties, and the acquisition of the divine eye. To see the light, one must become light oneself; to see God, one must become god oneself.[304]

In line with Palamas, Meyendorff claimed that the divine light contemplated by the saints is God himself. Its appearance is not a creaturely symbol of divinity (as Barlaam argued) but the uncreated glory of God. Although the light does not reveal the divine essence, the vision is a direct and immediate encounter with God "face to face."[305] However, it does not convey knowledge in any creaturely sense. As was noted in the context of apophatic theology, the vision is "knowledge through ignorance," "greater than knowledge"; "strictly speaking, it is not a knowledge."[306] The vision grants what can be experienced and participated in rather than what can be known, and is therefore suprarational but not supraexperiential.

Meyendorff's most original contribution to this theme was his recognition of the paramount importance of the incarnation of Christ for immediate communion with God. Generally speaking, Meyendorff rarely made any negative remarks about the Eastern church fathers and preferred to interpret them favorably through his own lenses rather than openly criticizing them. One notable exception was pseudo-Dionysius, to whom Meyendorff attributes "the absence of all Christology."[307] According to Meyendorff, the doctrine of revelation in pseudo-Dionysius was dominated by his idea of hierarchy, in which the mediating function of the angels played a crucial role. The system of hierarchy was not influenced by the incarnation and did not allow for the immediate vision of God even in the New Testament.[308] Although Meyendorff was sharply criticized for his interpretation of pseudo-Dionysius, he never changed his suspicious attitude toward the

---

304. Meyendorff may appear inconsistent when on the same page he first speaks of "the vision of an uncreated light by created eyes," and then states that "created faculties, whether bodily or intellectual, are not enough for man to see God" (*Study of Gregory Palamas*, 173). But what he means is that our created faculties must be transformed in order to acquire divine, uncreated capacities (necessary for the contemplation of the light) yet without ceasing to be creaturely.

305. Meyendorff, *Byzantine Theology*, 187; Meyendorff, *Study of Gregory Palamas*, 191.

306. Meyendorff, "Theosis in the Eastern Christian Tradition," 476; Meyendorff, *Byzantine Theology*, 13; Meyendorff, *Study of Gregory Palamas*, 168.

307. Meyendorff, *Study of Gregory Palamas*, 209.

308. Meyendorff, *Study of Gregory Palamas*, 189–91; Meyendorff, *Christ in Eastern Christian Thought*, 107–8; Meyendorff, *Byzantine Theology*, 28.

Corpus Areopagiticum, and in his late lectures he emphatically states that the hierarchical system of pseudo-Dionysius leaves "no room for faith in the incarnation" and even "completely ignores the incarnation."[309]

Understandably, Meyendorff attempted to find support for his critical attitude toward the Areopagite in the Eastern tradition itself. He ascribed to his theological heroes, Maximus and especially Palamas, a "Christological corrective," which they supposedly applied to pseudo-Dionysius.[310] The corrective consisted of purging the *Corpus Areopagiticum* from any remaining dependence on Neoplatonism and recovering the crucial importance of the incarnation, which made the immediate vision of God possible, independent of any symbolic intermediaries. With Jesus' coming in the flesh, the symbols were abolished, and the very reality appeared. According to Meyendorff, in the Old Testament the vision of the divine light was accessible only to Moses, while others had to content themselves with symbolic knowledge alone. In the New Testament, however, the immediate vision

309. Meyendorf, *Vvedenie v svyatootecheskoe bogoslovie*, 277–78. See also Van Rossum, "Otets Ioann Meyendorf," xi.

310. Meyendorff, *Study of Gregory Palamas*, 133, 189, 206; Meyendorff, "Notes sur l'influence dionysienne," 550; Meyendorf, *Vvedenie v svyatootecheskoe bogoslovie*, 277. Romanides insists that Meyendorff is wrong in attributing a christological corrective to Palamas, because there was no fundamental difference between the views of pseudo-Dionysius and Palamas and, consequently, no need for such a "corrective" ("Notes on the Palamite Controversy and Related Topics. Part 2," 236–70). According to Romanides, both the Areopagite and the Doctor of Hesychasm believed that the patriarchs, prophets, apostles, and saints in the OT and NT could all see the uncreated glory and have immediate contact with God, but they were "initiated into the meaning of their immediate vision of the glory of God by angels" (259). The role of the angels is, therefore, not revelatory or mediatory but, so to speak, interpretive: they do not produce the vision itself and do not become symbolic substitutes of God, but rather explain and interpret the vision. Later, Hieromonk Alexander Golitzin criticized the alleged corrective as "a scholarly invention" that reveals a "misapprehension of the meaning and function of the Dionysian hierarchies." See Golitzin, "Dionysius Areopagites in the Works of Saint Gregory Palamas: On the Question of a 'Christological Corrective' and Related Matters," *SVTQ* 46 (2002): 167. Following Romanides, Golitzin states that in the thought of pseudo-Dionysius, the angels were not "mediators" in the sense of blocking direct access to the experience of the divine light, but guides leading to that experience, as well as explaining, and testing it (175).

The legitimacy of the christological corrective was defended by Adolf Maria Ritter, and more recently by Joost van Rossum, who points out that "Romanides and Golitzin have overlooked Palamas's stress on the *superiority* of human beings over the angels, and on the meaning of the Incarnation as a radical *change* in the relation between God and man. These two 'Palamite' themes are not very 'Dionysian.'" See Ritter, "Gregor Palamas als Leser des Dionysius Pseudo-Areopagita," in *Denys l'Areopagite et sa postérité en Orient et en Occident*, ed. Ysabel De Andia (Paris: Études Augustiniennes, 1997), 565–79; van Rossum, "Dionysius the Areopagite and Gregory Palamas: A 'Christological Corrective'?," *Studia Patristica* 42 (2006), 350, emphasis original.

is accessible to all those who are in Christ.[311] Thus, although the dispute over the vision was originally related to the practice of monks, Meyendorff turned it in a more ecclesiastical and ethical direction. The light of Thabor penetrates Christ's humanity as communicated through the church and her sacraments. Therefore, it is accessible to all Christians and not merely to individual mystics. By participating in the sacraments, keeping God's commandments, and developing a life of prayer, Christians really participate in the divine energy and enjoy the vision of God.[312]

Energies as Grace. For many Christians, the entire discussion about energies as light may sound somewhat enigmatic and esoteric, and the focus on Christ's transfiguration may seem to overshadow the far more significant events of the crucifixion and resurrection. However, Meyendorff tried to bring the main issue of hesychast polemics closer to ordinary Christian life by stating that the light is simply *grace*. In the Eastern tradition, he noted, divine presence and grace were often described as light. Thus, defending the hesychasts, in Meyendorff's view, defended the gospel itself, understood as "the message of deification."[313] This deification is not a psychological experience or a figure of speech but real union with God.

In expounding his doctrine of grace, Meyendorff often compared Eastern and Western approaches. Quite surprisingly, he traces the resounding similarities between Augustine and Palamas: "As Augustine had done in his writings against Pelagius, Palamas insists on the basic incapacity of man to reach God by his own efforts: in this respect Palamas is one of the most 'Augustinian' writers of the Christian East." Later in this paragraph, Meyendorff claims that, in Palamas's view, man always "remains entirely dependent on divine grace in his knowledge of God"—a view that would

311. Meyendorff, *Study of Gregory Palamas*, 195. Although Meyendorff clearly says that "only Moses" was blessed with supernatural vision in OT dispensation, elsewhere he allows that some "other righteous men of the Old Testament" had the vision ("Doctrine of Grace," 22). In both publications Meyendorff is quick to add that in the NT not only particular individuals but all Christians can enjoy immediate communion with God.

312. Meyendorff, *Study of Gregory Palamas*, 161, 162, 168, 195; Meyendorff, *Christ in Eastern Christian Thought*, 202. Meyendorff even went so far as to claim that those apostles present at the transfiguration of Jesus did not enjoy the true vision we enjoy now that Christ's body and our bodies have entered eucharistic communion (Meyendorff, "Le thème," 200). See also Romanides, "Notes on the Palamite Controversy and Related Topics. Part 2," 243.

313. Meyendorff, *Study of Gregory Palamas*, 151; Meyendorff, "Mount Athos in the Fourteenth Century," 163.

perhaps prove to be too categorical even for Augustine, who believed in the existence of a certain natural knowledge of God.[314] Furthermore, according to Meyendorff, Palamas, *"d'une manière très augustinienne,"* affirms that achieving the likeness of God is "an effect of grace."[315] Meyendorff, however, immediately negates the similarity by emphasizing the crucial role of synergy in Palamism. In addition to the similarity between Augustine and Palamas, Meyendorff saw a convergence of the Eastern and Western views on grace in the Reformers' rejection of meritorious means between God and humanity and in their unwillingness to consider saving grace as created.[316]

Despite these arguably strained similarities, Meyendorff's overall attitude to the Western doctrine(s) of grace is predominantly negative. Although he seemed to realize the diversity of Roman Catholic theology of his time and acknowledged the fundamental difference between the medieval doctrine of grace and its Reformation counterpart, he typically identified the "Western" doctrine with a certain interpretation of Thomistic thought and attacked it on several fronts. First, as we already saw in "Underlying Characteristics of Meyendorff's Approach" (pages 143–55), Meyendorff maintained that, in contrast to Western theology, characterized by a dichotomy between nature and grace, Eastern theologians considered grace as originally being part of human nature. From the prelapsarian Adam onward, humanity participates in God by grace, and human nature is truly human nature in the fullest sense insofar as it exists in grace.[317] Second, Meyendorff maintained that the East, unlike the West, does not describe grace as a gift that exists apart from God and is then conferred on people. Strictly speaking, grace is not something God *gives*; rather, grace is what God *does* and what he *is* for us.[318] Meyendorff believed that for the West,

314. Meyendorff, *Study of Gregory Palamas*, 118.

315. Meyendorff, *Introduction à l'étude*, 179 (for some reason, this text does not appear in the English edition); Meyendorff, *Study of Gregory Palamas*, 121.

316. Meyendorff, "Significance of the Reformation," 172.

317. Meyendorff, *Byzantine Theology*, 138; Meyendorff, *Study of Gregory Palamas*, 121; Meyendorff, "New Life," 488.

318. Meyendorff, *Study of Gregory Palamas*, 163; see also Meyendorff, *Gregory Palamas*, 122–23. From Meyendorff's identification of the divine energy with grace, it seems to follow that God's activities are always gracious. This leaves no place in his theology for judgment and punishment as divine acts.

grace is extrinsic to both humanity and God, while for the East it is "natural" for humanity, and it is God himself in his revelation. Third, whereas Western theology, according to Meyendorff, is captivated by the forensic categories of justification, imputation, and forgiveness, and reduces salvation to a mere amnesty, Eastern thought recognizes the broader operation of grace: it does not simply cause humanity to be justified or forgiven, but unites it with God.[319] Fourth, Meyendorff notices a historical and methodological difference between West and East. The doctrine of grace emerged in the West as an answer to the Pelagian challenge, while in the East it was formulated in the context of the christological debates and monastic spirituality.[320] The central issue in the East related to the union of the two natures in Christ, which had to explain how Christ's humanity becomes the channel for the communication of grace. Eastern theologians emphasized that Christ "communicates to all Christians the divine energy—in other words, sanctifying grace—of which he is the source."[321]

Last, and most importantly for Meyendorff, grace is not a created reality. When speaking about the Western doctrine, Meyendorff did not make a distinction between God's uncreated gracious agency and the created fruits of grace, but simply stated that the West believes in created grace. In the East, on the contrary, a notion such as "created grace" would have seemed "a flagrant contradiction in terms," according to Meyendorff.[322] His argument is quite simple: God's grace must be uncreated, otherwise it would not be divine. If grace were created, the direct and personal union of God and humanity would be impossible. Since grace is the same as the divine energy *ad extra*, it cannot be created, because the createdness of the energy would imply the createdness of the essence. Thus, divine grace is

319. Meyendorf, *Vvedenie v svyatootecheskoe bogoslovie*, 329–30.

320. Meyendorff, "Doctrine of Grace," 17.

321. Meyendorff, *Study of Gregory Palamas*, 183.

322. Meyendorff, "Doctrine of Grace," 24. Similarly: "The notion of created grace is completely foreign to Greek patristics" (*Christ in Eastern Christian Thought*, 79). Such statements seem to contradict Meyendorff's admission that Palamas identified "a new heart" (Ezra 36:26) and "a new creature" (2 Cor 5:17; Gal 6:15) with "created grace" (Meyendorff, *Study of Gregory Palamas*, 164). Nikolaos Loudovikos, however, charges Meyendorff with misreading Palamas and insists that Palamas spoke of created grace only in the sense of the beauty and harmony of creation. See Loudovikos, "Striving for Participation: Palamite Analogy as Dialogical Synenergy and Thomist Analogy as Emanational Similitude," in Athanasopoulos and Schneider, *Divine Essence and Divine Energies*, 128.

not external to God and "not distinct from God."[323] It is God himself in his self-communication.[324]

According to Meyendorff, the maxim "all divine is necessarily uncreated" holds true also for deified human beings. To be saved by grace is to become deified by grace, which in turn is to become uncreated.[325] "By participation in God Himself, in His uncreated grace man himself becomes God."[326] Deified humanity does not simply begin to conform to God, but transcends the limitations of its created nature and becomes, so to speak, an instantiation of God. Normally, Meyendorff ascribed the ability to transcend creatureliness to a human *person*, but he also spoke of deified and uncreated human *nature*. If God is uncreated and God and humanity truly become one, then humanity must also somehow become uncreated in this union.[327] Similarly, since "no creaturely being has ever seen God" and yet the saints really do contemplate him, then their faculties must have previously become uncreated too.[328] Underlying these statements is Palamas's extremely realistic mysticism, nurtured by a few biblical

---

323. Meyendorff, *Study of Gregory Palamas*, 176.

324. Meyendorff, "'Defense of the Holy Hesychasts,'" 187.

325. Meyendorff obviously follows Palamas, who, while not rejecting the term "created grace" (as indicated in a footnote above), nevertheless insisted that the deifying power of grace makes the saints "uncreated by grace." Indeed, this for Palamas was proof of the uncreatedness of grace: "How could every saint become uncreated by grace, if this grace is created?" (*Triads*, 86). Meyendorff claims that "the traditional concept of deification [means that] by participating in God, the creature acquires 'divinity' and becomes uncreated" (*Vvedenie v svyatootecheskoe bogoslovie*, 329; see also Meyendorff, "Palamas [Grégoire]," 97). Furthermore, Meyendorff prefers not to differentiate between categories of grace and consistently speaks of it as being uncreated. Meyendorff also argues that in the mystical union between God and humanity "the obstacle of createdness is eliminated" ("Istoricheskoe znachenie," 6) and "all distinction between created and uncreated is inadmissible" (*Study of Gregory Palamas*, 177). However different their wordings may be, both Palamas and Meyendorff sought to prove that God's energy is wholly uncreated, while the deified saints remain created in one sense and become uncreated in another.

326. Meyendorff, *Gregory Palamas*, 118.

327. Certainly, the union is asymmetrical: while humanity becomes uncreated without ceasing to be created, God in his energy always remains uncreated.

328. Meyendorff, "Doctrine of Grace," 24. In this context, Meyendorff says: "It is precisely the gulf which exists between the Creator and the creatures that makes [it] necessary to admit the uncreated character of ... Divine energies" (24). Thus, the gulf does not mean that humankind can never acquire uncreated capabilities. Rather, it means that nothing created can see or have direct communion with God. Meyendorff deduces two conclusions from this: the energy (that which is participated) must be uncreated, and the saint (the one who participates) must also become uncreated in some sense.

passages and fully shared by Meyendorff. For example, John 3:6 means that the saints become "God" and "Spirit" because of the identification between that which is begotten and the begetter. Second Corinthians 12:2–5 means that in his ecstatic experience Paul was "that to which he was united. … Paul was Light and Spirit." Galatians 2:20 means that "the Christian no longer has any life of his own, but acquires that of Christ, the divine and uncreated life."[329]

Thus, Meyendorff's statement that God "alone [is] the Uncreated" should not be taken too literally because he means that only God is uncreated *by nature*. This does not preclude people from becoming uncreated as well, provided that they become uncreated by participating in the uncreatedness of God. Not surprisingly, Meyendorff goes on to say that God shares "with man His own uncreated existence." Meyendorff also mentions that Palamas "indignantly rejects the imputation that he had said that the *humanity* of Christ was uncreated," but in the footnote omitted in the English translation, Meyendorff cites Palamas stating that Christ's body did not become uncreated "by nature."[330] This passage is included in the section in which Meyendorff expounds the difference between essential union and the hypostatic union, attempting to prove that Christ's humanity is deified not naturally but by virtue of the hypostatic union. Neither Palamas nor Meyendorff, therefore, has objections to the idea of humanity becoming deified and uncreated: what they reject is the idea that humanity can become God *by nature*.

Energies as Life. As stated above, for Meyendorff the notions of energy, grace, and life signify one and the same reality. However, there is a difference between grace and life. According to Meyendorff's definitions, grace is "the divine life … when it is granted to man," or "the life of the one God communicated to men."[331] The two definitions presuppose that while grace is the energy of God in his relations with people, life is the divine energy both *ad intra* and *ad extra*. This makes the concept of life most suitable for considering the relation between God's internal and external energy.

---

329. Meyendorff, *Study of Gregory Palamas*, 174–75, 179; Meyendorff, *Gregory Palamas*, 118.

330. Meyendorff, *Study of Gregory Palamas*, 122, 183, emphasis original; Meyendorff, *Introduction* à l'étude, 254.

331. Meyendorff, *Study of Gregory Palamas*, 61, 176, 217.

Dealing with Meyendorff's position on the internal energies, we saw that he eventually identified them with the eternal circle of love within the Godhead. This section will discuss Meyendorff's understanding of the communication of this love *ad extra*. Three relatively long citations are of special interest in this respect. Replying to one of Jürgen Moltmann's articles, Meyendorff says:

> Because the three divine Persons are indeed three utterly distinct, loving and inviting subjects, human persons are saved precisely by entering into and participating in their interpersonal unity ("that they may be one in Us"—Jn. 17:21). To be sure, such an emphasis may be misunderstood as implying a kind of pantheism, with the Trinity of hypostases becoming a "myriad" of hypostases. It is important, therefore, to maintain that the divine, transcendent divine nature will always remain distinct and transcendent; it is by grace that human persons enter into the loving circle of the Three Divine Persons.[332]

In an ecumenical volume, Meyendorff writes:

> Deification ... is an acceptance of human persons within a divine life, which already is itself a fellowship of love between three coeternal Persons, welcoming humanity within their mutuality. Jesus prayed: "As you, Father, are in me and I in you, let them also be in us" (John 17:21). ... Of course, human participation ... in the life of the Trinity does not mean pantheism. The gulf between the Creator and the creatures remains. It is being bridged by *divine* love (or "grace," or "energy"). ... The essence of God is absolutely transcendent.[333]

Finally, in what would be his last publication, Meyendorff states:

> In Christ ... this divine love becomes accessible to created human persons: "that they may be one in Us" (Jn. 17:21). While in this life, this intratrinitarian love becomes accessible to created human beings, it cannot be reduced to pantheism. The absolute difference between Creator and creature remains intact. But it is overcome

332. See also Meyendorff, "Reply to Jürgen Moltmann's," 187.

333. Meyendorff, "Theosis in the Eastern Christian Tradition," 475–76, emphasis original.

> by the boundless divine love which is expressed in theology with the terms "grace" or "energy." … The divine essence remains completely transcendent.[334]

These three passages obviously have much in common. First, in none of them does Meyendorff draw any distinction between the internal divine love/life and the communicated love/life: what becomes accessible to human beings is *intra-Trinitarian* love.[335] Believers are included in the very life of the three divine persons and are admitted into their interpersonal fellowship of love. As Meyendorff states elsewhere, "human hypostases can become divine … by receiving the *fullness* of the Divine Life."[336] Second, normally sparing with biblical references, Meyendorff cites John 17:21 in all the quoted passages. Jesus' high-priestly prayer includes a variety of parallels with different subjects and meanings.[337] Although Meyendorff does not offer exegesis of this verse, it seems clear that with this reference he wishes to illustrate the inclusion of believers in the life of the Trinity. His reading is so realistic that he hastens to clarify that such inclusion does not result in "a 'myriad' of hypostases"—as if this verse says "they will be one *of* us." Third, in each passage Meyendorff finds it necessary to counter potential pantheist deductions, which may indicate that he envisages the fellowship between the divine and human persons as intimate enough to warrant such reservations. It is also remarkable that Meyendorff does not distinguish between the divine and human lives *in* this fellowship, but appeals instead to different ways of *entering* into this fellowship: "by nature" for the divine persons and "by grace" for the human ones. Fourth, Meyendorff clearly specifies the reason any conclusion of pantheism can be excluded: the absolute transcendence of the divine essence.[338] Thus, the difference between the divine and human persons consists not in the quality or mode

---

334. Meyendorff, "Une théologie," 292.

335. Similarly: "*God is Trinity* and, therefore, God is Love (1 John 4:8). He could not be *love*, if He were alone: love is always a relationship, and God is that love which eternally unites the Father, the Son, and the Spirit. Uniting the three divine persons by nature, that divine love is, by the power of grace, becoming accessible to men" (Meyendorff, "Theological Thought in the Christian East," 206).

336. Meyendorff, "Doctrine of Grace," 25, emphasis original.

337. A helpful analysis can be found in Burger, *Being in Christ*, 295–99.

338. See also Meyendorff, "Holy Trinity," 30–32; Meyendorff, "New Life," 489.

of their lives in fellowship with each other but in the remoteness of the divine essence, which transcends the fellowship.[339]

The concluding sentences of the second and third passages have a somewhat dialectical character (atypical of Meyendorff). "The gulf between the Creator and the creatures" first "remains" and then is "bridged"; "the absolute difference between the Creator and the creature" is first said to "remain intact" and then be "overcome." However, by using these wordings, Meyendorff hardly expresses anything different from his usual approach: "the gulf" ("the absolute difference") is preserved by the incommunicability of the divine essence/nature and is overcome by the communicability of the divine energy/love/life/grace. When he elsewhere writes about the "accessible divine life,"[340] he does not differentiate it from an inaccessible divine life but from the divine essence. The divine infinite and uncreated life is, therefore, fully accessible and communicable. There is no difference between the internal divine life and its manifestation to creatures. At the same time, the divine essence, being distinct from the divine life, always remains inaccessible.

The concept of energy as life helped Meyendorff to explain how the position he advocated for fundamentally differed from the Neoplatonic emanationist metaphysics. Although he occasionally used phrases that may sound Neoplatonic,[341] Meyendorff was eager to demonstrate that the Orthodox doctrine of revelation has nothing to do with an unconscious emanation of God. To be sure, he generally appealed to the distinction between essence and will for this purpose, and pointed out that external revelation is a free act of God. However, he also appealed to the dynamic and personal character of divine revelation in Christianity. In doing so he employed the concept of life as an antithesis to the concept of emanation: "divine energies, far from being emanations or 'ideas,' ... are nothing else, in fact, as the Divine *life*."[342] According to Meyendorff, the manifestation of the fullness of divine life also proves that the energies in Orthodox thought are not a lower divinity: "The energies ... are never considered as divine

339. Meyendorff, *Study of Gregory Palamas*, 175, 179, 180.

340. Meyendorff, "Mount Athos in the Fourteenth Century," 163.

341. Meyendorff, "Holy Trinity," 34.

342. Meyendorff, "Doctrine of Grace," 24, emphasis original.

emanations, or as a diminished God. They are divine life, as given by God to His creatures."[343] The energies, therefore, are not necessary, unconscious, inactive, lifeless emanations, but are free and full manifestations of the living God of the Bible. They are God himself (but not God *in* himself).

In discussing Meyendorff's views on energy as light, I have already noted the Christocentric nature of his doctrine of energies. The same can be recognized in his reasoning about divine life. After the incarnation, Meyendorff posited, it was "no longer possible ... to speak in any absolute way of the unknowability of God," because in Christ the hidden uncreated divine life had been made accessible to humanity.[344] Later he states: "To say, after the Incarnation, that God remains unknown to man, or to say that his acts do not put us in contact with the very reality of his uncreated life, is to abolish the Christian mystery."[345] Meyendorff certainly does not refer to the unknowability and incommunicability of the divine essence here, because in his theology it always remains absolutely unknowable and incommunicable—both after the incarnation and in the age to come. Thus, one has no choice but to conclude that, according to Meyendorff, before the incarnation God was unknowable and incommunicable in an "absolute way" also according to energies. For it is only "since the Incarnation [that] he himself acts in us and through us," and his love becomes accessible to us.[346] This, of course, raises the question of how communion with God and salvation

343. Meyendorff, *Byzantine Theology*, 77; see also 28. Meyendorff also defends Palamas, whose "ancient and modern critics" accredit him with the view that the divine energies are an inferior divinity distinct from God himself (*Study of Gregory Palamas*, 214). Meyendorff dismisses the charge by arguing that, according to Palamas, God appears in his energies "*in his very wholeness*" and unites himself to believers "to the extent of coming to dwell in his entirety in their entireties" (*Study of Gregory Palamas*, 213). Meyendorff admits that Palamas occasionally used the expression θεότης ὑφειμένη (lower divinity) but adds that the term was introduced into the polemics by Palamas's opponents and in any case can be understood in an Orthodox sense as describing divine energies and not presupposing two separate divine realities (*Study of Gregory Palamas*, 61; see also 218, 224; "Le dogme," 97). For an alternative evaluation of Palamas, see John A. Demetracopoulos, "Palamas Transformed. Palamite Interpretations of the Distinction between God's 'Essence' and 'Energies' in Late Byzantium," in *Greeks, Latins, and Intellectual History 1204–1500*, ed. Martin Hinterberger and Chris Schabel (Leuven: Peeters, 2011), 277–78.

344. Meyendorff, *Study of Gregory Palamas*, 186; Meyendorff, *Byzantine Theology*, 94; John Meyendorff, "Confessing Christ Today," in *Living Tradition*, 117.

345. Meyendorff, *Study of Gregory Palamas*, 186.

346. Meyendorff, "Notes sur l'influence dionysienne," 550; Meyendorff, "Une théologie," 292.

was possible in the Old Testament era. Meyendorff did not directly answer it, but he seemed to admit that a special kind of grace was granted in the Old Testament—but only as in anticipation of the incarnation. Thus, even the mystical experience of the Old Testament saints was made possible by the coming of Christ. Although Meyendorff made such concessions, his main intention was to emphasize "the reality of the *radical change* which took place in the relations between God and man as a consequence of the Incarnation."[347] Salvation can only be found in Christ.

Energies as Properties. In the Christian doctrine of God, the word "property" has at least two principal meanings. First, there are hypostatic properties (fatherhood, sonship, and spiration), which denote relations of origin between the Father, the Son, and the Spirit. These properties are unique for each of the divine persons and are obviously not communicable, either within the Godhead or to creation. Second, there are properties (also called attributes, qualities, or perfections) that denote what is common to all the three persons. Such properties are normally called essential or natural, because they are supposed to convey, however imperfectly, what God is in his very being. This section will not focus on hypostatic properties and will deal only with the properties common to all the divine persons.

Meyendorff did not repudiate the term "essential property" as such. He mentioned impassibility and immutability often as "the characteristics" or "the attributes and properties" of the *divine essence*.[348] Although these attributes are negative, they function, as we saw above (pages 176–79), as *opposites* of the corresponding human attributes (passibility and mutability) and thus receive a kind of a positive meaning. Furthermore, when Meyendorff discerned such properties of the divine essence as creativity or immortality (which obviously has a positive meaning, since it denotes the ability to live forever), it is difficult not to conclude that such properties denote something positive in God's nature rather than merely transcending all affirmations and negations.[349] This becomes especially evident when

347. Meyendorff, *Study of Gregory Palamas*, 149, emphasis original.

348. Meyendorff, *Byzantine Theology*, 155–56; Meyendorff, "Holy Trinity," 33; see also Meyendorff, *Christ in Eastern Christian Thought*, 160.

349. On creativity: Meyendorff, "Christ's Humanity," 13; see also Meyendorff, "Holy Trinity," 37, where he says that "the property of being the Creator—and not a creature—belongs to God in his unique nature." On immortality: Meyendorff, *Byzantine Theology*, 155.

Meyendorff speaks about natural properties in the christological context: he refers to the Chalcedonian definition as speaking about the "properties" or "characteristics" (both words in the plural) of each nature.[350] This seems to imply Meyendorff's agreement with the idea that Christ's divine nature has a set of properties that somehow characterize this nature and can hardly be considered as only purely negative.

Nevertheless, when it comes to the doctrine of God, and especially to the relation between essence and energy, Meyendorff was more cautious in his formulations. His main concern was that recognizing certain of properties of God's nature might conflict with its unknowability and incommunicability. To be sure, he retained the term "*natural* properties" to indicate that nature is the source or cause for the properties. However, when enumerating divine properties, Meyendorff argues that they reflect the divine energies and not the essence: "the concepts of beauty, being, goodness, and the like, reflect God, but not His essence, only His 'powers' and 'energies.'" Similarly, Meyendorff believes that Athanasius's notion of creation "leads to a distinction in God between His transcendent essence and His properties, such as 'power' or 'goodness,' which express His existence and action *ad extra*, not His essence."[351] Meyendorff did not simply state that it is impossible to predicate certain things of the divine nature in the same way as we predicate them of finite creatures or in the same way as they are predicated of the divine energy. Nor did he simply say that the divine properties cannot be predicated of God's nature *properly* and *proportionally* or that divine nature cannot be described *comprehensively*. His thought was more radical: the divine essence remains completely beyond description and predication.[352] All that can be said about God can be said *only* about his energies.[353] The issue is not the limitations of human language (which

350. Meyendorff, "*Eastern Orthodoxy*," section "Christ"; Meyendorff, *Byzantine Theology*, 33; Meyendorff, "Christ's Humanity," 12. See John Meyendorff, "Christ as Savior in the East," in *Christian Spirituality: Origins to the Twelfth Century*, ed. Bernard McGinn, John Meyendorff, and Jean Leclercq (New York: Crossroad, 1989), 237–38.

351. Meyendorff, *Byzantine Theology*, 27, 130.

352. Moreover, given Meyendorff's insistence that the revelation of God in his energy and the mystical communion with him (which alone provides true knowledge of God) transcend any conceptualization, it remains doubtful that "the *concepts* of beauty, being, goodness, and the like" may be applied even to the divine energies (*Byzantine Theology*, 27, emphasis added).

353. In his Palamite studies, Meyendorff often referred to the decisions of the councils between 1341 and 1351 where Palamas's doctrine was endorsed. One of the questions of the

is obviously too weak even to fully describe the divine energies) but the "point of reference": energy *and not* essence.[354]

In identifying the divine properties with God's energy, Meyendorff appealed to the Cappadocians, pseudo-Dionysius, and Maximus, but his main source, as usual, was Palamas.[355] Meyendorff's constant refrain was that God in his essence transcends the divine life, glory, and all the attributes. According to Palamas, foreknowledge, will, providence, self-contemplation, prescience, predetermination, and so forth are the "works" and "virtues" of God, collectively referred to as τα περί αὐτόν ("things around God").[356] The idea of the things around God stems from Plotinus's ontology and was widely used in the Eastern tradition since the Cappadocians.[357] It denotes the sphere of God's manifestation and becomes for Meyendorff another conceptual tool for differentiating between God's inconceivable essence and his communicable energy: "in God" and "around God" indicate God's essence and energy, respectively. We can apply certain properties to God's revelatory energy and identify it with them, but we cannot project them onto the divine nature.[358] Thus, the saints perceive divine properties "without however knowing his 'essence.'"[359]

1351 Council was whether the term θεότης could be used with respect to the divine energy without falling into ditheism. It was taken for granted that it could be applied to the essence (Lourié, "Kommentarii," 394). As Ware indicates, the council answered affirmatively as follows: "The term 'deity' (θεότης) may be applied not only to the essence of God but to the energies." ("God Hidden and Revealed," 130). Meyendorff, however, reproduces the conciliar decision as if it says "*not* to the essence" instead of "not *only* to the essence" and immediately appeals to the "*consensus* of the Eastern fathers" that the word θεός "etymologically means the divine energy rather than essence" (*Introduction* à l'étude, 298–99, emphasis added; see also *Study of Gregory Palamas*, 98).

354. The interrelation between the terms "attribute" and "energy" can be formulated in a twofold way: energies reflect attributes (in the sense that we know God's attributes by means of his energies/acts) and attributes reflect energies (in the sense that we apply certain names/attributes to describe energies/acts). In any case, for Meyendorff it is important to conjoin the terms without allowing them to testify to something more (that is, to God's nature/essence). One should always bear in mind that the divine energy is both what God *is* and what he *does*.

355. Meyendorff, *Gregory Palamas*, 38–39.

356. Palamas, *Triads*, 94.

357. See Tollefsen, *Activity and Participation*, 24, 78, 91–92, 127; Bradshaw, *Aristotle East and West*, 84–86, 132, 166–67, 189–96, 206–8, 237–38.

358. Meyendorff, *Study of Gregory Palamas*, 214; Palamas, *Triads*, 95.

359. Meyendorff, *Study of Gregory Palamas*, 208. As Palamas puts it, "None of these things is the essence of God—neither the uncreated goodness, nor the unoriginate eternal life; all these exist not in Him, but around Him" (*Triads*, 97). Nevertheless, Meyendorff makes a casual remark that, according to Palamas, it is justified to apply properties such as goodness,

The divine properties not only are perceived by humans but are also *communicated* to them. The idea of the *communicatio idiomatum* (communication of properties) was essential for Meyendorff's christological and anthropological constructions. When it comes to the communication of the *human* properties in Christ, Meyendorff's thinking was very straightforward: they are to be ascribed to his divine person and not to his divine nature. In this section, however, we are interested in the movement in the opposite direction, in which the concept of energy comes to the fore. In dealing with Meyendorff's view on the communication of the *divine* properties, I will first examine how they are communicated to the humanity of Christ and then to those who are in Christ.

Although Meyendorff defines the *communicatio idiomatum* in Christ as "a mutual exchange of properties *between the divine and human natures*," such a definition should be taken as a rather imprecise expression of his view, because it can hardly be reconciled with what Meyendorff clearly and repeatedly claimed elsewhere.[360] In explaining the mechanism of the *communicatio idiomatum* more carefully, Meyendorff made clear that the divine nature is not the recipient of human properties. The same holds true for the *divine* properties: the divine nature is not involved in their communication to Christ's humanity. The real and sole source of the communication of the divine properties is the divine *person* of the Son.[361]

---

wisdom, and majesty to the divine essence. He immediately adds, however, that, "as this essence is imparticipable, these appellations in fact apply to it alone and all signify the same thing" (*Study of Gregory Palamas*, 221). In other words, Palamas's phrase implies that we can call God's essence good, or wise, or majestic, but these words will have a totally different, indeterminate meaning, and contribute nothing to our understanding of the divine essence. Meyendorff, however, prefers to simply deny the applicability of the divine properties to the divine essence outright instead of applying them to it using equivocal language.

360. Meyendorf, *Vvedenie v svyatootecheskoe bogoslovie*, 294, emphasis added. See also Meyendorff, "Christ as Savior," 244, 246.

361. Meyendorff, *Christ in Eastern Christian Thought*, 170, 204. In his dissertation on Christ's humanity in the works of Meyendorff, Barth, and von Balthasar, Patrick Patterson mentions "Meyendorff's interpretation of the *communicatio idiomatum* or *perichoresis* ('interpenetration') of the natures," but immediately (and rightly) adds that, "strictly speaking, the *communicatio* applies to the hypostasis of the Son and to his human nature." See Patterson, "By Thine Agony and Bloody Sweat: A Dogmatic Description of the Double Agencies of Christ - A Modest Proposal" (ThD diss., Wycliffe College of University of Toronto, 2012), 49. Patterson does not elaborate on this topic further, but it is preferable to avoid speaking of "natures" in the plural in this connection: not just "strictly speaking" (as Meyendorff and Patterson say), but "factually speaking" Meyendorff's Christology does not allow the participation of the divine nature in the *communicatio idiomatum*.

What the person of the Son communicates is the divine properties, understood as *energies*. Even when Meyendorff—imprecisely—defines the *communicatio idiomatum* as taking place between the *natures*, he adds that it results in the penetration of Christ's humanity: not with the divine nature but with the divine *energy*: "the resurrected and glorified humanity of Christ [is] ... —in virtue of the 'communication of idioms' between the two natures—penetrated with divine life, or 'energies,' or 'grace.'"[362] The term "penetration" (περιχώρησις) is today known more as a means of describing the relationships between the three divine persons, but Meyendorff used it extensively in its original theological locus—Christology. Although the term is often understood as being weaker than the term "communication," for Meyendorff both terms signified the same reality. He placed them side by side as synonyms and indicated that Christ's humanity is penetrated with the divine energy precisely "through" or "in virtue of" the *communicatio idiomatum*.[363]

The recipient of the divine properties/energies is Christ's human nature (soul and body). Hence the asymmetry of the *communicatio idiomatum*: the divine nature remains totally unaffected, whereas the human nature becomes deified. The communication Meyendorff had in mind is certainly not simply a *dialectica prædicatio* but a *realis communicatio*: Christ's human nature really acquires the properties "that normally belong only to the divinity" (without, of course, participating in the divine *nature*).[364] One such property is uncreatedness. Meyendorff states that (un)createdness is not a "fixed" given of a concrete nature: rather, it "is a quality that can be transferred from one nature to another"—just as other properties are transferred.[365] To be sure, this does not mean that Christ's human nature

362. Meyendorff, "Christ as Savior," 244, emphasis added. See also Meyendorf, *Vvedenie v svyatootecheskoe bogoslovie*, 329.

363. Meyendorff, *Byzantine Theology*, 77, 163–64; Meyendorff, *Christ in Eastern Christian Thought*, 203; Meyendorff, "Christ as Savior," 242, 244; Meyendorff, "New Life," 498; Meyendorff, "'Defense of the Holy Hesychasts,'" 189.

364. Meyendorff, *Christ in Eastern Christian Thought*, 170. See the same formulation in Meyendorff, "Holy Trinity," 34.

365. Meyendorf, *Vvedenie v svyatootecheskoe bogoslovie*, 329. Notice again the words "from one *nature*": it is difficult for Meyendorff to remain consistent when setting the divine nature aside from the *communicatio idiomatum*. See also *Study of Gregory Palamas*, 181, and "Christ's Humanity," 31, where Meyendorff states that the divine and human *natures* are "open to communion" and "permeable" to each other.

disappears or loses the characteristics proper to it. On the contrary, man's "true humanity is realized only when he lives 'in God' and possesses divine qualities."[366] Deification does not suppress or destroy human nature, but rather brings it to its destiny and fulfillment.[367]

In sum, the definition of the communication of the divine properties in Christ can be formulated as follows: it is a *penetration* of Christ's human *nature* with the divine *energy* coming from the divine *person* of the Son.[368] This nature is also the unique channel for the communication of the divine properties to those who are in Christ. To be in Christ is to have communion with the body of Christ, which is the source and locus of deification. Here again Meyendorff found it necessary to repeat that by acquiring the divine properties believers do not share in the divine *nature*.[369] What they receive from the theurgic body of Christ is the divine energy, which penetrates

---

366. Meyendorff, *Byzantine Theology*, 139.

367. This is the central notion of Meyendorff's anthropology, but it is difficult to grasp the logic behind it. If the human nature originally had the property "createdness" and, being deified, acquires the property "uncreatedness" without losing the property "createdness," then it appears to now possess two contradictory properties (the same holds true for many other human and divine properties). Realizing the problems inherent in this idea, Meyendorff appeals to the thought that human nature was created to be deified and acquire the divine properties. Human properties, he states, "become even more real and authentic by contact with the divine model according to which they were created" (*Byzantine Theology*, 164). It is not clear, however, how a property such as createdness could become "even more real and authentic" by adding uncreatedness to the human nature. Meyendorff further complicates the matter by saying that deification makes human nature "fully human" (*Christ in Eastern Christian Thought*, 86) and brings it "to its original state, its fully natural state" (189). But again: how was a property such as uncreatedness "fully natural" for humanity from the very beginning? Referring to Maximus and Palamas, Meyendorff uses other terminology that seems more promising: "the human nature of Christ, created by nature, is 'uncreated by participation'" (*Christ in Eastern Christian Thought*, 205). Here createdness is at least interpreted as a natural state without uncreatedness as a "fully natural" state. It can be said, then, that just as in Christology two properties with the opposite meanings can be applied to Christ's person with some qualifications (e.g., Christ is omniscient *according to his divine nature* and limited in knowledge *according to his human nature*), so in Meyendorff's anthropology two opposite properties can be applied with some qualifications to human nature (see above: human nature is created *by nature* and uncreated *by participation in God*). This leads to the distinction between "natural" and "deified" modes/states of the human nature: just as in Christology the person has simultaneously two natures, so in Meyendorff's anthropology the glorified human nature has two modes, with two corresponding sets of properties, simultaneously. But even such terminology is somewhat confusing and does not permit one to define nature as a set of properties (because the human nature, at least, can have two sets of properties with opposite meanings!)

368. See Meyendorff, "Christ as Savior," 242.

369. Meyendorff, "Holy Trinity," 34; Meyendorff, *Christ in Eastern Christian Thought*, 207.

his human nature and—through their communion with his body—also their natures. Believers become one with God in his light, grace, life, and properties—that is, they become god by energy, but not God by essence.[370]

Christians are called to participate in Christ's body through sacramental life; in particular, the deified body of Christ as offered in the Eucharist.[371] Consistently, Meyendorff carefully distinguished between God's energy and essence on this point too. He concurs with Palamas, who "conceived the Eucharist as a participation in the *deified human nature* of Christ and, in it, in the uncreated energies of God."[372] He further criticizes Palamas's opponent Akindynos, who insisted that the eucharistic communion implies participation in the *divine* nature.[373] In the words of Meyendorff, "the sacrament of the Eucharist is ... the personal union with the *Person* of the Word and a real participation in his *energy*," but not in his *nature*.[374]

THE RELATION OF GOD'S HIDDENNESS AND HIS REVELATION

Knowledge and Participation

In this concluding section, I will investigate the relation between God's hiddenness and his revelation in Meyendorff's theology. As the preceding sections show, this relation can be easily presented as the relation between

---

370. Meyendorff approvingly cites Palamas's statement that the saints have "one single *energy* with Christ" (Meyendorff, *Study of Gregory Palamas*, 180, emphasis original).

371. Meyendorff, *Study of Gregory Palamas*, 183; Meyendorff, *Byzantine Theology*, 164; Meyendorff, "New Life," 497.

372. Meyendorff, *Christ in Eastern Christian Thought*, 205, emphasis original; Meyendorff, "Le dogme," 96.

373. Meyendorff, "Le dogme," 94–95; Meyendorff, *Christ in Eastern Christian Thought*, 205.

374. Meyendorff, "Le dogme," 98, emphasis added. Having said that through the Eucharist the saints do not partake in the divine essence, it is strange that Meyendorff tries to find support for this statement by citing a passage of John of Damascus where he says that people (unlike angels, who partake only in grace but not in the divine nature) "do share in and become partakers of the divine nature, as many of them as receive the holy body of Christ and drink His blood; for the body and blood of Christ are hypostatically united to the divinity, and in the body of Christ with which we are in communion, there are two natures inseparably united in the hypostasis. We thus partake of both natures—of the body, corporally, and of the divinity, spiritually." See *De sacris imaginibus III*, 26 (PG 94:1348 A–B), cited in Meyendorff, "Christ as Savior," 244; the same citation with another translation can be found in Meyendorff, *Christ in Eastern Christian Thought*, 189. It is simply impossible to interpret this citation in a way that supports Meyendorff's claims.

essence and energy. To put things into perspective and make the subsequent analysis of Meyendorff's thought clearer, I will start with a short historical overview. In doing so, I will loosely follow the methodology of Meyendorff himself, who, being no less a historian than a theologian, preferred to expound his views by interweaving them with the history of Christian thought. Taking the risk of generalization and the oversimplification of complex issues that deserve individual inquiry, I will mention what I consider to be differences between the approaches of Eastern theologians to such concepts as knowledge of God and participation in him, even if Meyendorff would not have agreed with my reconstruction.

Proponents of the distinction between God's essence and energy emphasize that it was by no means Palamas's innovation but that it is traceable to earlier periods and was clearly articulated by the Cappadocians. Basil famously writes: "We know our God from His operations [ἐνεργειῶν], but do not undertake to approach near to His essence [οὐσίᾳ]. His operations come down to us, but His essence remains beyond our reach."[375] What is less often emphasized is that not only was this distinction peculiar to the Cappadocians' doctrine of God, but it reflected their modest ontological language in general. Basil believed that we not only have no access to the essence of God, but indeed that we have no access to *any* essence. In dismissing his opponents' claims of unbegottenness as ontologically defining the divine essence, Basil first mentions the hiddenness of the divine essence. But, in the following paragraph, he also refers to a similar hiddenness of the earth that can never be comprehended by our reason, senses, or concepts.[376] Likewise, Gregory of Nyssa argues that if even "the lower creation, which is within range of our perceptive faculties, lies beyond the limits of human knowledge, how can the one who by his mere will constituted the universe be within the grasp of our mind?"[377] Replying to

375. Basil of Caesarea, *Epistle* 234.1, in *A Select Library of the Nicene and Post-Nicene Fathers of the Christian Church*, vol. II/8, ed. Philip Schaff and Henry Wace (New York: Christian Literature Company, 1895), 8:274 (PG 32:872C–873B).

376. Basil of Caesarea, *Against Eunomius* 1.12, trans. Mark DelCogliano and Andrew Radde-Gallwitz, Fathers of the Church 122 (Washington, DC: Catholic University of America Press, 2006), 109 (PG 29:539–42).

377. Gregory of Nyssa, *The Second Book against Eunomius* 3.79, in *Gregory of Nyssa: Contra Eunomium II; An English Version with Supporting Studies*, ed. Lenka Karfíková, Scot Douglass, and Johannes Zachhuber, trans. Stuart George Hall (Leiden: Brill, 2007), 77. See also Tollefsen,

Eunomius's claims about the possibility of the knowledge of the divine essence, Gregory rhetorically asks him to explain the nature of the "smallest phenomena before us," such as an ant.[378] In a similar vein, Gregory of Nazianzus notices that human beings are even deprived of an accurate knowledge of creation, to say nothing of their inability to inquire into the nature of divine things.[379] To be sure, God is even more incomprehensible than all creation taken as a whole, but still the Cappadocians considered his hiddenness in the context of their *general* epistemological caution and wariness.

Furthermore, while clearly confessing the unknowability of all essences *in themselves*, the Cappadocians, though not entirely consistently, allowed some knowledge of essences based on their operations (energies). As John Behr writes, for Basil "any essence is beyond human comprehension, but is known only through its properties and activities."[380] Though we cannot understand and explain any nature, we can still legitimately apply certain names to it (keeping in mind that these names do not exhaustively and precisely describe the nature).[381] Jean-Philippe Houdret describes the Cappadocian approach as follows: "No name is able to express what the divine nature is in itself. But thanks to the multitude of names, which express our various notions about God, we form in our minds a knowledge of the divine nature, a knowledge that is very limited, but nevertheless sufficient."[382] So, admitting that "there is not one name which encompasses the entire nature of God and suffices to express it adequately," Basil states that certain negative and positive properties such as incorruptibility,

---

Activity and Participation, 90; Barry D. Smith, *The Indescribable God: Divine Otherness in Christian Theology* (Eugene, OR: Wipf & Stock, 2012), 36.

378. Gregory of Nyssa, *Against Eunomius Book Three* 8.2, in *Gregory of Nyssa: Contra Eunomium III; An English Version with Commentary and Supporting Studies*, ed. Johan Leemans and Matthieu Cassin, trans. Stuart George Hall (Leiden: Brill, 2014), 186. See also Tollefsen, *Activity and Participation*, 52; and other statements of Nyssen that reflect his epistemic humility in Hans Boersma, *Embodiment and Virtue in Gregory of Nyssa: An Anagogical Approach* (Oxford: Oxford University Press, 2013), 55.

379. Gregory of Nazianzus, *Second Theological Oration (Oration 28)* 5 (PG 36:32B).

380. Behr, *Nicene Faith*, 294; see also 297.

381. Georgias Martzelos, "The Significance of the Distinction between the Essence and Energies of God according to St. Basil the Great," in Athanasopoulos and Schneider, *Divine Essence and Divine Energies*, 156.

382. Jean-Philippe Houdret, "Palamas et les Cappadociens," *Istina* 19 (1974): 268.

immortality, invisibility, goodness, and righteousness can contribute to some notion of God's nature—a notion that is "altogether dim and trifling as regards the whole but that is at least sufficient for us."[383] Likewise, Gregory of Nazianzus acknowledges that no mind has "entirely comprehended, [n]or speech exhaustively contained the Being of God. But we sketch Him by His Attributes, and so obtain a certain faint and feeble and partial idea concerning Him."[384] As Tollefsen sums up: on the one hand, "according to the Cappadocian Fathers it is not possible for created minds to know the essence of any nature. ... Only God knows the nature of beings." On the other hand, "the general principle of the Cappadocian Fathers says that it is by observing and knowing the activities of a substance that we may grasp its essence."[385]

Without directly contradicting this approach, a bolder view on God's unknowability emerged in the Eastern tradition. In this view, although the hiddenness of created essences is not explicitly denied, the hiddenness of the divine essence is presented as completely unique, without any precedence or similarity in the created realm. According to pseudo-Dionysius, our knowledge is limited and bound to beings, but God absolutely transcends any being and is himself a nonbeing. God is irreducible to any concept and cannot be predicated in any way. This thought is repeated by Maximus: God "can in no way be associated by nature with any being and thus because of his superbeing is more fittingly referred [to] as nonbeing."[386] It means that the superiority of God should not be understood in the way of eminence, when creaturely things are ascribed to him in a supereminent manner, but in the way of negation, when all concepts and names, both

---

383. Basil of Caesarea, *Against Eunomius* 1.10, p. 105 (PG 29:533–34). See also 1.9, pp. 103–4 (PG 29:531–33).

384. Gregory of Nazianzus, *Fourth Theological Oration* 17, in *NPNF*^{2} 7:317 (PG 36:125). See also Beeley, *Gregory of Nazianzus*, 98–99.

385. Tollefsen, *Activity and Participation*, 77, 219. It must be admitted, however, that the Cappadocians were not always consistent and clear: "In their anxiety to deny Eunomian claims that we can know God's essence rationally, the Cappadocians appear sometimes to deny also that we can know God on the basis of his action in the world." See Colin Gunton, "Persons and Particularity," in *The Theology of John Zizioulas: Personhood and the Church*, ed. Douglas H. Knight (Burlington, VT: Ashgate, 2007), 107.

386. Cited in Maximus Confessor, *Maximus Confessor: Selected Writings*, ed. George Charles Berthold (Mahwah, NJ: Paulist, 1985), 185.

negative and positive, are denied him.[387] Although God is also beyond any essence and is thus *super*essential (or *non*essential), this utter otherness of God was frequently expressed (for the lack of a better term) through the idea of the hiddenness of God's *essence*. Thus, the distinction between essence and energy *in God* acquired a stricter meaning.

Returning to Meyendorff, one can relatively easily situate his views within this context.[388] Meyendorff takes the unknowability of the divine essence as something nonpareil and is not optimistic about the possibility of apprehending the divine essence to any degree. In his famous study, Meyendorff twice cites Palamas's confession of the radical otherness of God: "if God is nature, the other beings are not nature; and if the other beings are nature, God is not; in the same way, he is not a being, if the others are beings."[389] Furthermore, the names predicated of God do not reflect, according to Meyendorff, the divine essence, which remains completely unknowable. Even the knowledge of the divine energy, Meyendorff believes, surpasses natural and creaturely knowledge and is not knowledge at all; rather, it denotes the experience of encounter with God.

This brings us to the next important notion of Eastern theology: participation. Here I will also note two approaches. As Jeffrey Finch demonstrates, early fathers such as Irenaeus, Clement, and Athanasius believed that human participation in God is "the acquisition of a sanctifying, created likeness to God effected by and continually arising from the economic activity of the triune God."[390] To participate in God is primarily to share in the divine sonship and immortality of the Logos. Despite the several well-known, striking phrases already coined during this period (such as the classical "God became man so that man might become God" in its many variations), the fathers clearly recognized that creatures can never

387. See Tollefsen, *Activity and Participation*, 72–74.

388. Meyendorff, of course, interpreted Eastern thought differently and did not see any discontinuity between the Cappadocian and post-Dionysius theology. Although he admits that the Cappadocians "were not always consistent in their definitions of the essence-energy concept," he saw them as adherents, or at least precursors, of the Palamite sense of the distinction ("Holy Trinity," 36).

389. Meyendorff, *Study of Gregory Palamas*, 162, 210. Meyendorff adds that this passage was "plainly inspired by the Pseudo-Dionysius" (162).

390. Jeffrey David Finch, "Sanctity as Participation in the Divine Nature according to the Ante-Nicene Eastern Fathers, Considered in the Light of Palamism" (PhD diss., Drew University, 2002), 374.

be elevated to divine status, overcome their creatureliness, or become equal to or identical with the object of participation in any sense.[391] The Cappadocians understood participation along similar ethical and christological lines. As God created humanity in his image, humanity's constitution mirrors certain attributes of the divine nature, which is its archetype.[392] When arguing that Christians must participate in the divine virtues, Gregory of Nyssa offers this definition of the Christian faith: "Christianity is an imitation of the divine nature."[393] Participation in God is a growing likeness to his specific virtues/attributes (especially purity). Thus, the Cappadocians had no objections to the idea of participating in the divine nature, provided participation is understood as resemblance (implied in the relation between an image and its archetype) rather than complete identity. The saints become deified *by participating* in the divine nature, but they never possess divinity *by nature*.

With the development of mystical spirituality, however, a bolder view of participation in God emerged. In this view, creatures become so transparent to the divine activity that penetrates them that they literally become one with it. According to Maximus, the deified man no longer possesses a "beginning" or an "end"; he transcends his temporal existence.[394] Palamas further argues that through deification the saints become "uncreated, unoriginate and indescribable."[395] Since what is communicated by God becomes fully bestowed on creatures, so that they transcend the limitations of their nature and exist in a divine uncreated mode, there must be something in God that is not communicated at all. The belief in such an intimate

391. Vladimir Kharlamov, "Rhetorical Application of *Theosis* in Greek Patristic Theology," in *Partakers of the Divine Nature: The History and Development of Deification in the Christian Traditions*, ed. Michael J. Christensen and Jeffery A. Wittung (Grand Rapids: Baker Academic, 2007), 122.

392. As Huttinga rightly observes, "The conception of man as *imago dei* has been far more important for the development of Christian participatory thought than, for example, a single 'disturbing' text in the New Testament that speaks boldly about our 'partaking in the divine nature'" (*Participation and Communicability*, 57).

393. Gregory of Nyssa, *On What It Means to Call Oneself a Christian*, in *Ascetical Works*, trans. Virginia Woods Callahan, Fathers of the Church 58 (Washington, DC: Catholic University of America Press, 1999), 85.

394. Maximus, "Difficulty 10," in *Maximus the Confessor*, by Andrew Louth (London: Routledge, 2005), 119. See also Tollefsen, *Christocentric Cosmology*, 213–14; Tollefsen, *Activity and Participation*, 178–83.

395. Palamas, *Triads*, 86.

union with God demands the aforementioned bold view of the hiddenness of God's essence in order to secure his transcendence. Therefore, Maximus already notes that creatures become "all that God is, except for identity of essence," which Palamas later develops into a clear distinction between God's energy and essence, in which participation of creatures in the divine essence is seen as "the greatest absurdity."[396] Participation as an increasing likeness to God was thus overshadowed by two notions: (1) participation as an identification with God in his energy and (2) the complete otherness and incommunicability of the divine essence.[397] As Tollefsen sums up, God "differs radically [from the deified human] according to essence and is identical according to activity."[398]

As concerns Meyendorff, his thought represented a subsequent development of the Palamite view. Without denying, of course, the ethical dimensions of participation, he focuses on mystical union with God, strengthening its christological foundation and describing it in more existentialist terms such as "encounter" or "meeting." Although personalistic categories provide more opportunities for keeping the identity of each side of the union, Meyendorff is so preoccupied with their oneness that the key distinction for him is not between the two sides of the union (humanity and God) but between what is and what is not communicable *in God*. This distinction deserves its own separate consideration.

A Real Distinction

Meyendorff has been known as arguably the most assiduous and effective popularizer of the term "real distinction" as applied to the relation between God's essence and energy. The term proved to be controversial, and Meyendorff's views have been understood and evaluated in different ways. Nevertheless, although Meyendorff's formulations leave some room

396. Maximus, *Ambiguum 41* (PG 91:1308B); Palamas, *Triads*, 106. See also Tollefsen, *Christocentric Cosmology*, 213–14; Tollefsen, *Activity and Participation*, 178–83.

397. This required, of course, a clear differentiation between what can and what cannot be participated in God. Accordingly, the opposition "by participation – by essence/nature," typical in the early tradition, gave way to the Proclean triad of "unparticipated – participated – participating," which became part of Eastern theology through the works of pseudo-Dionysius. See Dmitry Biriukov, "On the Topic of Participation in the Divine Essence according to St Symeon the New Theologian in the Patristic Context," *Scrinium* 11 (2015): 301–5.

398. Tollefsen, *Christocentric Cosmology*, 222.

for interpretation, this room is not very wide, and before proceeding with my own analysis I will mention two understandings that, in my opinion, go beyond the bounds implied by Meyendorff.

In her book about deification in Aquinas and Palamas, Anna Ngaire Williams devotes a separate section to Palamas's essence-energy distinction and its interpretation in the twentieth century. She points out that the majority of Palamas's commentators have supposed that he intended the distinction to be real and includes in this group both modern opponents of Palamas and apologists for him (Lossky, in particular). Over and against this group Williams places a second, smaller one, in which she includes Meyendorff, noting that his "views on the matter are complex" and later claiming that his language "suggests, or at least admits" the possibility of viewing the distinction as merely conceptual.[399] She contrasts Lossky's reading with that of Meyendorff and wonders why "two such careful readers of Gregory can regard him so differently."[400] Such a fundamental difference, however, simply does not exist. The passages to which Williams refers do not prove that Meyendorff, in contrast to Lossky, did not consider the distinction as real. Williams twice cites a passage in which Meyendorff maintains that "the triple distinction—essence, hypostasis, energy—is not a division of God's being."[401] Such statements are indeed numerous in Meyendorff's works, but what they show is that he consistently used the term "distinction" (also "*real* distinction") as an intermediate term between identification and division/separation. Meyendorff's denial of a *division* in God by no means implied a denial of a *real distinction* in God. Williams bases another proof on a passage where Meyendorff says that Palamism "affirms in God a real distinction between the Persons and the common 'essence,' just as it maintains that the same God is both transcendent (in the 'essence') and immanent (in the 'energies')."[402] Williams reads this to mean that Meyendorff did not "claim [that] there is a real distinction between the essence and the energies, as he does between the persons and the common essence."[403] However, in this particular passage Meyendorff simply utilizes

399. Williams, *Ground of Union*, 139, 152.

400. Williams, *Ground of Union*, 152.

401. Meyendorff, *Byzantine Theology*, 187; Williams, *Ground of Union*, 139, 152.

402. Meyendorff, *Byzantine Theology*, 225.

403. Williams, *Ground of Union*, 139.

alternative terms to describe the relation between God's essence and energy. This does not mean that he is somehow hesitant about the term "real distinction" as applied to the relation. In the very book Williams references, Meyendorff clearly speaks of "the real distinction between essence and 'energy' in God maintained by Palamas," and claims that the decisions of the Palamite councils amounted to the recognition "of a real distinction between 'essence' and 'energy' in God." Furthermore, Meyendorff puts special emphasis on the word "real": "the distinction—a *real* distinction—between divine 'essence' and divine 'energy' is made unavoidable in the context of the doctrine of 'deification.'"[404] Meyendorff also used the term "real distinction" in his other works—when commenting on Palamas's views as well as when expounding his own position.[405]

A virtually opposite reading of Meyendorff is offered by Tollefsen, who, like Meyendorff, is convinced of the continuity of the Eastern tradition from the Cappadocians through pseudo-Dionysius and Maximus to Palamas. However, unlike Meyendorff, Tollefsen suggests that applying the term "real distinction" to Palamas's theology is prone to misunderstanding and may bring Palamas's faithfulness to prior currents of patristic thought into question.[406] Admitting that Meyendorff wrote "the classical introduction" to the Palamite controversy and "was a pioneer in the scholarly work on Palamas," Tollefsen believes that "it is about time to look critically at some of the claims he makes in his research." Tollefsen rightly corrects Meyendorff's depiction of Neoplatonism and insists that Eastern Christian thought had more in common with Neoplatonism than Meyendorff acknowledges. Tollefsen also rightly points out that Meyendorff's

---

404. Meyendorff, *Byzantine Theology*, 59, 103, 186, emphasis original.

405. Meyendorff, "Holy Trinity," 31; Meyendorff, *Christ in Eastern Christian Thought*, 210; Meyendorff, "'Defense of the Holy Hesychasts,'" 175; Meyendorf, "Svyatoy Grigoriy Palama," 165.

406. Recent scholarship produced a wide range of opinions as to whether the term "real distinction" accurately reflected Palamas's doctrine. To take only two examples: Milbank adamantly claims that Palamas "never suggested anything like a 'real distinction' in God between the reserved 'essence' and the shared 'energies.'" See John Milbank, "Christianity and Platonism," in Athanasopoulos and Schneider, *Divine Essence and Divine Energies*, 166. Demetracopoulos insists that Palamas "introduced a peculiar *distinctio realis* between the 'essence' or 'nature' of God and His 'powers' or 'energies'" ("Palamas Transformed," 272), and demonstrates how later Palamites tried to correct his formulations and even combine them with some Thomistic insights. Much depends, of course, on how each particular interpreter of Palamas defines the term "real distinction."

personalism cannot be traced back to the Cappadocians and is influenced by the de Régnon thesis. When it comes to the term "real distinction," however, Tollefsen's critical remarks about Meyendorff are less persuasive. Tollefsen is afraid "that the term 'real' distinction may suggest too much of a diversity" and "makes the distinction between essence and activity too radical."[407] In order to avoid unhappy connotations, Tollefsen offers the following correction: "When Meyendorff says that the distinction is *real*, this has to be balanced against the sayings of Palamas that the activity *differs from* the essence, but is *not separated from* it."[408] But Meyendorff's theology and his interpretation of Palamas do not need to be balanced in this way, because Meyendorff himself established such a balance. In his famous study, Meyendorff speaks of "Palamas's teaching about the 'inseparability' of essence and *energies*." According to Palamas, Meyendorff argues, "the energies are inseparable from the essence." They do "involve a certain 'distinction' (διαστολή) in the divine Being, but they do not divide it (οὐ μερισμός)."[409]

Thus, on the one hand, Meyendorff certainly and unapologetically affirmed a *real* distinction between God's essence and energy. There is no reason to suggest that he was hesitant about the term: Meyendorff believed that it faithfully reflected Palamas's theology and adequately expressed his own position. Like Palamas, Meyendorff refused to say that essence and energy differ only conceptually (κατ' ἐπίνοιαν).[410] On the other hand, Meyendorff also categorically denied that such a distinction separated energy from essence. The term "real distinction" as such cannot be discarded as something introducing a division in God's being, because Meyendorff clearly differentiates between distinction and separation or division.

However, even after excluding these two interpretive extremes, the precise meaning of the real distinction remains obscure. As with other terms that have been employed to describe the distinction between essence and

407. Tollefsen, *Activity and Participation*, 2, 198, 208, 211–12, 214; see also 86.

408. Tollefsen, *Christocentric Cosmology*, 141, emphasis original.

409. Meyendorff, *Study of Gregory Palamas*, 176–77, 225, emphasis original.

410. See Demetracopoulos, "Palamas Transformed," 275, 305. See also Ware, "God Hidden and Revealed," 133; Basil Krivoshein, "The Ascetic and Theological Teaching of Gregory Palamas," *Eastern Churches Quarterly* 3 (1938): 152.

energy in Eastern Orthodoxy—adverbial, conceptual, formal, fundamental, nominal, ontological, phenomenological, virtual, and so forth—the term "*real* distinction" is open to different interpretations. In what follows, I will try to establish what "real distinction" means for Meyendorff.

At first glance, Meyendorff's explanation as to why the distinction should be designated as "real" is disappointedly trivial. He states that the distinction is "*real* and not figurative, because the divine transcendence and the divine presence in the created world are equally *real*."[411] The Palamite councils endorsed "a theology of real 'participation' of man in God and, *therefore*, of a real distinction between 'essence' and 'energy' in God."[412] Elsewhere Meyendorff chooses other formulations to convey the same idea: the distinction is real, because the transcendence of God and the communion with him are real.[413] But is this not a simplistic and even naive justification of the term? Of course, most Christian theologians approve of the reality of God's transcendence and immanence. Does this sole fact make the term "real distinction" necessary or at least acceptable? Meyendorff's explanation, however, seems to be more than merely a rhetorical device to justify the term "real." Insisting on the reality of God's transcendence and immanence, he ascribed a kind of ontological status to them. This ontologizing of the distinction means that transcendence and immanence correspond to certain ontological orders in God's being. The distinction is not caused by the finite nature of humans and is not located solely on the human side.

Most importantly, one must bear in mind that, in Meyendorff's terms, *really* transcendent and *really* immanent mean *wholly* transcendent and *wholly* immanent. As indicated above, in Meyendorff's theology essence is a concept that refers to that which is hidden in God and not shared in mystical union. Meyendorff liberally used adverbs such as "absolutely," "completely," "totally," "wholly" to emphasize that the divine essence is inaccessible to creatures in any sense whatsoever. Any participation in

411. Meyendorf, "Svyatoy Grigoriy Palama," 165, emphasis original. See also Meyendorff, "Holy Trinity," 31.

412. Meyendorff, *Byzantine Theology*, 103, emphasis added.

413. Meyendorff, *Byzantine Theology*, 225; Meyendorff, "Theosis in the Eastern Christian Tradition," 476; Meyendorff, "Holy Trinity," 30, 31; Meyendorff, *Study of Gregory Palamas*, 216; Meyendorff, "Eastern Orthodoxy" (section "The Transcendence of God").

God's essence, Meyendorff contends, is inadmissible because it undermines his uniqueness and transcendence.[414] According to the Palamite axiom adopted by Meyendorff, participation in God's essence, even to the smallest degree, amounts to becoming God as he is in himself. In fact, there are no degrees of participation in the essence: to participate in it is to be identical with it. If God's essence were participable, there would be as many divine hypostases as there would be participants.[415] Likewise, knowledge of God's essence in the least degree amounts to possessing God and knowing him as he knows himself.[416] Meyendorff maintains the absolute unknowability of God on the grounds that any description of God entails an *identification* with something creaturely and, consequently, a limitation. "A known God is necessarily limited"; thus, his essence must be completely unknowable.[417]

Meyendorff recognized the same identification between the participated and the participating when speaking of God's energy, with the difference that whereas participation/identification in the divine essence is categorically denied, participation/identification in the divine energy is ardently affirmed. There are two aspects to the wholeness of God's communicability: in his energy, God communicates his *wholeness*; in mystical union, the *wholeness* of God is united with the *wholeness* of humanity. Concerning the former aspect (God is wholly communicated), Meyendorff maintains that divine energies confer the fullness of God's presence and manifest the totality of his life.[418] God "reveals Himself wholly in each energy," and the revelation in Jesus Christ is "total" and "full."[419] Meyendorff emphasizes—against Neoplatonic emanationism, which implies a diminution of God in his processions—that God *fully* communicates his being in his acts *ad extra*.[420] Against charges brought by the opponents of Palamism, Meyendorff argues that the divine energy is no "lower" divinity and indicates not only the acts of God but *God himself* in his action. Concerning the latter aspect (that God

---

414. Meyendorff, "Mount Athos in the Fourteenth Century," 164.

415. Meyendorff, *Study of Gregory Palamas*, 184.

416. Meyendorff, *Gregory Palamas*, 119.

417. Meyendorff, *Christ in Eastern Christian Thought*, 93. See also Meyendorff, *Byzantine Theology*, 11.

418. Meyendorff, "Le dogme," 98; Meyendorff, *Study of Gregory Palamas*, 214.

419. Meyendorff, *Gregory Palamas*, 119, 121–22.

420. Meyendorff, *Christ in Eastern Christian Thought*, 99–100; Meyendorf, *Vvedenie v svyatootecheskoe bogoslovie*, 274.

is wholly participated by the wholeness of humanity), Meyendorff cites the most realistic and bold statements found in the Orthodox tradition on the union between God and humanity.[421] Whole-humanity participates in whole-God in the same way that soul and body are united; by grace, the saints become unoriginated and indescribable; the life of God becomes their life, and his existence their existence; God unites "to the extent of coming to dwell in his entirety in their entireties."[422] Meyendorff's assertion of the completeness of union with God in his energies is based on the same principle that causes him to assert the impossibility of any participation in the divine essence: *to participate in* is *to be one with*.[423]

Naturally, all of this leads to one simple question: How can this be? If, as Meyendorff repeatedly asserts, God in essence and God in energy is one and the same God, how can he be *wholly* imparticipable and *wholly* participable at the same time? In answering this question, Meyendorff normally appeals to the limitations of our human language and understanding. He admits that the real distinction between essence and energy cannot be logically explained and demonstrated. It rests on a "paradoxical" idea, reflects "the *antinomy* of transcendence and union," and "involves a philosophical *antinomy*."[424] The paradox and antinomy are "located within God Himself."[425] However, according to Meyendorff, one should not be too anxious about the logical difficulties implied in the distinction, because God is not "subject to the limitations of our intellect," and Christian experience should not be "reduced to logical postulates."[426]

421. Meyendorff, *Study of Gregory Palamas*, 213; see also 183, 218, 220.

422. Meyendorff, "Christ as Savior," 241; Meyendorff, *Study of Gregory Palamas*, 175, 177, 213.

423. Remarkably, Meyendorff argues that John Scotus Eriugena's theology, like that of Palamas, affirmed "the full reality of deification." However, the absence in Eriugena's system of the essence-energy distinction "inevitably leads him to neoplatonic monism" ("Early Medieval Bridge-Builder," 69).

424. Meyendorff, *Byzantine Theology*, 185; Meyendorff, *Study of Gregory Palamas*, 209, emphasis added; Meyendorff, *Orthodox Church*, 186, emphasis added. See also Meyendorff, "Mount Athos in the Fourteenth Century," 164; Meyendorff, *Byzantine Theology*, 5; Meyendorff, "Doctrine of Grace," 19; Meyendorff, *Gregory Palamas*, 38, 39.

425. Meyendorff, "Early Medieval Bridge-Builder," 68.

426. Meyendorff, *Orthodox Church*, 186; Meyendorf, "Svyatoy Grigoriy Palama," 161.

Ways to Unify

The problem with the real distinction between essence and energy is not only that it does not fit our logical frameworks or expectations. More serious is the implication that the unity of God and humanity could jeopardize the unity of God himself. The divine energies appear to be more intimately united with deified people (indeed, in some sense identical with them!) than with the divine essence. Meyendorff realized the need to affirm and express a certain continuity between energy and essence. As we saw, he was eager to show that the term "real distinction" by no means suggested separation. Moreover, "distinction" as an intermediate term between identification and separation seems to bring us close to the concept of analogy, through which Western theologians sought to avoid simple univocity (identification) and pure equivocation (separation) in speaking about God. It is remarkable that Palamas's immediate followers, after Aquinas's works had appeared in Greek translation, attempted to explain the doctrine of their doctor in a Thomistic spirit, without necessarily using the term "analogy."[427] In what follows, I will examine several ways that would allow Meyendorff to unify essence and energy.

Essence as the Cause of Energies

In the philosophical tradition common to East and West, it was widely accepted that cause and effect are interrelated ontologically and epistemologically in such a way that the former transmits certain properties to the latter. Thus, a cause and its effects share some commonalities, albeit to different degrees: what is characteristic of an effect is also characteristic in a higher mode of its cause. This principle implies that knowledge of an effect allows one to infer some knowledge, however imperfect, of its cause. In this light, it is noteworthy that Meyendorff often referred to the divine essence as the *cause* of the divine energy. This seems to provide possibilities for demonstrating how essence and energy belong together. If some Christian theologians have held that *created* effects can give humanity a limited knowledge of the divine essence, then one might expect an even greater knowledge of the essence from the *uncreated* energy. Nevertheless, instead of accentuating a qualitative resemblance between essence and

427. Demetracopoulos, "Palamas Transformed," 292–368.

energy as the cause and its effect, Meyendorff uses this kind of causality to demonstrate the *difference* between essence and energy. Since essence is the cause (or "origin") of the energies, it is distinct from them and has "ontological" priority over them.[428] That the divine essence is the cause of the energies means "that God in his essence is higher than his energies."[429] In this, Meyendorff follows Palamas, who did not hesitate to affirm that as the cause of the energies the divine essence "infinitely" transcends them.[430] In his study about Palamas, Meyendorff wrote a short, separate section titled "The essence 'cause' of the energies." Here he also maintains that "in so far as it is the cause of the energies, this unknowable Essence remains 'transcendental' with respect to them and the energies are 'inferior' ... in relation to the essence." Meyendorff so strongly emphasizes this "transcendence of the essence-cause in relation to the caused energies" that he finds it necessary to explain why it does not break the unity of God.[431] Thus, instead of strengthening the unity of God, the causal relation between essence and energy, as Meyendorff develops it, seems rather to endanger it.

The Agent and His Acts

In Orthodox theology, the divine energies are sometimes presented as God's nature in motion. According to Tollefsen, "the divine activity, in the precise sense, is the divine nature or essence *qua* being active. The activities are 'around' God, and are a movement of His nature."[432] Palamas himself noted that the divine essence "possesses" energies and surpasses them as an agent surpasses his actions.[433] If the agent of the energies is God in his essence, it seems reasonable to suggest that these energies are somehow revealing of their agent and, consequently, of his essence. For Meyendorff,

---

428. Meyendorff, "Holy Trinity," 33, 37.

429. Meyendorf, *Vvedenie v svyatootecheskoe bogoslovie*, 332.

430. Palamas, *Triads*, 95. See also Demetracopoulos, "Palamas Transformed," 279–80.

431. Meyendorff, *Study of Gregory Palamas*, 218.

432. Tollefsen, *Activity and Participation*, 168. Tollefsen also notes that for the Cappadocians, God's activities reveal to us divine attributes "that are, basically, the divine nature being powerfully active" (36). Also, "Activity does not denote something other in God than essence, but is the same divine being as active" (Tollefsen, *Christocentric Cosmology*, 141). Similar definitions can be found in Dumitru Stăniloae, *Orthodox Dogmatic Theology* (Brookline, MA: Holy Cross, 1994), 1:125–26.

433. Palamas, *Triads*, 81, 97, 105.

however, such constructions are not personalistic enough. He advocates a more existential understanding of energy: the acting subject and real possessor of divine energies is not the divine essence but the divine persons. It is not that the essence possesses energies: rather, the divine persons possess both essence and energies. Meyendorff argues that energies "result from the divine hypostases," belong to them, and have existence only within them.[434] Energies as a divine gift can only be bestowed by persons: "indeed, only a Person (and in God always the Three Persons)—not an impersonal essence—can freely *give*."[435] Even if the energies *originate* in the essence, what they *reveal* is the Father, the Son, and the Spirit, but not their essence.[436]

Energy as the Manifestation of Essence

Another, similar way to demonstrate the unity between essence and energy is to view the energies as a manifestation of the essence. Referring to "St. Gregory of Nyssa and all the other Fathers," Palamas states that "the natural energy is the power which manifests every essence," implying that this ontological principle also applies to God. On the other hand, he immediately claims that what is manifested by the divine energies is God, but not God in his essence.[437] Elsewhere, Palamas proposed to regard everything manifested in God as his energy and not his essence.[438] Meyendorff was not always consistent on this matter, either. On the one hand, he plainly states that "energy is the manifestation of nature."[439] Although the essence is unknown *in itself*, it is manifested through energies.[440] However, normally the belief in the total incommunicability of the divine essence compelled Meyendorff to deny its manifestation through the energies. The energies "reflect God, but not His essence"; they "express His existence and action *ad extra*, not His essence"; they manifest the penetration of

434. Meyendorff, *Study of Gregory Palamas*, 216–19.

435. Meyendorff, "Theosis in the Eastern Christian Tradition," 476, emphasis original.

436. Meyendorff, "Holy Trinity," 38; Meyendorff, "Christ's Humanity," 12.

437. Palamas, *Triads*, 95–97.

438. Gregory Palamas, *Capita* 107, in *The One Hundred and Fifty Chapters*, ed. and trans. Robert E. Sinkewicz (Toronto: Pontifical Institute of Medieval Studies, 1988), 205, 243.

439. Meyendorf, *Pravoslavie i sovremennyy mir*, 47.

440. Meyendorff, "Two Visions," 47.

divine hypostases "without revealing the essence as such."[441] In previous sections, I already mentioned Meyendorff's dissatisfaction with the Aristotelian dyad essence-energy, "according to which each 'nature' (*physis*) has an 'energy' (*energeia*), i.e., an existentially perceivable manifestation." Christian theology, Meyendorff contends, transformed this dyad into the triad "person-essence-energy," which brought fundamental changes: now "energy reflects the common *life* of the three *persons*," while their common essence remains incommunicable and imparticipable.[442] God "manifests himself in concrete Persons and by concrete Acts"—that is, personally and energetically, but not essentially.[443] "Thus, the energies manifest the Living God, in Three Persons, although we continue not to know *what* God is, i.e. His essence."[444]

Inexhaustibility

In the Bible and subsequent Christian tradition, God's virtues have been imagined to be inexhaustible. The depth of the riches and wisdom of God is inexhaustible, and his ways are inscrutable (Rom 11:33). One can never grasp or experience God in his wholeness: whatever progress one has already made in the knowledge, vision, and imitation of God, something not yet explored and experienced always remains. Christian life is straining forward (ἐπεκτεινόμενος) to what lies ahead (Phil 3:13). The language of inexhaustibility presupposes that God is knowable and participable, at least in some mode or measure, because the term is applicable to that which is infinite and accessible in a limited way but not to that which is totally inaccessible. Putting it mathematically, it implies "more and more" and not a constant zero. Since the idea of inexhaustibility implies an ongoing knowledge and participation, it is noteworthy that Meyendorff—with his insistence that God is simultaneously totally incommunicable and wholly communicable and participable—also wove it into his doctrine of God.[445] He notes that the Eastern understanding of God's revelation presupposes

441. Meyendorff, *Byzantine Theology*, 27, 130; Meyendorff, "Palamas (Grégoire)," 99.

442. Meyendorff, *Byzantine Theology*, 185–86, emphasis added.

443. Meyendorff, *Study of Gregory Palamas*, 216.

444. Meyendorff, "Doctrine of Grace," 25, emphasis original.

445. Meyendorff, "'Defense of the Holy Hesychasts,'" 184, 188–89; Meyendorff, *Byzantine Theology*, 11, 219, 225; Meyendorf, *Vvedenie v svyatootecheskoe bogoslovie*, 165, 186, 276, 324.

that "*greater things* are always to come."[446] Elsewhere Meyendorff states that "an exhaustive vision of the *essence* of God is inaccessible to the created mind."[447] Statements of this kind would seem to presuppose the possibility of a limited, *nonexhaustive* vision of the essence of God. But despite such occasional remarks, Meyendorff typically used God's inexhaustibility not to discuss what potentially *could* be revealed but only that which is always hidden. God is inexhaustible because he is totally incommunicable in his essence, and not because there is always something more to be revealed. According to Meyendorff, participation in God is "a process that knows no end" precisely because he is absolutely transcendent in his essence.[448] To be sure, Meyendorff does not mean participation in God's essence here. Such participation is impossible: not because it has no end, but because it has no starting point! Thus, although Meyendorff refers to the divine essence as inexhaustible, he does not mean that the essence is more and more participated in through the divine energies; rather, he means that it always remains incommunicable. It is difficult to understand how Meyendorff intended to buttress the idea of dynamic and perpetually progressive participation in God by the total incommunicability of God's essence. What is clear is that the concept of God's inexhaustibility does not function in his theology to form a link between God's essence and energy, although on its own strength this concept could have been quite naturally employed to such purpose.[449]

Analogy and Degree

In Western theology, one of the key concepts that unites *God in himself* and *God for us* is that of analogy: God's revelation is accommodated to our finite capacities, but it does not communicate a totally different God, because it is analogically related to what God is in himself. In a similar vein, the concept

446. Meyendorff, "'Defense of the Holy Hesychasts,'" 184.

447. Meyendorf, *Vvedenie v svyatootecheskoe bogoslovie*, 324, emphasis added; see also 165.

448. Meyendorff, "'Defense of the Holy Hesychasts,'" 193.

449. Compare this with how the essence-energy distinction is interpreted by Bulgakov: "Energy proves to be the means of communicating *ousia*. ... On the foundation of the operation of God in the creature, what God is in himself becomes known. Although this cognition in essence is inadequate, that is precisely why it represents the possibility of infinite growth and deepening." See Bulgakov, *Unfading Light: Contemplations and Speculations*, trans. Thomas Allan Smith (Grand Rapids: Eerdmans, 2012), 133, 215–16.

of degree is used: although creatures cannot know and participate in the infinite fullness of God, they can enjoy a qualitatively partial knowledge of God and can participate in him to their own creaturely degree. Although the terms "analogy" and "degree" did not belong to the core of Meyendorff's theological vocabulary, one can discern at least two ways in which he uses the terms or the ideas behind them. First, he extensively uses the idea of humanity as the image of God. Humanity possesses a natural kinship to God, and its virtues participate in and roughly mirror God's attributes. Created beings can participate in God only "in the proportion and analogy proper to each."[450] Although such statements may restrict the "wholeness" of the mystical participation in God's energy advocated by Meyendorff, they do not question the absolute unknowability of his essence. To be sure, once Meyendorff admits that in the Greek patristic tradition "'image' implies *a participation in the divine nature*"—but this passing remark was never developed in his thought regarding God's essence and energy. Elsewhere, expressing the same idea, he clarifies the matter stating that humans as images of God participate in the divine *life* and *glory*. Second, Meyendorff uses the language of degree when he observes the limitations of human language in describing even that which is communicated by God. Although God has revealed himself and can be encountered personally, "not Scripture, not conciliar definitions, not theology can express Him fully. ... No human language ... is fully adequate to Truth itself."[451] This is why Meyendorff's affirmations about participation in God are always bolder than his affirmations concerning the knowledge of God: the human mind and human concepts are unable adequately to express what happens in mystical union with God. For our purposes, it is important to note that Meyendorff never used the language of analogy or degree when elaborating the relation between God's essence and energy. Our participation in God's attributes can be analogous to how he reveals them as his energies; our description of the revealed truth can be analogous to the reality of the mystical union; but neither our participation in energies nor the divine energies themselves are said to be analogous to the divine *essence*.

450. Meyendorff, *Byzantine Theology*, 28.

451. Meyendorff, *Christ in Eastern Christian Thought*, 114–15, 210, emphasis original; Meyendorff, *Byzantine Theology*, 11, 143, 169.

Internal Energy

As indicated above, Meyendorff does not develop a clear and consistent doctrine on God's *internal* energy. His passing remarks, however, lead to the following conclusions: internal divine energies exist; they are best understood as the divine life and the reciprocal love of the divine persons; this life is further communicated to creatures; there is no difference between the internal divine life and the communicated life; deified human beings become participants of this life. What Meyendorff does not specify, however, is how the divine essence is involved in the intra-Trinitarian circle of love. Given that Meyendorff does not object to identifying God's essence with *God in himself*, it is noteworthy that he unequivocally states that *God in himself* is love.[452] This statement not only suggests a positive description of God's essence, but also affirms that the intra-Trinitarian relations cannot be considered apart from God's essential existence. For, as Meyendorff makes clear, *God in himself* is love precisely by virtue of the loving relations of the three divine persons toward one another. Moreover, Meyendorff emphasizes that it is this loving circle within the Godhead that makes God's *external* manifestation of love possible and meaningful. Potentially, this approach could have linked God in himself (his essence), his internal energies (the intra-Trinitarian relations), and his external energies (his manifestation to creatures). However, Meyendorff does not explicitly establish such links and does not take the statement that *God in himself* is love as disclosing something of God's essence. Rather, he repeats that "God is totally transcendent and unknowable in his essence."[453]

No Two Entities

The previous sections described some motifs and terms employed by Meyendorff that had potential for clarifying how God's essence is united with his energies. Nevertheless, as we saw, he does not consistently use any of them to lessen the tension between the fullness of God's incommunicability and the fullness of his communicability. At the same time, he realizes the need to demonstrate that the real distinction that he maintained involves no separation. He tries to reach this goal both negatively

---

452. Meyendorff, *Byzantine Theology*, 12–13; Meyendorff, "Holy Trinity," 35.

453. Meyendorff, "Holy Trinity," 31, 35.

and positively. Negatively, by denying the existence of two entities in God; and positively, by including essence and energy in a common category—God's *being*.

The denial of the existence of two entities requires a clarification of the ontological status of energies. Meyendorff sympathetically describes Palamas's terminological hesitations: for Palamas, energies are in one sense identical with essence, while in another they differ; in one sense, they are not "things" (πράγματα) or "realities" (ὄντων), while in another they are; they can be viewed as accidents, but only in a limited sense; energies are in a sense qualities, but they are free, while qualities are not, and so forth.[454] While such wavering to other scholars is a sign of "the ineptitude of Palamas as a metaphysician,"[455] Meyendorff takes it as a sign of Palamas's desperate attempts to "free theology from Aristotle's philosophical categories which were clearly inadequate worthily to express the Mystery." Meyendorff hardly offers any new categories of his own, and in this sense he does not advance much further than Palamas. In giving an ontological account of divine energy, he normally restricts himself to saying what energy is not: it is not a discrete entity, which has an existence independent of the essence. Essence and energy are not "two essential realities, since both belong to one unique living God."[456]

The Concept of Being

As noted above, Meyendorff's personalism allows him to present divine essence and energy as two modes of existence of the divine persons. The persons possess both essence and energy and are equally present in both. Meyendorff employs the concept of the divine being (*l'être*) in a similar vein. Although in Christian theology this concept has been typically understood as a synonym of God's essence (nature, substance), Meyendorff uses it differently. In his terminology, the being of God, like the persons, "cannot be identified with the essence." God is not bound by his incommunicable essence, but freely imposes on himself a *communicable* mode for his

454. Meyendorff, *Study of Gregory Palamas*, 225.

455. Milbank, "Christianity and Platonism," 203.

456. Meyendorff, *Study of Gregory Palamas*, 98, 225.

being—his energies.[457] Consequently, just as each of the divine persons is simultaneously hidden and revealed, so also the being of God is hidden and revealed at the same time. Meyendorff's term "mode of being," therefore, differs from Barth's term "mode of being" and Rahner's term "mode of subsistence": while Barth and Rahner use these terms to refer to what other theologians have identified as "person," for Meyendorff each divine person, as well as God's being, has two modes: essence and energy. The distinction between essence and energy is drawn *within* God's being: energy exists outside essence, but not outside being.[458] In Meyendorff's Trinitarian grammar, the concept of "being" served as a unifying concept comprising God's essence and his energy. Generally speaking, in the context of the distinction between essence and energy, the being is a singular equivalent to the plurality of the persons—hence it is often called "*personal* being." Meyendorff's ultimate answer to the charges of introducing a division into God can be formulated as follows: since God's essence and energy express one and the same being of God and belong to him, they are not and cannot be separated.[459] It is precisely because the *fullness* of being is present in both essence and energy that God can be *fully* incommunicable and *fully* communicable.[460]

---

457. Meyendorff, *Study of Gregory Palamas*, 225–26; Meyendorff, "Holy Trinity," 33; Meyendorff, "Philosophy, Theology," 207–8.

458. Meyendorff, "'Defense of the Holy Hesychasts,'" 175; Meyendorff, *Study of Gregory Palamas*, 216; Meyendorff, "Early Medieval Bridge-Builder," 67.

459. Meyendorff, *Gregory Palamas*, 122.

460. Meyendorff, "Le dogme," 98. Meyendorff's definitions are somewhat confusing even for scholars who otherwise demonstrate a proper understanding of his theology. Daniel Paul Payne attributes to Meyendorff the idea that "the Divine Being, God in Himself, is unknowable." See Payne, "The Revival of Political Hesychasm in Contemporary Orthodox Thought" (PhD diss., Baylor University, 2006), 304. Meyendorff, however, clearly denies that "the divine being" is to be identified with God in himself: the essence of God (God in himself) is only one of two modes of the divine being. In his communicable mode (in energy), the being is revealed and participated: "God can manifest himself in his very being, while remaining imparticipable in his essence: that is the real significance of what is called 'Palamism'" (Meyendorff, *Study of Gregory Palamas*, 213; see also 208; Meyendorff, *Orthodox Church*, 175; Meyendorff, "Mount Athos in the Fourteenth Century," 164). Another scholar, Jeffrey Finch, in his insightful doctoral dissertation, suggests that Meyendorff's reading of Palamas can be presented as follows: "God transcends Himself, His essence transcending His being or existence and His being or existence transcending His essence" ("Sanctity as Participation," 28). Finch correctly identifies God's being with his existence, but the formulation that God's being and essence mutually transcend each other is unnecessarily paradoxical and complicated. God's being may be said to transcend the divine essence in the sense that it also encompasses divine energy, but the divine essence, according to Meyendorff, transcends only divine energy (as its cause) and not divine being (of

Divine Simplicity

The most often repeated objection against the Palamite distinction between essence and energy—in the time of Palamas as well as in modern times—has been that it compromises divine simplicity. Meyendorff embraces the doctrine of God's simplicity as important for Christian theology and therefore attempts to prove that the essence-energies distinction does not undermine it. Although he does not treat the doctrine systematically, one can discern two key elements in his defensive strategy. First, Meyendorff insists that the doctrine is not jeopardized by the plurality of God's energies. Second, he seeks to prove that the doctrine is not defeated by the distinction between essence and energy. I will analyze his views below in this order.

Simplicity and the Plurality of Energies

In his writings, Meyendorff refers to the divine energy or energies in both the singular and the plural. This usage reflects his persuasion that energy has two interwoven aspects: it is what God *is* and what he *does*. It is logical to refer to God in his revelation as energy and to his multiple acts as energies. The interplay of singular and plural is also caused by the multiplicity of God's attributes (hence plural) and the belief that God in his revelation is identical with them (hence singular).

The recognition of multiplicity in God, Meyendorff contended, should not surprise us, for God contains not only the plenitude of attributes or energies but also the triunity of persons. God is not composite, and as the three divine persons do not compose one God, so also the various energies do not compose one energy; and as each person contains the fullness of divinity, so also each energy is the fullness of God's being. God does not consist of beauty, wisdom, goodness, truth, and so forth, but *is* beauty, wisdom, goodness, and truth.[461] When he reveals himself as good or wise, he does not merely reveal this particular attribute, but manifests the fullness of his being. Individual attributes, Meyendorff argues, are not "different realities,"

---

which it is a mode). Finch draws his conclusion from the following words of Meyendorff (and Palamas): "The essence is necessarily being, but being is not necessarily essence" (*Byzantine Theology*, 188). But what this means for Meyendorff is that while essence is a mode of God's being (and hence cannot transcend it!), being is not bound by essence. On what these words meant for Palamas, see Demetracopoulos, *Is Gregory Palamas an Existentialist?*, 37–38.

461. Meyendorf, *Vvedenie v svyatootecheskoe bogoslovie*, 331–32; see also Meyendorff, *Gregory Palamas*, 121.

but are ontologically identical to each other. To be sure, the attributes are not synonymous (mercy is not identical to righteousness, nor is majesty identical to truth) and are experienced as manifold, but they are identical in the sense that they denote one and the same entity. The attributes are not parts of one God and therefore do not entail any composition in him.[462]

In sum, despite using different formulations, Meyendorff does not significantly diverge from Western theologians in demonstrating how the plurality of attributes is compatible with divine simplicity. The important difference is, of course, that Meyendorff links divine attributes to energy rather than to essence. But the principle of the reconciliation of oneness and plurality in God is virtually the same: although God has many attributes, he is not composed of them, because they have the same reference and are identical to him (as to his energy).

Simplicity and the Essence-Energy Distinction

The essence-energy distinction, which does not have an exact counterpart in Western theology, poses another challenge to the doctrine of divine simplicity and demands more creativity in answering it. Obviously Meyendorff cannot agree that God's attributes are identical with his essence, because he consistently locates them at the level of energy and asserts that the latter is not identical with essence. At the same time, he also does not want to leave the essence aside when defining God's simplicity. Another option would have been to apply God's simplicity to the divine persons, but to link simplicity to what is multiple in God would hardly be convincing. Meyendorff chose, therefore, to associate God's simplicity with the divine being, which is singular in God and is fully present in both essence and energy. To be sure, Meyendorff affirms that God's essence is simple, which was quite traditional (Basil states that "the operations of God are various, but his essence is simple)."[463] However, linking simplicity exclusively to

---

462. Meyendorff, *Study of Gregory Palamas*, 215, 220.

463. Basil of Caesarea, *Epistle* 234.1, *NPNF*[2] 8:274 (PG 32:872C–873B). Meyendorff mentions simplicity along with unchangeability and incorruptibility as "the attributes and properties of His [God's] essence" ("Holy Trinity," 33), although, as I argued above (pages 221–27), the very idea of essential attributes is problematic within the framework of Meyendorff's approach. In the English translation of Meyendorff's study about Palamas, one also encounters the phrase "the simplicity of the divine nature" (*Study of Gregory Palamas*, 219), but in the original French text Meyendorff writes about "la simplicité de l'être divin" (*Introduction à l'étude*, 300).

the essence of God has essentialistic overtones for Meyendorff, while the application of "the concept of divine 'simplicity' not to the essence but to the personal Divine Being" is nothing but "a personal existentialism."[464]

It is not a trivial task, however, to prove the unity of the divine being, let alone its simplicity, given Meyendorff's insistence on the total incommunicability of essence, the total communicability of energy, and the seeming lack of clearly unifying links between the two. The defense of divine simplicity in face of the multiplicity of divine attributes normally amounts to saying that they differ only in our apprehension, but Meyendorff cannot follow this strategy in the case of the distinction between essence and energy, because he consistently denies that they are identical and affirms instead that they *really* differ. By revealing himself fully in his acts, God does not identify these acts with his essence.[465] Some of Meyendorff's formulations suggest that he might prefer a "soft" version of divine simplicity: referring to Palamas, he claims that "the simplicity of the personal Being of God" is not blemished by divine energy because the energy is "pure action foreign to all passivity." Meyendorff means that composition is caused by being acted on from without, but since God *himself* assumes a really diversified mode of existence, it cannot endanger his simplicity. Likewise, Meyendorff states that one could talk about "'complexity' in the Being of God" if the existence of the world, created by his energies, were *necessary* for God. Meyendorff himself, however, seems to realize that such an understanding of divine simplicity was somewhat deficient. Therefore, referring to Palamas, he offers another reason why the essence-energy distinction involves no composition: there can be no synthesis "of thing moved and movement."[466] This citation, however, implies that the agent is the essence itself—an idea that, as we saw, finds no place in Meyendorff's personalistic approach. Meyendorff transforms this notion into the idea that one and the same personal agent dwells equally in his essence and energy:

> What is called the divine "simplicity" does not manifest itself in the identity of the whole divine Being with the essence—which, for the Greek tradition, would be an abstract and philosophical conception

464. Meyendorff, *Gregory Palamas*, 123. See also Meyendorff, *Study of Gregory Palamas*, 220.

465. Meyendorff, *Gregory Palamas*, 119.

466. Meyendorff, *Study of Gregory Palamas*, 223, 226.

> of that simplicity—but in the fact that there is only one sole God living and acting in the imparticipable essence as in the energies.[467]

The simplicity of God consists not in the claim that essence and energy are "one sole thing" but that they belong "to one sole God."[468]

Meyendorff finds a solution, therefore, in the idea that divine simplicity amounts to the recognition of the fullness of the presence of the divine being in both essence and energy. He seems to believe that divine simplicity would have been compromised only if energy and essence *complemented* each other. But since God's being is wholly represented in both essence and energy, it entails no composition. "God appears complete in the total simplicity of his personal being" because "through each of his energies one shares in the whole of God." Essence and energy neither divide God's being, nor are they composite parts of it. "Unchangeableness and movement, unknowability and revelation, supratemporality and action in time ... [are] united in the simplicity and mystery of the personal Being of God."[469]

Conclusion

Meyendorff's distinction between God's essence and energy springs from his desire to affirm both the deification of humans—their transformation through union with God and their acceptance within the divine life—and the otherness of God. The distinction, as Meyendorff interprets it, allows him to state that "while uniting himself fully with man, God remains inapproachable in his essence."[470] Meyendorff unequivocally considers this distinction as real and not merely nominal: it reflects that which objectively exists in God. What is more, this real distinction between God's essence and energy means for Meyendorff that God is *wholly* incommunicable and

467. Meyendorff, *Study of Gregory Palamas*, 215.

468. Meyendorff, *Study of Gregory Palamas*, 215. Similarly, the essence-energy distinction "does not involve complexity in God, for it is not a question of two essential realities, since both belong to one unique living God" (98).

469. Meyendorff, *Study of Gregory Palamas*, 220, 223; see also 214. Interestingly, Meyendorff even tries to prove the unity of God's being and the fullness of his presence in his two modes *through* divine simplicity: "*in virtue* of the simplicity of His being, God is wholly and entirely present both in His essence and His energies" (*Gregory Palamas*, 122). Less explicitly: the Palamite distinction "does not break the unity of the divine being since God in His simplicity is wholly present in the essence and in the energy" (119).

470. Meyendorff, *Study of Gregory Palamas*, 184.

wholly communicable. God is not partly concealed and partly revealed: rather, he is completely inaccessible in one mode and totally present and participable in another, making the saints sharers of his uncreated life.

His affirmation of this distinction would seem to pose an insoluble paradox. Meyendorff himself admits that the distinction involves "the antinomy of two logically incompatible truths: first, that God is unknowable by nature, second, that the revelation of God in Jesus Christ is full."[471] The difficulties are not only logical, but also dogmatic: a distinction implying the existence of two objectively different modes in God seems to threaten his unity. Meyendorff, however, continually and consistently emphasizes that the divine energies, though really distinct from the divine essence, are inseparable from it. For him, the term "real distinction" does not imply a division within God.

While Meyendorff clearly states that God's essence and energies are united rather than separated, he is less clear as to *how* they are united. Although he employs several concepts that could potentially have clarified the relationship between God's essence and energy, he does not develop them in a manner that strengthens the link between these two modes of God's existence. In particular, while he asserts that God's essence is the cause of the energies, Meyendorff does not in turn conclude that the energies (as the effects of the essence) somehow disclose it. Rather, he argues that it is precisely as the cause of the energies that the divine essence infinitely transcends them. Meyendorff also refuses to consider the divine energies as God's essence at work. He claims instead that the agents behind the energies are the divine *persons* who possess both essence and energy: in essence, they remain totally unknown and reveal themselves only through the energies. With a similarly personalistic emphasis, Meyendorff elaborates the idea of God's manifestation. He argues that the energies manifest the life of their possessors—the divine persons—but *not* their essence. Thus, "even when He [God] manifests Himself, He remains unknowable in His essence."[472] That God's revelation is inexhaustible does not mean for Meyendorff that the divine essence becomes increasingly knowable and participable. Rather, God's inexhaustibility means that however much he

471. Meyendorf, *Vvedenie v svyatootecheskoe bogoslovie*, 330.

472. Meyendorff, *Gregory Palamas*, 118.

communicates through his energies, he remains totally transcendent in his essence. Further, while Meyendorff uses the concepts of analogy and degree in his anthropology and soteriology, he does not use analogical reasoning in his doctrine of revelation. That is, he does not argue that God's revelation is analogically related to what God is in himself and, consequently, he never establishes an analogical relation between God's essence and energy. Finally, Meyendorff notes that the doctrine of uncreated energies describes not only the divine manifestation *ad extra* but also the intra-Trinitarian communion of self-opening and love. He does not clarify, however, how these internal energies are related to the divine essence.

Meyendorff's defense of the inseparability of essence and energies boils down to two main assertions. First, he maintains that God's energies are inseparable from God's essence, because they are uncreated and do not exist independently of it. Second, Meyendorff argues that the essence and the energies are united by virtue of belonging to the one sole being of God. Thus, they are not two discrete, separable entities but two inseparable modes of God's existence.

Meyendorff is also convinced that his doctrine of the divine energies does not jeopardize divine simplicity. The plurality of energies does not introduce composition into God's being, because God does not consist of his energies as if they were his parts, but rather he reveals his fullness in each of his energies. Although the energies are experienced by humans as manifold and varied, each of them is God himself. Likewise, the essence-energy distinction does not involve composition, because God's being is *completely* present in his essence as well as in his energies. It is the totality of God that is simultaneously manifested and unmanifested, participable and unparticipable, knowable and unknowable.

4

COMPARISON AND EVALUATION

COMPARISON

Mutual Assessment

In chapters 2 and 3, I have tried to explain and systematize the views of Bavinck and Meyendorff using their own terms and in light of their own contexts. In this chapter, by contrast, my convictions and concerns will become more explicit. But before proceeding with a comparison and evaluation of their viewpoints, it is worth listening a little more to Bavinck's and Meyendorff's own voices. This will help us to discern how they themselves understood the differences between their respective traditions regarding the relationship between God's hiddenness and his revelation. However, I will not dwell long on this, primarily because both theologians, though generally open-minded and catholic in their theological endeavors, nonetheless lacked a substantial interest in each other's traditions. What is more, they presented the other's tradition in ways that betrayed the assumptions and limitations of the dogmatic and historical constructs that they themselves inherited from their respective contexts and mentors. Historical circumstances and different scholarly priorities did not allow them to treat each other's traditions with the precision and breadth of expertise that they demonstrated in dealing with other matters. Even where their descriptions of the other's tradition are questionable, they are nonetheless instructive in showing us their own underlying theological commitments, which also informed their evaluations of other traditions.

Bavinck on Eastern Orthodox Doctrine

Bavinck's knowledge and treatment of Eastern Orthodoxy were typical for a Western theologian of his time. He readily admitted the decisive role of the East in formulating the fundamental Christian dogmas about Christ and the Trinity, and recognized the liveliness of the christological debates in the East up until the eighth century. The Eastern doctrine, Bavinck notes, was summarized by John of Damascus, and after him the East dedicated itself to preserving the legacy of the fathers.[1] In what follows, I will briefly analyze Bavinck's scattered remarks about the Cappadocians, the influence of pseudo-Dionysius, the *filioque* clause, and the Palamite councils.

Bavinck understood God's simplicity as implying that each of God's attributes is identical to his essence. Bavinck admitted, however, that some church fathers made a distinction between God's essence and his attributes. In the first edition of his *Reformed Dogmatics*, Bavinck notes that in resisting Eunomius's claims about the knowability of the divine essence, Gregory of Nyssa differentiated between God's οὐσία on the one hand and properties related to it on the other. According to Bavinck, Gregory of Nyssa and his brother Basil maintained that no name can express God's essence, but that there are names and properties through which we receive a certain likeness of God. Such a distinction, Bavinck argues, immediately begged the question of what belongs to the essence and what to the attributes, and marked the point of departure from sound theology. Bavinck recognizes that the Cappadocians used this distinction mainly to emphasize God's incomprehensibility in their opposition to Eunomius, but he adds that the distinction acquired a more unfortunate meaning when the notion of God's incomprehensibility lost its significance. Instead of following the Cappadocians in this respect, Bavinck aligns himself with those church fathers who, supposedly, in describing God as being (or essence), had in mind not God's being *in distinction to* his attributes but God's being *as it is revealed in* his attributes. The being ascribed to God in this way was not an abstract or empty concept but the summation of all perfections. In the second edition, Bavinck removed his critical remarks about the Cappadocians, but he did not change his critical attitude toward differentiating between God's essence and attributes.[2]

1. *RD* 1:128, 132, 135; Bavinck, *Christendom*, 28. According to Bavinck, "a history of theology and dogmatics in the Eastern church after John of Damascus does not yet exist" (*RD* 1:131).

2. *RD* 2:118, 120, 125; *GD*[1] 2:86–87 (Moreover, in the second edition, Bavinck attributes to the Cappadocians the position that "every attribute is identical with the divine being," though the attributes themselves are distinct).

In the later Eastern tradition, Bavinck took special note of pseudo-Dionysius, whose works were pervasively influential in the East as well as in the West. Bavinck observes that the *Corpus Areopagiticum* used "neoplatonic philosophy and pantheistic mysticism" to elaborate Christian doctrine, which had detrimental consequences for the development of Christian theology and spirituality. In the West, Bavinck viewed the adoption of this "neoplatonic mysticism" via pseudo-Dionysius as leading to the affirmation of the possibility to contemplate God in his essence and to the development of the doctrine of "divinization (ϑεωσις), *such as Rome teaches*." Although Bavinck uses the Greek word ϑεωσις, he does not discuss the specifically *Eastern* doctrine of deification here. He seems to realize that it differed from what he regards as the "Roman" doctrine, because he consistently presents the latter as connected with the vision of God as to his essence—an idea hostile to Eastern apophaticism.[3]

In the East, the influence of pseudo-Dionysius expressed itself differently. Bavinck reveals his understanding of this influence when he maintains that the recognition of the ectypal character of our knowledge of God enables us to avoid two extremes. The first extreme is the theology of "those who consider an essential, quidditative, adequate knowledge of God a possibility." Here Bavinck includes "Catholic theologians who teach a vision of God in terms of his essence in the state of glory." The second extreme is represented by "those who, though regarding the use of creaturely names unavoidable in referring to God's being, see in them nothing more than symbols, products of the poetic imagination." Bavinck says that pseudo-Dionysius and John of Damascus belong to this category "in a sense," because "they claim that all those names merely make God known as the cause of all things." Elsewhere, when rejecting the idea that God's names "merely denote God as the cause of things," Bavinck refers to John of Damascus's *Exact Exposition of the Orthodox Faith*, where he says that we do not apprehend the "absolutely incomprehensible and unknowable" divine essence, but only its attributes.[4] By contrast, Bavinck states in this context that the revealed names of God "furnish, however feebly and

3. *RD* 1:131, 148; 2:188–91, emphasis added; 409, 453, 539; 4:72–73.

4. *RD* 2:107–8, 128; John of Damascus, *Exact Exposition of the Orthodox Faith* 1.4, 10, in *NPNF*[2], vol. 9 .

inadequately, some inkling of the divine essence."[5] According to Bavinck, therefore, "neoplatonic mysticism" transmitted through pseudo-Dionysius deeply influenced the West and the East, though they appropriated it differently: while it led to the affirmation of the vision of God as to his essence in the medieval West, in the East it consolidated the view that creaturely names are not applicable to God's essence, which should be regarded as totally unknowable and unnamable.

Bavinck's treatment of the *filioque* clause also demonstrates his uneasiness with mysticism. For Bavinck, the rejection of the *filioque* not only represents "a last lingering remnant of subordinationism," but also expresses what Bavinck regarded as a dualistic tension between doctrine and life in Eastern Christianity.[6] Bavinck saw the denial of the procession of the Spirit from the Son as implying that the Father reveals himself in the Son and in the Spirit "more or less independent[ly] of each other." Emotions and mysticism are associated with the work of the Spirit, thus receiving their own source and becoming independent from knowledge and orthodoxy, which are associated with the Son. Moreover, Bavinck claims that Eastern theologians not only separated the head from the heart in this way, but also gave higher priority to the heart, insisting that the religious life has more to do with feelings than with thought.[7]

For the purposes of the present study, it is also worth noting how Bavinck evaluates the Palamite controversy, to which he refers twice. Bavinck attributes "a kind of emanation theory" to Palamas, who regarded divine attributes "as eternal emissions of light from the unknowable divine essence, emissions that were essentially distinct from the divine essence and had to be viewed as a kind of inferior deities [*sic*]." Although Bavinck does not comment on this, the words he chooses ("emanation," "inferior deities") indicate his dismissive attitude toward this theory. Elsewhere he mentions and immediately rejects the decision of the Palamite Council of Constantinople that "approved the doctrine of an uncreated divine light that is distinct from the divine being."[8] Bavinck believed that postulat-

5. *RD* 2:128.

6. *RD* 2:137; Bavinck, *Christendom*, 30.

7. *RD* 2:317; Bavinck, *Christendom*, 29.

8. *RD* 2:125, 253. Usually very careful with respect to factual material, Bavinck dates the council in Constantinople as occurring in 1431 instead of 1341 (*GD*[1] 2:193; *GD*[4] 2:224), although

ing the existence of an uncreated reality in God distinct from his essence contradicts his simplicity. Bavinck himself uses the concept of energy (without referring to Palamas), stating that "the divine energy is the source of all powers and energies in creatures," so that things exist and work through the "divine δύναμις, divine ἐνέργεια."[9] However, he does not attempt to clarify the ontological status of the divine energy in the Godhead. In sum, Bavinck's brief remarks show that his interpretation of Palamas relies on the views predominant among his Western contemporaries.

Meyendorff on Reformed Doctrine

During the half-century or more separating the most productive periods of Bavinck and Meyendorff, the ecumenical movement appeared and developed on an international scale. As previously mentioned, Meyendorff himself actively participated in this movement: attending numerous conferences as an Orthodox delegate, serving as moderator of the World Council of Churches' Commission on Faith and Order, and working as a coeditor on ecumenical volumes with Lutheran and Reformed theologians. When one further considers the intense activity of Western theology, especially during and after the Reformation, and that Meyendorff lived his entire life in the West, it comes as no surprise that Meyendorff's engagement with Western theology was more substantial than Bavinck's with the East. Like his Orthodox contemporaries, however, Meyendorff typically identified the West as a whole with Thomistic thought (or rather with its reception in neo-Thomist scholasticism) and rarely dealt with the peculiarities of particular Western traditions, such as the Reformed tradition.[10] However, one of the few exceptions is directly related to our topic and deserves closer consideration.

---

the resource to which he refers gives the accurate date, 1341–1351. See Johann Heinrich Kurtz, *Lehrbuch der Kirchengeschichte* (Mitau: Aug. Neumann, 1849), §69, 2. The error of almost a century is likely mechanical, but the fact that Bavinck did not notice this oversight when preparing the second edition of his *Reformed Dogmatics* may suggest that he was personally unaware of the historical context of the Palamite controversies.

9. *RD* 2:253–54; Herman Bavinck, *Christelijke wereldbeschouwing: Rede bij de overdracht van het Rectoraat aan de Vrije Universiteit te Amsterdam op 20 October 1904* (Kampen: Bos, 1904), 50, 77, 87–88. See also *RD* 2:232, 241.

10. R. C. Walls, who presents a sympathetic account of Palamite theology, states nonetheless that Meyendorff's works are "spoilt by his inability to understand the reformed tradition." See Walls, "St. Gregory Palamas," *Scottish Journal of Theology* 21 (1968): 435). Although I agree

In his only publication fully devoted to Protestantism, Meyendorff suggests that Orthodoxy and the Reformation are united in rejecting "created grace—the created habitus of Thomism—which grants to the actions of human free will a meritorious character." Meyendorff admits that the Orthodox view of grace differs from the views of the Reformers in some important respects. Specifically, Orthodoxy does not share a juridical understanding of salvation, it denies "the purely passive role of man in his own salvation," and it does not accept the "lucid Calvinistic logic," according to which God saves and condemns whom he pleases. Nevertheless, Meyendorff argues that "the main intuition of both Luther and Calvin" was their rejection of created grace, and that in this rejection we have "a fundamental encounter between them and Orthodoxy"—an encounter "based on a common understanding of the gospel of Christ liberated from all philosophical reinterpretations."[11] But given this similarity, why, Meyendorff asks, do Orthodoxy and Protestantism so widely diverge on many points? Meyendorff maintains that the most fundamental cause of this divergence is to be found in the doctrine of God.

After describing Orthodox doctrine, which asserts the absolute transcendence of the divine essence while also affirming communion with God and participation in his life, Meyendorff claims that "the Reformers were quite close to that notion in their idea of *Deus revelatus qua absconditus*, but the whole intellectual tradition to which they belonged prevented them from drawing further conclusions." The tradition to which Meyendorff refers stems from Augustine, who, according to Meyendorff, perceived God as transcendent only in light of the deficiencies of creatures: once the soul is liberated from its present dependence on the body, humanity is able intellectually to know and directly to contemplate the essence of God. For Meyendorff, this amounted to denying the absolute character of God's transcendence. Although Luther and Calvin tried to recover a sense of the mystery of God, they could not overcome the essentialism of the Augustinian tradition. Meyendorff further comments as follows: "It is from this tradition that there comes the idea that God, being identical with His

---

that Meyendorff's interpretation of Western theology was often unnuanced, he hardly merits such a strong censure—if only for the simple reason that he almost never engaged with specifically Reformed doctrines.

11. Meyendorff, "Significance of the Reformation," 165, 168, 172–73.

essence, cannot be participated otherwise than in His essence. Since participation in the essence of God—being admitted in the *visio beatifica* of the Scholastics—is irreconcilable with the transcendentalism of the Reformed theology, it is clear that no real *participation* in God is possible." It is not clear whether, and if so how, the Reformers were able, in Meyendorff's view, to acknowledge the absolute transcendence of God in contrast to Augustine. Meyendorff's main charge, however, is perfectly clear: Reformed doctrine does not allow for "real participation in God," while it is precisely such participation, Meyendorff contends, that is able to justify veneration of the Virgin Mary and of the saints, sacramental realism, and other issues that divide the Orthodox and Reformed traditions.[12] Meyendorff concludes that at the root of this deficiency in Reformed theology lies an inadequate doctrine of God, namely, the refusal to recognize in God anything distinct from his imparticipable essence.

In other works, Meyendorff contrasts Orthodox and Protestant theologies along the same lines. In the East, humanity was conceived as "an open being" dynamically oriented upward: "man is truly man when he participates in the life of God."[13] Humanity was not created as self-sufficient but as those called to grow in their natural capacity to live in God and in grace. By contrast, in Western thought (medieval, Reformation, and modern), Meyendorff argues, humanity has been understood as "an autonomous being," who was only "declared" guilty or justified.[14] Meyendorff believed that Augustine posited a dichotomy between grace and nature,

---

12. Meyendorff, "Significance of the Reformation," 165, 167, 170, 172–73. Such an evaluation of the Reformed tradition was, of course, not unique to Meyendorff. Julie Canlis, having cited these words of Meyendorff, notes that "this bias" has been held by both insiders and outsiders to the Reformed tradition (*Calvin's Ladder*, 15). Canlis's judgment reflects the efforts of a number of Reformed theologians to identify and conceptualize a distinct theology of participation/deification in Calvin. See Canlis, "Calvin, Osiander and Participation in God," *IJST* 6 (2004): 169–84; Mosser, "Greatest Possible Blessing," 36–57; Billings, "John Calvin," 200–218; Heleen E. Zorgdrager, "On the Fullness of Salvation: Tracking *theosis* in Reformed Theology," *Journal of Reformed Theology* 8 (2014): 357–81. For an alternative view, see Bruce L. McCormack, "Union with Christ in Calvin's Theology: Grounds for a Divinization Theory?," in *Tributes to John Calvin: A Celebration of His Quincentenary*, ed. David W. Hall (Phillipsburg, NJ: Presbyterian & Reformed, 2010), 504–29. McCormack argues that it is a misnomer to present Calvin's theology in terms of deification and participation in God's uncreated life, because he refused the idea of an interpenetration of the divine and human natures and was careful to speak only of a participation in Christ's humanity.

13. Meyendorff, *Byzantine Theology*, 152; see also 138.

14. Meyendorff, "Confessing Christ Today," 123.

which shaped the entire history of Western theology and amounted to a "dichotomy between God and man." The Reformers "remained faithful" to this dichotomy and "even emphasized it more strongly," because their soteriology sharply contrasted the absolute powerlessness of humanity with the all-powerful transcendence of God: God proclaimed his grace, but it always remains external to humanity.[15] Meyendorff emphasized that while the East focused on Christ's hypostatic union, in which the divine life is made accessible to all people through the work of the Holy Spirit, the West chose to follow the Anselmian concept of redemption, in which Christ's work is treated in terms of satisfaction rather than participation, and, consequently, Christology becomes (almost) isolated from pneumatology and anthropology.[16]

According to Meyendorff, the false dichotomy between nature and grace is inextricably linked with another unfortunate part of the Augustinian legacy: essentialism. It is the failure to distinguish between essence and energies/grace/life/will in God that makes it impossible for the West to affirm—without running the risk of degenerating into pantheism—that grace permeates human nature and that this nature actually shares in the divine life.[17] Furthermore, the identification of God's essence with his will makes it impossible to distinguish between the generation of the Son and the procession of the Spirit on the one hand, and creation as a contingent act of God on the other.[18] Another aspect of essentialism—the prioritization of essence over person—implies that the West (Catholics and Protestants alike) views God primarily as a simple essence and considers the persons in terms of internal relations.[19] As is typical in Orthodox circles, Meyendorff traced the tensions between West and East back to this difference in approach to the Trinity.[20] According to Meyendorff, it is this difference that eventually gave rise to the *filioque* clause, which was the

15. Meyendorff, "Orthodox Theology," 169.

16. Meyendorff, *Byzantine Theology*, 32. See also Meyendorff, "Orthodox Theology," 177.

17. Meyendorff, "Mount Athos in the Fourteenth Century," 164.

18. Meyendorff, *Study of Gregory Palamas*, 221–22.

19. Meyendorff, *Byzantine Theology*, 61.

20. Meyendorff, "Holy Trinity," 43. To be sure, Meyendorff realized that the importance of this difference has its limits, and he was skeptical about the attempts of Lossky to use this difference as a universal explanation of the divergences between East and West (Meyendorf, *Vvedenie v svyatootecheskoe bogoslovie*, 230).

formal reason for the Great Schism of 1054.[21] In short, Meyendorff argued that Augustine's essentialism had devastating consequences for Western theology, observable in its inability to properly formulate a doctrine of God and an ontology of divine-human communion. According to Meyendorff, Western theologians, with few exceptions,[22] are infected by this essentialism, although the problems inherent in the Augustinian legacy may manifest themselves differently in Protestantism than in Catholicism.

Key Topics

The issues Bavinck and Meyendorff considered decisive for understanding the differences between the Reformed and Orthodox traditions will be analyzed in more detail below. I will also raise some noteworthy questions related to God's hiddenness and revelation. Structurally, I will follow the threefold pattern I used in the previous chapters. My analysis will begin by discerning two recurring motifs that, in my view, are important for understanding the differences between Bavinck and Meyendorff. Their importance stems from the fact that neither theologian formulated his doctrine of God in a vacuum, but, rather, did so in close connection with other doctrines. Their understanding of the relation between God's hiddenness and revelation was soteriologically motivated and guided, if not determined. Second, I will compare the views of Bavinck and Meyendorff on the hiddenness of God, paying special attention to the idea of the unknowability of the divine essence. Then I will discuss their understanding of God's revelation, seeking to point out common ground between them as well as identifying where and why they diverge.

Certainty of Faith versus Certainty of Experience

Bavinck was a son of the Reformation, which arose as a quest for certainty. Luther's famous declaration—"What is more miserable than uncertainty?"—is mirrored in Bavinck's conviction that certainty is the deepest need of the human soul and that doubt is *the* sickness of modern society.[23] The Reformation quest for certitude was soteriological: it was fulfilled

21. Meyendorff, *Byzantine Theology*, 61.

22. Meyendorff, "Orthodox Theology," 169–70.

23. Luther, *Bondage of the Will*, 10; Bavinck, *Certainty of Faith*, 8.

when the Reformers discovered justification by faith alone and understood faith not only as a matter of intellectual affirmation, but also, and primarily, as consisting in certainty. Bavinck, however, lived in an era in which the emphasis shifted from the question of soteriological certainty to that of epistemic certainty. The question was not so much "How can I be certain that God in heaven is merciful to me?" as it was "How can I be certain that God in heaven has revealed himself in Jesus Christ and Scripture?"[24]

According to Bavinck, one of the tasks of theology is to provide certainty of faith.[25] Bavinck was convinced that this certainty should have a positive content. Agnosticism or strict apophaticism does not provide the certainty that allows one to approach death without fear: "a negation inspires no martyrs."[26] To have peace of mind and die happily, one must be certain of the invisible and eternal things above. True certainty must be based on what God himself has promised. Therefore, it presupposes not only the reality and knowability of God's revelation but also revelation's correspondence to God in his very self. The allowance that God in himself can be different from what he has revealed can never bring us comfort and peace.

Bavinck's concern over the issue of certainty is, of course, unsurprising in view of the fact that the preoccupation with certainty was typical for the Western theological and philosophical tradition. What is remarkable, however, is that Eastern theology, as Meyendorff expounds it, also has the task of providing and defending a kind of certainty. Meyendorff argues that in the Byzantine tradition the mystical experience of Christians in union with God was regarded "as inner 'certainty,'" while the denial of the possibility of achieving this experience was considered "the greatest 'heresy.'"[27] Palamas's theology was aimed at explaining and vindicating the experience

24. To be sure, the issue of the reliability of revelation was not altogether missing even in the Reformation period. Still, it was far from being a primary focus of the Reformers. As Huijgen observes, "Calvin shows little awareness of the urgency of the question how we can know that God's self-manifestation is reliable; in other words, that God in Himself (*in se*), His essence or majesty, is no other than God as He reveals Himself (*quoad nos*)" (*Divine Accommodation*, 282).

25. "History and experience show us every day what is most [*allereerst en allerminst*] expected from theology: it must nurture [*verschaffen*] our certainty of faith" (Bavinck, *Certainty of Faith*, 19); see also *RD* 1:574.

26. Bavinck, *Certainty of Faith*, 13.

27. Meyendorff, *Byzantine Theology*, 212.

of those monks who claimed to contemplate the uncreated divine light.[28] The very distinction between essence and energies was accentuated to affirm the reality of this mystical experience—an experience that, as Meyendorff emphasizes, is accessible not only to particular individuals but to all Christians.[29] While Luther was consumed by the quest for a merciful God, Palamas, as Meyendorff emphasizes, searched for a participable God: "In a word, we must seek a God who can be shared in one way or another, so that each of us by participating therein receives ... being, life and deification."[30]

To be sure, the contrast between Meyendorff and Bavinck is not absolute: in conceiving the divine-human relationship, Meyendorff tried not to downplay the importance of faith, and Bavinck assigned a significant role to union with Christ and even defined faith as consisting in this union.[31] Nevertheless, the differences in their emphases and presuppositions are substantial enough to have an impact on their understanding of the relation between God's hiddenness and revelation. For Bavinck, theology must foster the certainty of faith, which rests on the promises of God in Scripture. As an act of trust, faith is impossible without presupposing God's ethical truthfulness, which Bavinck interprets as "complete correspondence between his being and his revelation."[32] Faith would never be certain if it allowed that God in himself can be different from what he has revealed. Furthermore, although faith unites the believer with Christ, it also preserves a difference and in a sense a distance between them. Faith is an act of the intellect and leads to the knowledge of God, but this knowledge always presupposes an epistemic distance between the knower and the known that infinitely

28. Meyendorff, "Holy Trinity," 30.

29. Meyendorff also insists that for Palamas "theology was a most certain knowledge" based on the reality of God's revelation ("Doctrine of Grace," 19). While Barlaam represented "theological relativism" claiming that it is impossible to prove anything about God, Palamas argued that theology is a domain of demonstration and proofs (Meyendorff, "Les débuts," 109, 113). Although the main purpose of Palamas's arguments was to defend the legitimacy and reality of a *mystical* experience, he was not a visionary but "a speculative thinker and a dogmatician" (119).

30. Meyendorff, *Study of Gregory Palamas*, 221.

31. *RD* 1:573; Ronald N. Gleason, "The Centrality of the *Unio Mystica* in the Theology of Herman Bavinck" (ThD diss., Westminster Theological Seminary, 2001); Burger, *Being in Christ*, 101–8.

32. *RD* 2:209.

surpasses him. Consequently, God's revelation is understood by Bavinck as always limited, and human knowledge of God as ever-deepening.

By contrast, Meyendorff conceives of salvation in experiential terms, focusing on the categories of deification and union with God. Meyendorff interprets this union as implying that God and humanity have one life and existence, and humanity acquires divine properties including uncreatedness. The belief in such an intimate union requires recognizing in God something beyond the union—hence the emphasis on the distinction between essence and energies. The distinction is supposed to demonstrate that the mystical experience (originally in Palamism it was the experience of the hesychasts, but more broadly it is the experience of all Christians) is not a pretense, but is genuine and theologically sound, because it is really possible and indeed necessary for a Christian to contemplate God and participate in him without seeing or sharing his inaccessible essence. According to the conventional Orthodox opinion shared by Meyendorff, it is two doctrines—the reality of the mystical union with God and the inaccessibility of his essence—that make the doctrine of God's energies necessary. God is certainly communicable (as the experience of the saints testifies), but he is not communicable in his essence—hence, he must be communicable otherwise, namely, in his energies. However, taking into consideration the importance of union with God in Meyendorff's theology, it is plausible that mystical union *alone* makes *both* the incommunicability of God's essence *and* the doctrine of God's energies necessary. To be orthodox and attainable, the union demands both doctrines: without the incommunicability of God's essence, mystical union is heretical (pantheist), and without the doctrine of God's energies, mystical union is impossible. In both cases, mystical union is decisive for the Orthodox understanding of God, his essence and energies. Given the primacy of experience in Eastern theology and spirituality, it is not surprising that the reality of the union precedes all reflections about God and, at least in some respects, determines the Orthodox doctrine of God.

God Hidden

For Bavinck and Meyendorff, it was axiomatic that God cannot be comprehended by humans. The immense metaphysical distance between divinity and humanity leaves much room for mystery in Christian theology. Both theologians considered this mystery as a starting point in the doctrine of God and suggested that it should be stressed in any dialogue with atheists and agnostics, who are often unsatisfied with simplistic rational accounts of God.

Both Bavinck and Meyendorff believed that apart from revelation God is completely hidden. Humanity can never start a relationship with God or move toward God "from below" by its own initiative. Revelation, as well as creation, is a free and sovereign act of God and comes out of his good pleasure. The existence and development of the world does not enrich or perfect God, who is complete within himself. In receiving revelation, humanity does not become its master and can never "possess" God. Bavinck and Meyendorff agreed that even as God reveals himself, there remains something irrevocably other about him. They were not inclined, however, to reflect on this abiding hiddenness in dialectical and dynamic terms.

Bavinck and Meyendorff were also united in denying the possibility of the beatific vision of the divine essence. This denial formed part of their broader criticism of Roman Catholic doctrine, but they arrived at it for different reasons. While Bavinck's position was dictated by his suspicion that "a corollary of vision of God in his essence would be the deification of humanity," Meyendorff's motivation in rejecting the vision was precisely the opposite, namely, to prove the orthodoxy of the Palamite concept of deification. Meyendorff viewed the scholastic *visio beatifica* as an implication of Augustinian essentialism and even seemed to believe that it somehow implies an *exhaustive* vision of the divine essence.[33] Bavinck was more careful to emphasize that the scholastics did not consider perfect knowledge of God possible, but he nevertheless did not accept the *visio per essentiam*, because, in *his* terminology, it amounts to comprehensive (that is, exhaustive) knowledge of God, which is never attainable for human beings.

Both theologians recognized the consequences of sin for human knowledge and communion with God and held, albeit with different emphases, to the principle that God can be known only by God. For Meyendorff, this principle meant that the way to mystical knowledge of God lies through the transformation of creaturely faculties. Nothing created can enjoy the true vision of God: to see God, humanity must participate in uncreated

33. *RD* 2:190; Meyendorf, *Vvedenie v svyatootecheskoe bogoslovie*, 164–65.

energies and must itself become uncreated (without ceasing to be created). For Bavinck, the principle that God can be known only by God emphasizes that the activity of the Spirit in believers enables them to receive external revelation (without making them uncreated). Furthermore, Bavinck paid attention to the New Testament idea of mystery, which denotes a matter previously hidden but now made known in the gospel and understood by believers. Meyendorff did not discuss this idea, but, as we saw, Bavinck himself was not consistent in using the idea of mystery in this sense, referring to it as something incomprehensible to all humans.[34]

The points mentioned above demonstrate that Bavinck and Meyendorff shared much in common. They part company, however, when it comes to the cornerstone of God's hiddenness—the divine essence. Neither of them provide a clear-cut definition of the essence: Bavinck did not seem to sense any urgency for precision in this matter, while Meyendorff's radical apophaticism regarding the divine essence restrained him from any attempt to define it. A reluctance to speak boldly on the essence of God recurs throughout the Christian tradition. John of Damascus famously comments that "it is impossible to explain what He is in His essence."[35] Aquinas, however, referring to these words, suggests that although we cannot know of what the essence of God consists, we can make use of God's effects and define his essence through them.[36] That is, by observing the effects of God in creation, we can arrive at valid, albeit only analogical, statements about their cause. Later, this schema was developed in post-Reformational scholasticism.

Bavinck's treatment of the essence of God and his attributes was undoubtedly in line with the Thomistic tradition and boiled down to two central principles: (1) an *analogy* between creaturely perfections and divine perfections, and (2) the *identity* between divine perfections and divine essence. The first principle means that God created the world in such a way that it is able to reproduce his own perfections (also called attributes, virtues, properties, qualities, or characteristics). In this sense, all his attributes are communicable and knowable. At the same time, all attributes

---

34. See "God's Hiddenness from Unbelievers" (pages 71–74).

35. John of Damascus, *Exact Exposition* 1.4.

36. Aquinas, *Summa Theologiae* I, q. 1, art. 7, reply to obj. 1. See also I, q. 13, art. 2, reply to obj. 1.

are also incommunicable, because God possesses them in a manner that infinitely surpasses our comprehension. Divine attributes as such—that is, in their original, perfect, archetypal form—cannot be known by humans, but they can be known partly and analogically based on their creaturely ectypes. Bavinck emphasizes, however, that the likeness implied in analogy is "faint," "weak," and "pale."[37] Therefore, the concept of analogy linking divine infinity with creaturely finiteness is rather modest. The connection between the two sides of analogy can never be explained, and the proportion between them can never be measured.

The second principle asserts the identification of all the attributes as they subsist in God with his essence. God *is* what he *possesses*. Bavinck emphasizes that theology obtains the concept of God's essence "by attributing to God in an absolute sense all the perfections that occur in creatures." The divine essence, therefore, is a set, or summation, of divine attributes. In a sense, God in himself does not have discernable attributes, because all of them are identical to his essence. The variety of attributes is necessary for *our* understanding: our finite mind is not capable of conceiving the divine essence as a single reality, but we can define and describe it as that which "encompasses all God's attributes."[38]

But if creaturely revelation provides analogical knowledge of the divine attributes, it seems irrefutable that it also provides analogical knowledge of the divine essence, which is nothing but a set of divine attributes. If the divine attributes are knowable insofar as they are reflected in their creaturely analogues, it must be this way also with the essence. Indeed, Bavinck admits the possibility of knowing God's essence to a certain degree. However, he also asserts the unknowability of God's essence on the grounds that no name makes God's essence known to us. As indicated above, Bavinck believed that knowledge of God in his essence implies perfect knowledge and that reasoning about the essence usually arises from idle speculation.[39] Therefore, he clearly denied the knowledge of God's essence in two senses: in the sense that we are not able to know God perfectly and in the sense that we are not able to know him apart from revelation. However, Bavinck

37. *RD* 2:110, 152, 420.

38. *RD* 2:121, 123, 135.

39. *RD* 2:136–37; see 2:40, 130, 133; see "God's Hiddenness in Revealedness" (pages 74–80).

was less clear as to whether the essence could be known analogically—as the divine attributes are known. It is difficult to reconcile his insistence that knowledge as to essence is necessarily perfect with his suggestion that one can describe God's essence based on his attributes that are analogically present in creatures.[40] What is clear is that Bavinck avoided starting with the speculative idea of an absolute being and then deducing attributes from it. Rather, he insisted on reversing the order: from revealed attributes to essence.[41]

The approach of Meyendorff was different. He would not have affirmed the two principles mentioned above as fundamental for understanding Bavinck's approach. First, Meyendorff clearly and repeatedly denies the identification of God's properties with his essence. He locates the properties instead at the level of energies, which form a kind of concentric sphere around the essence. On this view, the essence of God is his unknowable and imparticipable inner core, the utterly inaccessible and mysterious center of the Godhead. Referring to the phrase τὰ περὶ τὴν οὐσίαν, which was well-established in the Eastern tradition, Meyendorff argues that essence and energies are interrelated as that which is "in God" and "around God." Correspondingly, the divine properties characterize that which is around and comes forth from the essence but not the essence itself. Meyendorff insists that the divine properties and names such as beauty, wisdom, and goodness indicate the divine energies *and not* the divine essence.[42] Furthermore, although admitting that the essence is the cause of the energies, Meyendorff does not deduce from this that the energies somehow reveal their cause. As noted above, he used the notion of causality to demonstrate the *difference* between essence and energies rather than an affinity between them. As the cause of the energies, the essence infinitely transcends them.[43] The essence is not traceable in the energies and remains, therefore, beyond any communication or attribution.

---

40. Moreover, Bavinck argues that in all creatures, and especially in humanity, "there is something analogous to the divine *being* [*Wezen*]" (*RD* 2:135, emphasis added).

41. In the first edition of his *Reformed Dogmatics*, Bavinck argues that the distinction between essence and attributes should be rejected for the reason that the divine essence is not knowable without the attributes (*GD*[1] 2:90). That is, the denial of the identification of essence and attributes deprives us of the only means of knowing the essence.

42. See "Energies as Properties" (pages 221–27).

43. See "Ways to Unify" (pages 240–48).

Second, unlike Bavinck, Meyendorff does not feel any pressure to emphasize the difference between an attribute as it relates to creatures and an attribute as it relates to God. His insistence that deified saints in union with God receive divine attributes, including no less than the attribute of uncreatedness, seems to relativize, if not undermine, this difference. In Meyendorff's view, to participate in a divine property is not to acquire its creaturely resemblance but to become one with God in his energies and to transcend the limitations of created nature. Man fulfils his true destiny "when he lives 'in God' and possesses divine qualities."[44] All energies are divine and uncreated, and humans are called to share in the energies of God and have one life with him. Besides that, the analogical relation between human and divine perfections has been used in Western theology to preserve meaningful predication about God. But Meyendorff does not have much concern for proper predication and emphasizes instead that mystical knowledge goes beyond intellectual or semantic inquiry. True knowledge of God is neither conceptual nor discursive, but is instead experiential, immediate, intuitive, and accessible only to the spiritual senses. We are not to describe God but to be united with him.

Therefore, instead of linking God's hiddenness to the limitations of analogical reasoning, Meyendorff emphasizes, first, that even in his energies God is hidden to the discursive intellect, and, second and more importantly, that God in his essence is totally inaccessible, with regard to knowledge and participation alike. Conceiving of God's essence as completely hidden within the depths of God's interiority, Meyendorff feels free to allude to the most daring phrases of the Eastern fathers regarding union with God, epitomized by Maximus's statement that the saints become all that God is, except for the identity of essence. Meyendorff was convinced that this utter inaccessibility of the divine essence safely protects Orthodox mysticism from slipping into pantheist categories.

According to Meyendorff, his approach fundamentally differs from Western Trinitarianism also in understanding the relation between essence and person. As shown above, Meyendorff believed that the Eastern tradition, in contrast to Western "essentialism," emphasizes the priority of

44. Meyendorff, *Byzantine Theology*, 139.

person over essence.[45] Meyendorff argues that the reversed methodological order, from essence to persons, suffers from excessive preoccupation with God's essential unity and leads to the neglect of Trinitarian doctrine in the West. Despite his casual remarks about the compatibility of the two orders, he clearly prefers the "Eastern" order and concurs for the most part with those theologians who repudiate the "Western" order as a concession to natural theology, and an underestimation of the role of the history of salvation in establishing the doctrine of God.[46]

Although such criticism became a commonplace only in the second part of the twentieth century, Bavinck was not unaware of the objections to the traditional "Western" order, which were already being raised in his time. Nevertheless, he deliberately followed his Reformed predecessors in first considering the attributes of the divine essence and only then the Trinity.[47] Bavinck, however, insists that his organizational decision by no means implies "a desire to gradually proceed from 'natural' to 'revealed' theology, from a natural to the Christian concept of God." He emphasizes that in starting with the essence of God, he does not set biblical revelation aside for the moment but treats the essence "as it is revealed to us in Scripture, is confessed by the Christian faith, and exists—as will be evident in the locus of the Trinity—in a threefold manner."[48] According to Bavinck, before discussing the idea that the Father, the Son, and the Spirit share the same nature, one must understand what makes up this nature and how it differs from every created nature. Furthermore, Bavinck maintains that the arrangement he chooses follows the course of redemptive history, in which the nature of God is shown earlier and more clearly than his Trinitarian existence.[49] For Bavinck, the methodological prioritization of the essential unity does not necessarily imply downplaying the

45. See "The Priority of Person over Essence" (pages 188–202).

46. See "The Methodological Aspect" (pages 189–92).

47. *RD* 2:149. Understandably, this decision disappointed Karl Barth, who appreciated Bavinck's high estimation of the Trinity but regretted that it did not come to expression in the arrangement of his doctrine of God (*Göttingen Dogmatics*, 97).

48. *RD* 2:149–50. It must be added that, in line with the typical structure in Reformed orthodoxy, Bavinck deals with the divine essence and attributes *after* discussing the biblical names for God. This demonstrates his desire to remain within the bounds of revelation from the outset.

49. *RD* 2:150, 261. This corresponds with the remark of Muller, who notices that the traditional arrangement in Reformed Orthodox dogmatics was shaped by the order within the

significance of Trinitarian doctrine: it is even argued that this doctrine governs the whole structure of Bavinck's dogmatics and has important implications for other doctrines.[50]

So, although Bavinck and Meyendorff prefer different arrangements of the content of theology proper, their approaches cannot be contrasted as philosophical/speculative/essentialist versus revelational/personalist. This is the case not only because Bavinck does not consider the treatment of God's attributes and essence as a philosophical enterprise detached from revelation, but also because it can be questioned whether Meyendorff's approach is, in fact, consistently personalistic and revelational. First, as was indicated above, Meyendorff maintains that the divine essence is completely unknowable, transcending all negations as well as affirmations. So also, in dealing with the arrangement of the doctrine of God, he emphatically states that "God remains unknowable in his unique essence, but he has revealed himself as a Trinity of Three Persons."[51] At the same time, Meyendorff argues that "the starting point of any Christian discourse about God" in the writings of the fathers is the confession of God's incomprehensibility—that is, the incomprehensibility of his *essence*.[52] The same order is seen in Meyendorff's explanation of Palamas's doctrine of the divine essence and energies: he starts with the hidden God and only later moves to the divine persons and energies.[53] God's incomprehensibility is "the basis" or one of "the basic axioms of Greek patristics."[54] But if Eastern theology, as Meyendorff explains it, starts with God's unknowability with

Bible itself, where God first revealed his oneness in the OT and only later, in the NT, disclosed the mystery of the threeness of the one God (*Post-Reformation Reformed Dogmatics*, 3:158–59).

In addition, Bavinck contended that in an organic worldview unity always precedes diversity (*Christelijke wereldbeschouwing*, 44), although it is doubtful whether he also applied this logic in choosing a starting point in the doctrine of God.

50. Eglinton, *Trinity and Organism*, 89–90, 96–97. Burger notes, however, that Bavinck's doctrine of God itself is not controlled by the doctrine of the Trinity or by the narrative of Scripture. See Hans Burger, "God's Character and the Plot of the Bible," in *Reading and Listening: Meeting One God in Many Texts*, ed. Jaap Dekker and Gert Kwakkel (Bergambacht: 2VM, 2018), 242. In discussing the problem of structuring dogmatic content, Bavinck notes that the trinitarian scheme is not satisfactory (*RD* 1:109–10).

51. Meyendorff, *Orthodox Church*, 178; see also 176–77; Meyendorff, "Reply to Jürgen Moltmann's," 187; Meyendorff, "Christ's Humanity," 12; Meyendorff, "Justinian, the Empire," 60.

52. Meyendorff, "'Defense of the Holy Hesychasts,'" 183.

53. Meyendorff, *Study of Gregory Palamas*, 202–27.

54. Meyendorff, "Christian Theology," 63; Meyendorff, *Gregory Palamas*, 122.

regard to his essence, then it also starts from the divine essence and not from the persons, even if it seeks to keep a reverential silence about the divine essence.[55]

Second, in asserting the unknowability of the divine essence, Meyendorff makes no appeal to biblical evidence. Rather, as we saw above, he admits that even non-Christian philosophers had been aware of apophaticism, and he notes that for Palamas apophatic theology as such was "available without revelation" and contained "nothing specifically Christian."[56] Rejecting cataphatic speculations about God's essence and the attribution to it of a set of preconceived superlative properties such as omnipotence, omniscience, or omnipresence, Meyendorff rather promotes a radical apophaticism regarding the essence, which, however, seems to be just as natural in origin. Moreover, as indicated above, Meyendorff postulates the impassibility and immutability of the divine essence—again, without referring to concrete biblical passages.[57] Not only is this hardly compatible with the alleged complete unknowability of the divine essence, but—given the lack of biblical argumentation—it also sounds suspiciously similar to the claims of natural theology.

God Revealed

Whatever emphasis Bavinck and Meyendorff may place on the hiddenness of God, they focus more on interpreting what God has actually revealed to us rather than on denying that God is subject to the limitations of created reality. This is clearly evident with Bavinck, whose theology, although permeated by the sense of God's incomprehensibility, had nonetheless a distinctly positive orientation. But even for Meyendorff, apophaticism had

55. I seriously doubt whether the issue of order (from essence to persons or from persons to essence) can even exist in a theology that maintains the absolute unknowability of the divine essence. The differences in order make sense if by "person" one understands that which is particular to the Father, the Son, and the Spirit, and likewise if by "essence" one has in view that which is common to the Father, the Son, and the Spirit. Then the question arises whether we should start from the particularities, or from the unity, of God. But if the essence is completely unknown, then we cannot meaningfully move from or to the essence: if the essence transcends any theological discourse by definition, then discussion about it must be limited to proclaiming its unknowability. Any treatment of what is common to the persons is then possible only at the level of the divine energies.

56. Meyendorff, "Doctrine of Grace," 19. See "Apophatic Theology" (pages 170–76).

57. See "Impassibility and Immutability" (pages 176–79).

value as a preliminary step toward a *positive* experience, namely, mystical union with God.[58] In his theology, the utter inaccessibility of the divine essence does not have much significance in isolation, but rather serves to protect the reality and intimacy of this union from undesirable implications. It is also obvious that the views of Bavinck and Meyendorff about the revelation of God are inseparable from their conceptualization of the divine-human relationship. On this matter the breadth of topics worthy of attention is immense, but, due to limitations of space, the following analysis is restricted to the most important issues.

First, Bavinck and Meyendorff are both at pains to show that in revelation we encounter God himself. To be sure, they consider communion with God from different perspectives: Bavinck prefers to speak about it in terms of genuine knowledge of God, while Meyendorff describes it in more experiential terms. Accordingly, Bavinck emphasizes that the knowledge God has of himself is "materially one" with the knowledge that he grants in revelation, has recorded in the Bible, and introduces into the human consciousness. For his part, Meyendorff persistently repeats that the energies of God as understood in the Eastern tradition are not "a diminished form of deity, or mere emanations, but [are] themselves fully God."[59] Both theologians are also united in adding a certain qualification: in revelation we do encounter God, but not God as he is *in himself*. While insisting that the knowledge of God is the exclusive content of all dogmatics, Bavinck clarifies that the object of theology is not God in his essence but God as he has revealed himself. Meyendorff expresses a similar reservation, stating that the saints participate in divine energies but never in the divine essence.

Second, Bavinck and Meyendorff both attempt to build their concepts of revelation on a Trinitarian foundation. Bavinck claims that if God were not triune, revelation would be impossible, because God's external communication is grounded in his internal communication. If God could not communicate his fullness to the Son in generation, he would be even less able to communicate a pale image of himself to his creatures. In Meyendorff, one notices a similar link between God's inner life and his external communication. To be sure, Meyendorff refrains from identifying internal energies

58. See "Apophatic Theology" (pages 170–76).

59. *RD* 1:213–14; Meyendorff, *Byzantine Theology*, 28.

with the generation of the Son and the procession of the Spirit. However, he does identify energies with love, which abounds in the internal divine relationships and is poured out in creatures. The external manifestation of love, Meyendorff argues, "would be both impossible and meaningless if God were not Love *in Himself*, if he were not Trinity."[60] For both theologians, therefore, divine operations *ad extra* result from the plenitude of life that God has eternally in his Trinitarian being.

Third, both Bavinck and Meyendorff equally maintain that divine revelation is conscious and voluntary. Bavinck thought it necessary to affirm the intentional character of revelation in view of the pantheist tendencies of his time, while for Meyendorff it was important to show the difference between the Orthodox understanding of divine energies and Neoplatonic emanationist metaphysics. Both theologians affirm that eternal generation is an act of essence, while creation in time is an act of God's will.[61] In Meyendorff's theology, the recognition of the voluntary nature of revelation reinforced his personalistic emphasis: revelation can flow only from persons, because only a person—conceived not as an expression of essence, but as irreducible to it—can freely give.[62]

Fourth, both Bavinck and Meyendorff clearly deny that revelation somehow affects the divine essence. Bavinck sharply contrasts the

---

60. Meyendorff, "Holy Trinity," 35.

61. Nevertheless, both seem to avoid drawing this distinction too sharply. Bavinck emphasizes, on the one hand, that generation is not an unwilled emanation and, although it is not an act of an *antecedent decreeing* will, it does not nonetheless occur apart from the will of the Father (*RD* 2:310). On the other hand, Bavinck, while strongly affirming *creatio ex nihilo* and the distinctiveness of the world's being from God's being, maintains nonetheless that the world owes its existence to God's fecund productivity and is analogous to his being (*RD* 2:332). As Huttinga sums up Bavinck's position, "generation also involves God's will, and creation also involves God's being" (*Participation and Communicability*, 116). According to Meyendorff, the distinction between generation and creation proves the necessity of the distinction between essence and energy/will. He argues that essentialism, which identifies God's essence with his will, cannot properly distinguish between the acts of essence and will, and leads therefore either to pantheism or to reducing the Son and the Spirit to the status of creatures. Nevertheless, as we saw in "The Internal Energies" (pages 203–8), the existence of internal energies makes it difficult to link the concept of energies exclusively to God's will. Furthermore, although Meyendorff, unlike other proponents of Orthodox personalism such as Zizioulas, never seemed to speak of the existence of the Son and the Spirit as enacted by the *free will* of the Father, his emphasis on the *hypostasis* of the Father as the source of all divinity stands in some tension with the idea of generation as an act of essence *rather than* of will.

62. John Meyendorff, "Creation in the History of Orthodox Theology," *SVTQ* 27 (1983): 34; Meyendorff, "Theosis in the Eastern Christian Tradition," 476.

categories of being and becoming and argues that a confusion between the two leads to an obliteration of the distinction between God and creature. Since God's being is immutable and antecedent to his revelation, the outward works of the Trinity disclose it without constituting it. Similarly, in Meyendorff's theology, the divine essence is so safely shielded within the depths of God that any influence on it from the outside is by definition excluded. Meyendorff adds, however, that the immutability and impassibility of God's essence is not binding on his personal existence. This existential priority of person over essence is, as we saw, especially important for Meyendorff's Christology, because it allows him to state that the person of the Logos *became* man and really *suffered*, while his essence was not subjected to change and passion.

Finally, an obvious similarity between Bavinck and Meyendorff lies in their polemical rejection of any opposition between nature and the supernatural. Although Bavinck identifies such opposition as a characteristically "Roman" doctrine, while Meyendorff even depicts it as inherent in the entire post-Augustinian Western tradition, the real object of their criticism is neo-Thomist scholasticism, which dominated Roman Catholic theology in the late nineteenth and early twentieth centuries. According to Bavinck, the root of the problem is that the state of glory gradually came to be viewed in the church as a condition that far transcends natural human capacities. This—unfortunate and unbiblical, in Bavinck's opinion—understanding of humanity's final destiny led to the idea that Adam, even before sin, needed supernatural grace. On this view, Bavinck argued, grace is not a response to sin but a superadded gift to attain the supernatural *visio Dei*; grace does not renew nature, but complements it and elevates humanity above its nature. Instead of emphasizing the ethical antithesis between sin and grace, Rome, according to Bavinck, asserts a contrast—indeed, a separation and dualism—between nature and grace, the natural and the supernatural, creation and re-creation.[63] Over against this Roman view, Bavinck contends, the Reformation, especially its Reformed branch, proclaimed that grace neither stands in opposition to nature nor complements it; rather, grace affirms it, restores it, penetrates it, and purifies it from within. Furthermore, grace

63. Herman Bavinck, "The Catholicity of Christianity and the Church," trans. John Bolt, *CTJ* 27 (1992): 229, 231, 235, 237.

does not simply rehabilitate nature to its prelapsarian state, but engenders its normal development and raises it to its highest fulfillment, which would have been reached by Adam had he not sinned.

Although Meyendorff's criticism of the separation between nature and the supernatural is no less incisive, he proceeds quite differently. Unlike Bavinck, Meyendorff wholeheartedly embraces the idea that the state of glory—namely, deification—transcends natural capacities. However, this does not mean for Meyendorff that the supernatural forms a separate realm superimposed on humanity alongside its self-contained nature.[64] Rather, the natural is always already "engraced" and can never be conceived as purely natural. It is natural for humanity to be one with the supernatural, to become supernatural, and to become God. The full realization of human nature as it was created by God leads to the *overcoming* its creaturely limitations.[65] God and humanity are, so to speak, compatible, and the divinization of humankind is the true fulfillment of its humanity.[66] Thus, although Bavinck and Meyendorff are united in rejecting the autonomous character of the natural and in affirming the transformative impact of grace on nature, their respective understandings of the relation between nature and the supernatural are far from identical. Bavinck differentiates between nature and grace primarily by arguing that grace, "in its real sense," was not necessary for Adam before the fall—a viewpoint Meyendorff explicitly rejects.[67] However, the inapplicability of the term "grace" to the prelapsarian condition does not imply for Bavinck the absence of the supernatural dimension in human life, provided this dimension is not understood as being detached from nature.[68] Humanity *by nature* was oriented toward the supernatural: its original righteousness was "not for a second

64. See "Theocentric Anthropology" (pages 144–47).

65. According to Meyendorff, the Orthodox Christology "implies the positive concept of man as a being called to overcome constantly his own created limitations" (*Byzantine Theology*, 4). See also Meyendorff, "Palamas (Grégoire)," 93.

66. Meyendorff, "Continuities and Discontinuities," 73. See also Meyendorff, *Byzantine Theology*, 78; Meyendorff, *Christ in Eastern Christian Thought*, 150; John Meyendorff, "A Christian Theology of Creation," in *John XXIII Lectures*, vol. 1, *Byzantine Christian Heritage* (Fordham, NY: Fordham University Press, 1966), 65.

67. *RD* 3:577; Meyendorff, *Byzantine Theology*, 138; Meyendorff, "New Life," 488.

68. Although Bavinck argues that revelation "is always an act of grace" (*RD* 1:310), this phrase is rather more a rhetorical tool to emphasize the accommodative character of revelation than a doctrinal statement about the necessity of grace before the fall.

conceivable without communion with God"; its nature was fitting for the indwelling of the Holy Spirit; and its conformity to God—which was not yet fully developed—was not superadded, but belonged to his very nature.[69] Meyendorff's differentiation between nature and the supernatural implies that grace enables humanity to *transcend* its nature, even if such transcendence was anticipated by and in accordance with the original design of his nature. The famous Orthodox maxim that the deified human is by grace what God is by nature implies that grace makes humanity what it is *not* by nature.[70]

This difference between Bavinck and Meyendorff is of great significance for understanding the other dissimilarities between them. In particular, it suggests reasons why Meyendorff would probably have rejected six out of the eight characteristics of revelation that I distinguished in Bavinck's theology. While Meyendorff would undoubtedly have confirmed that revelation is voluntary and trustworthy, he would hardly have agreed, or at least not without serious qualifications, that revelation is accommodated, creaturely, analogical, mediated, limited, and intelligible. First, although Meyendorff, like Bavinck, appeals to the idea of condescension in describing the nature of revelation, he does not put much emphasis on God's accommodation to the finite capacities of his creatures. Rather, Meyendorff interprets God's movement toward creatures in terms of *ecstasis*: God comes out of his unapproachable essence, imposes on himself a communicable mode of existence, and reaches humans in his energies—not by accommodating himself to their creatureliness, but rather by enabling them to perform a similar ecstatic act of self-transcendence, through which they can transcend the limitations of their created nature. As a Western theologian, Bavinck begins with the question of human capacity to receive God's revelation and, for that reason, focuses on how God

69. *RD* 2:558; 3:292. Thus, "the supernatural is not at odds with human nature, nor with the nature of creatures; it belongs, so to speak, to humanity's essence" (*RD* 1:308). Moreover, Bavinck maintains that even after the fall, this orientation to the supernatural remains characteristic for human beings despite their depravity: "However far man may wander from God, he remains bound to heaven; in the depths of his soul he is linked to a world of unseen and supernatural things; in his heart he is a supernatural being" (*Philosophy of Revelation*, 142). See also Bavinck, *Our Reasonable Faith*, 17.

70. To be sure, this does not mean for Meyendorff that the person ceases to be a creature: rather, the deified person "is transported into a different state and ... gratuitously acquires a condition fundamentally foreign to that of nature" (*Study of Gregory Palamas*, 178).

must accommodate to the human condition in order to reveal himself. By contrast, Meyendorff is more preoccupied with God's capacity to reveal himself, since he takes it for granted that the human condition can indeed be transformed, if necessary, to become receptive to God's communication.[71] Speaking about God's external activities, Bavinck and Meyendorff differ in their emphases quite substantially: Bavinck primarily maintains that these activities imply "a kind of humanization of God," while Meyendorff emphasizes that they lead to the "deification of man."[72]

Second, Bavinck and Meyendorff clearly part company on the question of the created or uncreated character of revelation. Bavinck—with his affirmation of the goodness of creation and the neo-Calvinist commitment to reforming the natural—insists that revelation occurs in the created realm and therefore bears a creaturely character. Meyendorff, to the contrary, maintains that the divine energies are uncreated and enable their recipients to transcend their creatureliness. The contrast between the two theologians becomes somewhat less stark when we keep in mind that for Meyendorff the term "uncreated" is synonymous with the term "supernatural." Meyendorff never makes a distinction between these terms and argues that the Eastern tradition "never had recourse to the idea of a created supernature."[73] Bavinck, for his part, is cautious with the distinction between nature and the supernatural and argues that "all revelation, also that in nature, is supernatural"—primarily because it has a supernatural origin and points to a supernatural reality.[74] Still, the fundamental difference between Bavinck and Meyendorff remains, and it becomes apparent in locating the arena of encounter between God and humanity. For Bavinck, revelation *as we receive it* is always and necessarily bound to creaturely realities. God reaches us with his revelation in our creatureliness. By contrast, Meyendorff argued that the divine energies are always uncreated, and the

---

71. See Eric Lionel Mascall, *The Openness of Being: Natural Theology Today* (London: Darton, Longman & Todd, 1971), 220.

72. *RD* 1:310. To be sure, this contrast is not absolute, because Bavinck also believes that God's grace leads humanity to have a growing likeness to God, while Meyendorff, of course, does not deny the indisputable fact of God's humanization in the incarnation of the Son.

73. Meyendorff, *Gregory Palamas*, 122.

74. *RD* 1:307. According to Bavinck, revelation is also supernatural in the sense that it exceeds the thoughts of sinful human beings and also when it occurs contrary to the ordinary course of nature and history.

saints, being penetrated by these energies, are brought into this uncreated reality. Where Bavinck speaks of a reformation of creation (re-creation), Meyendorff speaks of a transcending of its limitations. Although both Bavinck and Meyendorff believed in the existence of the gulf between Creator and creatures, they interpret it differently. For Bavinck, it means that the creature cannot become uncreated in any sense. For Meyendorff, it has another meaning: nothing created can see or have direct communion with God. Thus, in order to contemplate God and be united with him, creatures must first become uncreated in the sense of being endowed with uncreated capacities.

Third, Bavinck and Meyendorff differ in their estimation of the usefulness, or indeed acceptability, of analogical reasoning. To be sure, in anthropology Meyendorff does employ a kind of analogical language, affirming, just as Bavinck, that God is the archetype of humanity, who is created in his image.[75] However, when it comes to the doctrine of God, Meyendorff does not appeal to the idea of analogy, and, in particular, he never presents the relationship between essence and energies in analogical terms. His understanding of human knowledge of God and participation in him is based on univocal assumptions. In Meyendorff's thought, to know God's essence would be to possess God, and to participate in God's essence would necessarily amount to becoming God essentially.[76] On the other hand, God reveals himself wholly in his energies, and to have communion with God in his energies is to literally become one with him. In summary, God is fully revealed and participated in just in his energies, but he is totally inaccessible in his essence, because, according to Meyendorff, "a revelation of the divine essence would bring God down to the level of creatures and make man a 'God by nature.'"[77] By contrast, Bavinck argues that analogical predication is the only means of communicating the knowledge of God. Creatures, and especially humans, were made analogous to their Creator, which vindicates the application of human terms to God. According to Bavinck, limited ontological similarity between human beings and God

---

75. Meyendorff, *Christ in Eastern Christian Thought*, 125; *RD* 2:129.
76. Meyendorff, "Doctrine of Grace," 25.
77. Meyendorff, *Gregory Palamas*, 118.

ensures that, although analogical revelation will never allow us to know God exhaustively, it nevertheless conveys true and reliable knowledge.

Fourth, Bavinck and Meyendorff diverge in their respective approaches to the idea of mediation in revelation. Bavinck argues that direct perception of God is unattainable due to the fundamental difference between Creator and creature. In revealing himself, God always uses means—natural, historical, psychological. Bavinck identifies immediate vision of God with vision of his essence, which, for Bavinck, implies perfect knowledge of God. Since such knowledge is unattainable for humans, an immediate vision of God is impossible even in the life to come. In contrast to Bavinck, Meyendorff not only allows for immediate vision of God, but praises it as the final end of human existence. He argues that the key point in Palamite disputes was Palamas's insistence, against his adversaries, on the possibility of an immediate and mystical contemplation of God in his uncreated energies. Although Meyendorff asserts that God reveals himself "through" his energies, his conviction that these energies *are* God himself does not permit us to interpret his "through" as indicating a mediatory function for energies. Rather, in these energies humans directly encounter God in his fullness. The differences between Bavinck and Meyendorff on this point stem from their different perspectives on communion with God. Despite his recognition of the mystical side of union with Christ, Bavinck prefers to describe it in covenantal terms, with a clear differentiation between the two parties involved. Speaking about human knowledge of God, Bavinck tries to preserve the distinct identities of the knower and the known. For Meyendorff, by contrast, mystical knowledge implies union, in which God and humanity have one life (possessing, to be sure, different and indeed totally separated *natures*). Immediate communion is communion without distance, where the known is no longer exterior to the knower.

Fifth, one of Bavinck's most often recurring statements about revelation is that it is necessarily limited. Building on the metaphysical axiom *finitum non est capax infiniti*, Bavinck asserts that God does not communicate himself in his infinite fullness but only according to the limited capacities of human nature. Revelation, accordingly, is partial and relative compared to the exhaustive and absolute self-knowledge of God. Meyendorff too recognizes the limitations of human knowledge. However, being committed to univocal reasoning, he does not deduce from this that we can have a *limited* knowledge of the *limitless* God, but rather that God cannot be known at all. Meyendorff argues that in the Eastern tradition any positive definition of God is regarded as putting a limitation on his being: "A known God is necessarily limited, since our created intelligence is limited by its very creation."[78] Consequently, God is totally unknowable by human reason. At the same time, Meyendorff contends that God *wholly* reveals himself in his energies and can be contemplated (that is, mystically known) by transformed human faculties, freed from their creaturely limitations.[79]

Last, Bavinck and Meyendorff diverge in their understandings of the role of human language and of the intellect in the communication and reception of God's revelation. Bavinck argues that in revealing himself God uses words and concepts derived from human experience and relations. Communicating revelation in human language, and in the written word in particular, is part of God's accommodating relationship with people. Meyendorff does not deny this, because he does not want to downplay the role of Scripture. However, he emphasizes that the *telos* of human life—union with God—surpasses linguistic expression and requires the cessation of all intellectual activity, because the created mind is feeble in the face of ultimate uncreated reality. People enter union with God through mystical ecstasy, leaving human knowledge and language behind and perceiving the presence of God in ignorance and silence. It is noteworthy in this context how negative and positive ways of knowing God are interwoven in the thought of both Bavinck and Meyendorff. Bavinck's apophaticism does not do away with cataphatic theology, but rather points to the limitations of analogical attribution and functions as a counterweight to the uncontrolled humanization of God. Such apophaticism does not deny creaturely perfections to God, but denies that they are present in him in the same way as in the created realm. For Meyendorff, however, apophatic theology does not give rise to chastened conceptual affirmations,

---

78. Meyendorff, *Christ in Eastern Christian Thought*, 93.

79. Meyendorff seems to proceed from the premise that the quality of the perceived object and the capacities of the knower must be identical. Given this premise, it is clear why the admission that God can be known by a finite intellect would necessarily lead to impoverishing the divine being, as well as why the perception of God in his uncreated energies requires transcending creaturely limits.

but rather exposes the utter inadequacy of all affirmations and negations concerning God, and prepares the way for a mystical knowledge of God beyond the boundaries of the creaturely mind. In Bavinck's understanding, the apophatic approach serves to qualify affirmations about God, while Meyendorff insists that it points us to a higher realm, where union with God occurs in a state of unknowing.

Conclusion

When it comes to determining the relation between God's hiddenness and revelation, there is much that separates Bavinck and Meyendorff. Certainly, Bavinck, at least on the surface, comes close to the Orthodox doctrine when asserting the unknowability of the divine essence. However, as we have seen, this claim stands in some tension with his clear belief that God's essence and his attributes are identical and that, based on their creaturely analogues, the attributes are knowable. Likewise, Meyendorff seems to be close to Western thinking when he denies any separation between God's essence and energies. However, he does not clearly unify these two modes of God's being—despite occasional statements that could potentially clarify how they belong together (essence as the cause of the energies; energies as actions of God in his essence; energies as the manifestation of God's essence; internal energies; etc.). Ironically, *creaturely* revelation in Bavinck's thought appears to be more closely, or at least more clearly, linked with the divine essence than the *uncreated* energies are linked with God's essence in Meyendorff's works.

Had Western theologians been familiar with neo-Palamite theology in Bavinck's time, Bavinck probably would have detected the same tendencies that he observed and criticized in the modernist theologies of his day: separation of God *in se* from God *pro nobis* on the one hand, and identification of God with his revelation on the other. Concerning separation, we saw that Bavinck criticizes distinguishing between God's essence and his attributes, arguing that divine simplicity requires their identity. The (neo-)Palamite understanding of God's essence as totally incommunicable, and of God's energies as wholly communicable, makes this distinction rather sharp, and this was unacceptable to Bavinck. Concerning identification, Meyendorff's realistic exegesis of the New Testament descriptions of union with God and his insistence on the necessity of transcending creaturely limitations in this union would have reinforced Bavinck's suspicious attitude towards Orthodox mysticism. For the neo-Palamite doctrine proclaims not only that God's energies are revealed fully, but also that the saints are wholly united with the fullness of God.

For his part, Meyendorff would probably have identified Bavinck's theology as insufficiently apophatic and insufficiently experiential. Despite his remarks on the unknowability of the divine essence, Bavinck was hardly consistent on this point, making him vulnerable to Meyendorff's criticism of the essentialist Western tradition. After all, Bavinck was a typical Western theologian who did not recognize in God anything distinct from his essence, which, as we saw, Meyendorff interprets as a failure that explains many of the problems with Western theology. In general, Bavinck pays much more attention to the knowledge of God than Meyendorff, which, from the perspective of Eastern apophaticism, could be characterized as an obsession with knowledge. Moreover, Bavinck insists that this knowledge is analogical, mediated, and based on the accommodated revelation of God in creation. This puts Bavinck in sharp contrast with Meyendorff's skepticism about creaturely knowledge of God and his appreciation of the mystical cognition that occurs in union with God. Compared to Meyendorff, Bavinck's approach is excessively bound to this world and is insensitive to the intrusion of the uncreated, otherworldly reality into the created realm.

In general, Meyendorff's understanding of the divine essence and energies provides greater precision in its conceptualization of the relation between God's hiddenness and revelation. He does not merely argue that God is simultaneously incommunicable and communicable, but also treats incommunicability and communicability as two modes of God's being, and assigns specific terms to them (namely, essence and energy). Compared to such subtle metaphysics, Bavinck's correspondence model, based on the concept of analogy, is vaguer. However, Bavinck believed that it is precisely this analogical reasoning that enables us to preserve both God's hiddenness and his revelation: univocal reasoning would compromise God's hiddenness by pretending that our concepts fully coincide with God's self-knowledge, while equivocal reasoning would compromise God's revelation by supplying concepts that are familiar when applied to ourselves with a totally foreign and unfamiliar content when applied to God.

EVALUATION

In this final section, I will present my evaluation of the views of Bavinck and Meyendorff. Before analyzing their views, however, I will sketch my own position on the relevant issues in order to clarify the basic commitments, concerns, and presuppositions that form the background of my evaluation.

John of Damascus's classical exposition of the Orthodox faith opens with a citation from the prologue of the Gospel of John: "No man hath seen God at any time; the Only-begotten Son, which is in the bosom of the Father, He hath declared Him" (John 1:18).[80] From this verse, Damascene concludes that the Deity is "ineffable and incomprehensible." While he later asserts that God has revealed himself in various ways, Damascene's emphasis remains on the incomprehensibility of God or, to be more precise, on the incomprehensibility of his essence. The second part of this verse does not seem to receive the same degree of emphasis in Damascene's exposition.

However, it is precisely this second part that is decisive and revolutionary: Jesus Christ has revealed God in a way that no Old Testament theophany could. John uses the rare expression ἐξηγέομαι, from which the English word "exegesis" is derived. For this reason, Ambrose called Jesus "the interpreter of the Godhead."[81] In the Lukan corpus, the word has the sense of "telling the whole story," such that the Son has presented a detailed description, or narration, of the Father.[82]

The evangelist makes clear that Jesus' narration is unique because it is based on his close relationship with the Father, as implied by the phrase "in the bosom of the Father"—a phrase that conveys the most intimate communion between the Son and the Father. Furthermore, Jesus emphasizes that he does not speak on his own authority but proclaims the message he has received from the Father (John 12:49; 14:10). While this statement evidences the Jewish principle of representation, according to which the messenger represents the one who sends him, Jesus' claims transcend this

80. John of Damascus, *Exact Exposition* 1.1. The Bible is cited according to the translation used in the English edition of Damascene's book.

81. Ambrose, *Joseph* 14.84, in *Seven Exegetical Works*, trans. Michael P. McHugh, Fathers of the Church 65 (Washington, DC: Catholic University of America Press, 1982), 237.

82. Andreas J. Köstenberger, *John*, Baker Exegetical Commentary on the New Testament (Grand Rapids: Baker Academic, 2004), 50. See Donald A. Carson, *The Gospel according to John* (Grand Rapids: Eerdmans, 1991), 135, 294.

principle.[83] He is not only an emissary commissioned to speak and act on behalf of God—he is *one* with God. "I and the Father are one" (John 10:30). Jesus can reveal the Father in an unprecedented way because he does not need to speak of the Father as an external object. He reveals the Father by revealing himself because that which Jesus reveals *in himself* is held in common with the Father. "Whoever has seen me has seen the Father" (John 14:9). As Irenaeus puts it, "The Son reveals the knowledge of the Father through his own manifestation."[84]

But what is the nature of the oneness between the Son and the Father? In many passages, John highlights the oneness of their agency and determination: Jesus does the works of the Father (10:32, 37–38) and seeks and fulfills his will (4:34; 5:30). The Son and the Father are one in power (5:21), message (7:16), judgment (8:16), and authority (17:2). Furthermore, John emphasizes the mutual indwelling of the Father and the Son: each is in the other (10:38; 14:10). According to Rudolf Schnackenburg, such dual "in-ness" is "a linguistic way of describing ... the complete unity between Jesus and the Father." This unity is emphasized to an even greater degree in John 10:30. Although the immediate context of the verse suggests primarily the oneness of redemptive power (the Son and the Father are one in taking care of their sheep), Schnackenburg rightly observes that the verse points out "the metaphysical depths contained in the relationship between Jesus and the Father."[85] Granted, as George Beasley-Murray indicates, the evangelist "has not spelled out the nature of those 'metaphysical depths.'"[86] However, his depiction of the unified agency of the Father and the Son is grounded on something much deeper.[87] Without offering a complex ontological system, the Fourth Gospel carried metaphysical implications that were conceptualized by later generations of Christian theologians, who met the challenge of formulating an ontological answer to the question of the identity of the one who came to save us.

---

83. Köstenberger, *John*, 393, 432.

84. Irenaeus, *Against Heresies* 4.6.3, *ANF* 1:468.

85. Rudolf Schnackenburg, *The Gospel according to St. John* (London: Burns & Oates, 1968–1982), 2:308; 3:69.

86. George R. Beasley-Murray, *John*, Word Biblical Commentary 36 (Dallas: Word, 2002), 174.

87. This is confirmed by the reaction of the Jews, who interpreted Jesus' statement as involving a claim to deity and prepared to stone him for blasphemy (John 10:31–33).

The church fathers responded to this challenge by asserting that the Son is consubstantial (ὁμοούσιος) with the Father.[88] The ultimate reason that the Son is united with the Father in agency and is uniquely qualified to make him known is their exact equivalence in essence. Jesus can reveal God because he himself is God, and he reveals in himself that which he holds in common with the Father—namely, the divine essence. Thus, in answering how the disciples could know the Father through knowing the Son, Hilary of Poitiers states that under Jesus' flesh his Father's nature dwells within him and, consequently, the knowledge of the Son entails "the knowledge of that nature on which, in him, they had gazed for so long."[89] According to Hilary, perceiving the power of the divine nature in the Son is inseparable from perceiving the nature itself.[90]

---

88. In modern scholarship, the patristic commentators have been often criticized for reading back the key terms of later controversies into the Johannine texts. Even earlier, Calvin rebuked ancient theologians for misusing John 10:30 in attempting to prove ontological statements. See John Calvin, *Commentary on the Gospel according to John*, trans. William Pringle (Grand Rapids: Eerdmans, 1949), 416. Although transferring the developed Trinitarian language to the biblical narratives would indeed be anachronistic (Bernard), this does not nullify the legitimacy—and, indeed, necessity, in view of the challenges mentioned above—of transcending biblical language in expressing the oneness of the Son with the Father. See John Henry Bernard, *A Critical and Exegetical Commentary on the Gospel according to St. John* (New York: Scribner's Sons, 1929], 2:365–66. As Donald Carson argues, if, according to John, "Jesus' will is exhaustively one with his Father's will, some kind of metaphysical unity is presupposed, even if not articulated. ... [John's Christology] demands that some more essential unity [than merely functional] is presupposed, quite in line with the first verse of the Gospel" (*Gospel according to John*, 395). Similarly, William Hendriksen maintains that the Gospel of John clearly shows "that the oneness is a matter not only of outward operation but also (and basically) of inner essence." See Hendriksen, *Exposition of the Gospel according to John*, (Grand Rapids: Baker Book House), 2:126.

89. Hilary of Poitiers, *On the Trinity* 7.34, *NPNF*[2] 9:132–33 (PL 10:228).

90. "The Son, who is equal with the Father, showed by his works that the Father could be seen in him so that when we perceived in the Son a nature like the Father's in its power, we might know that in Father and Son there is no distinction of nature" (Hilary of Poitiers, *On the Trinity* 9.52, *NPNF*[2] 9:173 [PL 10, 325]).

In his dissertation on the concept of participation in the ante-Nicene fathers, Jeffrey Finch argues that church fathers such as Irenaeus, Clement, and Origen "implicitly ident[i]fied God's essence with the fulness of His being" ("Sanctity as Participation," 377). Therefore, according to Finch, they did not conceive the divine essence as something totally incommunicable and did not exclude it when describing what God has revealed to us in Christ. Based on Irenaeus's passages about the revelatory activity of the Son, Finch concludes: "The essence of the Father does not now remain absolutely inaccessible and/or unknowable, Irenaeus insists, for the knowledge of the Son is the knowledge of the Father. ... The essence of the God who has revealed Himself in Christ remains unknowable after His self-disclosure, then, only in the specific sense that God can never be measured, fathomed, circumscribed, or encapsulated" (378). Finch further refers to Origen's passage where he maintains that through the knowledge of the incarnate Son one "may come to behold the essence (οὐσία), or the power and nature

The most ardent advocate of the term ὁμοούσιος, Athanasius, argues that it is precisely the Son's consubstantiality with his Father that enables him to impart to us knowledge of the Father: "Beholding the Son, we see the Father; for the thought and comprehension of the Son, is knowledge concerning the Father, because He is His proper offspring from His essence." Later, Athanasius writes: "Whoso sees the Son, sees what is proper to the Father, and knows that the Son's Being, because from the Father, is therefore in the Father. ... Whoso thus contemplates the Son, contemplates what is proper to the Father's Essence, and knows that the Father is in the Son." One of Athanasius's key arguments for the divinity of the Son rests on the Son's deifying power. If the Son merely *participated* in the essence of the Father, he would not be able to impart what he had partaken of to others. But precisely because he is coessential with the Father, he can make us participants of that which he has in common with God.[91]

As I noted in the introduction, the implications of the doctrine of ὁμοούσιος for the relation between God's hiddenness and revelation have been highlighted especially by prominent Athanasius scholar Thomas F. Torrance. He maintains that this doctrine was revolutionary, because it expressed the truth that what God is toward us in Jesus Christ he is inherently and eternally in himself.[92] In Athanasius's thought, Torrance argues, the knowledge of the Father, to which the knowledge of the Son leads, is

(φύσει) of God beyond the essence" (247; Origen, *Commentary on the Gospel of John* 19.37, trans. Ronald E. Heine, Fathers of the Church 89 [Washington, DC: Catholic University of America Press, 1993], 176 [PG 14:536]). While I concur with Finch's position on the knowability (and at the same time incomprehensibility) of the divine essence, I am less persuaded by his attempts to prove this based on the ante-Nicene fathers, primarily because of the variability of ontological terminology in Christian theology in that time. Finch is right, however, in observing that early theologians did not recognize any intrinsically incommunicable mode of God's being, which would be totally outside his revelation in the Son. After all, the issue is not about the term οὐσία as such, but rather about whether God reveals his very self—his character and inner life.

91. Athanasius, *Four Discourses against the Arians* 1.16; 3.3, *NPNF*[2] 4:316, 395 (PG 26:45, 328); Athanasius, *On the Councils of Ariminum and Seleucia* 51, *NPNF*[2] 4:477 (PG 26:784). Athanasius resorts to similar arguments concerning the divinity of the Spirit. "If the Holy Spirit were a creature, we should have no participation of God in him. If indeed we were joined to a creature, we should be strangers to the divine nature [φύσεως] inasmuch as we did not partake therein. ... But if, by participation in the Spirit, we are made 'sharers in the divine nature,' we should be mad to say that the Spirit has a created nature." See Athanasius, *Ad Serapionem* 1.23, in *The Letters of Saint Athanasius Concerning the Holy Spirit*, trans. C. R. B. Shapland (New York: Philosophical Library, 1951), 125 (PG 26:586).

92. Torrance, *Trinitarian Faith*, 130; Torrance, *Christian Doctrine*, 130, 243–44.

nothing but the knowledge of his very essence: "For us to know the Son is to know the Father in accordance with what he is in his own essential Nature, in the indivisibility of the Father from the Son and of the Son from the Father, and thus to know God in the *internal* relations of his eternal Being."[93] The Nicene phrase ὁμοούσιος τῷ Πατρί states, according to Torrance, that "the Son of God in his incarnate Person is the place where we may know the Father as he is in himself, and know him accurately and truly in accordance with his own divine nature."[94] It may be that Torrance could not fully resist the temptation to consider ancient texts from the perspective of modern problems.[95] However, Torrance is right in claiming that the ὁμοούσιος provides the real ontological ground for asserting the relation of absolute fidelity between God in himself and God in his revelation.[96]

The subsequent development of the doctrine of God, especially in the East, was much influenced by the Eunomian controversy. Eunomius claimed that the essence of God can be properly designated and grasped by the term "unbegotten" (ἀγέννητος). This provoked a response from theologians such as Basil and Chrysostom, who insisted on the inadequacy of human language to properly describe God's essence. However, it is remarkable that the revelatory power of Christ as evidenced in the Gospels compelled even these theologians occasionally to admit the knowability of the divine essence. According to Basil, created objects do not communicate the essence of their maker. However, the Son is not a created work but the Only-Begotten of the Father, which is proved precisely by his ability to make the Father known:

> It is not from the products of the artisan that we comprehend the artisan's substance [οὐσίας], but ... it is from that which has been begotten that we come to know the nature [φύσιν] of the begetter. After all, it is impossible to comprehend the substance of the house builder from the house. But on the basis of that which is begotten it is easy to conceive of the nature of the begetter. Consequently, if

---

93. Torrance, *Trinitarian Perspectives*, 8, emphasis original.

94. Torrance, *Trinitarian Faith*, 135, emphasis original.

95. See the reservations about Torrance's reading of Athanasius in Vladimir Cvetković, "T. F. Torrance as Interpreter of St. Athanasius," in *T. F. Torrance and Eastern Orthodoxy: Theology in Reconciliation*, ed. Matthew Baker and Todd Speidell (Eugene, OR: Wipf & Stock, 2015), 81–82.

96. Torrance, *Trinitarian Perspectives*, 81.

> the Only-Begotten is a created work, he does not communicate to us the substance of the Father [τοῦ Πατρὸς τὴν οὐσίαν]. But if he makes the Father known to us through himself, he is not a created work but rather the true Son.[97]

Although Basil does not explicitly state here that the Son reveals the nature/substance of the Father, the logic of his argument leads to this conclusion: the Son is begotten of the Father precisely because he is able to reveal the Father's substance through revealing himself. As mentioned above, Basil, while claiming, against Eunomius, that "there is not one name which encompasses the entire nature of God and suffices to express it adequately," maintains nonetheless that certain properties contribute to "a notion that is altogether dim and trifling as regards the whole but that is at least sufficient for us."[98] Similarly, Chrysostom, who adamantly rejected the possibility of obtaining knowledge of God's essence on the grounds that such knowledge would not differ from perfect knowledge of God, when preaching on John 14:8–15 admits that Jesus' words "Whoever has seen me has seen the Father" were spoken out of "the desire to stress the fact of His consubstantiality" with the Father and can be accurately paraphrased as "He who knows my essence knows also that of the Father."[99] According to Chrysostom, if Christ were of a different essence from the Father, he would not be able to claim that whoever knows him also knows the Father, because "it is not possible to gain knowledge of one substance or power by means of another."[100]

Thus, on the basis of the biblical witness, as well as its creative reception in the early church, we can state that in redemptive history with its pinnacle in Christ, God reveals his character, his very self, his *essence*. As Colin Gunton puts it, "In the light of the gospel we must be free to confess that we are granted to know the very being of God. ... If we *know* the hypostases,

---

97. Basil of Caesarea, *Against Eunomius* 2.32, pp. 180–81 (PG 29:647–48).

98. Basil of Caesarea, *Against Eunomius* 1.10, p. 105 (PG 29:533–34). See "Knowledge and Participation" (pages 227–33).

99. Chrysostom, *Homily* 74, in *Commentary on Saint John the Apostle and Evangelist: Homilies 48–88*, trans. Sister Thomas Aquinas Goggin, Fathers of the Church 41 (Washington, DC: Catholic University of America Press, 2000), 294 (PG 59:401).

100. Chrysostom, *Homily* 61, in *Commentary on Saint John*, 158 (PG 59:339).

... then we *know* the substance, being, essence, *Wesen*, etc., of God, for there is nothing else to be known."[101] God reveals himself as good, holy, wise, merciful, and so forth, because he *is* good, holy, wise, and merciful. His essence can be discerned in his acts and words and is therefore predicable.

In Christ, we behold the divine nature clothed with flesh. We cannot know and imitate God deeper than we know and imitate the man Jesus Christ. Our knowledge of God's essence is therefore mediated. This does not detract, however, from the revelatory power of Christ: although his divinity is clothed with flesh, it is not thereby completely hidden from our eyes. Not only is the Son visible on account of the flesh he assumed, but, as John 14:9 implies, the Father is also visible on account of the Son's incarnation. There is no need to transcend creatureliness to know God, because we can know God and participate in him by knowing the man Jesus Christ and participating in him.

It was to emphasize this significance of the incarnation that early Christian theologians formulated the stirring maxim: God became man so that man might become God.[102] It did not imply the necessity of overcoming creatureliness, but rather expressed the truth that through Christ we become children of God and attain incorruptibility and immortality. However, taken literally and in isolation, the maxim appears to contain an unqualified symmetrical inversion, which hardly does justice to the dramatic implications of the incarnation. To affirm the goodness of creatureliness as evidenced in the incarnation and the resurrection, it seems better to paraphrase the maxim as follows: God became man so that man might *stop wanting to* become God—or at least to stop wanting to become the not-yet-incarnate God (mentioned in the first clause of the patristic maxim.) Just as Philip's plea, "Show us the Father," was answered by pointing out the sufficiency (and abundance!) of the revelation in Christ's humanity, so human striving to become God must be tempered by pointing out the sufficiency of being conformed to the image of the incarnate Son.

---

101. Gunton, *Act and Being*, 111–12, emphasis original. To be sure, Orthodox theologians, including Meyendorff, would have objected that Gunton mistakenly assumes that the hypostases possess only essence, whereas Eastern theology affirms *three* realities in God: hypostases, essence, *and* energies. On the Orthodox view, in knowing the Son, we can know the energies of the Father rather than his essence. I will discuss this point later in this chapter.

102. Athanasius, *On the Incarnation* 8.54 (*PG* 25:192B); Irenaeus, *Against Heresies* 10.5–9 (*PG* 37:465).

It is in our humanness—without overcoming creatureliness—that we can eternally grow in the likeness of God through ever increasing participation in Christ's humanity.

Since Christ sits at the right hand of God, Paul urges us pilgrims to set our minds "on things that are above, not on things that are on earth" (Col 3:2). Our knowledge of God through Christ also has a supernatural dimension that transcends all created reality both in heaven and on earth. Jesus' answer to Philip affirms, rather than suppresses, Philip's longing for the supernatural. When Jesus points out the revelatory significance of his humanity, it presupposes that this humanity points beyond itself to him who "dwells in unapproachable light, whom no one has ever seen or can see" (1 Tim 6:16). While recognizing the abundance of the revelation in Christ, one should not forget, therefore, that God eludes our creaturely capacities and always surpasses our understanding. Primitive pictures of God (for example, as an old man with a long gray beard who sits on a throne in heaven) are not typically held by those who truly know him; rather, it is precisely by knowing him that they realize his incomprehensibility. To be sure, an attempt to define the incomprehensibility of God in a precise way would run the risk of violating the very idea of incomprehensibility. It is enough to say that the acts of God, while allowing humans a glimpse of his essence, also point to a mystery that is ineffable and can never fully be perceived. Biblical confessions of God's incomprehensibility are made not in the context of speculative reasoning about God but in response to his mighty acts (Ps 92:5; Eccl 3:11; Rom 11:33). It is worth noting that the recognition of this incomprehensibility does not lead to apophatic silence but to doxology (1 Tim 6:16).

The incomprehensibility of God is presupposed in the Christian idea of ever-increasing knowledge of God and ever-deepening communion with him: there is always more in him that can still be known and experienced. The riches of God are inexhaustible, and the process of our assimilation to him is endless. As Robert Jenson concludes, "Since God's ability to communicate himself is infinite, this conformity can and must increase indefinitely, without ever coming to rest."[103] The infinitude of God's being also

103. Robert Jenson, *Systematic Theology*, vol. 1, *The Triune God* (Oxford: Oxford University Press, 2001), 234.

means that our knowledge of God and our recognition of his incomprehensibility should not be thought of as being inversely proportionate. It is not that God's incomprehensibility diminishes in proportion to the increase of revealed knowledge. Rather, revelation progressively discloses new facets of his *incomprehensible* being. For example, God reveals his mercy more fully in the New Testament than he did in the Old Testament. However, this fuller revelation does not subtract from the mysteriousness of God's mercy, but rather demonstrates more clearly that his mercy is immeasurable and exceeds our understanding.

The recognition of the progressive character of God's communicability informs our understanding of the relation between God's hiddenness and revelation in two ways. First, the distinction between what is and what is not (yet) revealed is determined by our limited capacity to appropriate divine realities rather than by some innate distinction in God himself. The distinction lies, so to speak, on our side rather than on God's. Building on biblical testimony and developing Platonic insights, Christian tradition has insisted that we can know God and assimilate to him as far as it is possible for human nature.[104] Second, the capacity of human nature is not a constant, and so the relation between God's hiddenness and revelation is also in flux. Scripture speaks about our future cautiously: "what we will be has not yet appeared" (1 John 3:2). The apostle continues that "we shall be like him," but he does not specify the nature and measure of this likeness.

Therefore, it does not seem to be reasonable to conceptualize and eternalize God's incommunicability and communicability as two distinct modes of his being and assign specific terms to them. By doing so, we would project the dynamic limitations of our nature into God's very being. Instead, we must confess that one and the same reality—God's character, God's life, God's essence—is more and more revealed to humans without its depths ever being exhausted. In thinking about God's incommunicability and communicability, we must allow for fluidity. In sum, the relation between God's hiddenness and revelation should not imply a clear, static

104. "We ought to fly away from earth to heaven as quickly as we can; and to fly away means to become like God, as far as this is possible; and to become like him, means to become holy, just, and wise." See Plato, *Theaetetus* 176B, trans. Benjamin Jowett (New York: Random House, 1953). See also Clement, *Stromata* 6.12; Athanasius, *On the Incarnation* 9.57; pseudo-Dionysius, *The Ecclesiastical Hierarchy* 1.3.

boundary and should be formulated with less conceptual precision than, in my view, is presupposed in the distinction between the totally incommunicable essence and the fully communicable energies. As it has been said, "It is better to be vaguely right than to be exactly wrong."[105]

God's Incomprehensibility

In light of the above considerations, my evaluation of Bavinck's and Meyendorff's views in the following sections will hopefully be clearer. As mentioned in the introduction, I will use three criteria for evaluation: the preservation of God's incomprehensibility, the reality of union with God, and the oneness of God.

Bavinck

Bavinck's commitment to preserving the incomprehensibility of God is evident in both the structure and content of his *Reformed Dogmatics*. He believed that Christian theologians, including his Reformed predecessors, often downplayed the significance of God's incomprehensibility. Bavinck attempted to correct this shortcoming by beginning his doctrine of God with the emphatic confession of God's incomprehensibility, by stressing the limitations of human knowledge, and by respecting the role of mystery in theology. As we have noted, his efforts in this regard were met with appreciation by other theologians—Karl Barth, in particular.

However, Bavinck's expression of the doctrine of God's incomprehensibility leaves room for debate. The most questionable aspect of his approach is the denial of the knowability of God in his essence.[106] In previous sections,

105. Carveth Read, *Logic, Deductive and Inductive* (London: Grant Richards, 1898), 351.

106. It is remarkable that while *asserting* the unknowability of God's essence (*RD* 2:36, 40, 70, 130, 133), Bavinck *criticizes* the vision rather than the knowledge of God's essence (*RD* 2:187–91, 539, 543; 4:73; *Christendom*, 33). The two, of course, belong together, but for Bavinck the idea of *seeing* the essence may have had several additional negative connotations. First, although the beatific vision had a rich meaning for the medieval tradition, the idea of gazing on God's essence may have seemed too passive an activity for Bavinck's neo-Calvinist mindset. As Hans Boersma puts it, "Bavinck seems more at ease with an eschaton that continues the regular workweek than an eschaton that celebrates Sabbath rest." See Boersma, *Seeing God: The Beatific Vision in Christian Tradition* (Grand Rapids: Eerdmans, 2018), 39. Second, as a theologian of the Protestant tradition, focused on hearing the word rather than on seeing visual representations, Bavinck probably tried to avoid what may have seemed to him an excessive reliance on the faculty of sight. (To be sure, according to Aquinas, God's essence, even in the life to come, cannot be seen by the sense or the imagination, but only by the

I argued that Bavinck denied this for two reasons.[107] First, knowledge of God as to his essence, in Bavinck's view, amounts to perfect knowledge of God, which is unattainable for humans. Second, inquiring into the divine essence is associated with speculative thinking, while we must fully rely only on God's revelation and abandon all attempts to perceive God from below. Of course, Bavinck's concerns are valid. Furthermore, they are well established in the Christian tradition. Chrysostom, to mention only one, clearly identifies the knowledge of God's essence with full and exact knowledge of God, and urges his listeners to guard against the temptation of speculating about the divine essence.[108] Similar cautions were not

---

intellect. Furthermore, I admit that Bavinck does not overtly express such reservations himself, and Protestant theologians were not unanimous in their attitudes toward the role of sight. As Boersma notes, several Calvinists, including Kuyper, treated vision as the noblest of the senses [27 n. 24, 280]). Most importantly, Bavinck's opposition to *seeing* God's essence is determined by the fact that the "Roman" doctrines he criticizes—divinization, elevation of humans, the notion of merits, the separation of nature and grace (see "God's Revelation as Mediated" [pages 99–103] and "God Revealed" in [pages 274–84])—are connected, in his opinion, with what has become known as the *vision* of God's essence.

107. See "God's Hiddenness in Revealedness" (pages 74–80).

108. Chrysostom attributes the claim of having "entire, perfect, and complete" knowledge of God to his adversaries, the Eunomians. See *On the Incomprehensible Nature of God* 1.21, trans. Paul W. Harkins, Fathers of the Church 72 (Washington, DC: Catholic University of America Press, 1984), 176 (*PG* 48:704). The Eunomians, Chrysostom argues, pretended to know God's essence "with all exactness" (*Incomprehensible Nature* 3.23), and, indeed, to "know God as God himself knows himself" (2.17). Repeatedly and consistently, Chrysostom identifies the pretended knowledge of God's essence with "exact knowledge," "full and perfect knowledge," "a pure and perfect knowledge," "a clear knowledge and perfect comprehension of God" (4.27, 31, 23, 19). The knowledge of God's essence, according to Chrysostom, implies not only knowledge of the divine properties, but also of their "measure" and "degree." For example, to know God's essence is not only to know that God is wise, but also "how great his wisdom is" (1.33). Referring to Heb 11:6, Chrysostom notes that the apostle "did not say what his [God's] substance is: this can be known by no one. That he is loving, that he is kind, that he is good we know, but to what degree we do not know." See *Commentary on the Psalms*, trans. Robert Charles Hill (Brookline, MA: Holy Cross Orthodox Press, 1998), 2:255. To put it in the terms Bavinck preferred, the knowledge of a divine *attribute* implies the knowledge of its *creaturely analogue*, while the knowledge of God's *essence* implies the knowledge of all his attributes *in their divine, archetypal form*. Accordingly, Chrysostom refutes the possibility of knowing God's essence on the grounds that our knowledge is partial and imperfect (*Incomprehensible Nature* 2.40). Exact knowledge of God is unattainable for human beings, who, Chrysostom argues, "do not have any knowledge whatsoever" even of the essence of their own souls, or of the nature of the sky they see (5.27; 2.50). Furthermore, Chrysostom *contrasts* the pretension to know God's essence with knowing God according to his condescension and accommodation (3.17, 24). The Eunomians, Chrysostom writes, "are obstinately striving to know what God is in his essence" (1.22). Chrysostom warns his audience not to follow these "curious busybodies" in their "meddlesome investigations" and not to "be inquisitive about his [God's] essence" (1.35–36; 5.40).

only expressed by other contemporary opponents of Eunomianism such as Basil, but were also put forward by later theologians in one form or another. Respect for this deep-rooted tradition was an important, if not decisive, reason why Bavinck accepted the idea of the unknowability of the divine essence.

Though driven by legitimate concerns, this idea, however, downplays the Bible's emphasis on God's self-revelation and detaches God's essence from his revealed character. Essence has been traditionally understood as that which determines what an entity is. In the case of God, the divine essence is, as Rowan Williams notes, "a *concrete reality*—the 'stuff' which constitutes the God-ness of God."[109] To put it simply, God's essence is what makes God distinctively who he is.[110] Consequently, by denying the knowability of God in his essence, a theologian seems to maintain agnosticism about the very identity of God. To be sure, Bavinck seeks to avoid such a conclusion and postulates the unknowability of God in his essence on the grounds that the alternative is the impossible position of creatures having perfect knowledge of God. However, the choice Bavinck offers—either to have no knowledge of God in his essence or to possess perfect knowledge of God—would appear to be a false dilemma. The same holds true for his second concern. It is not clear why the knowledge of God's essence should necessarily be identified as speculative probing into his being and be contrasted with the knowledge of God we have on account of his accommodation.

Not only is the assertion of the unknowability of the divine essence in itself questionable, but it also does not naturally integrate into other aspects of Bavinck's theology. As noted above, Bavinck, unlike Meyendorff, does not differentiate between God's essence and attributes, and insists that they are identical. If, then, the divine attributes are partially knowable through their creaturely reflections (as Bavinck maintains), the divine

109. Williams, "Philosophical Structures," 34.

110. I concur with the approach of John M. Frame, who argues that "God's essence is not some dark, unrevealed entity behind God's revealed character. Rather, God's revelation tells us his essence. It tells us what he really and truly is." See Frame, *Systematic Theology: An Introduction to Christian Belief* (Phillipsburg, NJ: Presbyterian & Reformed, 2013), 431. Elsewhere Frame rightly states that the divine essence as comprising all the divine attributes revealed in Scripture "is knowable, but not exhaustively." See Frame, *The Doctrine of God* (Phillipsburg, NJ: Presbyterian & Reformed, 2002), 204–5.

essence, by the same token, should also be partially knowable.[111] The assertion of the unknowability God's essence undermines Bavinck's criticism of the distinction between essence and attributes, because the knowability of the attributes coupled with the unknowability of the essence does indeed imply such a distinction. Several of Bavinck's statements reveal that it was difficult for him to maintain consistency in his assertion of the unknowability of the essence. Bavinck admits that, inasmuch as "there is in his creatures an analogy to what is present in God himself," creaturely names "furnish, however feebly and inadequately, some inkling [*enige conceptie*] of the divine essence." However modest the phrase "some inkling" may sound, it implies nonetheless that the essence is not *altogether* unknowable. In the same paragraph, Bavinck argues that in his many perfections God displays before our eyes his being, or essence (*Wezen*). When denying to God all creaturely imperfections, Bavinck maintains, we can come to a positive appreciation of God as the absolute essence. Furthermore, Bavinck emphasizes that by revelation "we do have true and authentic knowledge of God's incomprehensible and adorable being [*Wezen*]." Thus, although Bavinck occasionally speaks of the unknowability of God's essence, his intention seems to be to deny the knowability of God *in* his essence.[112] If so, his point can be formulated as follows: God's essence is knowable based on his revelation, but God *in* his essence (or God in himself) is not knowable. However, such distinction would be rather unfortunate, because it creates the impression that God in his essence can be totally different from his essence as it is revealed through his attributes. In the end, Bavinck did come to distinguish clearly between God's unknowability and incomprehensibility, making it more natural to speak of the incomprehensibility rather than the total unknowability of God in his essence.[113]

Another problematic aspect of Bavinck's doctrine is his understanding of the distinction between the hidden and revealed will of God. As previously noted, Bavinck argues that the revealed will does not disclose God's

111. The conclusion seems to be inevitable, especially if one defines God's essence in terms of his character and his attributes as his characteristics. It would be odd then to say that we can know (in part, to be sure) God's characteristics without knowing his character as a summation of characteristics.

112. *RD* 2:36–37, 70, 128, 130, 190; *GD*[4] 2:14.

113. See "Comprehension and Knowledge" (pages 132–34).

own pleasure, but serves only as the norm for our conduct.[114] Bavinck's approach seems to have paradoxical implications for the relationship between God's hiddenness and revelation. If God's hidden will is the efficacious cause of everything that actually happens in the world, and if we encounter this reality in our daily life, then God's hidden will reveals something about God. To put it differently, if our reality is the direct and necessary result of God's hidden will, then, based on our experience of this reality, we can say something about God's hidden will and thus also about God's very being (with which, according to Bavinck, it is identical). On the other hand, if what God says in his revealed will pertains only to our conduct, then God's revealed will does not actually reveal his character. It is not his *actual* will and does not in any way inform our knowledge of God but merely indicates what we must do. Thus, paradoxically, God's attributes, character, and pleasure are in some sense revealed by God's hidden will rather than by his revealed will.[115] To be sure, Scripture—for example, in the story of Abraham's sacrifice of Isaac—does presuppose that God's revealed will may not reflect his ultimate purpose and volition. However, such exceptions do not negate the principle that the revealed will of God, contained in the law and the gospel, springs from and corresponds to God's character.[116] They do not, therefore, warrant Bavinck's decision to associate the revealed will exclusively with the regulation of human conduct.

Meyendorff

Although Bavinck asserts the unknowability of the divine essence, this seems to be an isolated and almost alien element in his dogmatic constructions. By contrast, Meyendorff considers this unknowability indispensable, because it allows him to postulate the realism and fullness of human union with God. However, despite fitting more naturally within Meyendorff's

---

114. See "The Hiddenness of God's Will" (pages 80–83).

115. Such a conclusion, of course, inevitably leads to further questions. If, on the one hand, the revealed will is "stated in law and gospel" (*RD* 2:243) and thus constitutes a part of God's revelation in the Bible, but on the other hand, this revealed will does not inform our knowledge of God, then does this not mean that we must seek God's character and being in his hidden will (in his decisions, as it were, behind the scenes) rather than in biblical revelation?

116. Muller observes that for the Reformed scholastics, the *voluntas signi* "is not a 'mere sign' but one that corresponds with something that is truly in God" (*Post-Reformation Reformed Dogmatics*, 3:458).

theology, his agnosticism concerning the essence poses its own dilemmas, as I hope to demonstrate below.

Meyendorff—quite rightly, in my view—defines the divine essence as "that which makes God to be God."[117] He also follows the traditional path of identifying God's essence with "God in himself." For Meyendorff, this identification means that God *in himself* is absolutely unknowable for us. God performs all his activities in the world *outside* his essence. In the act of creation, Meyendorff argues, God came out of his inaccessible essence "to act outside *himself*."[118] This means that God's identity—"that which makes God to be God"—as well as his very self, resides, so to speak, in his essence. While I agree that God's identity is bound to his essence, this idea becomes problematic in Meyendorff's theology, because it implies that what is absolutely concealed by the impenetrable clouds of apophaticism is precisely God's deepest intentions and his very self.

By placing God's essence beyond all characterization, Meyendorff's approach questions the very necessity of this concept in Christian theology, for the divine essence appears to collapse into a category devoid of any discernible content for human beings. Even Constantinos Athanasopoulos, who defends Palamas, admits that in Palamism "divine essence is something that remains apophatic, i.e., epistemologically and ontologically unknown and thus *theologically and philosophically unusable* (more or less)."[119] If nothing can be predicated of God's essence, then even to use the term seems pointless.[120] Furthermore, while Meyendorff aims to emphasize

---

117. Meyendorff, "Philosophy, Theology," 207.

118. Meyendorff, *Study of Gregory Palamas*, 223, emphasis added. Similarly, Lossky argues that God's energies make "him known outside himself, while concealing what he is in himself." See Vladimir Lossky, "The Procession of the Holy Spirit in Orthodox Trinitarian Theology," in *Eastern Orthodox Theology: A Contemporary Reader*, ed. Daniel B. Clendenin (Grand Rapids: Baker Academic, 2003), 178.

119. Constantinos Athanasopoulos, "St. Gregory Palamas as the Response of Orthodox Mystical Theology to (Neo)Platonist and Aristotelian Metaphysics," in Athanasopoulos and Schneider, *Divine Essence and Divine Energies*, 64, emphasis added.

120. Describing Palamas's Trinitarian theology, Meyendorff notes that "the common nature of the hypostases was, for him, a 'superessential essence,' an unknowable entity" (*Study of Gregory Palamas*, 216). The two parts of this quotation illustrate a shift of emphasis in interpreting God's essence in Eastern theology. In the early church, the essence signified that which is *common* in the Trinity and was typically coupled with the concept of person, which signified that which is *particular* to the Father, the Son, and the Spirit. Palamism preserved this old usage, but preferred to employ the concept of essence in the context of another distinction—that between essence and energies. The divine essence, therefore, pointed primarily

the otherness of God, his assertion of the total unknowability of God's essence deprives God of any *concrete* uniqueness and any *concrete* dissimilarity from his creatures.

Meyendorff also experiences difficulties in remaining consistently agnostic with regard to God's essence. As noted above, he cannot avoid attributing some properties to God's essence (such as impassibility and immutability), but he thereby violates the very apophatic limitations that he himself has imposed on the treatment of it.[121] These properties are not purely suprarational, but entail a statement—negative or even tacitly positive—concerning the divine essence. This also holds true for another essential property—God's immortality, which can naturally be interpreted positively as the ability to live forever. Meyendorff's contrast between the impassibility and immutability of the divine nature and the passibility and mutability of human nature makes clear that, in his view, passibility and mutability should be denied to God's essence not because it is apophatically *beyond* such characteristics but because it is *at variance* with them. Likewise, the alleged total unknowability of the essence seems to be at odds with Meyendorff's belief that the external manifestation of God's love "would be both impossible and meaningless if God were not Love *in Himself*."[122] While I agree with this statement about God's love, I doubt that it can be reconciled with Meyendorff's agnosticism regarding God in himself.

Similar tensions can be seen in Meyendorff's treatment of the relation between essence and person. His insistence that the hypostasis of the Father is the primordial reality in the Godhead presupposes more knowledge about God's interiority than his apophaticism seems to allow. Furthermore, the features of Eastern personalism as described by Meyendorff—the causal relation between person and essence and the consideration of "the who ... independently of the what"—lead to the question of the content of the person.[123] Although Meyendorff reproaches Western

to what is *hidden* in the Trinity (in contradistinction to the revealed energies) rather than to what is *common* in the Trinity (in contradistinction to the particular persons). A positive description of what is common in the Trinity was now made at the level of the divine energies.

121. See "Impassibility and Immutability" (pages 176–79).

122. Meyendorff, "Holy Trinity," 35, emphasis original.

123. Meyendorff, "Continuities and Discontinuities," 75.

theology for its commitment to abstract thinking, it seems that at this point his own theology suffers from the same weakness; if the person is logically prior to the essence and conceived independently of it, it would seem to be a pure abstraction. As follows from the brief analysis of his works above, Meyendorff does not simply repeat the Cappadocians' notion of the monarchy of the Father, but transforms it and develops it much further.[124] The priority of the Father over the Son and the Spirit becomes in his theology the priority of the *hypostasis* of the Father over the *nature* of the Son and the Spirit; the priority of the hypostasis of the Father over the *common* divine nature; and, finally, the priority of *all* hypostases over the common divine nature. Meyendorff seems to believe that all these various types of priority are identical with the Cappadocian notion, or, at least, naturally result from it, but his case would be more compelling if he could demonstrate how his conclusions follow from what the Cappadocians actually taught. Despite Meyendorff's reluctance to call such priorities ontological, it seems that he vests an ontological meaning in these priorities.

While the concept of God's essence does not play a significant role in Meyendorff's theological discourse and is only invoked by him in the attempt to preclude pantheist implications, in my opinion the same cannot be said of the doctrine of the Trinity in his theology, which is by no means neglected. It has often been argued that (neo-)Palamism runs the risk of depersonalizing God's economy of salvation and moving the Trinity into the hidden depth of God's being. In her seminal article, Dorothea Wendebourg claims that Palamas's system is "nothing less than the complete defeat of trinitarian theology." Wendebourg reaches this conclusion on the grounds that the Palamite identification of God's saving activities with his *energies* leaves no particular soteriological role for the *persons* of the Father, the Son, and the Spirit. "The *hypostaseis* do not enter the created world, they simply *are*," because "they belong to that level in God which is defined as being unalterably beyond the sphere of soteriological contact with his energies, namely, the level of divine essence."[125] According to the Palamite doctrine, Wendebourg argues, we know from the Bible that God is Trinitarian at a

124. See "The (Onto)logical Aspect," (pages 195–99).

125. Dorothea Wendebourg, "From the Cappadocian Fathers to Gregory Palamas: The Defeat of Trinitarian Theology," *Studia Patristica* 17 (1981): 196.

level which is totally inaccessible for us, but we do not encounter God as Trinity in the course of our salvation.[126]

However justified this criticism may be with regard to Palamas's own views, I do not think that one can easily apply it to Meyendorff's theology (or, for that matter, to the theologies of other neo-Palamites such as Lossky). First, Meyendorff repeatedly and consistently states that the divine persons possess both essence and energies. Therefore, they cannot be located only at the unknowable level of divinity. Rather, the persons are "unknown in essence and revealed in energy."[127] Second, Meyendorff is at pains to show that the divine energies "are not impersonal manifestations," but "result from the divine hypostases" and manifest their life.[128] Energies are always en-hypostatized: they belong to particular (divine) persons and are communicated to particular (human) persons. Third, Meyendorff affirms the idea of appropriation by stating that certain actions of God can be more properly attributed to a particular person.[129] To be sure, Meyendorff adds that all God's acts imply the involvement of all three persons. But this does not differ from the generally accepted idea (shared also by Bavinck) that all God's works *ad extra* are indivisible. As Meyendorff puts it, "None of

126. After Wendebourg, several Orthodox, Catholic, and Protestant theologians criticized (neo)Palamism along the same lines. As mentioned in the introduction, Zizioulas regrets that the neo-Palamite overemphasis on the divine energies tends to undermine the involvement of the divine persons in salvation. In a volume dedicated to Zizioulas's theology, Gunton also maintains that "the development of trinitarian theology from Cappadocia to Palamas drove the three hypostases deeper into the being of God, at the expense of their economic action. God the Father is no longer conceived to operate by his two hands; rather, the triune mystery of Father, Son and Spirit operates by means of the divine energies" ("Persons and Particularity," 106). According to Catherine LaCugna, "by locating the divine persons in the inaccessible, imparticipable divine essence, Gregory [Palamas] in effect has removed the Trinity from our salvation" (*God for Us*, 197). LaCugna is convinced that "the primary weakness of Palamite theology" lies in its assertion that the creatures have communion with the divine energies rather than the divine persons (186, 192). Likewise, Jenson argues that Palamism suffers from a "pneumatological deficit," because it implies that, "at least in the case of the Spirit, the energies replace the person in the historical actuality of salvation." Jenson substantiates his charge by Palamas's statement that the Son gives to his disciples the grace, or energies, of the Spirit rather than the Spirit himself (*Systematic Theology* 1:157–58). In his critical appraisal of Lossky's theology, Papanikolaou suggests that in neo-Palamism "the Son and Spirit simply become conveyors of the divine energies," which detracts from the Trinitarian nature of God, because "one could easily conceive a non-trinitarian God who communicates the divine energies" (*Being with God*, 125).

127. Meyendorff, "Philosophy, Theology," 208.

128. Meyendorff, "Christ's Humanity," 22; Meyendorff, *Study of Gregory Palamas*, 216.

129. Meyendorff, "Holy Trinity," 39.

the divine persons works independently of the others. Therefore, belief in the Trinitarian God is … the experience of his tri-personal acts, which cannot be separated."[130] Fourth, as we saw as we saw above (pages 192–95), Meyendorff's personalism has an experiential aspect. He argues that salvation consists in restoring communion with the divine persons, each of whom "is met or encountered in a unique, personal way."[131] Finally, it is noteworthy that Meyendorff has been criticized for *over*personalizing his doctrine of the divine energies. In explaining Palamas's theology, Meyendorff argues that energies are "personal acts," and it is "by virtue of their 'Perichoresis' [that] the three hypostases have only 'one sole energy.'"[132] Lourié takes these statements as implying that, in Meyendorff's view (one must bear in mind that Meyendorff's interpretation of Palamas reveals his own views no less than Palamas's), each of the divine persons has his own energy, and only the perichoresis of their energies leads to the oneness of the divine energy.[133] Whether Lourié's remarks are correct, they demonstrate how diligently Meyendorff tries to emphasize the personal aspect of the divine energies.[134]

The assertion of a real distinction between God's essence and energies, and the identification of the latter with God's life and acts, leads Meyendorff to differentiate between God's essence on the one hand, and his life and acts on the other. Meyendorff argues that the saints share in God's life, even in the *intra-Trinitarian* life, while his essence remains completely transcendent.[135] However, it is not clear how the intra-Trinitarian life can be distinguished from God in himself, who, according to Meyendorff, is absolutely inaccessible even for deified humans. The real distinction between God's unknowable essence and his knowable acts is equally dubious. Instead of arguing that God's energies signify the presence and activity of his essence in the world, Meyendorff maintains that God's activity occurs outside his

---

130. Meyendorff, *Vvedenie v svyatootecheskoe bogoslovie*, 176.

131. Meyendorff, "Christ's Humanity," 11–12.

132. Meyendorff, *Study of Gregory Palamas*, 215, 218.

133. Lourié, "Kommentarii," 439.

134. I am not persuaded that Lourié's criticism is valid, because, contrary to his claims, Meyendorff does not use the phrase "perichoresis of energies," and in explaining why all the divine persons have one energy he points also to "their consubstantial unity" ("Holy Trinity," 39; Meyendorff, *Study of Gregory Palamas*, 215).

135. Meyendorff, "Une théologie," 292.

essence. This implies that God is inactive with respect to his essence and that his activity constitutes another mode of his existence—one outside his essence. The real distinction between God's essence and his acts seems to be untenable, because in the Bible it is precisely God's awesome deeds that are praised as unsearchable (Pss 92:5; 145:1–7). The loving and holy *acts* of God are as incomprehensible (but in some measure knowable!) as his *being* love and holiness. God's acts plumb the same hidden depths as his essence. The distinction should be drawn not between God's unknowable essence on the one hand and his knowable acts on the other, but between his inexhaustible essence and inexhaustible acts on the one hand, and our limited capacity to understand them on the other.

The Reality of Encounter and Union with God

Bavinck

In determining my second criterion of evaluation, I have proceeded mostly from the Eastern Orthodox understanding of revelation, which emphasizes that God's external acts do not merely provide information about God, but secure the possibility of a real encounter and union with God. From Meyendorff's perspective, Western theology has both epistemological and soteriological deficiencies in this regard. Epistemologically, it reduces God's revelation to Scripture and creaturely reflections of God in nature without showing how human beings can directly encounter the uncreated reality of God himself. Soteriologically, it reduces salvation to an imputation of Christ's righteousness to believers and declaring them forgiven before God—who remains totally distant. Western theology, according to Meyendorff, fails to show how believers can participate in the very life of God and become deified.[136] The degree to which Meyendorff's epistemological and soteriological concerns are justified will occupy us in the next

136. Meyendorff expresses similar criticism of Barlaam, Palamas's main opponent. Epistemologically, Meyendorff charges Barlaam with holding that God can be known only indirectly. Soteriologically, Barlaam, according to Meyendorff, taught that in Christ, "humanity and divinity, inalienable natures impermeable one by the other, are in a purely external relation of juxtaposition" (*Study of Gregory Palamas*, 181). Such a "static" notion of nature, Meyendorff argues, signaled a return to Nestorianism and did not allow for the communication of the idioms, without which neither Christ's humanity nor the saints could be deified.

section. This section, however, will focus on how Bavinck demonstrates that revelation is concerned with God himself.

In his doctrine of revelation, Bavinck makes ample use of the concept of the Logos. The prologue of John's Gospel states that the Logos was in the beginning with God and himself was God. Bavinck describes the divinity of the Logos in terms of communicability, participation, and perfect image: God communicated himself to the Logos and expressed his entire being in him; the Son participates from all eternity in the Father's nature, life, and love; the Logos is the image of God in an absolute sense. Such participatory language allows Bavinck to establish an analogical relation between the Logos on the one hand and creation, revelation, and human beings on the other. While God communicated himself to the Logos in all his fullness, he also partially communicated himself in creation and revelation; while the Logos is the perfect image of God, human beings are images of God in a relative sense; and so forth. It was Bavinck's conviction that the Logos shines throughout the entirety of creation.[137] Just as the intelligibility of the world and the possibility of natural science is grounded in the horizontal correspondence between the logos inherent in human beings and the logos implicit in other creatures, so the knowability of God and the possibility of theology is grounded in the vertical analogy between the divine Logos and his creaturely reflections.

Thus, according to Bavinck, the Logos is able to reveal God for two reasons: first, because he is God himself, and second, because the created means of his revelation, as well as the created recipients of his revelation, are made in his image. Creation is not an obstacle to encountering God but is a well-prepared arena for it. Bavinck, therefore, unapologetically affirms that all revelation is creaturely in form, rather than ever lamenting revelation as merely creaturely. He holds that his doctrine of the Logos demonstrates the creation's ability truly to reflect God's perfections, and simultaneously avoids the mixing of divine and human realities by establishing an *analogical* relationship between them. Bavinck rejects the mystics' yearning for an immediate knowledge of God as implying a confusion of "our logos" with "the Logos of God."[138]

---

137. *RD* 1:233; 2:273–74, 309, 533.

138. *RD* 2:69.

The necessity of accommodating God's absoluteness to a creaturely level is amply demonstrated by Bavinck's parallel between incarnation and inscripturation, that is, between the Logos assuming flesh and the Logos becoming Scripture. According to Bavinck, "the Logos, in becoming flesh ... enters into human nature, prepares and shapes it by the Spirit into his own appropriate medium. ... So also the word, the revelation of God, entered the world of creatureliness, the life and history of humanity, in all the human forms of dream and vision, of investigation and reflection." However, the subject of incarnation and inscripturation is divine and remains divine despite entering the world of creatureliness. Although in our human experience we deal with creaturely realities in Scripture (with human words and concepts), it has a divine origin and a divine subject: "Always it is God who stands behind that word."[139] The same holds true for the incarnation: although those who encountered Jesus on earth saw a creature, in seeing Jesus they could also see the divine Logos, consubstantial with the Father. Creaturely means of revelation, therefore, point beyond themselves to God, who truly communicates himself through them.

According to Bavinck, revelation not only makes God known, but also involves all God's activities in (re-)creating humanity according to his image.[140] Thus, Bavinck's doctrine of revelation is closely interwoven with his doctrine of creation and salvation. In elaborating these doctrines, he tries to demonstrate that God communicates himself to his creatures—yet without merging with them or violating their creaturely integrity. For Bavinck, union with God is the essence of religion. He argues that the word *ethisch* (ethical, existential) is too weak to describe this union and prefers to call it "mystical." Apart from this union, humans "cannot be truly and completely human." Bavinck affirms that humans participate in the divine nature through this mystical union. However, he does not move beyond merely acknowledging this idea in the New Testament, and he finds it more important to dispel its various distortions than positively to explain its meaning. Bavinck notes that even the union of the two natures in Christ is not natural but personal. He distances himself from the Lutheran doctrine, which states that properties of Christ's divine nature are communicated

139. *RD* 1:434; 4:449.

140. See "The Necessity of God's Revelation," (pages 84–86).

to his human nature, and from the Roman Catholic position, according to which the two natures of Christ interpenetrate and inwardly affect each other, leading to the deification of the human nature. Bavinck concurs with Reformed theologians who taught that in Christ only the person is immediately united with the human nature, while the divine nature is united with it *mediately*.[141]

According to Bavinck, the distinction between divinity and humanity is even more clearly preserved in the mystical union between God and his people, established in the *pactum salutis* and objectively realized by Christ.[142] Bavinck repeatedly asserts that believers have communion with the person of Christ rather than with his divine nature. In this communion, believers preserve their human identities: if even the hypostatic union does not diminish the genuineness of Christ's humanity, it is all the more clear that the union between Christ and his people does not lead to the dissolution of their identities. Bavinck also emphasizes that communion with Christ as a person is mediated by the Spirit. It is in the pneumatological context that Bavinck makes his boldest statements about divine-human communion. He maintains that the communion with the Father and the Son to which the Spirit leads us is "direct and immediate."[143] In the Lord's Supper, the Spirit brings about our special communion with the whole Christ, both in his divine and in his human natures. Bavinck further argues that the Spirit communicates the Father and the Son to us with all their benefits, among which Bavinck includes the divine nature.[144] In general, Bavinck speaks with greater boldness about the Spirit's indwelling us than about our participation in God's life. Although these two themes can

141. *RD* 3:276, 304, 309.

142. For a helpful overview of the different semantic and theological contexts in which Bavinck develops his doctrine of the *unio mystica*, see Burger, *Being in Christ*, 101–8, 117–25.

143. Bavinck, *RD* 2:278. The assertion of an "immediate" communion mediated by the Spirit may seem oxymoronic, but Bavinck's point behind it is to indicate the unity of the three divine persons in their relations with humans: if the Spirit is immediately present in us, this also implies our immediate communion with the Father and the Son, who are one with the Spirit. This does not change the fact that Bavinck is rather inconsistent in applying the term "immediate" to our knowledge of God (as we saw in "God's Revelation as Mediated" [pp. 99–103]). On the one hand, he rejects the possibility of an immediate vision of God on the grounds that it implies a perfect knowledge of God; on the other hand, he maintains that in the state of blessedness the redeemed will know God directly and immediately (*RD* 4:722).

144. *RD* 2:312; 4:576–78.

be understood as mirroring each other rather than competing with each other, Bavinck's desire to emphasize the asymmetry in divine-human communion (God condescends to our creaturely existence, while we are not elevated to a supernatural realm) causes him to focus almost exclusively on God's activity within us. In light of this asymmetry, Bavinck's relative reticence concerning salvific participation in the divine nature becomes more understandable. This asymmetry also shows that Bavinck—rightly, in my view—sees all the possibilities for a genuine encounter and communion with God as happening in the midst of the created order and within our creaturely limitations.

Meyendorff

As noted above, Meyendorff argues that the failure to recognize in God anything distinct from his imparticipable essence prevents Reformed theologians from affirming a real participation of humanity in God.[145] By contrast, in Orthodox theology the distinction between God's essence and energies provides a dogmatic backdrop for affirming participation in the most realistic terms. However, while this affirmation forms the very core of the gospel message for Meyendorff, in my view it constitutes the root of what I consider to be problematic in the (neo-)Palamite formulation of the relation between God's hiddenness and revelation.

Meyendorff's understanding of participation becomes evident both from what he denies and from what he affirms. Negatively, Meyendorff rejects human participation in God's essence on the grounds that it would abolish the ontological distinction between God and humanity and make humanity as divine as the three hypostases. Following Palamas, Meyendorff maintains that an essence has as many hypostases as there are partakers of it.[146] Positively, Meyendorff states that humanity's fullness becomes united with God's fullness through deification.[147] Meyendorff alludes to Palamas's interpretation of Paul's heavenly journey described in 2 Corinthians 12,

---

145. See "Meyendorff on Reformed Doctrine" (pp. 259–63).

146. See "A Real Distinction" (pages 233–39).

147. See "A Real Distinction" (pages 233–39). It must be added, however, that in Meyendorff's theology participation in God also has some weaker aspects. In particular, Meyendorff affirms the idea of universal participation in God (*Christ in Eastern Christian Thought*, 135). In this weaker sense, participation is far from identification. See also "Ways to Unify" (pages 240–48) about Meyendorff's use of the concept of analogy.

where Palamas explains that the apostle "was that to which he was united."[148] Thus, the manner in which Meyendorff denies participation in God's essence and affirms participation in God's energies indicates that, in his view, participation is hardly distinguishable from identification.

Such a view, however, goes beyond the participatory language and imagery employed by the church fathers, who carefully distinguished participation from identification and maintained that partakers share in God to a limited degree and in a distinct manner.[149] The Son's *identity* with the Father by nature was sharply contrasted with our *similarity* to God by participation. Meyendorff seeks to preserve this contrast by insisting that the deified saints are united with God by grace, rather than by nature. This distinction should be understood in light of Meyendorff's real distinction between the participated and the unparticipated in God: the Son is one with God the Father in all aspects (both in essence and energies), while the saints are one with God only in what is participated in him (that is, in his energies). However, Meyendorff does not clearly differentiate between the character of each of the two unions: in both cases the union is presented in terms of unrestricted oneness. While God's imparticipable nature and human created nature indeed remain outside human union with God (thus preserving the distinction between God and humanity), that which *is* united—God in his energies and the saints in the deified mode of their existence—really are *one*. It is worth noting that Meyendorff never denies the validity of pantheist deductions by specifying any limitations to the union between humanity and God in his energies. Rather, he denies them by maintaining the absolute transcendence of the divine *essence*.[150]

Epistemologically, this "excessively realist and near-materialist view" of participation in God implies identification between the knower, the

---

148. Meyendorff, *Study of Gregory Palamas*, 174.

149. Friedrich Normann, *Teilhabe, ein Schlüsselwort der Vätertheologie* (Münster: Aschendorff, 1978), 73–74.

150. Meyendorff, *Study of Gregory Palamas*, 218. As I argued above, Meyendorff's radical apophaticism concerning God's essence rests primarily on the necessity to avoid pantheist implications in asserting his concept of deification. In this regard, Gunton notes that the negative way "is insidiously a way of a merging with God," and the apparent modesty and humility of apophaticism masks "an almost Promethean aspiration to unity with the divine" (*Act and Being*, 63, 65).

known, and the act of knowing.[151] According to Meyendorff, since mystical knowledge involves uniting with its object, it does not presuppose epistemic distance and is not knowledge in the usual sense of the term.[152] Meyendorff does not explain how this concept preserves the distinct identity of the human knower, but he does not seem to be worried about its possible loss.[153] What is more troubling for Meyendorff's purposes is that, despite his emphasis on the dynamic character of participation, the identification between the knower and the known leaves little, if any, room for progress in the knower's knowledge of God.

Moreover, Meyendorff's insistence that God's revelation to the "spiritual senses" occurs beyond the conceptual process hardly gives due weight to the cognitive and verbal aspects of God's revelation. To be sure, in defining God's revelation, one can legitimately emphasize that its content is God himself and that he reveals himself through his gracious works in the world. However, this emphasis on God's self-giving and on his revealing acts should not be at the expense of downplaying his communication by words, as if we were to transcend it. The God of Scripture reveals himself primarily through his *speech* acts. Likewise, *our appropriation* of God's revelation should not be purged of cognitive and verbal content. Certainly, knowledge of God can be acquired through personal relationship rather than intellectual observation or speculative thought. However, we express our knowledge of God through confession, praise, and thanksgiving, all of which presuppose predicative discourse.

Meyendorff's attitude toward the categories of knowledge and language is dismissive—chiefly because he views them as "creaturely" concepts. They belong to the domain of created things and cannot, therefore, serve us in

---

151. Williams, "Philosophical Structures," 44.

152. Lossky puts it even more clearly: "It would even be inaccurate to say that it [mystical theology] has God for its object. ... God no longer presents Himself as object, *for it is no more a question of knowledge but of union*" (*Mystical Theology*, 28, emphasis added).

153. Letham, however, goes too far when he claims that since the neo-Palamite position implies that God "has wholly revealed himself, we can be the masters of this revelation, and so can determine for ourselves the details of what we can and ought to be and do" (*Holy Trinity*, 341). This charge seems to presuppose that in neo-Palamite thought God's revelation is a reality external to the deified saints, who can somehow master it. But this is not the case: rather, God's revelation is God's life, which becomes one with the lives of the saints. The problem with the neo-Palamite perspective is not that the deified recipients of revelation become its masters or self-determined subjects, but rather that their subjectivity, or distinctive identity, virtually dissolves.

approaching the reality of the uncreated God. By contrast, personalistic and experiential categories such as encounter, meeting, contact, experience, communion, contemplation, and deification have no such strict connotations for Meyendorff and remain positive and meaningful when applied to mystical union with God.[154] Meyendorff, however, does not attempt to substantiate his selectivity. He does not explain why God's uncreatedness allows a positive *experience* of God and simultaneously does not allow a positive *knowledge* of God. If human senses, as Meyendorff maintains, can be transformed and endowed with uncreated capacities to see God experientially, it is not clear why, by analogy, human reason and language cannot be empowered and transformed to express God's truth conceptually.[155]

What seems to be crucial, however, is that the very need to become "uncreated" for real communion with God to occur cannot be properly substantiated from Scripture. Scripture, in fact, bears witness to the opposite cosmological movement—from the uncreated *to* the created. It speaks about the incarnation, which, as James Smith puts it, was "God's refusal to avoid speaking."[156] After God has spoken to us in human form, we should not lament our inability to speak of God in divine language, or language that is proper of him in every way—perfectly expressing his divine majesty. While such language is indeed unattainable for us, God urges us to speak of him in human language—the language he has first spoken to us through his Logos. The same holds true for all aspects of our existence:

---

154. When it comes to experience or communion, Meyendorff does not use paradoxical expressions such as "the communion with God's incommunicability." But when it comes to knowledge, Meyendorff employs oxymora such as "the knowledge of the Unknowable" (*Byzantine theology*, 12). Although Meyendorff defines revelation as "a free and sovereign act of God, by which ... the Unknowable makes himself known," this knowability is not intellectual or conceptual (*Study of Gregory Palamas*, 209; see also 220). True knowledge of God is the knowledge of his unknowability ("the knowledge that God is unknowable," *Study of Gregory Palamas*, 131). Thus, paradoxically, through revelation the Unknowable makes himself known precisely as the Unknowable.

155. Historically, apophaticism has often been connected with the devaluation of materiality and temporality. Meyendorff, however, maintains that deification involves a transfiguration of the whole person: body and soul together. His appreciation of the human body, stemming from Palamas's defense of hesychast practices, shows that his apophatic strategy does not imply ascending from the material to the immaterial. This positive view of corporeality stands in some tension with Meyendorff's skepticism about knowledge and language. Furthermore, one must bear in mind that Meyendorff celebrates materiality in so far as it is endowed with *uncreated* capacities.

156. James K. A. Smith, *Speech and Theology: Language and the Logic of Incarnation* (London: Routledge, 2002), 185.

after the Son has reached us in our creatureliness, one should not seek to get rid of it in order to reach God in his divinity. In Christ, we become new *creatures* rather than transcending the limitations of creatureliness.

As noted above, Meyendorff's understanding of union with God lies at the root of the differentiation between God's wholly incommunicable essence and his fully communicable energies. Meyendorff himself argues that the essence-energy distinction "inevitably results" from the doctrine of deification.[157] The reason seems to be clear: since Meyendorff, following Palamas, interprets deification, or participation, in terms of oneness between God and humanity, God's otherness can be safeguarded only by affirming a mode of his existence that lies entirely beyond participation. In this regard, Jenson observes that the distinction between God's essence and energies results from Palamas's desire to "reserve some final reality of God from creaturely participation."[158] In Palamism, as Thomas Anastos correctly explains, "the inaccessibility of God is preserved by the radical transcendence of the divine essence, *a transcendence which is a necessary reaction to the intimacy of the union in the divine energies*."[159] Meyendorff is thus right that, *given his doctrine of deification*, a kind of essence-energy distinction needs to be postulated within God in order to balance his far-reaching view on God's communicability in his energies with an equally far-reaching view on his incommunicability in essence and to integrate these two elements into one coherent system. However, the necessity of this distinction becomes questionable when human participation in God is understood in a less comprehensive way.

The Oneness of God

Bavinck

Bavinck's theology proper is not original: even the most cursory reading of his works reveals his deep indebtedness to the preceding tradition,

---

157. Meyendorf, "Svyatoy Grigoriy Palama," 164. Elsewhere he writes that the real distinction between God's essence and energies "is made unavoidable in the context of the doctrine of 'deification'" (*Byzantine Theology*, 186).

158. Jenson, *Systematic Theology*, 1:152.

159. Thomas L. Anastos, "Gregory Palamas' Radicalization of the Essence, Energies, and Hypostasis Model of God," *The Greek Orthodox Theological Review* 38 (1993): 343, emphasis added.

particularly Augustine, medieval scholasticism, and Reformed orthodoxy. This tradition has been criticized for the many supposed defects in its doctrine of God, but not for undermining or underestimating God's oneness. On the contrary, many theologians have argued that its preoccupation with the essential oneness of God has resulted in a neglect of God's Trinitarian existence and that its metaphysical concept of God as pure act has led to his being and his external activity being indistinguishable. In this section, therefore, I will not discuss whether Bavinck succeeded in preserving God's oneness—hardly anyone would call this into question. Instead, I will analyze whether Bavinck avoided a one-sided emphasis on the oneness of God and whether he was consistent in his approach.

As noted above, Western essentialism is one of the main targets of Meyendorff's criticism. He contends that essentialism, among other things, threatens God's freedom, particularly in the act of creation. According to Meyendorff, the identification of God with his essence does not allow one "to say that divine acts are voluntary acts, and that, therefore, the act of creation is not a 'necessary' effulgence of divine essence but a result of the omnipotent divine will."[160] If Western essentialism were correct, Meyendorff argues, God "would then lose His freedom in the acts of Grace."[161] Recently, these criticisms have been taken up and developed more systematically by David Bradshaw. Bradshaw notes that the Thomistic account of divine simplicity, as well as its less sophisticated version in Augustine, entails that God's essence is identical to his will (not simply to his will as a faculty or to his capacity to will but to God's determinate will as actually realized). According to Bradshaw, this view turns out to be incompatible with human libertarian freedom for the following reason: if God's will is identical with his essence, it cannot respond to free human decisions, as then human agency would be partly constitutive of God's essence, which, in turn, would be incompatible with divine aseity. Thus, the identification of God's essence with his will necessarily results in the denial of humans' free choices and in the postulation of the divine will as determined solely by God. What is more, divine simplicity, as Aquinas understood it, also contradicts *divine* free choice, as it implies that in order to will or to act

160. Meyendorff, "Creation in the History," 34.
161. Meyendorff, "Doctrine of Grace," 25.

differently God must *be* different. The identity of God's essence with his will makes these two equally necessary. To be sure, Bradshaw realizes that Aquinas affirmed the contingency of the world. However, he argues that Aquinas failed to demonstrate how his account of divine simplicity is compatible with God's capacity to choose among opposites (for example, whether to create and what to create). Bradshaw finds a much better alternative in the essence-energy distinction, which enabled Palamas "to say what Aquinas so much wanted to say, but could not: that God can *do* otherwise without *being* otherwise."[162]

Bavinck's doctrine of God seems to be susceptible to such criticism, not only because in general he follows the Augustinian-Thomist line but also because he explicitly affirms that God's will is identical with his essence. However, Bavinck's account of divine simplicity shows that this doctrine should not necessarily be understood in a strict sense, but, rather, is capable of accommodating distinctions in God. Bavinck distinguishes between God's will as directed toward God himself and God's will as related to the world. The former indicates that God eternally loves himself and is completely blessed within himself. "God eternally wills himself with the will of delight."[163] The latter indicates his propensity toward creatures and is the final cause of all that exists.

According to Bavinck, God's will in relation to himself and his will in relation to creatures differ not only with regard to their objects but also with regard to their character. The former is necessary: God "eternally, and with divine necessity, delights in himself."[164] By contrast, the latter is free: he was free to create or not create the world, or to create things in a greater or lesser number than he did. Bavinck, however, seeks to avoid a nominalist understanding of freedom as absolute arbitrariness. For this reason, he emphasizes that God's will with regard to creatures is not severed from the divine nature but flows from divine, natural[165] wisdom, goodness, and other attributes.

---

162. Bradshaw, *Aristotle East and West*, 272, emphasis original.

163. *RD* 2:232, 240, 243–44, 247, 373.

164. *RD* 2:223. The necessary character of this kind of will, of course, does not rule out freedom, for the latter is understood as God's willing in full accord with his own desires and without external compulsion.

165. *RD* 2:234.

By Bavinck's account, therefore, God's will in relation to himself is indeed necessary and fully identical with his essence and attributes. God's will in relation to creatures, however, is not a necessity for him and does not coincide with his essence, but rather corresponds to it. This stance may or may not allow for the existence of libertarian human freedom, depending on whether one affirms that human decisions can affect God's will in relation to creatures. But for the Calvinist Bavinck, this is not an issue. What is clear, and what is important for him, is that his account of God's will does affirm *divine* freedom.

This is not to say that Bavinck's approach is fully free from internal tensions or that his terminology is perfectly consistent. Although Bavinck insists that "God wills himself and his creatures with one and the same simple act," one may question whether the word "simple" is indeed the best term to describe a twofold will. Elsewhere, Bavinck argues that the term "simple" is not an antonym of "twofold" or "threefold" but of "composite." I am not sure, however, whether every hint of composition is excluded in a will, one aspect of which is necessary and the other is not. If the world is contingent, then God could have willed himself without willing his creatures. Correspondingly, the latter willing is not essential to God's willing of himself, and it does not seem justified to insist that a whole, which contains something that is not essential to it, is simple. It is equally doubtful that Bavinck, given his clear distinction between the necessary divine will and the free divine will, can consistently identify God's will—as a whole—with the divine essence. This difficulty can be seen in Bavinck's own hesitations with regard to terminology. For example, he argues that God's plan for all that exists and will happen in time is "the willing and deciding *God himself*, not something accidental in God, but *one with his being*, as his eternally active will." However, he immediately clarifies that "this world plan, though closely connected with God's being, may not be equated with that being." I agree with this clarification, but I doubt that it fits well with Bavinck's assertion concerning the identity of God's will and his essence/being.[166]

---

166. *RD* 2:176–77, 223, 373, emphasis added. In explaining how God wills himself and his creatures in one simple act, Matthew Levering argues that "God *can* be said to will *necessarily* everything that he wills" in the sense that "there is no God 'prior' to God's will to create." See Levering, *Engaging the Doctrine of Creation* (Grand Rapids: Baker Academic, 2017), 103,

For the present work, the most intriguing question is to what extent Bavinck's distinction between God's necessary and free will corresponds with Bradshaw's (and more generally the (neo-)Palamite) distinction between necessary and contingent aspects of God. Speaking about God's free will, Bavinck calls it "a rich and powerful divine energy."[167] To be sure, Bavinck does not use the word "energy" in the specifically Palamite sense, and the word "power" could substitute it without any change in meaning. However, Bavinck's word choice makes the issue even more pressing: Was Bavinck's position close to the essence-energy distinction? The simple answer would be no; it was not. The reason is not only that it is difficult to consider the Palamite essence-energy distinction in isolation from the other doctrinal commitments and the specific forms of spirituality of Palamism, which Bavinck obviously did not support. As with any other fundamental doctrine, this distinction is connected by many ties to its historical and theological context, and it is not easy to transplant it into new theological soil. More important, however, is that Bavinck's affirmation of the distinction between God's necessary and free will, between God's self-consciousness and his world-consciousness, between God's being and his works *ad extra*, does not imply the existence of two eternal modes in God's existence, one of which is communicable and the other of which is not. Rather, all these distinctions mean that the same divine attributes

---

emphasis original. In support of this claim, Levering cites James E. Dolezal: "There has never been a temporal or logical 'moment' in the divine life in which God stood volitionally open to other possible worlds. The actual world is conditionally necessary and every other possible world is conditionally impossible by virtue of the fact that God has *eternally* willed this particular world." See *God without Parts: Divine Simplicity and the Metaphysics of God's Absoluteness* (Eugene, OR: Pickwick, 2011), 207. I agree that the eternity of God's will excludes temporal succession in God's will and knowledge. However, I don't see why it should also exclude *logical* succession. The denial of the existence of a logical moment in which God decided to create the world, and to create it exactly as it is, binds God and the world too tightly. I believe this is what Bavinck sought to avoid when stressing that God's self-consciousness should be distinguished from his world-consciousness, and that the content of God's self-knowledge should be logically distinguished from his eternal knowledge of the world (*RD* 2:195, 343). If God indeed *chose* to create, then it follows that, in the logical sense, there was when the world was not [in God's decision]. I also suspect that Dolezal's denial of logical moments in the divine life renders the lapsarian question meaningless. Bavinck's position differs also in this respect, since he, without expressing a strong preference for either infra- or supralapsarianism, nonetheless takes the question seriously and does not object to the idea of a logical order in God's eternal decrees. Thus, I don't think that Bavinck would have approved of the explanation of Levering and Dolezal, but I must also note that he does not offer a clear alternative.

167. *RD* 2:241. In the original (Dutch) edition, Bavinck uses the Greek term ἐνέργεια.

(goodness, love, wisdom, and so forth) are expressed not only necessarily within God's being but also freely outside it—in his acts. Although our understanding of these acts is necessarily limited, while God's understanding of them is perfect, Bavinck is right to emphasize that these two understandings are not completely different but, rather, analogically related. The concept of analogy brings structure and integrity to Bavinck's system and favorably distinguishes it from Meyendorff's system, in which this concept is missing.

Importantly, Bavinck, unlike Meyendorff, Bradshaw, and other neo-Palamites, unambiguously identifies God's essence and attributes.[168] In light of this identification, one would have expected him to affirm the possibility of analogical knowledge of God's essence. Such an affirmation would have fit very well with Bavinck's antinominalistic leanings, which are felt in his contention that God's will toward the world should not be severed from his essence. In fact, everything in Bavinck's theology leads to the conclusion that God's essence may be partially known through his acts, in which he reveals his attributes.[169] However, as indicated above, Bavinck

---

168. Although I question the validity of Bavinck's identification of God's essence and his determinate *will*, I believe that Bavinck's assertion of the identity of God's essence and his *attributes* is correct—at least when considered within the framework of Bavinck's metaphysical system (which, borrowing Nicholas Wolterstorff's term, could be characterized as constituent ontology in contradistinction to relation ontology). See Wolterstorff, "Divine Simplicity," *Philosophical Perspectives* 5 (1991): 541. Whatever effects God could have caused outside himself, and in whatever ways he could have willed to reveal his attributes, his essence and attributes remain identical and unchanged. His "being Creator and Sustainer of the world as it is" is not an attribute, but rather one of the possible ways in which he could have acted in accordance with his essential attributes. Thus, if God had decided not to create the world, or to create it differently, that would not affect his essence *and attributes*. In sum, Palamas and his followers differentiate between God's essence on the one hand, and his properties and will (subsumed under the term "energy") on the other hand (and further differentiate between different kinds of energies). Bavinck argues that God's essence, attributes/properties, and will are identical, although he does not seem to be consistent in asserting this identity. I would differentiate between God's essence and attributes on the one hand, and his will concerning the world on the other (which does not mean, of course, that this will is arbitrary: rather, it flows from, and corresponds with, God's essence and attributes).

169. Recent publications about the essence-energy distinction by several scholars connected to the Reformed tradition demonstrate why the formulation "God's essence is revealed through his acts" is helpful in avoiding some misunderstanding. Myk Habets holds that "a basic difference between Reformed theology and Eastern Orthodoxy" lies in the fact that the former takes *homoousion* to mean "that God reveals himself not simply through his impersonal *energies* but in a very real way through his personal *essence*: in the incarnation God gives *himself* in grace." See Habets, "'Reformed Theosis?' A Response to Gannon Murphy," *Theology Today* 65 (2009): 494, emphasis original. Apart from doubting that Reformed theology

is not consistent on this point, asserting the unknowability of God in his essence. To be sure, this does not bring him much closer to the Palamite essence-energy distinction because, as noted above, Bavinck's position is based on different premises and driven by different concerns.

Meyendorff

Positing a real distinction in God, Meyendorff realizes the need to demonstrate its coherence and to explain why it does not imply a breach between the totally unknowable essence and the fully communicable energies. As we saw above, while Meyendorff insists on the inadequacy of human logic in explaining "the antinomian poles" of God's existence, he also employs more positive apologetic strategies.[170] In particular, he takes pains to show that God's essence and energies are not discrete entities existing independently of each other. Rather, they are two inseparable modes of God's existence. Meyendorff also interprets God's being as a uniting concept that comprises both essence and energies. Essence and energies are not separated, because God's being is fully present in both of them, albeit in different modes. It is not that one half of God is communicated and another is not: rather, the fullness of God is communicable in one *sense* (or mode) and incommunicable in another. In the same vein, Meyendorff interprets the doctrine of God's simplicity: God is simple not because his essence and attributes are identical, but because both essence and energies belong to

describes God's essence in a more personal way than Eastern Orthodox theology describes God's energies, I am not sure what it means that God reveals himself not simply through his energies, but through his essence. In my view, God's essence is not the *means* of revelation, but that which is (partly) revealed through (the means of) his acts/words/energies. On the other hand, Michael Horton, in trying to explain the importance of the essence-energy distinction, argues that we know God "from his acts and not from his essence" (*Lord and Servant*, 117). However, Horton's formulation presents a false dilemma. The issue is not whether we know God from his essence or from his acts. The real issue is whether we know God's essence from his acts, or whether it remains shrouded despite God's revelatory activity. The knowability of the essence by no means diminishes the necessity and importance of God's revelatory acts. On the contrary, it strengthens their revelatory power by implying that what they reveal is the very essence of God. Although Habets and Horton take diametrically different positions concerning the essence-energy distinction (Habets holds that it is "thoroughly incompatible with Reformed theology" and should be rejected ["Reformed Theosis," 492], while Horton, as we saw, maintains that the distinction is not only compatible with Reformed theology, but indeed indispensable to it), I suspect that the following simple formulation could be acceptable for both of them: we know [what?] God's essence [how?] "through" (or "from") his acts/words.

170. See also "Ways to Unify" (pages 240–48).

the one single being of God. Furthermore, Meyendorff seeks to strengthen God's unity through his personalistic emphasis. God's essence and energies are inseparable, because the Father, the Son, and the Spirit possess them both. Each of the divine persons is simultaneously hidden and revealed.

These arguments of Meyendorff notwithstanding, I am not convinced that he succeeds in demonstrating that the essence-energy distinction does not endanger God's oneness. Meyendorff's insistence that "even when He [God] manifests Himself, He remains unknowable in His essence" proves that the two modes of divine being remain disconnected.[171] As shown in the previous section, although Meyendorff occasionally speaks of the divine energies as a manifestation of God's essence, he insists that they "reflect God, but not His essence."[172] Meyendorff also argues that God's properties such as goodness "express His existence and action *ad extra*, not His essence."[173] This inevitably begs the question as to what the energies actually reflect or reveal. The only answer Meyendorff's system allows is that the energies reveal nothing but the energies themselves (or, to put it in more personalistic terms, the persons in their energies reveal their own energies, or life). The energies do not reveal the divine essence, because, as Meyendorff repeatedly emphasizes, the latter "can never be known or seen even in the life to come": it "remains transcendent and totally unparticipable," "totally unknowable and transcendent," and "absolutely incommunicable to creatures."[174] The energies do not reveal anything that stands

171. Meyendorff, *Gregory Palamas*, 118.

172. See "Ways to Unify" (pages 240–48).; Meyendorff, *Byzantine Theology*, 27. At first glance, Meyendorff seems to be inconsistent on this point. However, a recent article by David Bradshaw demonstrates that even an unambiguous acceptance of the idea that God's energies manifest his essence does not necessarily mean that the energies actually reveal the essence in any measure. Bradshaw rejects the assumption that "there must be a qualitative resemblance between a manifestation and its source." He suggests that this is far from the case, and gives several examples: "There is no non-trivial resemblance between lung disease and the shortened breath that manifests it, nor between a man's love for his wife and the flowers he brings home, nor between the mind of Mark Twain and Huckleberry Finn. The relationship between a source and its manifestation is far too varied to be captured simply in terms of resemblance, and this is especially true when the source is a free agent capable of sustained, creative action." See Bradshaw, "In Defence of the Essence/Energies Distinction: A Reply to Critics," in Athanasopoulos and Schneider, *Divine Essence and Divine Energies*, 263–64.

173. Meyendorff, *Byzantine Theology*, 130.

174. Meyendorff, "Significance of the Reformation," 169; Meyendorff, *Byzantine Theology*, 186; Meyendorff, "Orthodox Theology," 184; Meyendorff, "Holy Trinity," 31. As mentioned above (pages 179–84), Meyendorff occasionally remarks that deified saints participate in the

'behind' them and do not point to a reality beyond them. They do not presuppose a Revealer who is *inexhaustibly* revealed through them. Rowan Williams rightly describes this (neo-)Palamite standpoint as follows: "Our ultimate encounter is not with the οὐσία through πρόοδοι, but with the πρόοδοι or ἐνέργειαι 'in themselves', whatever that may mean."[175]

Contrary to Meyendorff's intentions, the denial of the revealing function of God's energies as to his essence leads to speculation and uncertainty. If God's essence is not revealed through his energies, it inevitably becomes a matter of speculative reasoning. Without revelation, even the unknowability of God's essence can only be speculated rather than asserted.[176] Conversely, if theology is based on revelation, then the total unknowability of the essence must actually be revealed in order for us to able to believe in it. What is more, Meyendorff's essence-energy distinction deprives us of the certainty that God's revelation corresponds to what he is in himself. In the biblical narrative, God's words and acts do not merely have the salvation of people as their objective, but they also reveal his own heart. The denial of any knowledge of God in himself seems to undervalue the openness and trust that characterize God's revelation in Scripture.

While Meyendorff's theology, as I argued above, does not make the doctrine of the Trinity irrelevant for salvation, it fails consistently to show how the economic Trinity is related to the ontological Trinity.[177] The Trinitarian relations as revealed in the Bible, especially in John's Gospel, are not restricted to the economy of salvation but point beyond it to eternal relationships within the Trinity.[178] Meyendorff takes this into account when describing the inner relations of the Trinity in terms of internal

divine nature. This may suggest that he was not fully consistent as to the communicability of the divine essence/nature. In most of his works, however, he states consistently and repeatedly that God is totally unknowable and inaccessible in his essence.

175. Rowan Williams, *Wrestling with Angels: Conversations in Modern Theology* (Grand Rapids: Eerdmans, 2007), 11.

176. By *reductio ad absurdum*, one can claim that if God's essence is really unknowable then we cannot assert anything about it, not even its alleged unknowability.

177. David Coffey rightly observes that "an unfortunate corollary of Palamism, found in both Palamas and his modern followers, is the denial of a necessary correspondence between the economic and the immanent Trinity." See Coffey, *Deus Trinitas: The Doctrine of the Triune God* (Oxford: Oxford University Press, 1999), 26.

178. Even the names by which God reveals himself as the Trinity indicate that his revelation is grounded in the primal Trinitarian relations: God reveals himself as Father, Son, and Spirit, rather than as "Creator, Liberator and Comforter," "Ground, Logos, and Spirit," or "Creator,

divine energies and life, which are knowable and communicable to creatures. However, it is not clear how the intra-Trinitarian relations can be so fundamentally different from God's essence that the former are fully communicable while the latter is totally incommunicable.

Meyendorff's account of the essence-energy distinction also makes it difficult to infer the unity of the essence from the unity of the energies. As Meyendorff correctly notes, the Greek fathers argued that the fundamental oneness of the acts of the Father, the Son, and the Spirit proves that they share one and the same nature.[179] For example, according to Athanasius and the Cappadocians, if the Father, the Son, and the Spirit are one in performing such activities as creation, sanctification, illumination, and comforting, they must necessarily also be one in nature. This argument of identity seems to be based on the premise that what characterizes an activity also characterizes the nature from which the activity flows.[180] The activities of the Father, the Son, and the Spirit are not alien to their essence, but flow from it. However, the argument loses its strength if the relation between essence and energy is indefinite. Meyendorff's real distinction between essence and energy, therefore, hardly permits him to deduce consubstantiality from conenergiality.[181]

Although Meyendorff asserts that God's essence and energies are not two entities, it is difficult to understand how one and the same entity can

Redeemer, and Sanctifier," as has been suggested by those theologians who are uneasy with traditional biblical names and look for more inclusive language about the persons of the Trinity.

179. Meyendorff, *Byzantine Theology*, 185. See also Meyendorff, *Christ in Eastern Christian Thought*, 144; Meyendorff, "Holy Trinity," 25.

180. Hart rightly states: "Logically, if the divine energies are genuine *manifestations* of God, however limited, then whatever names apply to the energies also necessarily apply to the essence, even if only defectively, immeasurably remotely, incomprehensibly, and 'improperly'" ("Hidden and the Manifest," 212).

181. In order to illustrate their understanding of the relation between essence and energies, Palamas and his followers frequently alluded to the metaphor of the sun, representing God's essence, and its rays, which represent the communicable and participable energies. Meyendorff agrees that this analogy is appropriate and emphasizes that it was a commonplace of the Greek patristic tradition. However, it is not clear how this metaphor strengthens the Palamite point. While it is true, of course, that we do not know the sun directly, it is equally true that the rays communicate some knowledge of the sun rather than leaving us totally ignorant about it. The metaphor of the sun and its rays fits well in analogical reasoning (which Meyendorff seeks to escape), because the properties of heat and light communicated by the rays presuppose that the sun itself possesses these properties, albeit in a different measure—with greater temperature and luminosity. Thus, the metaphor illustrates that while we do not know God's essence directly, we do know it in some measure based on its operations.

be totally incommunicable and wholly communicable at the same time. The denial of the existence of two entities becomes even more problematic in view of Meyendorff's claims that "God manifests himself *outside* his unknowable essence."[182] What he means is that God's essence is not involved in the revelation of God. As Milbank argues, the Palamite position "suggests a literally regional reserve beyond any communication," which means that "that which is communicated is turned into too literal a part of God."[183] Energies are almost *spatially* different from essence, which is, so to speak, left behind in God's ecstatic movement toward creatures. The wedge between essence and energies, driven by such statements, becomes even more obvious when Meyendorff elsewhere identifies the "outside" of God's essence with creation.[184] Since the essence is defined as "an unknowable entity," the knowable mode of God's being seems still to be another *entity*—not necessarily self-standing or diminished but still "quite distinct" from the *unknowable* entity.[185]

Whether the two modes in God can be designated as two distinct entities or not, the choice of terms does not change the fact that in Meyendorff's theology an impenetrable wall exists between God's essence and his energies. If energies stand for what is *wholly* communicable in God and essence for that which is *wholly* incommunicable, one cannot escape the conclusion that they are *wholly* distinct from each other. Meyendorff does not show how these two wholly distinct modes are united, apart from embracing them under the concept of God's being. Presented as two modes within a single concept, however, God's essence and energy remain isolated from each other without any interpenetration. It is this lack of ontological continuity between essence and energies that I see as the greatest problem in Meyendorff's theology.[186] The problem would not be so significant—and the

182. Meyendorff, *Study of Gregory Palamas*, 216, emphasis added; see also Meyendorff, *Byzantine Theology*, 27.

183. Milbank, "Christianity and Platonism," 201.

184. "The divine energies represent God's existence, His outpouring love *outside* of His essence, i.e., in creation" (Meyendorff, "Holy Trinity," 34, emphasis original). See also Meyendorff, *Study of Gregory Palamas*, 223.

185. Meyendorff, *Study of Gregory Palamas*, 216, 231.Meyendorff also does not explain how the idea that energies are outside the essence can be reconciled with the existence of *internal* energy.

186. Rowan Williams describes this problem as follows: "What Meyendorff apparently does not understand is that it is no answer ... to say that God's *ousia* is immutable and His

contrast with Bavinck would be less poignant—if Meyendorff interpreted God's energies in an analogical sense as designating God's activities, which, on the one hand, bring us into communion with God without transgressing the Creator-creature boundary and, on the other hand, do not leave God's essence wholly unknowable, but disclose it to us without violating its incomprehensibility. Reinterpreting the essence-energy distinction along these lines would be a promising contribution to the dialogue between the Orthodox and Reformed traditions.

Conclusion

Early Christianity unanimously asserted that knowledge of God is attainable by looking hard at Jesus Christ.[187] One can see God the Father in Christ because Jesus is one with the Father. Later theologians expressed the ground for this oneness in the concept of consubstantiality. Jesus does not need to reveal God by speaking of him in the third person; rather, he can reveal God by disclosing in himself—in his powerful words, mighty works, and humble service—that which he holds in common with the Father and Spirit: divine character, divine attributes, divine *essence*. This essence, however, is infinite and far transcends human perception. Therefore, though knowable to a certain extent, God always remains beyond the grasp of human comprehension.

Both Bavinck and Meyendorff seek to do equal justice to God's transcendence and his condescendence. Emphasizing God's otherness, both theologians assert—albeit with different motivation, assumptions, emphasis, and reasoning—that God in his essence is unknowable. The assumption of this assertion is that if we want to emphasize the mysteriousness of God, we must affirm his unknowability (namely, the unknowability of his essence) in the strongest terms. If we want to somehow temper the

energeiai mutable, as this drives a very considerable wedge between the two terms: what is true of one 'mode' or aspect of God is *not* true of another. The unity of God is far more gravely imperilled by this than any Palamite or neo-Palamite seems to have grasped; it is the purest Neoplatonism, an affirmation of two *wholly* distinct orders of reality in God. ... Since the second and inferior order exists (strictly) only as a means of participation for yet further orders, we are faced with the prospect of two eternal realities, God *in se* and God as participated by creatures" ("Philosophical Structures," 38, emphasis original).

187. N. T. Wright, "Christian Origins and the Question of God," in *Engaging the Doctrine of God: Contemporary Protestant Perspectives*, ed. Bruce L. McCormack (Grand Rapids: Baker Academic, 2008), 21.

Reformed obsession with knowledge, or if we want to somehow restrict the Orthodox aspiration to the closest union with God, we must proclaim God's essence to be completely unknowable, imparticipable, and inaccessible. I am not convinced, however, that such assertion serves its purpose. The problem is that if we argue that God's essence is unknowable, then it appears to collapse into a category devoid of any discernible content for us. If the essence is unknowable, we cannot say anything about it, and thus we cannot meaningfully use it in theology. If so, we focus exclusively on that which is actually revealed and communicated, and tend to clearly demarcate that which is revealed from that which is not. While the Reformed focus on what is revealed and the Orthodox on what is communicable in God, God's mystery drops out of theological discourse.

As explained above, the better approach in my view is to say that God's essence is knowable from what God has revealed to us, but only to a very limited extent. We are constantly reminded then that whatever attribute we apply to God based on his revelation, he infinitely surpasses it. But while God is always more than we can possibly know or imagine, this more is not inconsistent with what he has revealed to us. That said, I recognize the validity of Bavinck's and Meyendorff's concerns and their desire to follow well-established Christian tradition in this regard. By denying knowledge of God as to his essence, Bavinck emphasizes our inability to have perfect knowledge of God and our epistemological dependence on God's revelation. He also clearly identifies God's attributes with his essence and admits their knowability, which demonstrates that he does not remain agnostic concerning God's inner character and does not treat his essence as an entity devoid of properties. Meyendorff's assertion of the utter unknowability of God's essence is more marked and fits better with his overall theological system, although he is not perfectly consistent either, especially when speaking of God's *essential* properties. Meyendorff's motivation is also understandable: given his high view of humanity's union with God, the refusal to admit any communicability of God's essence reflects his commendable desire to avoid a complete melding of God and humanity.

Although both Bavinck and Meyendorff claim that union with God is at the heart of the Christian faith, they diverge on many points in formulating an ontology of divine/human communion. Bavinck's understanding of salvific participation in the divine nature is not clear—primarily because he focuses more on dispelling distortions of this New Testament idea rather than on explaining its meaning. Furthermore, his cosmological interest in the Logos as the bearer of the world/idea and in God's eternal decrees and thoughts runs the risk of overshadowing the actual history of salvation and the centrality of the resurrected, eschatological Christ. By placing an even greater emphasis on Jesus Christ, rather than focusing on the preexisting Logos, Bavinck would have reinforced his main biblical intuition: we obtain knowledge of God through creaturely revelation, of which the focal point is Jesus Christ. Meyendorff explains his view on participation in God with more clarity and detail. However, participation in God, at least in its highest form, becomes in his theology indistinguishable from the closest interpenetration of human and divine energies, owing to his realistic exegesis and emphasis on the mystical oneness of God and humanity. To be sure, this does not compromise God's transcendence, since Meyendorff argues that humans can never participate in the divine *essence*. However, Meyendorff's insistence that the vision of God and communion with him require transcending the limitations of created nature lacks scriptural support and goes beyond early patristic accounts of participation. Furthermore, Meyendorff's skepticism regarding human knowledge and language as applied to union with God in his energies downplays the significance of the cognitive and verbal content of revelation.

Both Bavinck and Meyendorff maintain that the twofold claim of God being transcendent and yet deeply involved in the world does not lead to a division in God's being. Although eclectic in his use of the preceding tradition, Bavinck holds to a strong doctrine of divine simplicity when he identifies God's essence not only with his attributes but also with his will as actually realized. However, affirming the contingency and nonnecessity of the world, he differentiates between God's necessary will toward himself and his free will toward creatures. It remains unclear how this distinction can be reconciled with the identification of God's will as a whole with his essence and with Bavinck's persuasion that God wills himself and his creatures with one and the same simple act. Meyendorff clearly rejects the identification of God's essence with his attributes or will, and posits a real distinction between God's essence and energies. What is more, he argues that in his energies God is wholly present and manifested, while in his essence he remains absolutely transcendent and totally unmanifested.

While this approach shows how God acts freely in the world, it does not explain how God can be totally incommunicable and wholly communicable at the same time. Although Meyendorff clearly asserts the inseparability of God's essence and energies, his case would be more compelling if he demonstrated particular ways in which these two modes of God's being are united.

The difficulties that Bavinck and Meyendorff have in explaining the relation between God's hiddenness and his revelation demonstrate the weakness of our logical and linguistic constructions. Bavinck explicitly recognizes the problem of doing equal justice to God's absoluteness and his nearness and likeness to us, while Meyendorff even suggests that God's unknowability in his nature and his full revelation in Christ are two logically incompatible truths. In the final analysis, the relation between God's hiddenness and revelation remains a mystery—not in the sense that it is completely inexpressible and one must remain silent about it, but in the sense that any theological explanation that seeks to understand and describe it will fall short of complete clarification. This mystery, however, should be embraced for its ability to humble us, which may lead us to greater amazement and admiration. As Gregory of Nazianzus notes, God draws us to himself by means of that which is knowable in him, whereas he uses that which is unknowable in him to excite in us yet greater wonder, desire, and thirst.[188]

188. Gregory of Nazianzus, *Oration* 38, 7 (*PG* 36:317).

BIBLIOGRAPHY

—

PRIMARY SOURCES

The following primary sources are arranged chronologically in accordance with their date of publication.

Herman Bavinck

"De hedendaagsche wereldbeschouwing." *De Vrije Kerk* 9 (1883): 435–61.

De wetenschap der H. Godgeleerdheid: Rede ter aanvaarding van het leeraarsambt aan de Theologische School te Kampen, uitgesproken den 10 jan. 1883. Kampen: Zalsman, 1883.

"Het dualisme in de Theologie." *De Vrije Kerk* 13 (1887): 11–39.

"De theologie van Albrecht Ritschl." *Theologische Studiën* 6 (1888): 369–403.

"Calvinistisch en Gereformeerd." *De Vrije Kerk* 19 (1893): 49–71.

"The Future of Calvinism." Translated by Geerhardus Vos. *PRR* 5 (1894): 1–24.

Beginselen der Psychologie. Kampen: Bos, 1897.

Godsdienst en Godgeleerdheid: Rede gehouden bij de aanvaarding van het hoogleeraarsambt in de Theologie aan de Vrije Universiteit te Amsterdam op woensdag 17 december 1902. Wageningen: Vada, 1902.

Christelijke wereldbeschouwing: Rede bij de overdacht van het Rectoraat aan de Vrije Universiteit te Amsterdam op 20 October 1904. Kampen: Bos, 1904.

"Calvin and Common Grace." Translated by Geerhardus Vos. *PTR* 7 (1909): 437–65.

Magnalia Dei: Onderwijzing in de christelijke religie naar gereformeerde belijdenis. Kampen: Kok, 1909.

The Philosophy of Revelation. New York: Longmans & Green, 1909.

*Modernisme en Orthodoxie: Rede gehouden bij de overdracht van het rectoraat aan de

Vrije Universiteit op 20 October 1911. Kampen: Kok, 1911.

Het Christendom. Groote Godsdiensten 2.7. Baarn: Hollandia, 1912.

Handleiding bij het onderwijs in den christelijken godsdienst. Kampen: Kok, 1913.

Mental, Religious and Social Forces in the Netherlands. A General View of the Netherlands 17. The Hague: Commercial Department of the Netherlands Ministry of Agriculture, Industry, and Commerce, 1915.

Kennis en Leven. Opstellen en artikelen uit vroegere Jaren. Kampen: Kok, 1922.

Our Reasonable Faith. Translated by Henry Zylstra. Grand Rapids: Baker Book House, 1977.

"The Problem of War." Translated by Stephen Voorwinde. *Banner of Truth* (July-August 1977): 46–53.

The Certainty of Faith. Translated by Harry der Nederlanden. St. Catharines, ON: Paideia, 1980.

"The Catholicity of Christianity and the Church." Translated by John Bolt. *CTJ* 27 (1992): 220–51.

"Foreword to the First Edition (Volume 1) of the *Gereformeerde Dogmatiek*." Translated by John Bolt. *CTJ* 45 (2010): 9–10.

"The Theology of Albrecht Ritschl." Translated by John Bolt. *BavRev* 3 (2012): 123–63.

"Modernism and Orthodoxy." Translated by Bruce Pass. *BavRev* 7 (2016): 68–114.

John Meyendorff

"Doctrine of Grace in St. Gregory Palamas." *SVTQ* 2 (1954): 17–26.

"Istoricheskoe znachenie ucheniya sv. Grigoriya Palamy" [The Historical Significance of the Teaching of St. Gregory Palamas]. *Vestnik Russkogo Studencheskogo Khristianskogo Dvizheniya [Bulletin of the Russian Student Christian Movement]* 46 (1957): 3–9.

"Le dogme eucharistique dans les controverses théologiques du XIVe siècle." Γρηγόροις ὁ Παλαμᾶς 42 (1959): 93–100.

Introduction à l'étude de Grégoire Palamas. Paris: Éditions du Seuil, 1959.

The Orthodox Church: Its Past and Its Role in the World Today. New York: Pantheon, 1962.

"The Significance of the Reformation in the History of Christendom." *Ecumenical Review* 14 (1964): 164–79.

"A Christian Theology of Creation." In *John XXIII Lectures*. Vol. 1, *Byzantine Christian Heritage*, 59–67. Fordham, NY: Fordham University Press, 1966.

"Philosophy, Theology, Palamism and Secular Christianity [Reply to P. Sherwood]." *SVTQ* 10 (1966): 203–8.

"Review of *Symvolai eis ten peri Nestoriou erevran (Contributions to the Study of Nestorius)*, by G. S. Bebis." *SVTQ* 10 (1966): 214–15.

"Justinian, the Empire and the Church." *Dumbarton Oaks Papers* 22 (1968): 45–60.

Byzantine Hesychasm: Historical, Theological and Social Problems. London: Variorum Reprints, 1974.

"Les débuts de la controverse hésyhaste." In *Byzantine Hesychasm*, 87–120.

"Notes sur l'influence dionysienne en Orient." In *Byzantine Hesychasm*, 547–52.

"O vizantiyskom isikhazme i ego roli v kul'turnom i istoricheskom razvitii Vostochnoy Evropy v XIV v" [Byzantine Hesychasm and Its Role in the Cultural and Historical Development of the Eastern Europe in the XIV Century]. In *Trudy otdela drevnerusskoy literatury* [The Works of the Department of Old Russian Literature], 291–305. Leningrad: Nauka, 1974.

A Study of Gregory Palamas. Translated by George Lawrence. 2nd ed. 1974. Reprint, Crestwood, NY: St Vladimir's Seminary Press, 1998.

"Le thème du 'retour en soi' dans la doctrine palamite du XIVe siècle." In *Byzantine Hesychasm*, 188–206.

Christ in Eastern Christian Thought. Crestwood, NY: St Vladimir's Seminary Press, 1975.

"The Holy Trinity in Palamite Theology." In *Trinitarian Theology East and West: St Thomas Aquinas–St Gregory Palamas*, edited by M. A. Fahey and J. Meyendorff, 25–43. Brookline, MA: Holy Cross Orthodox Press, 1977.

Living Tradition: Orthodox Witness in the Contemporary World. Crestwood, NY: St Vladimir's Seminary Press, 1978.

"The Time of Holy Saturday." In *Orthodox Synthesis: The Unity of Theological Thought*, edited by J. Allen, 51–63. Crestwood, NY: St Vladimir's Seminary Press, 1981.

The Byzantine Legacy in the Orthodox Church. Crestwood, NY: St Vladimir's Seminary Press, 1982.

Catholicity and the Church. Crestwood, NY: St Vladimir's Seminary Press, 1983.

"Creation in the History of Orthodox Theology." *SVTQ* 27 (1983): 27–37.

"Byzantium as Center of Theological Thought in the Christian East." In *Schools of Thought in the Christian Tradition*, edited by P. Henry, 65–74. Philadelphia: Fortress, 1984.

"Palamas (Grégoire), théologien byzantin, auteur spirituel, archevêque de Thessalonique, 1296-1359." *Dictionnaire de Spiritualité* 12 (1984): 81–107.

"Reply to Jürgen Moltmann's 'The Unity of the Triune God.'" *SVTQ* 28 (1984): 183–88.

"Christ as Savior in the East." In *Christian Spirituality: Origins to the Twelfth Century*, edited by Bernard McGinn, John Meyendorff, and Jean Leclercq, 231–51. New York: Crossroad, 1985.

"Review of *Biblical and Liturgical Symbols within the Pseudo-Dionysius Synthesis* by Paul Rorem." *SVTQ* 29 (1985): 364–65.

"The Mediterranean World in the Thirteenth Century Theology: East and West." In *The 17th International Byzantine Congress: Major Papers*, 669–82. New Rochelle, NY: Caratzas, 1986.

Byzantine Theology: Historical Trends and Doctrinal Themes. Fordham, NY: Fordham University Press, 1987.

"Christ's Humanity: The Paschal Mystery." *SVTQ* 31 (1987): 5–40.

"Theological Education in the Patristic and Byzantine Eras and Its Lessons for Today." *SVTQ* 31 (1987): 197–213.

"Mount Athos in the Fourteenth Century: Spiritual and Intellectual Legacy." *Dumbarton Oaks Papers* 42 (1988): 157–65.

"New Life in Christ: Salvation in Orthodox Theology." *Theological Studies* 50 (1989): 481–99.

"Theosis in the Eastern Christian Tradition." In *Christian Spirituality: Post-Reformation and Modern*, edited by Louis Dupré and Don E. Saliers, 470–76. New York: Crossroad, 1989.

"A Life Worth Living." In *Liturgy and Tradition: Theological Reflections of Alexander Schmemann*, edited by Thomas Fisch, 145–54. Crestwood, NY: St Vladimir's Seminary Press, 1990.

"The Nicene Creed: Uniting or Dividing Confession?" In *Faith to Creed: Ecumenical Perspectives on the Affirmation of the Apostolic Faith in the Fourth Century*, edited by S. M. Heim, 1–19. Grand Rapids: Eerdmans, 1991.

"Humanity: 'Old' and 'New' – Anthropological Considerations." In *Salvation in Christ: A Lutheran-Orthodox Dialogue*, edited by John Meyendorff and Robert Tobias, 59–66. Minneapolis: Augsburg, 1992.

"Une théologie mystique." *Christus: La spiritualité de l'Orient chrétien* 39, no. 155 (1992): 286–93.

"Continuities and Discontinuities in Byzantine Religious Thought." *Dumbarton Oaks Papers* 47 (1993): 69–81.

Pravoslavie i sovremennyy mir [Orthodoxy and the Contemporary World]. Minsk: Luchi Sofii, 1995.

Rome, Constantinople, Moscow: Historical and Theological Studies. Crestwood, NY: St Vladimir's Seminary Press, 1996.

Pravoslavie v sovremennom mire [Orthodoxy in the Modern World]. Moscow: Put', 1997.

St Gregory Palamas and Orthodox Spirituality. Translated by Adele Fiske. Crestwood, NY: St Vladimir's Seminary Press, 1998.

Vvedenie v svyatootecheskoe bogoslovie [Introduction to Patristic Theology]. 4th ed. Kiev: Khram prp. Agapita Pecherskogo, 2002.

Paskhal'naya tayna: Stat'i po bogosloviyu [Paschal Mystery: Theological Articles]. Moscow: Eksmo, 2013.

Secondary Sources

Agachi, Adrian. *The Neo-Palamite Synthesis of Father Dumitru Stăniloae*. Newcastle upon Tyne: Cambridge Scholars, 2013.

"Agreed Statement on the Holy Trinity." In vol. 2 of *Theological Dialogue between Orthodox and Reformed Churches*, edited by Thomas F. Torrance, 219–26.

Edinburgh: Scottish Academic, 1993.

Ambrose. *Joseph*. In *Seven Exegetical Works*. Translated by Michael P. McHugh. Fathers of the Church 65. Washington, DC: Catholic University of America Press, 1982.

Anastos, Thomas L. "Gregory Palamas' Radicalization of the Essence, Energies, and Hypostasis Model of God." *The Greek Orthodox Theological Review* 38 (1993): 335–49.

Asselt, Willem J. van. "The Fundamental Meaning of Theology: Archetypal and Ectypal Theology in Seventeenth-Century Reformed Thought." *WTJ* 64 (2002): 319–35.

Athanasius. *Ad Serapionem*. In *The Letters of Saint Athanasius Concerning the Holy Spirit*. Translated by C. R. B. Shapland. New York: Philosophical Library, 1951.

———. *Four Discourses against the Arians*. *NPNF*[2] 4.

———. *On the Councils of Ariminum and Seleucia*. In *Select Library*. *NPNF*[2] 4.

Athanasopoulos, Constantinos. "St. Gregory Palamas as the Response of Orthodox Mystical Theology to (Neo)Platonist and Aristotelian Metaphysics." In Athanasopoulos and Schneider, *Divine Essence and Divine Energies*, 50–67.

Athanasopoulos, Constantinos, and Christoph Schneider, eds. *Divine Essence and Divine Energies: Ecumenical Reflections on the Presence of God in Eastern Orthodoxy*. Cambridge: Clarke, 2013.

Barnes, Michel René. "De Régnon Reconsidered." *Augustinian Studies* 26 (1995): 51–79.

———. "Rereading Augustine's Theology of the Trinity." In *The Trinity: An Interdisciplinary Symposium on Trinity*, edited by Stephen T. Davis, Daniel Kendall, SJ, and Gerald O'Collins, SJ, 145–76. Oxford: Oxford University Press, 1999.

Barth, Karl. *The Göttingen Dogmatics: Instruction in the Christian Religion*. Translated by Geoffrey W. Bromiley. Grand Rapids: Eerdmans, 1991.

Basil of Caesarea. *Against Eunomius*. Translated by Mark DelCogliano and Andrew Radde-Gallwitz. Fathers of the Church 122. Washington, DC: Catholic University of America Press, 2011.

———. *Epistle 234*. *NPNF*² 8.

Beasley-Murray, George R. *John*. Word Biblical Commentary 36. Dallas: Word, 2002.

Beck, Andreas J. "Gisbertus Voetius (1589–1676): Basic Features of His Doctrine of God." In Van Asselt and Dekker, *Reformation and Scholasticism*, 205–26.

Beeley, Christopher A. *Gregory of Nazianzus on the Trinity and the Knowledge of God: In Your Light We Shall See Light*. Oxford: Oxford University Press, 2008.

Behr, John. "Calling upon God the Father: Augustine and the Legacy of Nicea." In Demacopoulos and Papanikolaou, *Orthodox Readings of Augustine*, 153–54.

———. *The Nicene Faith*. Part 2. Crestwood, NY: St Vladimir's Seminary Press, 2004.

Belt, Hendrik van den. "Autopistia: The Self-Convincing Authority of Scripture in Reformed Theology." PhD diss., Leiden University, 2006.

Berkouwer, Gerrit C. *Divine Election*. Translated by Hugo Bekker. Grand Rapids: Eerdmans, 1960.

———. *A Half Century of Theology: Movements and Motives*. Edited and translated by Lewis B. Smedes. Grand Rapids: Eerdmans, 1977.

———. *Sin*. Translated by Philip C. Holtrop. Grand Rapids: Eerdmans, 1971.

Bernard, John Henry. *A Critical and Exegetical Commentary on the Gospel according to St. John*. Vol. 2. New York: Scribner's Sons, 1929.

Billings, J. Todd. *Calvin, Participation, and the Gift: The Activity of Believers in Union with Christ*. Oxford: Oxford University Press, 2007.

———. "John Calvin: United to God through Christ." In Christensen and Wittung, *Partakers of the Divine Nature*, 200–18.

———. *Union with Christ: Reframing Theology and Ministry for the Church*. Grand Rapids: Baker Academic, 2011.

Biriukov, Dmitry. "On the Topic of Participation in the Divine Essence according to St Symeon the New Theologian in the Patristic Context." *Scrinium* 11 (2015): 295–305.

Boersma, Hans. *Embodiment and Virtue in Gregory of Nyssa: An Anagogical Approach*. Oxford: Oxford University Press, 2013.

———. *Seeing God: The Beatific Vision in Christian Tradition*. Grand Rapids: Eerdmans, 2018.

Bolt, John. "Editor's Introduction." In Bavinck, *RD* 1:11–19.

———. "Grand Rapids between Kampen and Amsterdam: Herman Bavinck's Reception and Influence in North America." *CTJ* 38 (2003): 263–80.

———. "A Pearl and a Leaven." *CTJ* 45 (2010): 7–8.

Bradshaw, David. *Aristotle East and West: Metaphysics and the Division of Christendom*. Cambridge: Cambridge University Press, 2004.

———. "Augustine the Metaphysician." In Demacopoulos and Papanikolaou, *Orthodox Readings of Augustine*, 227–51.

———. "The Concept of the Divine Energies." *Philosophy and Theology* 18 (2006): 93–120.

———. "In Defence of the Essence/Energies Distinction: A Reply to Critics." In Athanasopoulos and Schneider, *Divine Essence and Divine Energies*, 256–73.

———. "The Divine Energies in the New Testament." *SVTQ* 50 (2006): 189–223.

———. "The Divine Glory and the Divine Energies." *Faith and Philosophy* 23 (2006): 279–98.

Bratt, James D. "The Context of Herman Bavinck's Stone Lectures: Culture and Politics in 1908." *BavRev* 1 (2010): 4–24.

———. *Dutch Calvinism in Modern America: A History of a Conservative Subculture*. Grand Rapids: Eerdmans, 1984.

Bremmer, Rolf Hendrik. *Herman Bavinck als Dogmaticus*. Kampen: Kok, 1961.

Brouwer, Arie. *Ecumenical Testimony*. Grand Rapids: Eerdmans, 1991.

Bulgakov, Sergei. *The Lamb of God*. Translated by Boris Jakim. Grand Rapids: Eerdmans, 2008.

———. *Sophia, the Wisdom of God: An Outline of Sophiology*. Translated by Patrick Thompson, O. Fielding Clarke, and Xenia Braikevitc. Hudson, NY: Lindisfarne, 1993.

———. *Unfading Light: Contemplations and Speculations*. Translated by Thomas Allan Smith. Grand Rapids: Eerdmans, 2012.

Burger, Hans. *Being in Christ: A Biblical and Systematic Investigation in a Reformed Perspective*. Eugene, OR: Wipf & Stock, 2009.

———. "Christologisch én pneumatologisch: Herman Bavinck en de relatie tussen schriftleer en christologie." In *Weergaloze kennis: Opstellen over Jezus Christus, Openbaring en Schrift, Katholiciteit en Kerk aangeboden aan prof. dr. Barend Kamphuis*, edited by Ad de Bruijne, Hans Burger, and Dolf te Velde, 126–35. Zoetermeer: Boekencentrum, 2015.

———. "God's Character and the Plot of the Bible." In *Reading and Listening: Meeting One God in Many Texts*, edited by Jaap Dekker and Gert Kwakkel, 239–47. Bergambacht: 2VM, 2018.

Butner, D. Glenn. "For and against de Régnon." *IJST* 17 (2015): 399–412.

Calvin, John. *Commentaries on the Catholic Epistles*. Translated and edited by John Owen. Grand Rapids: Baker, 1996.

———. *Commentary on the Gospel according to John*. Translated by William Pringle. Grand Rapids: Eerdmans, 1949.

———. *Institutes of the Christian Religion*. Edited by John T. McNeill. Translated by Ford Lewis Battles. Philadelphia: Westminster, 1960.

Canlis, Julie. "Calvin, Osiander and Participation in God." *IJST* 6 (2004): 169–84.

———. *Calvin's Ladder: A Spiritual Theology of Ascent and Ascension*. Grand Rapids: Eerdmans, 2010.

Carey, Patrick W., and Joseph T. Lienhard. *Biographical Dictionary of Christian Theologians*. Westport, CT: Greenwood, 2000.

Carson, Donald A. *The Gospel according to John*. Grand Rapids: Eerdmans, 1991.

Chadwick, Henry. Foreword to Nassif, *New Perspectives*, ix–x.

Christensen, Michael J., and Jeffery A. Wittung, eds. *Partakers of the Divine Nature: The History and Development of Deification in the Christian Traditions*. Grand Rapids: Baker Academic, 2007.

Clark, Gordon H. , "The Answer to a Complaint against Several Actions and Decisions of the Presbytery of Philadelphia Taken in a Special Meeting Held on July 7, 1944." Unpublished defense paper, Philadelphia Orthodox Presbyterian Church.

———. *God's Hammer: The Bible and Its Critics*. Jefferson, MD: Trinity Foundation, 1987.

Clendenin, Daniel B. *Eastern Orthodox Christianity: A Western Perspective*. 2nd ed. Grand Rapids: Baker Academic, 2003.

Clouser, Roy. "Pancreation Lost: The Fall of Theology." In Athanasopoulos and Schneider, *Divine Essence and Divine Energies*, 68–95.

Coffey, David. *Deus Trinitas: The Doctrine of the Triune God*. Oxford: Oxford University Press, 1999.

———. "The Palamite Doctrine of God: A New Perspective." *SVTQ* 32 (1988): 329–58.

———. "Trinity." In *The Cambridge Companion to Karl Rahner*, edited by Declan Marmion, 98–111. Cambridge: Cambridge University Press, 2005.

Cvetković, Vladimir. "T. F. Torrance as Interpreter of St. Athanasius." In *T. F. Torrance and Eastern Orthodoxy: Theology in Reconciliation*, edited by Matthew Baker and Todd Speidell, 59–93. Eugene, OR: Wipf & Stock, 2015.

Demetracopoulos, John A. *Is Gregory Palamas an Existentialist? The Restoration of the True Meaning of His Comment on Exodus 3,14: "Ἐγώ εἰμι ὁ ὤν."* Athens: Parousia, 1996.

———. "Palamas Transformed: Palamite Interpretations of the Distinction between God's 'Essence' and 'Energies' in Late Byzantium." In *Greeks, Latins, and Intellectual History 1204–1500*, edited by Martin Hinterberger and Chris Schabel, 263–372. Leuven: Peeters, 2011.

DeVries, Dawn. "The Living God: The Problem of Divine Personality in Reformed Theology." In *Reformed Theology for the Third Christian Millennium*, edited by Brian Albert Gerrish, 61–81. Louisville: Westminster John Knox, 2003.

Dolezal, James E. *God without Parts: Divine Simplicity and the Metaphysics of God's Absoluteness*. Eugene, OR: Pickwick, 2011.

Donnelly, John Patrick. "Calvinist Thomism." *Viator* 7 (1976): 441–55.

Dosker, Henry Elias. "Herman Bavinck." *PTR* 20 (1922): 448–64.

Duby, Steven J. "Working with the Grain of Nature: Epistemic Underpinnings for Christian Witness in the Theology of Herman Bavinck." *BavRev* 3 (2012): 60–84.

Dulles, Avery Cardinal. *Church and Society: The Laurence J. McGinley Lectures, 1988–2007*. Fordham, NY: Fordham University Press, 2008.

Echeverría, Eduardo J. "The Reformed Objection to Natural Theology: A Catholic Response to Herman Bavinck." *CTJ* 45 (2010): 87–116.

Ecumenical Patriarch of Constantinople Bartholomew I. "Pastoral Reflections." In Nassif, *New Perspectives*, 3–4.

Eglinton, James. "Bavinck's Organic Motif: Questions Seeking Answers" *CTJ* 45 (2010): 51–71.

———. "How Many Herman Bavincks? De Gemeene Genade and the 'Two Bavincks' Hypothesis." In *The Kuyper Center Review*, vol. 2, *Revelation and Common Grace*, 279–301. Grand Rapids: Eerdmans, 2011.

———. *Trinity and Organism*. Edinburgh: T&T Clark, 2012.

Engelsma, David J. "Bavinck: The Man and His Theology." *Protestant Reformed Theological Journal* 46 (2012): 3–43.

Fairbairn, Donald. *Eastern Orthodoxy through Western Eyes*. Louisville: Westminster John Knox, 2002.

Finch, Jeffrey David. "Sanctity as Participation in the Divine Nature according to the Ante-Nicene Eastern Fathers, Considered in the Light of Palamism." PhD diss., Drew University, 2002.

Florovsky, Georges. *The Collected Works of Georges Florovsky*. 14 vols. Edited by Richard Haugh. Belmont, MA: Nordland, 1974–1989.

———. "The Quest for Christian Unity and the Orthodox Church." In Florovsky, *Collected Works*, 13:136–44.

———. "Patristic Theology and the Ethos of the Orthodox Church." In Florovsky, *Collected Works*, 4:11–30.

———. "Patristics and Modern Theology." In *Procès-verbaux du Premier Congrès de Théologie Orthodoxe à Athènes*, edited by Hamilcar S. Alivisatos, 238–42. Athènes: Pyrsos, 1939.

———. "St. Gregory Palamas and the Tradition of the Fathers." In Florovsky, *Collected Works*, 1:105–20.

———. "Western Influences in Russian Theology." In Florovsky, *Collected Works*, 4:157–82.

Frame, John M. *The Doctrine of God*. Phillipsburg, NJ: Presbyterian & Reformed, 2002.

———. *The Doctrine of the Knowledge of God*. Phillipsburg, NJ: Presbyterian & Reformed, 1987.

———. *Systematic Theology: An Introduction to Christian Belief*. Phillipsburg, NJ: Presbyterian & Reformed, 2013.

Gavrilyuk, Paul. *Georges Florovsky and the Russian Religious Renaissance*. Oxford: Oxford University Press, 2014.

———. "The Reception of Dionysius in Twentieth-Century Eastern Orthodoxy." In *Re-thinking Dionysius the Areopagite*, edited by Sarah Coakley and Charles Stang, 182–90. Oxford: Wiley and Sons, 2011.

Gelderen, Jan van, and Willem Velema. *Concise Reformed Dogmatics*. Phillipsburg, NJ: Presbyterian & Reformed, 2008.

Gilson, Étienne. *Thomism: The Philosophy of Thomas Aquinas*. 6th ed. Translated by Laurence K. Shook and Armand A. Maurer. Toronto: Pontifical Institute of Mediaeval Studies, 2002.

Gleason, Ronald N. "The Centrality of the *Unio Mystica* in the Theology of Herman Bavinck." ThD diss., Westminster Theological Seminary, 2001.

Golitzin, Alexander. "Dionysius Areopagites in the Works of Saint Gregory Palamas: On the Question of a 'Christological Corrective' and Related Matters." *SVTQ* 46 (2002): 163–90.

Gootjes, Nicolaas H. "De Struktuur van Bavincks Gereformeerde Dogmatiek." *Radix* 16 (1990): 136–57.

Goris, Harm. "Thomism in Zanchi's Doctrine of God." In Van Asselt and Dekker, *Reformation and Scholasticism*, 121–39.

Gregory of Nazianzus. *Fourth Theological Oration (Oration 30)*. *NPNF*[2] 7.

Gregory of Nyssa. *Against Eunomius Book Three*. Translated by Stuart George Hall. In *Gregory of Nyssa: Contra Eunomium III; An English Version with Commentary and Supporting Studies*, edited by Johan Leemans and Matthieu Cassin, 42–233. Leiden: Brill, 2014.

———. *On the Beatitudes*. Translated by Stuart George Hall. In *Gregory of Nyssa: Homilies on the Beatitudes*, edited by Hubertus R. Drobner and Albert Viciano, 21–90. Leiden: Brill, 2000.

———. *On What It Means to Call Oneself a Christian*. In *Ascetical Works*. Translated by Virginia Woods Callahan. Fathers of the Church 58. Washington, DC: Catholic University of America Press, 1990.

———. *The Second Book against Eunomius*. Translated by Stuart George Hall. In *Gregory of Nyssa: Contra Eunomium II; An English Version with Supporting Studies*, edited by Lenka Karfíková, Scot Douglass, and Johannes Zachhuber, 59–201. Leiden: Brill, 2007.

Gunton, Colin. *Act and Being: Towards a Theology of the Divine Attributes*. London: SCM, 2002.

———. *Father, Son and Holy Spirit: Toward a Fully Trinitarian Theology*. London: T&T Clark, 2003.

———. "Persons and Particularity." In *The Theology of John Zizioulas: Personhood and the Church*, edited by Douglas H. Knight, 97–107. Burlington, VT: Ashgate, 2007.

Habets, Myk. "'Reformed Theosis?' A Response to Gannon Murphy." *Theology Today* 65 (2009): 489–98.

———. *Theosis in the Theology of Thomas Torrance*. Farnham, UK: Ashgate, 2009.

Halleux, André de. "Palamisme et scolastique: Exclusivisme dogmatique ou pluriformite theologique?" *Revue theologique de Louvain* 4 (1973): 409–42.

Harinck, George. "Herman Bavinck and Geerhardus Vos." *CTJ* 45 (2010): 18–31.

Hart, David Bentley. *The Beauty of the Infinite: The Aesthetics of Christian Truth*. Grand Rapids: Eerdmans, 2004.

———. "Foreword." In *Encounter between Eastern Orthodoxy and Radical Orthodoxy: Transfiguring the World through the Word*, edited by Adrian Pabst and Christoph Schneider, xi–xiv. Farnham, UK: Ashgate, 2009.

———. *The Hidden and the Manifest: Essays in Theology and Metaphysics*. Grand Rapids: Eerdmans, 2017.

———. "The Hidden and the Manifest: Metaphysics after Nicaea." In Demacopoulos and Papanikolaou, *Orthodox Readings of Augustine*, 191–226.

Hegel, Georg Wilhelm Friedrich. *Lectures on the Philosophy of Religion*. Vol. 1. London: Kegan Paul, Trench, Trübner, 1895.

Heideman, Eugene. *The Relation of Revelation and Reason in E. Brunner and H. Bavinck*. Assen: Van Gorcum, 1959.

Hendriksen, William. *Exposition of the Gospel according to John*. Vol. 2. Grand Rapids: Baker Book House, 1985.

"Herman Bavinck." *PTR* 6 (1908): 529–43.

Herrick, Jennifer A. *Does God Change? Reconciling the Immutable God with the God of Love*. Parkland, FL: Universal, 2003.

Hilary of Poitiers. *On the Trinity*. *NPNF*[2] 9.

Hopko, Thomas. "John Meyendorff." In *A New Handbook of Christian Theologians*, edited by Donald W. Musser and Joseph L. Price, 297–303. Nashville: Abingdon, 1996.

Horton, Michael. *The Christian Faith: A Systematic Theology for Pilgrims on the Way*. Grand Rapids: Zondervan, 2011.

———. *Covenant and Eschatology: The Divine Drama*. Louisville: Westminster John Knox, 2002.

———. *Covenant and Salvation: Union with Christ*. Louisville: Westminster John Knox, 2007.

———. *Lord and Servant: A Covenant Christology*. Louisville: Westminster John Knox, 2005.

———. *People and Place: A Covenant Ecclesiology*. Louisville: Westminster John Knox, 2008.

Houdret, Jean-Philippe. "Palamas et les Cappadociens." *Istina* 19 (1974): 260–71.

Huijgen, Arnold. *Divine Accommodation in John Calvin's Theology*. Göttingen: Vandenhoeck & Ruprecht, 2011.

Huttinga, Wolter. *Participation and Communicability: Herman Bavinck and John Milbank on the Relation between God and the World*. Amsterdam: Buijten en Schipperheijn, 2014.

Irenaeus. *Against Heresies*. *ANF* 1.

Jansen, Henry. "Relationality and the Concept of God." PhD diss., Free University, 1995.

Jenson, Robert. *Systematic Theology*. Vol. 1, *The Triune God*. Oxford: Oxford University Press, 2001.

———. *The Triune Identity: God according to the Gospel*. Philadelphia: Fortress, 1982.

John Chrysostom. *Commentary on St John the Apostle and Evangelist: Homilies 48–88*. Translated by Sister Thomas Aquinas Goggin. Fathers of the Church 41. Washington, DC: Catholic University of America Press, 1984.

———. *Commentary on the Psalms*. Translated by Robert Charles Hill. Brookline, MA: Holy Cross Orthodox Press, 1998.

———. *On the Incomprehensible Nature of God*. Translated by Paul W. Harkins. Fathers of the Church 72. Washington, DC: Catholic University of America Press, 1984.

John of Damascus. *Exact Exposition of the Orthodox Faith*. *NPNF*[2] 9.

Johnson, Keith E. *Rethinking the Trinity and Religious Pluralism: An Augustinian Assessment*. Downers Grove, IL: IVP Academic, 2011.

Jowers, Dennis W. *The Trinitarian Axiom of Karl Rahner: The Economic Trinity Is the Immanent Trinity and Vice Versa*. Lewiston, NY: Edwin Mellen, 2006.

Jugie, Martin. "Palamas, Gregoire." In *Dictionnaire de théologie catholique* 11.2, edited by Jean Michel Alfred Vacant et al., 1736–76. Paris: Librairie Letouzey et Ané, 1932.

Jüngel, Eberhard. "The Revelation of the Hiddenness of God: A Contribution to the Protestant Understanding of the Hiddenness of Divine Action." In *Theological Essays II*, 120–44. Translated by Arnold Neufeldt-Fast and John B. Webster. London: Bloomsbury T&T Clark, 2014.

Kamphuis, Barend. "Alles in alles: Rehabilitatie van het panentheïsme?" *Theologia Reformata* 48 (2005): 194–206.

———. "Chalcedon in Kampen." *Theologia Reformata* 48 (2005): 26–40.

———. "Herman Bavinck on Catholicity." *Mid-America Journal of Theology* 24 (2013): 97–104.

Kant, Immanuel. "Preface to the Second Edition." In *Critique of Pure Reason*. Translated by John M. D. Meiklejohn. London: Bell & Sons, 1901.

Kapriev, Georgi. *Philosophie in Byzanz*. Würzburg: Königshausen und Neumann, 2005.

Kasper, Walter. *The Petrine Ministry: Catholics and Orthodox in Dialogue; Academic Symposium Held at the Pontifical Council for Promoting Christian Unity*. Mahwah, NJ: Paulist, 2006.

Kharlamov, Vladimir. "Basil of Caesarea and the Cappadocians on the Distinction between Essence and Energies in God and Its Relevance to the Deification Theme." In *Theōsis: Deification in Christian Theology*, edited by Vladimir Kharlamov, 2:100–145. Cambridge: Clarke, 2012.

———. "Rhetorical Application of *Theosis* in Greek Patristic Theology." In Christensen and Wittung, *Partakers of the Divine Nature*, 115–31.

Klooster, Fred H. *The Incomprehensibility of God in the Orthodox Presbyterian Conflict*. Franeker: Wever, 1951.

Köstenberger, Andreas J. *John*. Baker Exegetical Commentary on the New Testament. Grand Rapids: Baker Academic, 2004.

Koutloumousianos, Chrysostom. *The One and the Three: Nature, Person and Triadic Monarchy in the Greek and Irish Patristic Tradition*. Cambridge: Clarke, 2015.

Krivoshein, Basil. "The Ascetic and Theological Teaching of Gregory Palamas." *Eastern Churches Quarterly* 3 (1938): 26–33, 71–84, 138–56, 193–214.

———. "Svyatoy Grigoriy Palama. Lichnost' i uchenie po nedavno opublikovannym materialam" [Saint Gregory Palamas. His Life and Teaching According to Recently Published Materials]. *Vestnik Russkogo Zapadno-evropeyskogo Patriarshego Ekzarkhata* [Bulletin of the Russian West-European Patriarchal Exarchate] 33–34 (1960): 101–14.

Kurtz, Johann Heinrich. *Lehrbuch der Kirchengeschichte*. Mitau: Aug. Neumann, 1849.

Kuyper, Abraham. *Encyclopaedie der Heilige Godgeleerdheid, Tweede Deel, Algemeen deel*. Kampen: Kok, 1909.

LaCugna, Catherine Mowry. *God for Us: The Trinity and Christian Life*. San Francisco: HarperCollins, 1991.

Larchet, Jean-Claude. *La Théologie des énergies divines: Des origines à saint Jean Damascène*. Paris: Cerf, 2010.

Lauer, Quentin. *Hegel's Concept of God*. Albany, NY: State University of New York Press, 1982.

Letham, Robert. *The Holy Trinity: In Scripture, History, Theology, and Worship*. Phillipsburg, NJ: Presbyterian & Reformed, 2004.

———. *Through Western Eyes: Eastern Orthodoxy, A Reformed Perspective*. Fearn, UK: Mentor, 2007.

Levering, Matthew. *Engaging the Doctrine of Creation*. Grand Rapids: Baker Academic, 2017.

Lossky, Vladimir. "Elements of 'Negative Theology' in the Thought of St. Augustine." *SVTQ* 21 (1977): 67–75.

———. *The Mystical Theology of the Eastern Church*. Translated by Members of the Fellowship of St. Alban and St. Sergius. London: Clarke, 1968.

———. "The Procession of the Holy Spirit in Orthodox Trinitarian Theology." In *Eastern Orthodox Theology: A Contemporary Reader*, edited by Daniel B. Clendenin, 163–82. Grand Rapids: Baker Academic, 2003.

———. "Spor o Sofii" [The Controversy over Sophia]. In *Stat'i raznykh let* [Articles of Various Years], 7–79. Moscow: Svyato-Vladimirskoe Bratstvo, 1996.

Loudovikos, Nikolaos. "Striving for Participation: Palamite Analogy as Dialogical Syn-energy and Thomist Analogy as Emanational Similitude." In Athanasopoulos and Schneider, *Divine Essence and Divine Energies*, 122–48.

Lourié, Basil. "Kommentarii" [Commentaries]. In *Zhizn' i trudy svyatitelya Grigoriya Palamy: Vvedenie v izuchenie* [The Life and Works of St Gregory Palamas: Introduction], by Ioann Meyendorf, 373–460. Saint Petersburg: Vizantinorossika, 1997.

Louth, Andrew. *Modern Orthodox Thinkers: From the Philokalia to the Present*. Downers Grove, IL: InterVarsity Press, 2015.

Luther, Martin. *The Bondage of the Will*. Translated by Henry Cole. London: Bensley, 1823.

MacLeod, Donald. "Bavinck's Prolegomena: Fresh Light on Amsterdam, Old Princeton, and Cornelius van Til." *WTJ* 68 (2006): 261–82.

———. "Herman Bavinck and the Basis of Christian Certainty." *Scottish Bulletin of Evangelical Theology* 29 (2011): 92–107.

Maritain, Jacques. *A Preface to Metaphysics: Seven Lectures on Being*. New York: Sheed & Ward, 1958.

Martzelos, Georgias. "The Significance of the Distinction between the Essence and Energies of God according to St. Basil the Great." In Athanasopoulos and Schneider, *Divine Essence and Divine Energies*, 149–57.

Mascall, Eric Lionel. *The Openness of Being: Natural Theology Today*. London: Darton, Longman & Todd, 1971.

Mattson, Brian. *Restored to Our Destiny: Eschatology and the Image of God in Herman Bavinck's Reformed Dogmatics*. Leiden: Brill, 2012.

Maximus Confessor. "Difficulty 10." In *Maximus the Confessor*, by Andrew Louth. London: Routledge, 2005.

———. *Selected Writings*. Edited by George Charles Berthold. Mahwah, NJ: Paulist, 1985.

McCormack, Bruce L. *Karl Barth's Critically Realistic Dialectical Theology: Its Genesis and Development, 1909–1936*. Oxford: Clarendon, 1995.

———. *Orthodox and Modern: Studies in the Theology of Karl Barth*. Grand Rapids: Baker Academic, 2008.

———. "Union with Christ in Calvin's Theology: Grounds for a Divinization Theory?" In *Tributes to John Calvin: A Celebration of His Quincentenary*, edited by David W. Hall, 504–29. Phillipsburg, NJ: Presbyterian & Reformed, 2010.

McLelland, Joseph. "Sailing to Byzantium." In *The New Man: An Orthodox and Reformed Dialogue*, edited by John Meyendorff and Joseph C. McLelland, 10–25. New Brunswick, NJ: Agora, 1973.

Meyendorff, John, and Joseph McLelland, eds. *The New Man: An Orthodox and Reformed Dialogue*. New Brunswick, NJ: Agora, 1973.

Meyendorff, John, and Robert Tobias, eds. *Salvation in Christ: A Lutheran-Orthodox Dialogue*. Minneapolis: Augsburg, 1992.

Milbank, John. "Christianity and Platonism." In Athanasopoulos and Schneider, *Divine Essence and Divine Energies*, 158–209.

———. *The Word Made Strange: Theology, Language, Culture*. Oxford: Blackwell, 1997.

Moltmann, Jürgen. *The Crucified God: The Cross of Christ as the Foundation and Criticism of Christian Theology*. Translated by Robert A. Wilson and John Bowden. London: SCM, 1974.

Mosser, Carl. "The Greatest Possible Blessing: Calvin and Deification." *Scottish Journal of Theology* 55 (2002): 36–57.

Muller, Richard. "Christ—the Revelation or the Revealer? Brunner and Reformed Orthodoxy on the Doctrine of the Word of God." *Journal of the Evangelical Theological Society* 26 (September 1983): 307–19.

———. "Not Scotist: Understandings of Being, Univocity, and Analogy in Early-Modern Reformed Thought." *Reformation and Renaissance Review* 14 (2012): 127–50.

———. *Post-Reformation Reformed Dogmatics*. 3 vols. Grand Rapids: Baker Academic, 2003.

Nassif, Bradley, ed. *New Perspectives on Historical Theology: Essays in Memory of John Meyendorff*. Grand Rapids: Eerdmans, 1996.

———. Introduction to *New Perspectives*, xi–xvi.

Nassif, Bradley, Michael Horton, Vladimir Berzonsky, George Hancock-Stefan, and Edward Rommen. *Three Views on Eastern Orthodoxy and Evangelicalism*. Grand Rapids: Zondervan, 2004.

Normann, Friedrich. *Teilhabe – ein Schlüsselwort der Vätertheologie*. Münster: Aschendorff, 1978.

"Orient et occident: Grégoire Palamas." *Istina* 3 (1974): 257.

Origen. *Commentary on the Gospel of John*. Translated by Ronald E. Heine. Fathers of the Church 89. Washington, DC: Catholic University of America, 1993.

Ouwendorp, C. *Jeruzalem & Athene*. Delft: Eburon, 2012.

Palamas, Gregory. *Capita* 107. In *The One Hundred and Fifty Chapters*. Edited and translated by Robert E. Sinkewicz. Toronto: Pontifical Institute of Medieval Studies, 1988.

Pannenberg, Wolfhart. *Jesus: God and Man*. Translated by Lewis L. Wilkins and Duane A. Priebe. London: SCM, 1968.

———. *Systematic Theology*. Vol. 1. Translated by Geoffrey Bromiley. Grand Rapids: Eerdmans, 1991.

———. *Theology and the Kingdom of God*. Edited by Richard John Neuhaus. Louisville: Westminster John Knox, 1969.

Papanikolaou, Aristotle. *Being with God: Trinity, Apophaticism, and Divine-Human Communion*. Notre Dame, IN: Notre Dame University Press, 2006.

———. "Sophia, Apophasis, and Communion: The Trinity in Contemporary Orthodox Theology." In *Cambridge Companion to the Trinity*, edited by Peter C. Phan, 243–58. Cambridge: Cambridge University Press, 2011.

Pascal, Blaise. *Pensées*. Translated by A. J. Krailscheimer. Harmondsworth, UK: Penguin Classics, 1966.

Patterson, Patrick. "By Thine Agony and Bloody Sweat: A Dogmatic Description of the Double Agencies of Christ—A Modest Proposal." ThD diss., Wycliffe College of University of Toronto, 2012.

Payne, Daniel Paul. "The Revival of Political Hesychasm in Contemporary Orthodox Thought." PhD diss., Baylor University, 2006.

Payton, James R., Jr. *Light from the Christian East: An Introduction to the Orthodox Tradition*. Downers Grove, IL: InterVarsity Press, 2010.

Pelikan, Jaroslav. "In Memory of John Meyendorff." In Nassif, *New Perspectives*, 7–9.

———. Preface to *The Triads*, by Gregory Palamas, xi–xiii. Mahwah, NJ: Paulist, 1983.

Perepiska svyashchennika Pavla Aleksandrovicha Florenskogo so svyashchennikom Sergiem Nikolaevichem Bulgakovym [Correspondence of Rev. Pavel Aleksandrovich Florensky with Rev. Sergii Nikolaevich Bulgakov]. Tomsk: Vodolei, 2001.

Perl, Eric D. *Theophany: The Neoplatonic Philosophy of Dionysius the Areopagite*. Albany, NY: State University of New York Press, 2012.

Pinnock, Clark H., Richard Rice, John Sanders, William Hasker, and David Basinger. *The Openness of God: A Biblical Challenge to the Traditional Understanding of God*. Downers Grove, IL: InterVarsity Press, 1994.

"Pis'ma G. Florovskogo S. Bulgakovu i S. Tyshkevichu" [Letters of G. Florovsky to S. Bulgakov and S. Tyschkevich]. *Simvol* 29 (1993): 199–216.

Plato. *Theaetetus*. Translated by Benjamin Jowett. New York: Random House, 1953.

Plested, Marcus. "Gregory Palamas." In *Wiley Blackwell Companion to Patristics*, edited by Ken Parry, 293–306. Oxford: Wiley and Sons, 2015.

———. *Orthodox Readings of Aquinas*. Oxford: Oxford University Press, 2012.

"Pravoslavnaya pozitsiya - beseda s prof. prot. Ioannom Meyendorfom: Vremya osmysleniya" [The Orthodox Position—A Conversation with Prof. Prot. John Meyendorff: Time for Deep Reflection]. *Voronezhskiy eparhial'nyy vestnik* 8 (1992): 43–46.

Radcliff, Jason Robert. *Thomas F. Torrance and the Church Fathers: A Reformed, Evangelical, and Ecumenical Reconstruction of the Patristic Tradition*. Cambridge: Clarke, 2015.

Rahner, Karl. "Der Dreifaltige Gott als transzendenter Urgrund der Heilsgeschichte." In *Mysterium Salutis: Grundriß heilsgeschichtlicher Dogmatik*, edited by Johannes Feiner and Magnus Löhrer, 2:317–401. Einsiedeln: Benziger, 1967.

———. *The Trinity*. Translated by Joseph Donceel. New York: Herder and Herder, 1970.

Read, Carveth. *Logic, Deductive and Inductive*. London: Grant Richards, 1898.

Régnon, Théodore de. *Etudes de théologie positive sur la Sainte Trinité*. Vol. 1. Paris: Victor Retaux, 1892.

Reid, Duncan. *Energies of the Spirit: Trinitarian Models in Eastern Orthodox and Western Theology*. Atlanta: Scholars Press, 1997.

Ritter, Adolf Maria. "Gregor Palamas als Leser des Dionysius Pseudo-Areopagita." In *Denys l'Areopagite et sa postérité en Orient et en Occident*, edited by Ysabel De Andia, 565–79. Paris: Études Augustiniennes, 1997.

Roberts, Matthew P. W. "Thinking Like a Christian: The Prolegomena of Herman Bavinck." *Ecclesia Reformanda* 1 (2009): 70–91.

Rocca, Gregory. *Speaking the Incomprehensible God: Thomas Aquinas on the Interplay of Positive and Negative Theology*. Washington, DC: Catholic University of America Press, 2004.

Romanides, John. "Notes on the Palamite Controversy and Related Topics. Part 1." *The Greek Orthodox Theological Review* 6 (1960–1961): 186–205.

———. "Notes on the Palamite Controversy and Related Topics. Part 2." *The Greek Orthodox Theological Review* 9 (1963–1964): 225–70.

Rossum, Joost van. "Dionysius the Areopagite and Gregory Palamas: A 'Christological Corrective'?" *Studia Patristica* 42 (2006): 347–53.

———. "Otets Ioann Meyendorf: Zhizn', posvyashchennaya nauke i sluzheniyu Tserkvi" [Father John Meyendorff: A Life Dedicated to Science and Ministry to the Church]. In *Paskhal'naya tayna: Stat'i po bogosloviyu* [Paschal Mystery: Theological Articles], by Ioann Meyendorf, vi–xxii. Moscow: Eksmo, 2013.

———. "Palamas and Aquinas." *SVTQ* 59 (2015): 29–41.

Russell, Norman. "'Partakers of the Divine Nature' (2 Peter 1:4) in the Byzantine Tradition." In *Kathegetria: Essays Presented to Joan Hussey on Her Eightieth Birthday*, edited by Julian Chrysostomides, 51–67. Camberley, UK: Porphyrogenitus, 1988.

———. "The Reception of Palamas in the West Today." Θεολογία 83 (2012): 7–21.

———. "Theosis and Gregory Palamas: Continuity or Doctrinal Change?" *SVTQ* 50 (2006): 357–79.

Schnackenburg, Rudolf. *The Gospel according to St. John*. 3 vols. London: Burns & Oates, 1968–1982.

Schneider, Christoph. "Beyond Agnosticism and Pantheism." In Athanasopoulos and Schneider, *Divine Essence and Divine Energies*, 9–26.

Shaw, Lewis. "John Meyendorff and the Russian Theological Tradition." In Nassif, *New Perspectives*, 10–42.

Shevzov, Vera. "The Burdens of Tradition: Orthodox Constructions of the West in Russia (Late Nineteenth–Early Twentieth cc.)." In *Orthodox Constructions of the West*, edited by George E. Demacopoulos and Aristotle Papanikolaou, 83–101. Fordham, NY: Fordham University Press, 2013.

Smith, Barry D. *The Indescribable God: Divine Otherness in Christian Theology*. Eugene, OR: Wipf & Stock, 2012.

Smith, James K. A. *Speech and Theology: Language and the Logic of Incarnation*. London: Routledge, 2002.

Stăniloae, Dumitru. *Orthodox Dogmatic Theology*. Vol. 1. Brookline, MA: Holy Cross, 1994.

Suh, Chul Won. *The Creation-Mediatorship of Jesus Christ: A Study in the Relation of the Incarnation and the Creation*. Amsterdam: Rodopi, 1982.

Sytsma, David S. "Herman Bavinck's Thomistic Epistemology: The Argument and Sources of His *Principia* of Science." In *Five Studies in the Thought of Herman Bavinck*, edited by John Bolt, 1–56. Lewiston, NY: Edwin Mellen, 2011.

Tanev, Stoyan. "The Concept of Energy in T. F. Torrance and in Orthodox Theology." In *T. F. Torrance and Eastern Orthodoxy: Theology in Reconciliation*, edited by Matthew Baker and Todd Speidell, 194–217. Eugene, OR: Wipf & Stock, 2015.

Tertullian. *Against Praxeas*. *ANF* 3.

Tollefsen, Torstein. *Activity and Participation in Late Antique and Early Christian Thought*. Oxford: Oxford University Press, 2012.

———. *The Christocentric Cosmology of St Maximus the Confessor*. Oxford: Oxford University Press, 2008.

Torrance, Thomas F. *The Christian Doctrine of God: One Being, Three Persons*. Edinburgh: T&T Clark, 1996.

———. *Divine Meaning: Studies in Patristic Hermeneutics*. Edinburgh: T&T Clark, 1995.

———. "Memoranda on Orthodox/Reformed Relations." In *Theological Dialogue between Orthodox and Reformed Churches*, edited by Thomas F. Torrance, 1:3–18. Edinburgh: Scottish Academic Press, 1985.

———, ed. *Theological Dialogue between Orthodox and Reformed Churches*. Edinburgh: Scottish Academic Press, 1985.

———. *Trinitarian Faith: The Evangelical Theology of the Ancient Catholic Church*. Edinburgh: T&T Clark, 1995.

———. *Trinitarian Perspectives: Toward Doctrinal Agreement*. Edinburgh: T&T Clark, 1994.

Trueman, Carl R. *John Owen: Reformed Catholic, Renaissance Man*. Aldershot, UK: Ashgate, 2007.

Van Til, Cornelius. "Bavinck the Theologian: A Review Article." *WTJ* 24 (1961): 48–64.

———. "Common Grace: Part II. The Latest Debate about Common Grace." *WTJ* 8 (May 1946): 166–200.

———. *An Introduction to Systematic Theology: Prolegomena and the Doctrines of Revelation, Scripture, and God*. Phillipsburg, NJ: Presbyterian and Reformed, 2007.

———. "The Text of a Complaint against Actions of the Presbytery of Philadelphia in the Matter of the Licensure and Ordination of Dr. Gordon H. Clark." Unpublished complaint, Philadelphia Orthodox Presbyterian Church.

Veenhof, Cornelis. "Uit het leven van de Theologische Hogeschool 6." *De Reformatie* 30 (1955): 123–24.

Veenhof, Jan. "Bavinck en de Wijsbegeerte." In *Ontmoetingen met Bavinck*, edited by George Harinck and Gerrit Neven, 219–33. Barneveld: De Vuurbaak, 2006.

Velde, Dolf te. *The Doctrine of God in Reformed Orthodoxy, Karl Barth, and the Utrecht School*. Leiden: Brill, 2013.

Vissers, John. "Karl Barth's Appreciative Use of Herman Bavinck's Reformed Dogmatics." *CTJ* 45 (2010): 79–86.

Vos, Arvin. "Knowledge according to Bavinck and Aquinas." *BavRev* 6 (2015): 9–36.

Vos, Geerhardus. "Herman Bavinck. Gereformeerde Dogmatiek, Volume Two." *PRR* 10 (1899): 694–700.

Wallace, James Buchanan. *Snatched Into Paradise (2 Cor 12:1–10): Paul's Heavenly Journey in the Context of Early Christian Experience*. Berlin: de Gruyter, 2011.

Walls, R. C. "St. Gregory Palamas." *Scottish Journal of Theology* 21 (1968): 435–48.

Ware, Timothy (Kallistos). "The Debate about Palamism." *ECR* 9 (1977): 45–63.

———. "'Following the Holy Fathers': Is There a Future for Patristic Studies?" in *A Celebration of Living Theology: A Festschrift in Honour of Andrew Louth*, edited by Justin Mihoc and Leonard Aldea, 214–24. New York: Bloomsbury, 2014.

———. "God Hidden and Revealed: The Apophatic Way and the Essence-Energies Distinction." *ECR* 7 (1975): 125–36.

———. *The Orthodox Church: An Introduction to Eastern Christianity*. London: Penguin, 1993.

Wendebourg, Dorothea. "From the Cappadocian Fathers to Gregory Palamas: The Defeat of Trinitarian Theology." *Studia Patristica* 17 (1981): 194–99.

Williams, Anna Ngaire. *The Ground of Union: Deification in Aquinas and Palamas*. Oxford: Oxford University Press, 1999.

Williams, Rowan. "The Philosophical Structures of Palamism." *ECR* 9 (1977): 27–44.

———. "The Theology of Vladimir Nikolaievich Lossky: An Exposition and Critique." PhD diss., University of Oxford, 1975.

———. *Wrestling with Angels: Conversations in Modern Theology*. Grand Rapids: Eerdmans, 2007.

Wit, Willem J. de. *On the Way to the Living God: A Cathartic Reading of Herman Bavinck and an Invitation to Overcome the Plausibility Crisis of Christianity*. Amsterdam: VU University Press, 2011.

Wolterstorff, Nicholas. "Divine Simplicity." *Philosophical Perspectives* 5 (1991): 531–52.

———. "Herman Bavinck - Proto Reformed Epistemologist." *CTJ* 45 (2010): 133–46.

Wright, N. T. "Christian Origins and the Question of God." In *Engaging the Doctrine of God: Contemporary Protestant Perspectives*, edited by Bruce L. McCormack, 21–36. Grand Rapids: Baker Academic, 2008.

Yannaras, Christos. "The Distinction between Essence and Energies and Its Importance for Theology." *SVTQ* 19 (1975): 232–45.

———. *Orthodoxy and the* West. Translated by Peter Chamberas and Norman Russell. Brookline, NY: Holy Cross Orthodox Press, 2006.

Yarnell, Malcolm B. *The Formation of Christian Doctrine*. Nashville: B&H Academic, 2007.

Ziegler, Roland E. "Luther and Calvin on God: Origins of Lutheran and Reformed Differences." *Concordia Theological Quarterly* 75 (2011): 63–90.

Zizioulas, John. *Being as Communion: Studies in Personhood and the Church.* Crestwood, NY: St Vladimir's Seminary Press, 1997.

———. *Communion and Otherness: Further Studies in Personhood and the Church.* New York: T&T Clark, 2006.

———. "The Doctrine of the Holy Trinity: The Significance of the Cappadocian Contribution." In *Trinitarian Theology Today*, edited by Christoph Schwöbel, 44–60. Edinburgh: T&T Clark, 1995.

Zorgdrager, Heleen E. "On the Fullness of Salvation: Tracking *Theosis* in Reformed Theology." *Journal of Reformed Theology* 8 (2014): 357–81.

NAME INDEX

SUBJECT INDEX